Where Are They Now?

West Bromwich Albion

Ian Atkins

www.where-are-they-now.co.uk/club/west-bromwich-albion

First published in 2020 by
Media House Books

© Media House Books 2020

ISBN 978-1-912027-56-9

Original cover design by Marten Sealby

Introduction

I would like to dedicate this book to any of the 'Albion family' who might have passed away during the Covid-19 pandemic, or for any other reason, and to their families and friends.

A huge 'thank you' to all NHS workers, you are all Champions! To the other people too numerous to mention, who helped keep our Country going throughout the Corona Virus pandemic, 'A massive Thank You to all of you!'

West Bromwich Albion, Founder members of the Football League, 5 times FA Cup Winners. Football League Cup winners once, League Division One Champions 1919/20. One hundred years on from that famous Championship winning season, our only one to date, the 'Baggies' are now back in the Premier League for season 2020/21. How good does that sound?

We have become a bit of a yo-yo team in the 21st century bouncing or 'boing-ing' between the Championship and the Premier League.

With the 'promised land' again in sight nearing the end of the 2018/19 season, the Baggies faltered, losing on penalties to fierce local rivals from Aston, in the play-off semi-final. Then with the 'divine' appointment of Slaven Bilic as manager, promotion was achieved in July 2020 and our beloved West Bromwich Albion could once again call themselves a Premier League team in 2020/21.

The 2019/20 season was the strangest I have ever encountered, in my 62 years as a season-ticket holder at the Hawthorns. The season was 'abandoned' in March due to the Corona Virus pandemic, then 're-started' in June, finishing in somewhat strange circumstances with Promotion on the final day, almost a year after starting the previous pre-season friendlies, with no fans in the ground, and Albion failing to win any of their final four games.

That final July day in 2020 was probably the most nervous I have ever felt about football, watching the game against QPR via the Club's i-Follow platform.

The Jeff Astle Foundation

The Jeff Astle Foundation's ultimate goal is to establish a care home for former sports people with dementia or chronic neurological impairment, who are often younger at diagnosis and require specialist care.

Old Baggies is the WBA Former Players' Association

If you are an Old Baggie or would like further information please contact Secretary Geoff Snape
Tel: 07860 523866 or e-mail geoffsnape1@btinternet.com

Back in August 2019, myself and 22 other family members were invited to the Hawthorns for the official re-naming of the Manager's Room at the Hawthorns, as the 'Everiss Suite', in honour of the years of service given to West Bromwich Albion by my Grandfather, Fred Everiss.

He joined the staff in 1896, rising from office boy, Secretary, Secretary/manager, Director and Life Member until his death in 1951 and Alan Everiss, my Uncle, who joined the Albion office staff in 1933, becoming assistant Secretary in 1948, later Secretary, Board Member and Life Member until his death in 1999. We were treated like royalty and had the honour of meeting and chatting with Slaven Bilic. Thank you, West Bromwich Albion! 'One Family – One Club!'

I would like to acknowledge the following: I have had help from Tony Matthews, ex-WBA club statistician and had his permission to use information from some of his books; Laurie Rampling, one of the un-sung stars at the Hawthorns, usually seen in his shorts, snapping photos of the Albion, thank you for permission to use some of your photographs; Geoff Snape Secretary of the Old Baggies Former Players Association for his permission to use information and pictures from the Old Baggies website; Wikipedia and 'Albion Til We Die' for confirming stats etc.; Some of the former players who sent me information about their lives after football: Bernard McNally, Andy Hunt, Joost Volmer, Alan Merrick, Kevin Kent, Gary Owen, '68 Skipper Graham Williams, thank you.

Finally, thank you to my late Mom & Dad, my wonderful wife of 43 years, Linda, our four Children & partners Deborah & Mike, David & Caroline, Daniel & Emma, Matthew & Moyo, and my amazing little Grandchildren Freddie, Coralie plus 'Little Miss', due in October 2020. Love you all so much Boing! Boing!

I hope you enjoy reading about some of the Albion 'family' members from years gone by. Apologies if I missed out your favourite player but I was unable to include every former Baggie.

Ian

ADAMS James

Goalkeeper 5'10"

Born *3/1/1908 Norton Canes, Cannock*
Died *Birmingham 1983*
Playing Career: *Cannock Town, West Bromwich Albion (221 appearances Oct 1929 – May 1945)*

Nicknamed 'Doc'. He was a fine, competent goalkeeper, hefty but extremely mobile. He was in competition with Harold Pearson, George Ashmore and Billy Light for the keepers' position, playing 103 league matches. He was one of the club's heaviest players, tipping the scales at almost 15 stone during WW2 when he played 118 of his games for Albion. He retired in 1945 due to ill health.

ADAMSON Christopher 'Chris'

Goalkeeper 5'11"

Born *4/11/1978 Ashington, Northumberland*
Playing career: *West Bromwich Albion (14 appearances Apr 1995 – Apr 2003), IK Brage in Sweden (loan), Mansfield Town (loan), Halifax Town (loan), Plymouth Argyle (loan), Halesowen Town (loan), St. Patricks Athletic in Dublin, Solihull Borough, Sheffield Wednesday, Stockport County, Northwich Victoria (loan), Ilkeston Town, Hereford United (1997 – 2010)*

Adamson joined West Bromwich Albion as an apprentice in April 1995, turning professional in July 1997. Chris was a sound goalkeeper maybe lacking a few inches to be top class. His handling was sound but his kicking, especially when put under pressure, was nervy and inconsistent. He made his Albion début in a 2-1 defeat away at Stockport County on 11th April 1998. He generally found it difficult to break into the Albion first team, and remained an understudy to Alan Miller, Brian Jensen and Russell Hoult. He was a regular for Albion's reserve and youth sides during the late 1990's and early 2000's. Adamson spent time on loan at various clubs, including IK Brage in Sweden, Mansfield Town, Halifax Town, Plymouth Argyle and Halesowen Town. Adamson then signed for League of Ireland side St Patrick's Athletic in 2002. He made 66 league appearances for Athletic before returning to England. Adamson had a brief spell at Southern League Premier Division club Solihull Borough, before joining Sheffield Wednesday in January 2005. He made his Sheffield Wednesday debut as an 8th-minute substitute on 12th

March 2005 at home versus Blackpool in Football League One, helping to secure a 3–2 win. He was released on a free transfer following the Owls' promotion to the Championship at the end of the season. However, manager Sturrock was unsuccessful in finding a replacement back-up goalkeeper and Adamson re-signed for Wednesday in July 2005. Adamson made five appearances for the Owls in the 2005/06 season, Chris did however captain the Sheffield Wednesday reserve team to the title in the Pontins Central Reserve League. Adamson was released by Wednesday in May 2007 for the second time, after playing 12 first team games. In June 2007, Adamson signed a one-year deal with Stockport County, making just two appearances for the club. He joined Ilkeston Town in August 2008. After playing a major part in Ilkeston's promotion to the Conference North, playing in 32 league games, Adamson joined Hereford United in July 2009 on a 12-month contract as a player-goalkeeper coach. In April 2010 Adamson was involved in a car crash on the M5 motorway between Worcester and Droitwich Spa, he was taken to hospital for treatment to minor injuries. In May 2010, Adamson moved to Mansfield Town to become the club's goalkeeping coach. In 2014 he was coaching at Bustlehome FC in West Bromwich.

Chris Adamson

AGNEW Paul

Full back/Defender 5'9"

Born *15/8/1965 Lisburn, Northern Ireland*
Playing career: *Cliftonville, Grimsby Town, West Bromwich Albion (Cost £65,000 39 + 2 sub appearances 1 goal Feb 1995-1 June 1997), Ilkeston Town, Swansea City, Wisbech Town. (1982-1999)*

Nicknamed 'Aggy'. A strong tackling no nonsense defender, although not the quickest. Agnew was born in Northern Ireland in 1965, and joined Cliftonville in 1982. Two years later he joined Grimsby Town for £4,000, where he remained for the next 11 years. Whilst at Blundell Park he helped the club to two back to back promotions under manager Alan Buckley. In 1995 Agnew followed Buckley to West Bromwich Albion for £65,000, and was one of many players that transferred to and from Albion and Grimsby in the years during Buckley's time at the Albion. He took the captain's armband shortly after arriving at the Hawthorns, although he was continually troubled by injuries. After forty-one games for the Baggies, plus a dozen for the reserves, Agnew was released at the end of the 1996/97 season. After seven games for Swansea City, he then switched to non-league club Wisbech Town to play under his former Grimsby teammate Gary Childs. Paul now has his FA Coaching level 2 certificate trained in injury management, emergency first aid, and qualified to coach disabled footballers. He also spent time coaching for Birmingham County FA, Adidas and Sutton College Football Academy. Since 2000 he has run Saturday soccer classes for disabled children at Whittington FC. He was given the 2009 Staffordshire Coach of the year award. Teaching at Blackwood school 2019

Arthur Albiston

AITKEN Andrew 'Andy'

Winger 5'9"

Born *21/8/1934 Edinburgh, Scotland*
Died *28/2/2005 Edinburgh, Scotland*
Playing Career: *Hibernian, West Bromwich Albion (Cost £9,000 22 appearances 2 goals Sept 1959 – Feb 1961), Falkirk, Raith Rovers (1955 – 1963)*

He played for Cliftonville whilst doing his National Service in Northern Ireland. Signed for Hibernian on completing this in 1955. Aitken became a key player in the Hibs team over the next few years, including their run to the 1958 Scottish Cup Final. Aitken moved to West Bromwich Albion for £9,000 in September 1959, but was hindered by injury, making just 22 appearances, scoring 2 goals. He was a persevering winger who lacked that extra yard of pace needed to succeed at the top level. He returned to Scotland with Falkirk for £5,000, and helped them gain promotion to Scottish League Division One. He then moved on to Raith Rovers and Gala Fairydean before retiring from the game.

ALBISTON Arthur

Left back 5'7"

Born *14/7/1957 Edinburgh, Scotland*
Playing career: *Manchester United, West Bromwich Albion (Free transfer 47 appearances 2 goals August 1988 – June 1989), Dundee, Chesterfield, Chester-City, Molde, Ayr United, Sittingbourne, Witton Albion, Droylesden.(1974-1994) Scottish U-21 and Full international, 14 caps.*

A left back who holds the distinction of making his FA Cup debut, at Wembley, for Manchester United against Liverpool in the 1977 Final, celebrating with a winner's medal. Arthur won the second division title with Manchester United in 1974/75, FA Cup in 1977, 1983 & 1985 and the Charity Shield in 1977 and 1983, shared. Played 485 times for United scoring 7 goals. After 14 years and 379 league games at Old Trafford, Arthur joined Albion on a free transfer in August 1988, signing for his former boss, Ron Atkinson. He played in 47 games scoring twice. Arthur was skilful with good positional sense and a wealth of experience but he had obviously lost a yard of pace. He moved to Dundee, Chesterfield, Chester City, Molde on loan then Ayr United, drifting into non-league with Sittingbourne, Witton Albion and Droylsden. He became manager of Drolysden in the North West Counties League 1996/97.

Worked as a junior coach at Manchester United for four years from 2000 to 2004 and also worked as a summariser for Manchester Independent radio station. Arthur has worked for MUTV, Manchester United's official television channel, acting as match summariser during live coverage of the club's reserve and academy teams. Arthur is a witty and eloquent speaker, direct and anecdotal, available for after Dinner Speaker, Golf Events Motivational Speaking, Charity Events, Corporate Hospitality, Personal Appearances, Sportsman's Dinners, Question and Answer Sessions. Via Clubland Entertainments.

ALBRECHTSEN Martin

Full back/centre back 6'2"
Born *31/3/1980 Vaerlose, Denmark*
Playing career:: *Akademisk Bolbklub Gladsaxe, FC Copenhagen, West Bromwich Albion (Cost £2.5 million 118+20 sub appearances 4 goals Jul 2004 – June 2008), Derby County, FC Midtjylland, Brondby IF, AC Horsens, BK Avarta Vaerebro BoldKlub (1998 – 2018) He had 4 Full International caps for Denmark and also played at U-19 & U-21 International level.*

Born in Værløse in the Capital Region of Denmark, Albrechtsen started his career at Akadeisk Boldklub. He won the Danish Cup in 1999. Albrechtsen was sold to defending Superliga champions F.C. Copenhagen (FCK) in a DKK 9 million, £1.086 million, transfer deal in January 2002. He helped the club win the 2003 and 2004 Danish Superliga championships, as well as the 2004 Danish Cup trophy. In June 2004, he moved abroad to play for English club West Bromwich Albion in the FA Premier League. He was bought in a £2.5 million transfer deal, making him the most expensive player the club had ever bought at that point. Signed as a centre back, he played most of his Albion career at right back. Tough tackling, powerful on the ground and in the air, although sometimes beaten too easily, when playing as a full back, by a fast winger. He played 138 games for Albion, 20 as a substitute, scoring 4 goals. Albrechsten joined Derby County on a Bosman free transfer, signing a two-year contract with the club on 30 June 2008. He quickly fell out of favour with new manager Nigel Clough, however, and his contract at the club was cancelled by mutual consent on 30 August 2009. After a few days joining FC

Midtjylland, 2009-2012, Martin revealed the motives behind his decision to part ways with Derby County. He claimed to have been annoyed at being handed a number of fines by Clough for breaches of club rules. He continued playing in Denmark for Bondby IF 2012 – 2016, AC Horsens Dec 2016 – May 2017 where he suffered with groin problems that sidelined him for 3 months. He moved to BV Avarta where his brother Jacob was a player. In January 2018 he joined Vaerebro Boldklub. Nicknamed 'Dolph' due to his similarity to Dolph Lungren. He has two children and had their names displayed on a specially designed pair of football boots, which he wore in a league match against Sheffield United in February 2008. The boots were a present from his girlfriend Camilla Malmberg. However, Albrechtsen and Camilla got separated in 2011. He was later in a relationship with a Danish model named Emilie Posborg. It was revealed in 2016, that Albrechtsen's son, Justin, suffered from an extremely rare disease named Oesophageal atresia. He is now a personal trainer in Copenhagen.

ALLEN Ronald 'Ronnie'

Centre Forward/winger 5'9"
Born *15/1/1929 Fenton. Stoke-on-Trent*
Died *9/6/2001 Great Wyrley, Staffordshire*
Playing career: *Port Vale, West Bromwich Albion (£20,000 458 appearances 234 goals Mar 1950 – May 1961), Crystal Palace (1944 1965) 5 England Caps, also represented the Football League, England 'B', FA XI and the RAF*

The 'complete footballer' and the king-pin of Albion's wonderful attack of the 1950's. Initially a right winger. Allen was converted into a brilliant centre forward by Albion, although he played in every position across the front line. He possessed a powerful shot in both feet and was a superb volleyer of the ball. He was also an ace penalty taker scoring over 40 times from the spot for Albion including the FA Cup Semi Final at Villa Park and in the FA Cup Final in 1954. He was a vital member of that FA Cup Winning team of 1954 scoring twice in the 3-2 victory over Preston North End. Ronnie scored a Hat-trick at Wolverhampton in a 4-4 draw in the Charity Shield 1954. The following season Ron was the highest League scorer in Division One with 27 goals.

RON ALLEN
West Bromwich
Albion and
England

ALSOP Gilbert

Centre Forward 5'9½"
Born 2/9/1908 Fampton Cotterell
Died 16/4/1992 Walsall aged 83
Playing career: *Bath City, Coventry City, Walsall, West Bromwich Albion (Cost £3,000 1 appearance Nov 1935 – May 1937), Ipswich Town, Walsall. (1927-1948)*

After a remarkable scoring return of 40 goals in all competitions in 1933/34 and 48 goals in all competitions in 1934/35 for Walsall, Alsop attracted the attention of clubs further up the league and moved to First Division West Bromwich Albion for £3,000 in November 1935. However, Alsop found his first team opportunities were severely limited by the form of W. G. Richardson and Harry Jones, He was unlucky to be around when W.G. Richardson was still at his best at the Hawthorns, only making only one first team appearance. At Walsall he scored 194 goals in 266 games and a further 56 for the Saddlers during wartime action. In total he appeared in 447 matches in his 20year career scoring 297 goals He worked on Walsall's ground staff for twenty years and was groundsman of the playing fields adjoining Walsall Arboretum. He had a stand in the Bescot Stadium named in his honour after his death.

He holds the unique record of being the only player to have scored in each of the first 20 post WW2 seasons 1945/46 – 1964/65. Allen was an excellent golfer, twice winning the Professional Footballers' Golf title in 1959 and 1960, also being runner-up in 1963 & 1964. After finishing playing he became Wolverhampton Wanderers manager in 1966, gaining promotion from the Second Division in 1966/67. In the Summer 1967 he spent time coaching Los Angeles Wolves in USA. He moved to Spain to steer Athletic Bilbao to second place in La Liga in 1969/70. In 1972 Allen was appointed manager of Sporting Lisbon in Portugal. After one season he moved back to England to manage Walsall for a brief period. In 1977 Ronnie became Albion manager until, he was lured away to advise the Saudi Arabia national team. In 1980 he took charge of Greek club Panathinaikos . Allen returned to the Albion as, manager in 1981, taking the club to the Semi-Final of the FA Cup and the League Cup, losing both but only narrowly avoiding relegation. He was replaced as manager by Ron Wylie, but Ronnie stepped into a role as general manager for a year. He continued to coach and scout for the club during his retirement playing in a testimonial match at Cheltenham in 1995 at the age of 66. He spent his final few years in a nursing home, suffering with Alzheimers. Ronnie died in Great Wyrley aged 72.

Personal note: *Ronnie lived in an Albion club house in Frank Road, Smethwick in the late 1950's. I lived just around the corner in Devonshire Road. He could also often be seen playing golf at Sutton Park.*

AMALFITANO Morgan

Striker 5'9"
Born 20/3/1985 Nice, France
Playing career: *Sedan, Lorient, Marseille, West Bromwich Albion (loan 26+4 sub appearances 4 goals Sept 2013 – June 2014), West Ham United, Lille, Rennes (2003 – 2018) One French Cap.*

He started his professional career with CS Sedan Ardennes playing 126 league games from 2003-2008. In the summer of 2008, Amalfitano moved to Ligue 1 side Lorient. He played 110 league games scoring 14 goals. In July 2011, Amalfitano joined Marseille on a free transfer, signing a contract until 2015. Here he won the Coupe de la Ligue trophy in April 2012. On 1st September 2013, it was confirmed that Amalfitano had signed for West Bromwich Albion on a season-long loan deal. He scored an audacious lob from 35 yards in the thrilling 3–3 draw against fellow relegations rivals Cardiff City in March 2014. He usually played as a right winger, wide midfielder or even at right wing back.

Morgan played 30 games for Albion scoring 4 goals. He returned to Marseille but was soon transferred to West Ham United in September 2014 on a two-year deal. In August 2015, Amalfitano was disciplined for a breach of club rules by new manager Slaven Bilic. Amalfitano was banned from the first-team squad and ordered to train with the under-21 team. On 6th October 2015, Amalfitano left West Ham by mutual consent. In January 2016, he joined French side Lille. On the final day of the 2016/17 winter transfer window, Amalfitano agreed to the termination of his contract with Lille before re-joining his former coach, Christian Gourcuff, at Stade Rennais F.C. In August 2018, Amalfitano agreed the termination of his contract with Rennes. His younger brother Romain also plays professional football.

AMPADU (Patrick) Kwame

Midfielder 5'10"
Born *20/12/1970 Bradford*
Playing career: *Arsenal, Plymouth Argyle (loan), West Bromwich Albion (on loan then signed for £63,000 October 39+23 sub appearances 5 goals 1991 – Feb 1994), Swansea City, Leyton Orient, Exeter City, Newport County, Tiverton Town. Republic of Ireland U-21 International.*

Ampadu was born in Bradford, West Yorkshire, England, to an Irish mother and Ghanaian father. He subsequently moved with his parents to Dublin, Ireland, where he was raised. Ampadu first played in Irish youth football for Sherrard United and Belvedere before joining Arsenal in July 1988. He appeared in two league games at Highbury, going out to have loan spells with Plymouth Argyle and West Bromwich Albion the following season, before making a permanent move to the latter in June 1991. Signed by Bobby Goul d for £63,000 along with Winston White and the lanky Paul Williams, in a bid to stave off relegation to the third tier. Sadly, that was not successful and Albion were relegated to the Third Division for the first time in their history. Kwame was obviously a skilful footballer but he did not seem capable of stamping his mark upon a game. He made 62 appearances for the first XI, of which 23 were as a substitute. Ampadu spent three years at West Bromwich Albion, before moving to Swansea City in February 1994 for £19,000.

He played in Swansea City's 1994 Football League Trophy win at Wembley. He also reached the 1997 Football League Third Division Play Off Final with the Swans. Ampadu played 144 league games scoring 12 goals between 1994-1998. He went on to play for Leyton Orient (whose fans were less than impressed - labelling him the worst player to have played for the club), Exeter City, Newport County and Tiverton Town, retiring in 2006.He returned to Exeter City in July 2008 and was part of the coaching staff with the club's academy working with the U-18's. Ampadu moved to Arsenal in 2012 to become U-14's coach at Arsenal's Hale End Academy. His son Ethan, a Welsh International, played for Exeter and Chelsea and on loan at RB Leipzig.

ANDERSON Colin

Left back/midfield 5'8"
Born *26/4/1962 Newcastle-on-Tyne*
Playing career: *Burnley, North Shields, Torquay, West Bromwich Albion (on loan then signed Coat £25,000 140+12 appearances 12 goals Mar 1985 – Jun 1991), Walsall, Hereford United, Exeter City (1980 – 1995)*

Colin started his professional career at Burnley playing 6 league games. In 1982 he moved to Torquay United where he played 109 league games scoring 11 goals, before joining West Bromwich Albion in March 1985 initially on loan then signing permanently for £25,000. A utility player who started his Albion career at left back, where his lack of pace was often shown up. He really came into his own at the Hawthorns when he was moved into a left midfield role, often appearing very inventive and creative. He was injured against Everton in an FA Cup match in January 1989 and he never really reached the peak of his form again. After 140 league games and 10 goals, he moved to Walsall in July 1991 for a season making 26 league appearances. Then he moved to Hereford United for two seasons playing 70 league games, moving on to Exeter City in 1996. He made a total of 385 league appearances scoring 25 goals. After being released by Exeter at the end of the 1995/96 season, he later played Devon County League football for Teignmouth and then moved to Western League Dawlish Town in November 1997. He was a salesman in the Yeovil area.

ANELKA Nicolas

Striker 6'1"

Born *14/3/1979 Le Chesnay, Versailles, France*
Playing career: *Paris Saint-Germain, Arsenal, Real Madrid, Paris Saint-Germain,Liverpool (loan), Manchester City, Fenerbahce, Bolton Wanderers, Chelsea, Shanghai Shenhua (China), Juventus (loan), West Bromwich Albion (Free Transfer 11 +1 sub appearance and 2 goals July 2013 – March 2014), Mumbai City (player-manager), Trappes Saint-Quentin, Clairefontaine. (1996-2016)French International & U-18 and U-20 20 International.*

Anelka won the 'Double', League and FA Cup, with Arsenal in 1997/98 and the Charity Shield in 1998. He won the UEFA Champions League at Real Madrid in 1999/2000. In 2000 he was part of the France team that won the UEFA Championship. With PSG he won the Inter-Toto Cup in 2001. Won the Super Lig in Turkey with Fenerbahce 2004/05. With Chelsea he was league Cup and UEFA Champions League runner up in 2007/08. Anelka was not selected for the 2008 World Cup Squad. Back at Chelsea, he then won FA Cup & Charity Shield in 2009. 'Double Winner FA Cup and Premier League in 2009/10. At Juventus he won Serie A in 2012/13. In July 2013, 34-year-old France striker Anelka signed for West Bromwich Albion on an initial one-year deal. Albion manager Steve Clarke, who briefly worked with Anelka at Chelsea, said in a club statement, "We are missing a bit of firepower from last year – we're trying to put that right and to kick off with the signing of Nicolas at the start of the summer is a great boost for everyone at the club. The sole focus at the club is trying to build on what we did last season. The more quality players you can bring to the club the better and no-one can question Nicolas' quality. He's a player I have worked with before as I was at Chelsea when they signed him. He has got a great work ethic, looks after himself and is a consummate professional. If you add that to the obvious talent that he's got I think he can prove to be a really top signing for the club. His experience with some of the top clubs in England and Europe will stand the group in good stead. Hopefully he will be able to inspire the other players to even greater heights than we managed to achieve last year." Well Mr. Clarke, that did not go too well. He made 11 appearances plus one as a substitute and he scored his first,

and only, Albion goals, a first-half brace, in his first appearance in over two months for the WBA in a 3–3 draw with West Ham United on 28th December 2013. During his goal celebration he performed a quenelle, a hand gesture popularized by his comedian friend Dieudonné, described by some critics as an inverted Nazi salute. The FA and anti-racism organisations investigated the incident following allegations of anti-Semitism. Anelka was subsequently banned for five matches, fined £80,000 and ordered to complete an educational course. In the hearing, the FA disciplinary hearing panel concluded, "We did not find that Nicolas Anelka is an anti-Semite or that he intended to express or promote anti-Semitism by his use of the quenelle." He has since stated that this gesture was aimed at former WBA manager Steve Clarke with whom Anelka had fallen out. Anelka used social media to announce he was terminating his contract with WBA. West Brom responded that Anelka had given the club no official notification of his intention to leave, and later gave him 14-days notice of termination from the club for gross misconduct 2014/15. After 7 games for Mumbai City FC, he was supposed to join Algerian Side NR Hussein Dey but the moved was blocked. He returned to Mumbai as player/manager in July 2015. Anelka joined the technical staff of Dutch Eredivise side Roda JC in 2017, then moved to Lille as youth attacking coach in 2018.

Nicolas Anelka

ANGEL Mark
Left winger 5'10"
Born *23/8/1975 Newcastle-on-Tyne*
Playing career: *Sunderland, Oxford United, West Bromwich Albion (Free transfer 5+23 sub appearances 1 goal July 1998 – June 2000) Darlington, Queen of the South, Boston United, Kings Lynn, Cambridge United (loan), Wisbech Town (loan), Mildenhall Town, Newmarket Town, Bourne Town, Spalding United (1993 – 2009),*

Mark played for Boston United, Darlington, Oxford United, Sunderland and West Bromwich Albion. Used mainly as a substitute at the Hawthorns, only making 4 league starts in 2 seasons, losing them all. After a spell of coaching at Corby Glen, in May 2015 he was appointed manager of Boston Town but left in 2016.

ANGELL Brett
Striker 6'4"
Born *20/8/1968 Marlborough, Wiltshire*
Playing career: *Portsmouth, Cheltenham Town, Derby County, Stockport County, Southend United, Everton, Sunderland, Sheffield United (loan), West Bromwich Albion (loan 3 sub appearances March 1996), Stockport County, Notts County (loan), Preston North End (loan), Walsall, Rushden & Diamonds, Port Vale, QPR (1986-2003)*

Prolific striker who began his career at Pompey as a defender. Turning professional with Portsmouth in 1986, he made his mark as a striker the following year after moving to Cheltenham Town. In 1988, he joined Stockport County via Derby County, before signing with Southend United in 1990. Impressing at the club, he won a move to Everton four years later. However, the following year, he transferred to Sunderland, who then loaned him to West Bromwich Albion in March 1996. Manager Alan Buckley only used him as a substitute on three occasions, before he returned to Roker Park. He moved to Stockport later in the year. He retired in 2003 having scored 200 goals in 540 games, in all competitions. After knocking in goals for numerous clubs, he finally returned to Fratton Park as a coach in 2005. This role only lasted 5 months. Angell has since coached in Ecuador and taught coaching courses for the FFA before taking up a Central Football regional coaching job in New Zealand. Brett was appointed head coach at Hawke's Bay United, New Zealand September 2014 until 2019.

Victor Anichebe

ANICHEBE Victor
Striker 6'3"
Born *23/4/1988 Lagos, Nigeria*
Playing career: *Everton, West Bromwich Albion (Cost £6 million 31 + 32 sub appearances 9 goals Sept 2013 – June 2016), Sunderland, Beijing Enterprises in China. 11 Nigerian International caps plus 5 at U-23.*

Anichebe was born in Lagos, Lagos State, Nigeria but moved to Liverpool, Merseyside, England aged one. His family originally lived in Toxteth before settling in Crosby. He is the cousin of former professional football player Iffy Onuora, Olympian Anyika Onuora and professional basketball player Chiz Onuora. He is also an Olympic silver medallist, competing for Nigeria in football at the 2008 Olympics. A strong well-built striker whose career was blighted by injuries and inconsistent form. He burst onto the scene at Everton, making his reserve team debut in 2003 aged 15 and his first team debut as a sub in an FA Cup game, aged 17. On 7th May 2006, he scored his first Premier League goal, against West Bromwich Albion. He was awarded Everton's Reserve Player of the Season for the 2005/06 season. At the end of the 2006/07 season, he was voted by Everton fans as their Young Player of the Season. In February 2009, during a match against Newcastle United, a tackle from Kevin Nolan left Anichebe badly injured and unable to play for 11 months. Nolan, who received a straight red card for the foul, later settled out of court when Anichebe sued for loss of earnings. Victor suffered a groin injury while on international duty in September and did not play for the rest of 2011.

He made his return as a second-half substitute on 1st January 2012, against West Bromwich Albion and scored in the 87th minute to give Everton a 1–0 away win. In February he became Everton's most used substitute in the history of the club. In 2012/13 he missed a number of games due to a hamstring injury. In late March, Anichebe said he wanted to finish the season with a goal tally in double figures, but he finished with 8 goals from 32 matches, still the most he has scored in a single season in his career. In September 2013, Anichebe transferred to West Bromwich Albion in a deal which could rise to £6 million. Anichebe was signed by Steve Clarke, but he endured a slow start to his career with the Baggies and failed to score in his first eight matches for the club. He ended his first season with three goals in 24 Premier League appearances for Albion. The centre-forward struggled with injuries the following campaign, although he seemed to enjoy a new lease of life after Tony Pulis took charge of the club in January 2015. He ended the campaign with six goals in 25 appearances in all competitions. Anichebe really struggled to hold down a place in the team the following season and left West Bromwich Albion after his contract expired at the end of the campaign, making just three Premier League starts all season. In September 2016, Anichebe signed a one-year contract with Sunderland to play under his former Everton manager David Moyes. He started well at the Stadium of light nominated as PFA Fans Player of the Month in November, but injuries and a dip in form

meant that on in June 2017, Anichebe joined Chinese club Beijing Enterprises after he was released by Sunderland. In October 2018 it was reported that Anichebe stopped playing for his team, and reported his own club after alleging on two occasions he was encouraged to fix matches and not to try. When he raised the issue with his team mates, he was told: "This is China; we do as we're told." Moving to China he anticipated change and he welcomed the opportunity. His optimism was quickly deflated, realising that corruption and bribery rumoured in the sport was prevalent. He took his case to FIFA. He was soon asked to leave the club and instructed by his lawyer to return to China to negotiate a contract settlement. With no resolution in sight his contract was prematurely terminated. In January 2019 he was awaiting FIFA's response hoping for a fair public CAS hearing where the truth would come out. He summed up the situation by saying "It is during times like these you doubt yourself and question, why me? These are also the times that we must Trust in God with all our hearts and lean not on our own understanding and submit to Him." Still only 31, after an 18-month exile, he started training with Darren Moore's Doncaster Rovers with the manager suggesting a lack of fitness meant he was not offered a deal. In December 2019 he claimed this was untrue and that he was in fact offered various contracts but declined them, stating that "Doncaster was a great club with an incredible manager and most importantly an incredibly sic person in Darren Moore."

The Hawthorns 2018

ARMSTRONG Gerard 'Gerry'

Striker 5'11"

Born *23/5/1954 Belfast, Northern Ireland*

Playing career: *: Bangor, Tottenham Hotspur, Watford, Real Mallorca in Spain, West Bromwich Albion (Free transfer 10+1 sub appearances 1 goal Aug 1985 – May 1986), Chesterfield, Brighton & Hove Albion, Millwall (loan), Crawley Town, Glenavon, Bromley, Worthing, Whitehawk (1970 – 1998) Northern Ireland International 63 caps.*

Armstrong began his career in Northern Ireland with St Paul's Swifts. He only started playing football as a teenager whilst serving a ban from Gaelic football. He subsequently moved on to play for Cromac Albion and Bangor. In November 1975, Armstrong moved to England, signing for Tottenham Hotspur for a fee of £25,000. He made a total of 84 league appearances for Spurs, scoring 10 goals. In November 1980 he was signed by Second Division side Watford for £250,000. Watford were promoted to the First Division in the 1981/82 season. He represented the Northern Ireland national football team and won acclaim at the 1982 FIFA World Cup, where he was the highest scoring player from the UK; this included a shock winner against hosts Spain. In August 1983, he moved to Spain with RCD Mallorca for £200,000. Armstrong returned to England in August 1985, signed by Johnny Giles, as part of the Irish contingent, for West Bromwich Albion on a free transfer. Strong and powerful but lacking pace, he played just 8 league games. In January 1986 he was loaned to Chesterfield, whom he joined permanently in March 1986 until the end of the season. He signed for Brighton & Hove Albion on a free transfer in August 1986. In January 1987, he was loaned to Millwall. Whilst at Brighton he was appointed player/ coach in 1988 but left after an altercation with a fan. Took a similar position at Crawley Town February 1989 to March 1990 leaving after another confrontation with a fan. Armstrong joined Glenavon as a player the same month, and by April 1990 he was also playing midweek games for Bromley. In 1991 he was appointed manager of non-league Worthing, leading them to promotion in 1993. He became assistant manager to the Northern Ireland national team alongside Bryan Hamilton. In 1995 he left Worthing and was appointed youth coach in the county of Surrey.

Armstrong last played competitive football for Brighton based non-league side Whitehawk in 1997/98, making a scoring debut in December 1997 in 3-1 Sussex County League Cup defeat at Burgess Hill Town. He played twice more in the league for Whitehawk that season. In 2004 he returned to assistant manager role for Northern Ireland alongside Lawrie Sanchez. He left in 2006, as his wife Debby was expecting a child. He combined coaching with his employment in journalism, TV and radio. He was co-commentator for Sky Sports covering La Liga. Also worked for ESPN Star Sports analysing Premier League games. Worked for Talksport and has appeared on Singaporean media as analyst on Sing mio TV's 2014 World Cup coverage.

ASHCROFT Lee

Winger/striker 5'9"

Born *7/9/1972 Preston*

Playing career: *Preston North End, West Bromwich Albion (Cost £250,000 79 + 31 sub appearances 18 goals July 1993 – Nov 1996), Notts County (loan), Preston North End(loan then signed) , Grimsby Town, Wigan Athletic, Port Vale (loan), Huddersfield Town (loan), Southport, Chorley (loan), Kendal Town 2004, player-manager of non-league Kendal Town 2006-12. (1987 – 2010) Played once for England U-21's.*

Lee was a tricky, skilful winger, not the fastest, who sometimes played as a striker. An England under-21 international, the striker began his playing career at Preston North End in 1987. Six years later he was sold on to West Bromwich Albion for £250,000 in August 1993, where Ashcroft was signed by manager Keith Burkinshaw. He scored a vital headed goal on the final day of the 1993/94 season, in a 1–0 win at Portsmouth, to keep Albion in the First Division. Lee also scored a terrific hat-trick in the final home game of the 1994-95 season at the Hawthorns against Tranmere Rovers in a 5-1 victory. Ashcroft could produce something special, a mazy dribble, a terrific cross or a thrilling goal, but he did not do this on a regular enough basis. He was loaned out to Notts County in 1995. He returned to Preston North End for £150,000 in September 1996. Ashcroft was transferred to Grimsby Town £500,000 in August 1998, before again being sold on, to Wigan Athletic in August 2000 for £350,000. Loaned out to Port Vale and Huddersfield Town.

He was released in 2003 and joined Conference club Southport, before ending his career with a six-year spell with Kendal Town. He amassed over 400 league games scoring 91 goals After retiring from playing football Lee managed Northwich Victoria 2012/13 then took on the role of director of football. He manged Longridge Town in the West Lancashire League Premier Division winning the title in 2017/18. Won the North West Counties League Division One North title in 2018/19. Now in the North West Counties Premier Division but when lying 6th in the league, the season was abandoned in March 2020 due to Covd-19 pandemic and all results were expunged with no promotion or relegation.

ASHLEY Harry

Forward/half back/full back 5'9½"
Born *7/1/1913 Smethwick*
Died *Jan 1985 Birmingham*
Playing career: *West Bromwich Albion, Derby County, WBA (13 apps 6 goals, 1934-37 & 1942-43), Darlington (1934-42).Also guested for Nottingham Forest & Walsall during WW2.*

Nicknamed 'Caggy' he was a good, honest performer who spent his initial spell at the Hawthorns in the reserves, joined Derby County in 1937 for a fee of £525 but came back as a guest player during the hostilities of WW2. He re-joined Albion in 1942, making all of his senior appearances in the Wartime Leagues and Cup competitions. Harry was something of a dressing room comedian. Lye Town Manager 1948-50. Assistant-trainer at the Hawthorns 1950-64.

He was a publican in Leicester. Later returned to the Hawthorns as Steward and ground staff assistant from 1971to 1981, retiring through ill health aged 68.
Personal note: *I recall Harry having multiple jobs at the Hawthorns, like looking after the apprentices and the boot room. He always walked round in a white coat - a really funny man.*

ASHMORE George

Goalkeeper 5'11"
Born *5/5/1898 Plymouth, Devon*
Died *12/5/1973 Handsworth, Birmingham*
Playing career: *West Bromwich Albion (268 appearances Nov 1919 – October 1931), Chesterfield. (1919 – 1935) One England cap in 1926*

Nicknamed 'Cap'. An agile, daring goalkeeper. He was understudy to Hubert Pearson for a number of years, appeared mainly in the mid-twenties, losing his place to Harold Pearson, Hubert's son. George played for England once in 1926. George played in 268 games for Albion's first team in a 12-year career. His last Albion game was in the 1930/31 season when he deputised for Pearson in the FA Cup 3rd round 2nd replay against Charlton held at Villa Park when Albion won 3-1. He played 114 times for the reserves winning Birmingham & District championship medal in 1919/20 and Central League championship winners medal in 1922/23. He retired from football aged 37. George worked for the Midlands Electricity Board MEB for many years.

ASTLE Jeffrey 'Jeff'

Striker 6'0"
Born *13/5/1942 Eastwood, Notts*
Died *19/1/2002 Burton-on-Trent*
Playing career: *Notts County, West Bromwich Albion (Cost £25,000 359+2 sub appearances 174 goals Sep 1964 – July 1974) Hellenic (South Africa), Dunstable Town, Weymouth, Atherstone Town, Hillingdon Borough (loan). (1960-1977) England International 5 caps & Played twice for the Football League and played 3 games for an England XI scoring 7 goals, in South America prior to the 1970 World Cup Finals, in which he also made 2 appearances.*

Coming from a family of 7, with 3 brothers and 3 sisters, it wasn't an easy childhood. Jeff lost his father Samuel at the age of 4 and for him, like so many families in the post war years life, financially, was a struggle. Jeff's ability was first noticed by his old sports master who recommended Jeff to

West Notts Schools Boys team. After catching the eye of local footballing scouts, Jeff turned professional with Notts County when he was 17. His style was that of a classic centre forward, and he was the protege of the late great Tommy Lawton. In September 1964 Jeff signed for West Bromwich Albion for a fee of £25,000, and jumped from the old Division 4 to top flight football in Division 1, probably the best ever value for money transfer to the Albion when Jeff was signed by Albion manager Jimmy Hagan He scored two goals on his home debut against Black Country rivals Wolverhampton Wanderers in a 5-1 victory and he was an instant 'hit' with all Baggies fans. Whilst with the Albion Jeff won the League Cup in 1966 & the FA Cup in 1968, scoring in every round including the winner at Wembley. He was also a League Cup Final runner up in 1967 and 1970. Jeff was the first player to score in an F A Cup Final & League Cup Final at Wembley. He was voted as Midlands Footballer of the Year in 1968. Jeff as the highest League goal scorer in the First Division in 1969/70 with 25 goals. Known as the 'King' by all Albion fans. After leaving Albion in 1974 he joined the late great Bobby Moore at South African team Hellenic. He later enjoyed non-league football with Dunstable Town, where he teamed up with the legendary former Manchester United star George Best, later playing for Weymouth, Atherstone Town and Hillingdon Borough. He started a window cleaning business whilst still playing at Weymouth. Later Jeff ran his own industrial cleaning business in Ashby-de-la-Zouch. In 1994 his vocal talents were also exposed to the nation through his regular appearances as resident singer on BBC's cult programme 'Fantasy Football' with Frank Skinner and David Baddiel. Appeared for the Albion Old Stars and went on the road with the 'Jeff Astle Roadshow'. His last appearance on Fantasy Football, now on ITV, was during the 1998 World Cup finals. Jeff died tragically at home on 21st November 2002. South Staffordshire coroner concluded that he died from brain injuries caused by repeatedly heading a ball – dementia: footballers' migraine. Since his death, aged just 59, despite the growing understanding of issues around head injury in sport and in particular, chronic traumatic encephalopathy

(CTE), awareness of these important issues still remains low in the UK. From May 2014, he will be remembered as the first British professional footballer confirmed to have died from chronic traumatic encephalopathy (CTE), a progressive, degenerative brain disease found in individuals with a history of head injury, often as a result of multiple concussions. In Jeff Astle's case, it was the repeated, low level brain trauma believed to have been caused from the repeated heading of footballs. The family of Jeff Astle - his loving wife Laraine & Daughters Dorice, Dawn & Clare, launched the 'Jeff Astle Foundation' on 11th April 2015 established in memory of Jeff, as a fitting and lasting legacy to both raise awareness of brain injury in all forms of sport and to offer much needed support to those affected.

Personal note: *Jeff was a real character. Always willing to play a joke. One day at Spring Road training ground, John Osborne turned up in a flashy new suit. Jeff thought it would be funny to use scissors to cut the trousers at the knees. Ossie was fuming, but the players put together to buy him a new suit. I used to spend hours at the training ground in my school holidays, watching the players train and then collecting their autographs. Jeff was my first real footballing hero. I was fortunate to go to Wembley in 1968. I was seated two rows from the back in the stand opposite the Royal Box, with my Uncle Stan and cousin Roger. The players looked so tiny and rather strange in their white kit with red socks. When the 'King' scored the winning goal in extra time to win the FA Cup in 1968, that moment was totally euphoric. That was the pinnacle of my years watching Albion, although only 16 at the time. Here we are over 50 years later and still no major trophies at the Hawthorns. If I could make a wish for every Albion fan, it would be for us to win another FA Cup Final at Wembley.*

BACHE Harold
Centre forward 5'8"
Born *20/4/1889 Churchill, Worcestershire*
Died *15/2/1916 near Comines, Hainaut, Belgium in WW" aged 26*

Playing career: *Corinthians, West Bromwich Springfield, Staffordshire Youths, Eastbourne FC, West Bromwich Albion (14 appearances 4 goals Feb 1914 – Feb 1916) Amateur England International & played for the Football League XI. Killed in action in WW1.*

Born in Churchill, Worcestershire, Bache was educated at King Edward VI School in

Birmingham and Caius College, Cambridge. Harold was a brilliant amateur International. He was not very big for a centre forward, weighing barely 10st. However, Harold was so fast, skilful and positive in everything he did and his height and build proved insignificant. He sadly only played 14 games for Albion but he had been a regular performer for England Amateur FA international side and in one international against France at Ipswich 1910 he scored 7 goals in a 20-0 victory. He also played for the Football League XI in 1914. Destined for major honours until he was killed by a sniper near the Comines Canal, West Flanders in Belgium, aged just 26, whilst serving with the Lancashire Fusiliers in Belgium during WW1. Having no known grave, he is commemorated on the Menin Gate Memorial. He excelled in Rugby Union, Tennis and athletics, as well as being an all-round cricketer playing. He really was a grand sportsman in every sense of the word, liked, loved and respected throughout the sporting world. A sad loss to football.

BADDELEY George

Half back 5'9"

Born *8/5/1874 Stoke-on-Trent, Staffs*
Died *July 1952 West Bromwich, Staffs aged 78*
Playing career: *Stoke City, West Bromwich Albion (Cost £250 157 appearances 1 goal 1908 – 1914)*
He joined Stoke in May 1900 he made his debut in 1901/02. He was awarded the captaincy in his first full season of 1902–03. Although occasionally criticised for 'marring a clever display by trying to do much with the ball' Baddeley's consistency allowed him to play 208 league games between 1901 – 1908. Stoke struggled, first being relegated and then being liquidated which saw them leave the Football League at the end of the 1907–08 season. In July 1908 Baddeley, along with centre forward Freddie Brown, signed for West Bromwich Albion for £250 and made his debut away at Grimsby Town two months later. Strong and safe, extremely difficult to pass, also a fine feeder of the attack. He was a competent, confident right half. He won a Second Division championship medal with the club in 1910/11 and an FA Cup runners-up medal in 1912. George played 157 matches for Albion, scoring once. Baddeley's last game for Albion was against Sheffield Wednesday on

18 April 1914, at the age of 39 years, 345 days. He retired from football the following month after playing making 157 senior appearances for West Bromwich Albion. He subsequently became a publican at the Crown & Cushion in West Bromwich and also worked in the upholstery trade.

BAIRD Chris

Defender/midfielder 6'1"

Born *25/2/1982 Rasharkin, Northern Ireland*
Playing career: *Southampton, Walsall (loan), Watford (loan), Fulham, Reading, Burnley, West Bromwich Albion (Free transfer 12 + 12 sub appearances July 2014 – June 2015), Derby County, Fulham (loan) (2001 – 2019) Retired February 2019 Northern Ireland U-18, U-21 and Full International 79 caps.* Adaptable and reliable Baird played Right back, centre-half, defensive midfielder and central midfielder.
A solid and versatile player who played a no-frills game. He started his professional career at Southampton playing 68 league games between 2003- 2007. He had loan spells at Walsall and Watford. Baird left Southampton in July 2007 to move to Fulham for £3.025 million, where he linked up with manager Lawrie Sanchez. He played 127 league games scoring 4 goals between 2007-2013. Baird was one of twelve players released by Fulham at the end of the 2012/13 Premier League season. Baird signed for Reading in September 2013 on a deal until January 2014 then was left without a club after leaving Reading. In March he signed a short-term contract at Burnley making 7 league appearances helping them gain promotion to the Premier League. In July 2014 Baird signed a one-year contract for Albion, then in the Premier League. He played at left back and more as a defensive midfielder, making 19 appearances. He was released at the end of the season. Baird signed for Derby County in June 2015 on a two-year contract. Injuries, a drop in form and managerial changes resulted in him having a brief loan at one of his former clubs Fulham, playing 7 league games. Released by Derby at the end of 2017/18 season and unable to find a club, he announced his retirement in February 2019. Now working for first club Southampton, his aim is to make a seamless transition from a successful playing career into scouting and player recruitment whilst studying at the same time.

BANKS Ian
Midfielder 5'9"

Born *9/1/1961 Mexborough, Yorkshire*

Playing career: *Barnsley, Leicester City, Huddersfield Town, Bradford City, West Bromwich Albion (Cost £100,000 2+2sub appearances Mar 1989 - Barnsley, Rotherham United, Darlington, Emley AFC, AFC Emley (1978 – 1999)*

A competitive, hare-working midfielder with a thunderous shot. He started at Barnsley playing 164 league games scoring 37 goals 1978-1983, Leicester City 103 league games and 14 goals, Huddersfield Town 78 league games 17 goals. Bradford City was his next stop, making 30 appearances in the league and scoring 3 times. He had a disappointing time at the Hawthorns, signed by Brian Talbot for £100,000, only making 2 starting appearances and a further 2 as a substitute. Good ion the ball but he seemed to struggle with his weight. He moved on to play at Barnsley, then Rotherham United and Darlington before moving into non-league. He managed AFC Emley between 2008 and 2010 working alongside Grant Crookes, becoming the first person to manage the old Emley and the current AFC Emley. When celebrating a friend's 60th birthday with his wife Kaye at the Olive Lounge, a tapas bar and restaurant in Wickersley, Rotherham, in March 2019. As he was checking for the group's taxi, was attacked twice, inside the bar and again as he was standing on the pavement. Ian discharged himself from Rotherham Hospital the following day, and after some CT scans and seven stitches in the back of his head he was allowed to leave. He suffered dizzy spells, could not lie down on his left side. His concentration is affected and he suffers with fatigue and tiredness. South Yorkshire Police arrested a man but charges Had not yet been made. It was believed to be a case of mistaken identity but even though Ian's scars had healed it has obviously left him very shaken He works as a Mortgage advisor.

"DID YOU KNOW?"

"Ronnie Allen is the only player to have scored a league goal in every one of the 20 post-WW2 seasons"

BANNISTER Gary
Striker/forward 5'7"

Born *22/7/1960 Warrington, Lancashire*

Playing career: *Coventry City, Detroit Express (loan), Sheffield Wednesday, Queens Park Rangers, Coventry City, West Bromwich Albion (Cost £250,000 69 + 12 sub appearances 20 goals Mar 1990 – June 1992), Oxford United (loan), Nottingham Forest, Stoke City, Hong Kong Rangers, Lincoln City, Darlington, Poerthleven (1978 – 2001)*

Gary was a diminutive figure for a striker but relied upon his pace and skill. Quietly spoken both on and off the pitch. He was always personable with fans. He started at Coventry City playing just 22 league games and scored 3 goals before moving for £100,000 to Sheffield Wednesday, scoring 55 goals in 118 league games. He formed a deadly partnership with Imre Varadi in 1983/84 where they scored 41 goals between them as Wednesday were promoted to the First Division. In summer 1984 he moved to Queens Park Rangers for £200,000. Bannister made 168 appearances, scoring 66 goals in his three and a half seasons with them. He returned to Coventry City in March 1988 in a £300,000 deal. His second spell at Coventry lasted two years and was not a great success as he scored 13 goals in 44 appearances. He moved again, this time to West Bromwich Albion for £250,000 in March 1990 where he stayed until the summer of 1992, making 66 appearances and scoring 19 goals. Bannister had a spell at Oxford United on loan. He moved to Nottingham Forest where, he was unable the stop the team being relegated from the Premier League. Stoke City was his next team. He also spent one-year 1993/1994 playing for Hong Kong Rangers. Gary's final two teams were Lincoln City and Darlington before retiring at the end of the 1995/96 season. He had a long 17-year career lasting from 1978 to 1995 during which time he made 564 appearances in league and cup matches plus 42 as substitute. On leaving football Bannister moved to St. Ives in Cornwall becoming involved in Hotel Maintenance and Property Development. He played for, and coached, Porthleven in the South Western Football League for several seasons. After about 10 years in Cornwall, Bannister and his family moved back to the Midlands and he has a job in Hotel Maintenance in Birmingham.

BARHAM Mark
Right winger/Midfielder 5'7"
Born *12/7/1962 Folkestone, Kent*
Playing career: *Norwich City, Huddersfield Town, Middlesbrough, Hythe Town, West Bromwich Albion (1989), Brighton & Hove Albion, Shrewsbury Town, Kitchee in Hong Kong, Sittingbourne, Southwick, Fakenham Town, Mulbarton (1980 – 1998) 2 England International caps*

He played 213 times for Norwich and scored 25 times. While with the club he was capped twice by England on their 1983 trip to Australia. He was a member of the Norwich sides that won the League Cup in 1985 and the Second Division championship in 1986. Barham joined Huddersfield Town in July 1987 for £25,000. After only 27 league appearances, with a single goal, Barham then joined Middlesbrough in October 1988, and he played just four league matches for Boro where a serious knee injury threatened to end his full-time career. Following a short period at Hythe Town, Barham found himself playing another four league matches for West Bromwich Albion in 1989. From there, he joined Brighton & Hove Albion playing in 73 league appearances, scoring three times in three years. In 1992, he joined Shrewsbury Town, scoring once in eight league appearances.

He then dropped into the non-league scene, including Fakenham Town as manager from April 1996 until his resignation in December 1997, and Mulbarton in February 1998. As well as working on corporate hospitality for Norwich City, Barham spent three years with Hewden Hire Centre a tool-hire company, 4 years as Partner in Rent-a-Tool Hire & Sales in Norwich. The last 12 years with MITIE Group PLC as Business Development Manager at Wyngate School, Norwich.

BARLOW Raymond 'Ray'
Forward/Wing half 6'0"
Born *17/8/1926 Swindon, Wiltshire*
Died *14/3/2012 Bridgend, South Wales*
Playing career: *West Bromwich Albion (482 appearances 48 goals 1944 – 1960) Birmingham City, Stourbridge. (1944-1962) Played once for England, twice for England B and four times for the Football League, also went on an FA tour of South America.*

A tall, rangy player, who was poised, elegant, skilful and fast over a short distance. He was recommended to Albion by former striker Jimmy Cookson. Wholehearted with heaps of energy, big Ray started as an inside forward with Albion even playing centre forward and centre half but he developed into a classy wing half.

One of the finest footballers ever to don an Albion shirt. He made his first team debut in a 2-0 home Wartime League Cup defeat away at Walsall. In February 1945. His League debut was away at Newport County in Division Two in August 1946. Albion won 7-2 and Barlow scored one, Ike Clarke scored four. He could tackle soundly, strutted across the field majestically spraying passes straight to the feet of his colleagues from 40 yards. His powerful runs from deep carried him into the opposing penalty area where he caused all sorts of trouble. It was a forward dash that resulted in a penalty after being fouled by Tommy Docherty in the 1954 FA Cup Final at Wembley, which Ronnie Allen duly dispatched. He was extremely unlucky not to pick up more than the solitary England cap which came in a 2-0 victory against Northern Ireland in 1954.He sold furniture with Jimmy Dugdale marketing a gramophone record cabinet, whilst still playing, Ray did represent the 'B' team, the Football League and the FA XI as well as frequently being an England reserve at home and abroad. He skippered the Albion in the late 1950's. Ray played 482 times for Albion's first XI scoring 48 goals and a further 41 appearances with 10 goals for the Reserve side in the Central League. He moved to Birmingham City to play 5 games in the 1960/61 season.

Ray finished his footballing career in non-league with Stourbridge, although he did frequently turn out for the Old Players team in Charity events. He ran a Newsagents and Tobacconists shop in West Bromwich & later a Post Office in Stourbridge. Barlow was the last surviving member of the WBA team that won the FA Cup in 1954 against Preston North End. He lived in Pedmore near Stourbridge, until his death in March 2012, aged 85, after a long illness He was described by Bobby Robson as one of the best players he had played alongside. Ray was a very useful cricketer and played quite a few games for West Bromwich Dartmouth in the Birmingham League.

BARNES Giles

Forward/attacking midfielder 6'2"
Born *5/8/1988 Barking, London*
Playing career: *Derby County, Fulham (loan), West Bromwich Albion (Free transfer 7+21 sub appearances Feb 2010 – July 2011), Houston Dynamo in USA, Vancouver Whitecaps, Orlando City, Leon in Mexico, Colorado Rapids, Hyderabad in India.(2005 – 2019*
Signed professional with Derby County in August 2005 making his debut as a late substitute in a League Cup defeat to Grimsby. Although he picked up an injury towards the end of the season, Barnes was still able to make an impact in Derby's successful Championship play-off campaign in his two substitute appearances. It was his corner from which Leon Best scored an own goal in the second leg of the semi-final clash with Southampton and he also came off the bench to set up Stephen Pearson's winner in the 2007 Championship play-off Final victory over West Bromwich Albion. After this, it was found out that Barnes was playing with a broken foot and he missed all of the summer. His 2007/08 season ended early when it was discovered he had a knee injury which required major surgery. In 2008/09 after just three league appearances, on 31st January 2009, Barnes signed for Fulham on loan for the rest of the season with a view to a possible permanent transfer, with Derby receiving a substantial loan fee, and agreeing a fee of £2 million, raising to £4 million on appearances if he signed permanently. He did not make a single appearance due to fitness, but scored seven in eight reserve matches.

Giles Barnes

Roy Hodgson confirmed that Fulham would not be signing Barnes on a permanent basis. Barnes returned to Derby but sustained another injury in a pre-season friendly against Stoke City after a two footed lunge by Carl Dickinson, and was eventually released from his Derby contract in December 2009. In mid-January 2010 Barnes moved on to train with West Bromwich Albion of the Championship. On 3rd February 2010, Barnes signed for West Bromwich Albion on an 18-month contract, with an option for a further one-year extension. He made his debut in the 1–0 win against Sheffield Wednesday in March 2010, coming off the bench for the last 10 minutes of the match. Albion were promoted at the end of that season. Barnes never really established himself at the Hawthorns, showing only glimpses of the form of previous years. After 7 appearances plus another 21 as a substitute, it was announced that Barnes was being released by West Bromwich Albion in May 2011. He had not played any matches for the club since the arrival of manager Roy Hodgson in January 2011. In August 2011, Barnes signed a six-month contract with Doncaster Rovers following a successful trial at the club. Barnes signed with Major League Soccer club Houston Dynamo in August 2012. In March 2016, Barnes was appointed captain of the Houston Dynamo for the 2016 season. Barnes was traded to Vancouver Whitecaps FC on 30 July 2016 in exchange for general allocation money and the MLS rights to Keyner Brown. The deal also dictated that Houston will receive a percentage of any future transfer fees. Barnes was traded to fellow MLS club Orlando City SC in February 2017 in exchange for Brek Shea. Barnes signed with Mexican club León in January 2018. On 13th July 2018, Barnes signed a six-month deal with MLS side Colorado Rapids. In 2019 he signed for Indian side Hyderabad.

"DID YOU KNOW?"

"Jimmy Cookson once scored 6 goals in a match against Blackpool in the Second Division on 17 September 1927."

BARNES Peter

Winger 5'10"

Born 10/6/1957 Manchester

Playing career: *Manchester City, West Bromwich Albion (Cost £748,000 90+2 sub appearances 25 goals July 1979-July 1981), Leeds United, Real Betis, Leeds United, Manchester United (loan), Coventry City, Manchester United, Manchester City, Bolton Wanderers (loan), Port Vale (loan), Wimbledon (loan), Hull City, SC Farense Portugal,.Bolton Wanderers, Sunderland, Stockport County (loan), Footscray JUST Yugoslavia, Bury, Drogheda United, Tampa Bay Rowdies, Stafford Rangers, Northwich Victoria, Wrexham, Radcliffe Borough, Mossley, Hamrun Spartans Malta, SC Farense Portugal, Cliftonville. (1974-1992) 22 England International Caps also U-21.*

Nicknamed 'Barnesy' he started his career at Manchester City. He scored in the 1976 League Cup final at the age of 18. He was voted Young Player of the Year by the Professional Footballers' Association in 1976. Barnes was sold by new boss Malcolm Allison in 1979, and joined West Bromwich Albion for a fee of £748,000, a club transfer record, that was held until Kevin Kilbane broke the £1 million barrier over 18 years later. He finished as the club's leading scorer in 1979/80 season with 15 league goals. He showed flashes of brilliance with his superb dribbling, as in the game against Bolton Wanderers at the Hawthorns on 18th March 1980, when he scored a hat-trick. Albion finished fourth in 1980–81 under Ron Atkinson. Barnes frequently drifted out of games and the final delivery was often missing. He signed for Leeds United in 1981 for £748,000. Leeds' manager Allan Clarke played him as a striker but Barnes failed to adapt to his new role, scoring once in 30 games as Leeds were relegated into the Second Division in 1981/82. Assistant manager Martin Wilkinson stated that the club were not asking Peter to run his blood to water, but wanted to see him sweat occasionally. Barnes handed in a transfer request, and in February 1982 was given a £750 club fine following comments he made to newspapers. Barnes spent 1982/83 in La Liga with Real Betis, before returning to Elland Road for a run of 27 games and four goals in 1983/84. He was sold by Eddie Gray to Coventry City for £50,000 in 1984/85. Ron Atkinson subsequently signed him for Manchester United, where he was effectively an understudy to Danish winger Jesper Olsen.

His time at Old Trafford was limited when Atkinson was replaced as manager by Alex Ferguson. Barnes was transferred back to Manchester City in 1987, but soon fell out of favour and left Maine Road in 1988. He embarked on a remarkable tour of global football, playing for Hull City, SC Farense, Bolton Sunderland, Stockport County, Footscray JUST, Bury, Drogheda United, Tampa Bay Rowdies, Stafford Rangers, Northwich Victoria, Wrexham, Radcliffe Borough, Mossley, Hamrun Spartans, and Cliftonville. This took him to Portugal, Australia, Malta, the United States, and both the Republic of Ireland and Northern Ireland. After retiring from playing, Barnes had a brief spell managing Gibraltar and Runcorn, and has since worked behind the scenes at Manchester City and for BBC Radio Manchester. From August 2010, he was based in Kuala Lumpur, working as a Premier League pundit for Malaysian network Astro, and its thrice-weekly FourFourTwo TV programme. On the night that his former club Manchester City clinched the 2011/12 Premier League title, the normally reserved Barnes sang a rendition of "Blue Moon" during the post-game show in Astro's studios. Later returned to Maine Road to help out in the Social Club, and then to help coach the youngsters. He has worked in radio, TV, coaching and scouting. Was the director of Kick Off Soccer Centre, has been involved with a company that sells artificial pitches, and has also worked at City in their hospitality suites. He is the Son of former Southampton, Arsenal & Wales International player Wally Barnes.

Peter Barnes

BARNETT Leon
Defender/midfielder 6'1"
Born *30/11/1985 Stevenage, Herts*
Playing career: *Luton Town, Aylesbury (loan), West Bromwich Albion (Cost £3 million 51+5 sub appearances 3 goals Jul 2007 – July 2010), Coventry City (loan), Norwich City (loan then signed), Cardiff City (loan), Wigan Athletic, Bury, Northampton Town (21002 – 2018)*

A tall, rangy defender, he primarily played as a centre-back, but also as a full-back, central midfielder and striker. He began his career with Luton Town where he established himself in the first team. He played 59 league games, before signing for West Bromwich Albion in 2007 for an initial fee of £2.5 million which would rise by £250,000 depending upon appearances and another £250,000 after winning promotion, which was achieved in his first season. Leon lost his place in the side due to injury and loss of form, spending the majority of the 2009/10 season on loan with Coventry City. He joined Norwich City on loan in 2010 before completing a permanent transfer in January 2011. His first season with the club led to promotion from the Championship. He made 50 league appearances for the Canaries before, after a brief loan spell at Cardiff City, moving to Wigan for £500,000. Barnett started in a 2–0 defeat to Manchester United in the FA Community Shield at Wembley Stadium. He ended his first season with the club having made 53 appearances and scoring five goals in all competitions. Having made 21 appearances in all competitions Wigan were relegated to League One at the end of the 2014/15 season. The club announced that Barnett would be released at the end of 2015/16. He signed a two-year contract with League One club Bury in July 2016. However, on 31st May 2017, Barnett signed a two-year contract with League One club Northampton Town on a free transfer. Leon Barnett retired from playing on 26th November 2018, aged 32, as a result of a heart condition. He was fitted with a pacemaker after being diagnosed with myocarditis. Northampton honoured the remainder of his contract and offered him the opportunity to work at the club to gain coaching experience. Leon started his own football academy in the Luton area. Has done some media work co-commentating on Norwich City games.

BARTLETT Kevin

Forward 5'9"

Born *12/10/1962 Portsmouth*

Playing career: *Portsmouth, Fareham Town, Cardiff City, West Bromwich Albion (Cost £100,000 31+12 sub appearances 11goals Feb 1989 – Feb 1990), Notts County, Port Vale (loan), Cambridge United (1980 -1993)*

He began his career at hometown club Portsmouth in 1980, but dropped into non-league football with Fareham Town two years later. Signing with Cardiff City in September 1986, he helped the "Bluebirds" to the Welsh Cup and promotion out of the Fourth Division in 1987/88. He moved on to West Bromwich Albion in 1989 for £100,000. A pacey striker with a keen eye for goal. He made 31 starts for Albion and another 12 substitute appearances scoring 11 goals, before joining Notts County a year later. He helped the "Magpies" to promotion out of the Second Division in 1991 but retired due to injury in 1993, not long after joining Cambridge United. Kevin was a self-employed football coach 1995-96 and joined the voluntary sector as a housing advisor for Shelter. He was a welfare benefits advisor with Nottingham City Council 1996-98, then worked for 2 years with NACRO. Kevin became regional manager with Refugee Action between 2000-2003. Regional manager with Crime Concern from 2003 to 2005. He did Partnership Development with One Nottingham 2005 to 2011, and was a Trustee with Notts County Football in the Community between 2010 to 2018. In February 2015 Nottingham became the first City of Football and Kevin was Non-Executive Director from 2015 to 2018. His final role was Apprentice Service Manager with Nottingham City Council between 2017 and 2019 before retiring in July 2019.

BASSETT William 'Billy'

Right winger 5'5½"

Born *27/1/1869 West Bromwich, Staffs*

Died *8/4/1937 West Bromwich, Staffs aged 68*

West Bromwich Albion (311 appearances 77 goals Aug 1886 – Apr 1899) 16 England International caps

Billy Bassett is one of the great names in Albion's history. The eldest of six children whose Father was a coal merchant. He joined West Bromwich Albion in 1886, playing at outside-right. Bassett made his League debut for Albion on 8th September 1888 in a 2–0 win against Stoke City.

West Bromwich Albion
FIXTURES, 1908-9.

With **W. I. Bassett's**
Dartmouth Hotel,
West Bromwich.   Compliments.

When he made his League debut, he was 19 years 225 days old. That made him, on that first day of League football, West Bromwich Albion's youngest player. Including Cup, matches and friendlies, Billy made over 450 appearances for Albion, scoring over 125 goals. In his early days Bassett's weekly wage was 7s 6d. He was reported as being a writing clerk in the 1891 census, living in Nichols Street, West Bromwich. This was one of the first indications that footballers had to have second jobs to pay their bills. He played 261 Football League games for the club, scoring 61 goals, and he also won 16 England caps scoring eight goals, becoming one of the game's earliest celebrities. On 28th April 1894, Bassett became the first ever Albion player to be sent off for using "unparliamentary language" in a friendly match at Millwall. A quite brilliant player, fast and clever, determined and dedicated, he played mostly as an outside right, hugging the touchline and putting in many darting runs. His centres were immaculate and his shooting red hot. He was a great clubman. He appeared in three FA Cup Finals with Albion 1888, 1892 and 1895 collecting winners' medals in the first two.

He had the honour of being named 'finest footballer in Britain' in 1895. Bassett made his 311th and final competitive appearance for Albion on the last day of the 1898/99 season, lining up in a 7–1 defeat away against Aston Villa. He retired in 1899, aged 30, because he did not want to live on his reputation. He was married to Beatrice nee Birch in June 1900 and they had four children, Norman, Beatrice, Mary and Joan. He played hockey for a couple of years. Billy became a Football League linesman. He represented West Bromwich Dartmouth and West Bromwich Wednesbury cricket clubs. He also became a first-rate golfer. In the 1901 census Billy was registered as a licensed victualler, was licensee of the Globe, Reform Street, West Bromwich 1896 to 1900 , and ran the Anchor Inn at 303 High Street, West Bromwich. Bassett was a Freemason, a member of Noah's Ark Lodge, initiated on 15th April 1904. He held the tenancy of the Dartmouth Hotel between 1906 – 1920. He also had financial interests in the Cinema industry. In the 1911 census, Basset was still a victualler, running the Dartmouth Hotel at 2, Paradise Street in West Bromwich. He had a regular column in the Birmingham Mail in 1905, reporting every week on the Black Country's football news, and continued to supply articles for many newspapers afterwards. Bassett became an Albion director in 1905, following the resignation of the previous board in its entirety. The club was in deep financial trouble and had had a writ served upon them by their bank, but Bassett, returning chairman Harry Keys and Club Secretary Fred Everiss, rescued the club, aided by local fund-raising activities. Bassett became chairman in 1908, a position he held until his death, and helped the club to avoid bankruptcy once more in 1910 by paying the players' summer wages from his own pocket. His activities in the wider footballing world let him to take an active role in the development of both the Football Association and the Football League. The strength of England's rivalry with Scotland had led Bassett to develop a "distaste" for Scots during his playing days, and his 29-year chairmanship Albion did not sign a single Scottish player. In 1935 he was appointed as a local Magistrate. His final years were plagued by ill-health, but he celebrated 50 years with Albion in 1936.

Billy Bassett died of a heart attack on 8th April 1937 at the age of 68 at his home 'Kelvedon', 81, Beeches Road, West Bromwich. Two days after his death, a minute silence was held prior to Albion's 4–1 defeat to Preston North End in the FA Cup semi-final at Highbury. The Albion players were clearly affected, with Teddy Sandford saying "We were all too full up to play. Mr Bassett's death stunned the whole team. He was such a well-respected person. He taught me a lot and I must admit that I was tearful for most of the first half following the minute's silence before the kick off."

Notice of the Funeral: Monday, 12th April 1937: "The funeral will take place on Monday, the internment will be at All Saints' Parish Church, West Bromwich, after a service at St. Philip's Church, Beeches-road, at noon. The service will be conducted by the Rev. W. C. Jordan, Vicar of Darlington, ex-Albion amateur International centre-forward of pre-war days. He will be assisted by the Rev. Martin, of Smethwick, a personal friend of the late Mr. Bassett." - Birmingham Daily Gazette, Friday, 9th April 1937. More than 100,000 people lined the streets of West Bromwich for Bassett's funeral procession.

Notice of Probate: "Bassett- William Isaiah of Beeches Road, West Bromwich, Staffordshire died 8 April 1937. Probate London 16th June to Beatrice Bassett widow, William Ellery Jephcott journalist and Fred Everiss company secretary. Effects £51,162 13s. 4d."(equivalent to over £3.5 million in today's money). In 1998, he was listed among the Football League 100 Legends, while in 2004 he was named as one of West Bromwich Albion's 16 greatest players, in a poll organised as part of the club's 125th anniversary celebrations.

Personal note: *Rev. W. C. Jordan, Vicar of Darlington, ex-Albion amateur International centre-forward of pre-war days conducted the marriage service of my Mom Edna Everiss, Fred Everiss' daughter, to my Dad Charles Atkins in November 1940.*

"DID YOU KNOW?"

"West Bromwich Albion were one of the 12 Founder Members of the Football League in 1888/89."

BATSON Brendon MBE

Right back/defender 5'10"

Born *6/2/1953 St Georges, Grenada*

Playing career: *Arsenal, Cambridge United, West Bromwich Albion (Cost £30,000 220 appearances 2 goals Feb 1978 – May 1984) 3 England 'B' International caps. Retired through injury*

Brendon was a highly efficient right-back who began his playing career with Arsenal as either a midfielder or central defender. With the Gunners he won an FA Youth Cup winners' medal 1971. Playing only 10 league games in 3 years at Arsenal, he moved to Cambridge United in January 1974.

As Captain, Batson helped the team to the Fourth Division title in 1977. He played in 163 league games scoring 6 goals for Cambridge. Steady, easy-going and sincere, he was Ron Atkinson's first signing for Albion, signing him for £30,000 in February 1978. Whilst with Albion, he gained three England 'B' caps in 1980. He became known as one of Albion's 'three degrees' along with Laurie Cunningham and Cyrille Regis. Unfortunately, his career came to an abrupt end aged 31 in 1984 when, on doctor's advice, he was forced to quit competitive football through a knee injury.

Brendon Batson

Albion immediately granted him a Testimonial Match to say 'thank you' for his magnificent service to the club. Brendon assisted the WBA All-stars 1984-87. Batson played in 220 games in all competitions for Albion scoring 2 goals. He was elected assistant-secretary to the PFA in May 1984, later becoming deputy chief executive. He was managing director at the Hawthorns July 2002 – June 2003. He has assisted from time to time on local radio covering Midlands football. He has done a lot of Charity work including long cycle rides. He was awarded the MBE in 2001.He is a staunch supporter of the Old Baggies Former Players' Association. In 2020 he was part of a group of present and former players who sent messages or made phone calls to senior season ticket holders during the Corona Virus pandemic.

BEATTIE Craig

Striker 6'0"
Born *16/1/1984 Glasgow, Scotland*
Playing career: *Celtic, West Bromwich Albion (Cost £1.25 million + £500,000 performance-related add ons 13+28 sub appearances 7 goals July 2007 – July 2009), Preston North End (loan), Crystal Palace (loan), Sheffield United (loan), Swansea City, Watford (loan), Heart of Midlothian, St. Johnstone, Barnet, Dundee, Zebbug Rangers in Malta, Stirling Albion, Edinburgh City, Elgin City. (2003 – 2019) 7 Full caps for Scotland plus played for U-19's, U-21's and 'B' teams. At the Hawthorns*
Beattie was signed for Albion from Celtic by manager Tony Mowbray in the Summer of 2007 for £1.25 million rising by £500,000 performance-related add-ons. Craig scored his goals, a hat trick, for Albion in August 2007 in a pre-season friendly game against Dutch side SC Heerenveen at the Hawthorns. Promising much but failing to shine, he started the 2007/08 season as first choice number 9 alongside Kevin Phillips but competition, from Ishmael Miller and later Roman Bednar, pushed him down the pecking order. He scored just 4 times in that season as Albion won the Championship under Tony Mowbray. Craig was full of running but was lacking that extra yard of pace and had average close ball control skills. He never really got going for Albion making 13 starts and 28 substitute appearances, scoring 7 goals. He was sold for £800,000 to Swansea City in August 2009.

In 2014 he signed for Maltese side Zebbug Rangers on a one-year deal but left after less than 2 weeks for Ayr United. In April 2014, Beattie was declared bankrupt after finding himself with debts of £70,000. In 2016 he signed for newly promoted Scottish League Two side Edinburgh City. He spent two seasons there before leaving in May 2018. Beattie played for Elgin City until January 2019.

BEDNAR Roman

Striker 6'4"
Born *26/3/1983 Prague, Czechoslovakia*
Playing career: *FK Mladá Boleslav in Czech, FKB Kaunas in Lithuania, Heart of Midlothian (loan then signed), West Bromwich Albion (loan then signed Cost £2.5 million 70 + 36 sub appearances 34goals Aug 2007 – Jan 2012), Leicester City (loan), MKE Ankaragücü in Turkey (loan), Blackpool, Sivasspor in Turkey, Sparta Prague in Czech Republic, 1. FK Příbram in Czech Republic (loan then signed) (2002 – 2016) U20. U-21 & Full Czech Republic International with 8 caps.*
In 2002, after failing to break into the first team at Bohemians, he moved to Czech Second Division side FK Mladá Boleslav. Bednar finished the 2003/04 season as top scorer with 10 goals as Mladá Boleslav won the Second Division title. In July 2005, Hearts announced that they had completed the signing of Roman Bednar on a one-year loan deal from FBK Kaunas. He joined Hearts on a permanent deal on 31st August 2006, but exactly a year later he moved to West Bromwich Albion on a season-long loan deal which later became permanent. He made his first team debut for Albion as a substitute in a 3–0 away win against Watford in November 2007. He finished the 2007/08 season with 17 goals from 22 starts. Bednar joined Albion for £2.3 million in addition to the £200,000 loan fee they had paid previously. A tall, shaven-headed, powerful striker, good in the air and capable of holding the ball up well to bringing his fellow forwards into play, he knew exactly where the goal was. In summer 2008 he underwent a hernia operation. Bednar was suspended by West Bromwich Albion in May 2009 over allegations that he had purchased drugs. The following month he was cautioned by West Midlands Police regarding the incident, for possessing small amounts of class A drugs, principally cocaine, as well as cannabis, a class B drug.

Roman Bednar

In his own words: *Talking about his start at the Hawthorns, "When I first started here, I slept on a hotel bed and it was too soft and floppy. I hurt my back. It became tight and I couldn't move properly. So, when I'd worked hard to get my fitness here, I had to go back and sleep on this bed and it was terrible. For one month I could hardly move with my back. But then I moved into my own apartment and I had my bed delivered from Scotland so everything is cool now. My hard bed is the best."*

BEESLEY Paul

Defender 6'1"

Born *21/7/1965 Liverpool*

Playing career: *Wigan Athletic, Leyton Orient, Sheffield United, Leeds United, Manchester City, Port Vale (loan), West Bromwich Albion (loan 8 appearances March – May 1998), Port Vale, Blackpool, Chester City, Stalybridge Celtic, Ballymena United. (1984 – 2002)*

The FA granted permission for Roman to resume playing, following his suspensio but his form suffered and he appeared a shadow of the player he was. On 24 November 2010, Roman joined Leicester City on loan until January 2011. West Bromwich Albion accepted a £1.2 million offer from Bristol City in January 2011. However, Roman turned down the move. He subsequently joined Turkish club Ankaragücü on loan for the remainder of the 2010–11 season. Roman returned to the Baggies after his loan spell ended and the club took up the option to extend his contract until the end of 2011/12 season. He was assigned the squad number 43 after his previous squad number 9 had been assigned to new signing Shane Long. Bednar's only appearance during the 2011/12 season was as a substitute in a League Cup win over Bournemouth in August 2011. In four-and-a-half years with West Bromwich Albion, he made a total of 106 appearances scoring 34 goals. On 28th January 2012, he joined Blackpool on a free transfer, signing a six-month contract, making 8 league appearances scoring one goal. In August 2012, Bednar signed a two-year contract with Turkish Süper Lig side Sivasspor but left in 2013 without playing a league game. He played 39 league games for Sparta Prague between 2013-15. His final team was 1. FK Příbram who signed him after a loan spell. He made 37 league appearances scoring 12 goals 2015/16.

A tall one-paced defender. Beesley joined Wigan Athletic in September 1984, where he would spend five seasons. He played 185 games in all competitions in five years at Springfield Park, before joining Leyton Orient for £175,000 in October 1989. He joined Sheffield United for £300,000 in July 1990, and was voted Player of the Year at the Premier League club in 1993. Beesley was sold to Leeds United in August 1995 for a £250,000 fee, before moving on to Manchester City in February 1997 for £500,000. He had brief loan spells at Port Vale and West Bromwich Albion. Dennis Smith signed him on loan from March 1998 until the end of the season, making his debut in a 1-1 draw at Norwich alongside fellow debutants Jason Van Blerk and Steve Nicol. Albion won only one of the 8 games that he played. On returning to Manchester City, Paul was allowed to join Port Vale permanently in July 1999. He joined Chester City in the Conference in July 2000, and was voted the club's Player of the Season, before he signed with Stalybridge Celtic in October 2001. He later finished his career in Northern Ireland with Ballymena United. Paul Beesley worked as a youth team coach at Notts County, before he was appointed under-18 coach at Leeds United for a brief spell in 2007. In 2012 he was appointed as the kit man at Ipswich Town by manager Paul Jewell, before departing the role in July 2015

BENJAMIN Trevor

Forward/striker 6'0"

Born *8/2/1979 Kettering, Northamptonshire*
Playing career: *Cambridge United, Leicester City, Crystal Palace (loan), Norwich City (loan), West Bromwich Albion (loan 3 substitute appearances Mar-Apr2002), Gillingham (loan), Rushden & Diamonds (loan), Brighton & Hove Albion (loan), Northampton Town (loan then signed), Coventry City, Peterborough United, Watford (loan), Swindon Town (loan), Boston United (loan), Walsall (loan), Hereford United, Gainsborough Trinity, Northwich Victoria, Hednesford Town, Wellingborough Town, Kidsgrove Athletic, Tamworth, Harrogate Town, Woking, Sunshine George Cross in Australia, Beddington Terriers, Wroxham (loan), Morpeth Town (loan then signed), Seaton Delaval Amateurs (1995 – 2012)*
England U-21 International 1 cap, Jamaica 2 full caps

With the West Bromwich Albion, Benjamin arrived on loan towards the end of the 2001/02 season, appearing in 3 of the final 5 games, all as substitute, without scoring. Albion being promoted to the Premier League for the first time. He is famed for being a prime example of a journeyman footballer, having represented 29 teams in his career, making over 350 appearances in the Football League between 1995 and 2008. He also holds the record for the most league clubs played for - 16. He most notably spent time in the Premier League with Leicester City, having joined from Cambridge United.

He was capped by England U-21 but went on to feature for Jamaica as a full international, where he earned two caps. Benjamin has also played as a professional in the Football League for Crystal Palace, Norwich City, West Bromwich Albion, Gillingham, Rushden & Diamonds, Brighton & Hove Albion, Northampton Town, Coventry City, Peterborough United, Watford, Swindon Town, Boston United, Walsall and Hereford United. At the age of 28, Benjamin dropped out of the professional game and firstly signed for Conference North side Gainsborough Trinity. He went on to play for Northwich Victoria, Hednesford Town, Wellingborough Town, Kidsgrove Athletic, Tamworth, Harrogate Town and Woking. In 2010, he briefly joined Australian semi-pro side Sunshine George Cross, but failed to make an appearance and returned to the English non-league game where he went on to feature for Bedlington Terriers, Wroxham and Morpeth Town. Having initially been on loan at Morpeth from Bedlington, he was later appointed player-manager of the club in November 2010 and managed the club until the end of the 2010/11 season. After retiring from competitive football Benjamin has launched his own brand of goalkeeping gloves called Locust UK

Martyn Bennett

31

BENNETT Martyn

Centre back/defender 6'0"

Born *4/8/1961 Great Barr, Birmingham*

Playing career: *West Bromwich Albion (216 + 1 Sub appearances 10 goals Aug 1978 -June 1990) retired due to injury. 9 England Schoolboy International caps.*

Nicknamed 'Benno'. A tall, blonde talented, dominant defender, strong in the tackle and powerful in the air as well as quick in recovery. Martyn won 9 schoolboy caps for England. He understudied John Wile and Ally Robertson for a number of years before establishing himself in Albion's first XI in 1980-81. Injuries plagued him preventing him from representing his country at Full International level on a couple of occasions. Martyn was once described by ace goalscorer from yesteryear Jimmy Greaves as "the fastest covering defender I've ever seen." This was in the 1982/83 season when called up by England. He made the subs bench versus Wales in 1983. Albion named him as captain for the 1986-87 season but a niggling back injury sidelined him, eventually needing surgery to fuse vertebrae in his back. He managed to make only 18 starts for Albion between 1986 -1990, playing his final game for the club in 1989 in a 7-0 win over Barnsley. He made 217 appearances for Albion in all competitions. He was given a Testimonial game. Unfortunately, Benno had to retire in 1990. He had a couple of seasons at Worcester & Cheltenham, managing both until leaving football altogether. Martyn still lives in Streetly, Sutton Coldfield.

BLOOD Robert 'Bobby'

Centre forward 5'8"

Born *18/3/1894 Harpur Hill, Buxton, Derbyshire*
Died *12/8/1988 Buxton, Derbyshire aged 94*

Playing career: *Leek Alexandra, Port Vale, West Bromwich Albion (Cost £4,000 53 appearances 26 goals Feb 1921 – Dec 1924), Stockport County, Winsford United, MossleyFC, Buxton, Aston National FC (1912 – 1931)*

He was the youngest of 10 children and his Father was a quarry worker, whom he followed with his brothers, at the Hoffman Quarry. He played non-league football before joining Leek Alexandra. Playing at outside left he scored 6 goals on his debut in September 1913. In March 1915, he volunteered to serve the 16th Battalion Sherwood Foresters in World War I. On 5th June 1916, he was injured during a raid on the Béthune Front, and nearly lost his leg. Upon his recovery he was drafted into the 7th Battalion Sherwood Foresters and returned to France in March 1917. He also represented British Army in football matches against Belgium and France, and won both the Divisional Cup and the Brigade Cup with the 7th Sherwood Foresters. He rose to the rank of Sergeant major and returned to Buxton after the Allies declared victory on 11 November 1918. He began to strengthen his leg by spending many hours kicking a ball against a wall near his home in Harpur Hill. On returning to Leek Alexandra, playing at centre forward, he scored 11 goals in the first two months of the 1919/20 season. He was then signed by Port Vale for a fee of £50. His war service left him with a hole in his right leg, as well as having one leg shorter than the other, doctors said he was not fit enough to play professional football, though the management at The Port Vale felt otherwise. In the 1919/20 season he finished as top-scorer with 26 goals in 32 games. He continued his goal scoring feats in the 1920/21 season with 20 goals in 26 games. He demonstrated the fearsome power of his shot by striking a penalty which was saved by the Bristol City goalkeeper at the cost of a broken wrist. A Stockport player who headed the ball off the line to save a Blood shot had to be taken off the field with concussion. West Bromwich Albion secretary-manager Fred Everiss signed him in February 1921 for £4,750, then a club record fee. Vale fans were outraged at the sale, though Blood was informed that the club's financial situation meant that either he went or the club would go broke. He was a slight figure, but was a dynamic and brave centre forward, renowned for his cannon-ball shooting. When on target it is reported that his shots were nigh-on impossible to stop. Blood would primarily serve the reserve team, acquiring a Central League medal and scoring 73 goals in 72 Central League games. Blood finished as the club's top-scorer in 1923/24 with nine goals. He moved to Stockport County for a £3,000 fee in December 1924. He scored seven goals in 25 Second Division games during the 1924/25 campaign, though his eight goals in 16 league matches could not prevent County suffering relegation in last place in 1925/26.

After spending 1926/27 in the Third Division North, he moved on to Cheshire County League side Winsford United. He moved on to league rivals Mossley in 1928, scoring six goals in 17 league games. He then transferred to Ashton National Gas, before returning to Buxton in 1930. He did some scouting of young talent for Albion. He married Lily Mellor in 1922. Their only child, Robert, died within three hours of his birth on 9 October 1924. After his wife died, Bob resided in the Salvation Amy Hostel in Buxton for a number of years before passing away in 1988 aged 94.

Personal note: *Bobby Blood was my Dad's favourite player. What a thrill it was when in 1979 at Dartmouth Park, whilst standing with my Dad, Charles, watching some of the Albion Centenary celebrations, a helicopter landed and out stepped Bobby Blood, at the time one of the oldest living former WBA players. He had been flown in from his home in Derbyshire especially for this event. My Dad didn't recognise him at first as he was introduced to the crowd but Dad then he nearly burst into tears seeing his first Albion hero again. I think Bob might even have kicked off at the start of the Charity football match. Sadly, my Dad passed away the following year aged 69.*

BOERE Jeroen

Striker 6'4"

Born *18/11/1967 Arnhem, Netherlands*
Died *16/8/2007 Marbella, Spain*
Playing career: *SBV Excelsior, De Graafschap, VVV-Venlo, De Graafschap (loan), Roda JC, VVV-Venlo, Go Ahead Eagles, West Ham United, Portsmouth (loan), West Bromwich Albion (loan 5 appearances 1994), Crystal Palace, Southend United, Omiya Ardija (Japan) (1985 – 1999)*

He was a tall target man, not the most mobile, who spent his early years playing in Holland playing for 5 different teams and having a loan spell. Joined West Ham United for £250,000 signed by Billy Bonds in the summer of 1993. In two seasons he only played 25 league games scoring 6 times for the Hammers. After a loan spell at Portsmouth he arrived on loan at the Hawthorns playing just 5 games in September, alongside Bob Taylor, without scoring. Moved to Crystal Palace 1995/96, then played for two seasons at Southend United where he had his most successful run playing 73 league games scoring 25 goals.

He moved to Japan and played for local club, Omiya Ardija in the Japanese second division scoring 18 goals in 26 matches in the 1998/99 season. In May 1999, after dinner with his wife at a restaurant in Roppongi district of Tokyo, he was stabbed in his left eye and arm by two unknown men who reportedly appeared to be of Middle Eastern origin. His attacker was later reported to be an Israeli criminal who was later found shot through the head in a Bangkok river. Boere lost his eye in the incident, which forced his retirement from football at the age of 31. He returned to England and ran the Half Moon pub in Epping between 1999 and 2004 .The Dutchman moved to Spain in 2004 to work as a real estate agent. Sadly, he died in 2007 at the age of 39. There are conflicting reports about the cause of death and place of death. Some media reported that Boere died in a car crash, possibly on Ibiza, while other media reported that he was found dead in his home in Marbella. English newspaper Ilford Recorder stated that Boere had committed suicide

BOOKMAN Louis

Outside left 5'8"

Born *6/11/1890 Zagare, Russian Empire (Now Lithuania)*
Died *10/6/1943 Dublin, Ireland*
Playing career: *Belfast Celtic, Bradford City, West Bromwich Albion (18 appearances 1 goal July 1914 – June 1915), Glentoran, Shelbourne, Luton Town, Port Vale, Shelbourne (1910 – 1925) Played 4 times for Ireland*

His actual surname was Buckhalter, of Lithuanian Jewish origin. Born the son of a rabbi in Lithuania, he arrived in Ireland in 1895 when his family emigrated to escape antisemitism; his family subsequently adopted the name Bookman. He represented Ireland at both football and cricket. He joined Albion just before the beginning of the 1914/15 season, starting as first choice left winger he scored on his debut away at Newcastle in September 1914 in a 1-1 draw, this was his only Albion goal. He lost his place eventually to Ben Shearman and left Albion at the start of WW1. In a career disrupted by the War, he played 167 games scoring 11 times. A left-handed batsman and left-arm spin bowler, he played for Railway Union Cricket Club and the Leinster Cricket Club. After his career in sports was over, he worked in Ireland on the railways, and also entered the jewellery business.

BORTOLAZZI Mario

Midfielder 5'10"

Born: *10/1/1965 Verona, Italy*

Playing career: *Verona, Italy Playing career Mantova, Fiorentina, Milan, Parma, Milan, Verona, Atlanta, Genoa, West Bromwich Albion (Free transfer 26 +10 sub appearances 2 goals July 1998 – May 1999), Livorno, Lecco,Livorno (1980 – 2003)*

Bortolazzi changed clubs 11 times in Italy either side of his time at the Hawthorns. He was signed from Genoa on a free transfer after playing 241 games for them. He came to the Black Country merely as a minder for the young Enzo Maresca. Mario was 33 when he joined Albion as part of the deal to bring Enzo to the Albion. Mario had a certain Italian finesse and elegance, even if he did come to the Hawthorns towards the end of his career. It was obvious he had left his best footballing years on the football playing fields of Seria A, most notably two spells with Milan. He won Serie A with Milan in 1987/88 and the Anglo-Italian Cup with Genoa in 1995/96. Nonetheless, he was still a tidy player. A string of niggling injuries hampered him in the course of the 1998/99 campaign, although Mario played 25 league games and 10 more as a substitute, scoring twice. He was not the quickest but was a tidy, cultured player in the Albion midfield that took on a remarkably cosmopolitan look with Enzo Maresca, the Dutch master, Richard Sneekes and Sean Flynn. With Maresca acclimatising and increasingly taking Mario's starting place in the team, Bortolazzi was to return home to Italy with Livorno in the Summer of 1999. He made a total of 532 league appearances

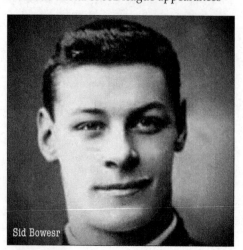

Sid Bowesr

scoring 44 goals over a 23-year playing career. He was assistant coach to his former Milan teammate Roberto Donadoni firstly at Livorno between 2005 and 2006, then with the Italian National team between 2006 and 2008, and later with Napoli 2009.

BOWSER Sidney 'Sid'

Inside left/centre half 5'10"

Born *6/4/1891 Handsworth, Birmingham*

Died *10/2/1961 Birmingham*

Playing career: *West Bromwich Albion (July 1908 – Apr 1913) Belfast Distillery 1913-14, West Bromwich Albion (Total in two spells 371 appearances 72 goals Feb 1914 – Aug 1924), Walsall. Guested for Southport Vulcan, Notts County & Stoke City in WW1. (1908 – 1927) He played once for England in 1919.*

Sid was a tenacious, resilient and hard-working professional who divided his immense talent between two completely different roles – those of a centre half and an inside forward. A big strong fellow, Sid had two spells at the Hawthorns achieving success in both, in 1910/11 he helped Albion win the Second Division title and in 1912 he played in the F A Cup Final, losing after a replay to Barnsley. He moved to Ireland and played for Belfast Distillery in May 1913 before turning to the Hawthorns in Feb 1914. In his second spell he was a key figure in the 1919/20 Championship winning side scoring 10 goals, 8 of them, penalties, including a hat-trick from centre half against Bradford City. A sterling performer in every sense of the word, he won only one England cap v Ireland in 1919. Whilst playing in Ireland, he did represent the Irish League. He finished his career moving to Walsall for £250 in August 1924. A genuine sportsman who loved his football. He played 371 games in all competitions for Albion scoring 72 goals. He became a publican in Dudley after retiring from football in 1927. He remained in the trade for 25 years.

BOYES Walter 'Wally'

Outside left 5'3½

Born: *5/1/1913 Killamarsh, Derbyshire*

Died *16/9/1960 aged 47*

Playing career: *Woodhouse Mills United, West Bromwich Albion (165 appearances 38 goals Feb 1931 – Feb 1938), Everton, Notts County, Scunthorpe United (1931 – 1951) Played 3 times for England He guested for Aldershot, Brentford, Clapton Orient, Leeds United, Manchester United, Middlesbrough, Millwall,*

Newcastle United, Preston North End and Sunderland during WW2. 3 England International caps.

Wally's strength was his goalscoring, in fact as a youngster in Sheffield he once found the net 17 times in one game as his side won 31-2, this despite having one leg shorter than the other. A spirited little footballer, perhaps best known as an outside left Wally 'Titty' Boyes also competed capably and with distinction at left half and inside left. He was purposeful, direct, had an accurate shot and allied to his quickness off the mark, and skilful footwork, he was indeed a big favourite with the fans. Boyes took over from Stan Wood. Wally turned professional in February 1931 but did not become a first team regular until the 1934/35 season.

Wally played in the 1935 FA Cup Final for Albion scoring one goal as they lost 4-2 to Sheffield Wednesday, the club Wally had supported as a boy. He left the Hawthorns after making 165 senior appearances scoring 38 goals. In February 1938 Boyes joined Everton for a £6000 fee and instantly formed a great left-wing partnership with Alex Stevenson, which helped the side clinch the 1938/39 league title He was player/coach at Notts County 1949/50, then became player/trainer for Scunthorpe United between 1950 and 1953. Walter later became player/manager of Retford Town in 1954 and also at Hyde United in 1958. Boyes joined Swansea as trainer in 1959 but retired due to illness in May 1960. He died in September of the same year aged just 47.

Darren Bradley

BRADLEY Darren

Midfielder 5'10½"

Born *24/11/1965 Kings Norton, Birmingham*

Playing career: *Aston Villa, West Bromwich Albion (£90,000 deal involving swap with Steve Hunt 270 +18 sub appearances 13 goals March 1986- June 1995), Walsall. England youth international (1984 – 1997).*

Darren started his career at Aston Villa playing 20 league games before moving to Albion in March 1986 in a deal that saw Steve Hunt move in the opposite direction. A hard working, tough tackling and capable midfielder, who was a natural leader on the field. He was Captain of Albion's 1992/93 Promotion winning team that won the 1993 Play-Off Final 3-0 against Port Vale at Wembley. Darren is probably best remembered for a spectacular 30-yard goal against arch rivals Wolverhampton Wanderers, helping the Baggies to a 3–2 victory in August 1993. Darren has since played for Aston Villa Old Stars, worked as a sales rep for a forklift company and involved in launching Intergarage in 2000, a business designing and manufacturing underground garages. He currently runs a Water Treatment Company, living just outside Coventry with his South African wife Ris. In 2018 & 2019 Darren played walking football for England over 50's team.

BRADSHAW Paul

Goalkeeper 6'2½"

Born *28/4/1956 Altrincham*

Playing career: *Blackburn Rovers, Wolverhampton Wanderers, Vancouver Whitecaps, West Bromwich Albion (Free Transfer Feb 1985- June 1986), Walsall coach June 1986, Bristol Rovers non-contract, Newport County, West Bromwich Albion (Free Transfer Aug 1988- June 1990 22 appearances in 2 spells), Peterborough United, Kettering Town (1973-1992) Won caps for England Youths and U-21's.*

Played 200 league games with Wolverhampton Wanderers. games. A fine goalkeeper, fearless, agile and a safe pair of hands. Won the Football League Cup with Wolves in 1980. He arrived at the Hawthorns in February 1985 on a free transfer as back up keeper and to compete with Tony Godden for the number 1 spot. He took up a coaching role at Walsall in June 1986 but soon returned to playing though, signing for Bristol Rovers on a non-contract basis, and later played in Newport County's final season in the Football League. He had a second spell with West Bromwich Albion from August 1988 to June 1990. In two spells with the Baggies he only played in a total of 22 games. Paul played for Peterborough United in the 1990/91 season and finished his career in non-league football with Kettering

Tony Brown

Town, retiring in 1992. He became a security advisor in Wolverhampton before moving to Altrincham where he became a baggage handler at Manchester Airport. However due to a back injury he is now unable to work. He still lives in his hometown of Altrincham.

BROWN Alistair 'Ally'
Forward 6'0"
Born *12/4/1951 Musselburgh, Scotland*
Playing career: *Leicester City, West Bromwich Albion (Cost £61,111 331 +28 sub appearances 85 goals March 1972-Feb 1983), Portland Timbers (loan), Crystal Palace, Walsall, Port Vale (1968 – 1986).*
A player who always gave a good account of himself whatever the circumstances. He was promoted as Leicester were Second Division Champions in 1970/71 finishing as their top scorer. A Charity Shield winner in 1971 beating Arsenal 1-0. As Arsenal were 'Double' winners, they played the 2nd Division Champions, Leicester City for the Shield. Ally joined Albion in March 1972 for a fee of £61,111. He had a couple of lean seasons when Don Howe was manager between 1973-75, but he usually served Albion with great consistency in every game. He was Albion's top scorer in the 1975/76 Albion's promotion winning team. He later formed a great partnership with Cyrille Regis. In 1978/79 he was voted Midlands Sportswriters' Footballer of the Year jointly with Tony Brown. He played 359 games for Albion, including 28 substitute appearances, scoring 85 goals. Brown played for Portland Timbers on loan in 1981, scoring nine goals and bagging six assists in 24 NASL appearances for Vic Crowe's side. He left for Crystal Palace in March until the end of the 1982/83 season scoring once in 11 games. Ally then moved on to Walsall in August 1983 for a season netting 13 times in 38 games. His final move was to Port Vale where he played two more seasons, scoring a further 22 goals in 67 games. He was often seen smoking a cigarette at half time or immediately after a game. In 18-years he appeared in 520 league games scoring 149 times including his spell in the USA. He was a publican in West Bromwich and later at the Cedar Tree Public House in Aldridge. He was also the steward at the Throstle Club in Halfords Lane. Later a warehouseman in an iron foundry in Walsall.

BROWN Anthony 'Tony'
Wing half/Inside forward 5'9"
Born *3/10/1945 Oldham, Lancashire*
Playing career: *West Bromwich Albion (704 + 16 sub appearances 279 goals Oct 1963 – Dec 1981), New England Tea Men 1980, Jacksonville Tea Men 1981, West Bromwich Albion (1981), Torquay United, Stafford Rangers (1963 – 1983) Played once for England at Senior level & also played for England Youth, and the Football League.*
Brown joined West Bromwich Albion as an apprentice on 13th April 1961, earning a wage of £6 a week. After two seasons playing youth football, he made his reserve team debut in the final Central League game of 1962–63, scoring in a 3–2 defeat to Manchester United reserves. He turned professional on 27 September 1963 and was immediately called up to the first team squad for the away match at Ipswich Town the following day. Eddie Readfern was unable to play game due to illness, which meant that Brown was given his league debut, just a few days before his 18th birthday. His equalising goal helped Albion to a 2–1 away win. Brown won the League Cup in 1966, scoring in every round, and the FA Cup in 1968 with Albion. He was also runner up in two League Cup Finals at Wembley in 1967 & 1970. He played a major role in Albion's return to the top flight in 1976, scoring the goal that clinched promotion in a 1–0 win away at his home town club Oldham Athletic. He appeared in more first team games: 826, scored more goals: 313, than any other Albion player ever. Tony Brown was voted Midlands Footballer of the Year on three occasions 1969, 1971 and again in 1979, jointly sharing it with Ally Brown. He topped the Football League Division One scoring chart in 1970/71 scoring 28 league goals. Tony scored 51 out of 61 penalties taken in all matches, and 51 goals in 66 reserve matches, and 51 goals for the third Intermediate team. He has attended numerous Supporters' Club events. Is an avid supporter of the Old Baggies Former Players' Association. He was coach at the Hawthorns under manager Johnny Giles, then Nobby Stiles and finally Ron Saunders. Then he coached at St Andrews, Birmingham under Garry Pendrey. He has a statue of himself erected outside the Club Shop behind the East Stand. He has had two hip replacement operations.

Tony was a columnist for a local paper. He was a match summariser working for many years with Tom Ross on Capital Radio. Recently heard on Radio WM co-commentating on Albion games.

BUCK Frederick 'Freddy'

Centre half / Inside forward 5'4"
Born *2/11/1879 Audley, Newcastle-under-Lyme, Staffordshire*
Died *05/06/1952 Stafford*
Playing career: *Stafford Rangers, West Bromwich Albion (Nov 1900 – May 1903), Liverpool, Plymouth Argyle, West Bromwich Albion (Total in two spells of 319 appearances 94 goals Apr 1906 – May 1914), Swansea Town. Played for the Football League in 1911 Retired 1917*

One of the greatest little players Albion have ever had on their books. In fact, he is the smallest centre half ever to don an Albion shirt. (There seems to be some uncertainty as to his actual height, various sources stating between 5'4" to 5'7") He was of slight physique but had a big heart, was fast and tricky, a real tough nut. Fred possessed wonderful judgement and was ever dangerous around goal. In his early Albion career, he was an inside forward, from where he scored most of his goals, but during his second spell he was converted to a very solid centre half, regarded at the time to be one of the finest, for his size, in the country. In the 1901 census he was described as an apprentice fitter. In 1902 he played in 22 second XI games for Albion, gaining a Birmingham & District League Championship medal. In 1903 he scored both goals when Albion won the Staffordshire Cup beating Stoke City 2-0.

During his brief spell at Liverpool in a game against Stoke City, Buck was sent off and suspended for kicking and punching opponent James Bradley. He won a Second Division Championship medal with Albion in 1911 when his penalty on the last day in the home game against Huddersfield clinched the title. He also played for the Football League team in 1911. In the 1911 census he was described as an Engineer Fitter. He won an FA Cup runners-up medal in 1912, after Albion lost to Barnsley after a replay. In two spells with Albion 1900 – 1903 and 1906 – 1914 he played in 319 games scoring 94 goals, of which 26 were penalties. He also played 22 games for the reserve team. From 1915 to 1918, he served as a private in the Army Service Corps in France, where he gained the British War Medal. After football he was a publican at the Victoria Inn, Rugby, Warwickshire for 24 years and later from 1945 until 1952 he was a clerk in the Grinding Wheel Works in Stafford. He died in 1952 aged 72.

BULL Stephen 'Steve'

Striker 5'11"
Born *28/3/1965 Tipton, Staffordshire*
Playing career: *Tipton Town, West Bromwich Albion (3 + 4 sub appearances 3 goals July 1984 – November 1986), Wolverhampton Wanderers, Hereford United.13 Full England caps, 5 'B' Internationals & 5 U-21 appearances (1984 – 2001)*

He began his professional career, aged 19, after being recommended to West Bromwich Albion in 1984 by his Tipton Town manager Sid Day, who also worked as a scout for the Albion. He made his senior debut in October 1985, replacing Garth Crooks in a 2–1 Full Members Cup win against Crystal Palace. He made his league debut against QPR in April 1986 and his full debut at home to Sheffield Wednesday on 22nd April. They were his only league appearances that season and only appearances in top flight football. In November 1986, he was sold by Albion manager Ron Saunders, to local rivals Wolverhampton Wanderers, along with Andy Thompson, for £65,000 where he remained until the end of his professional career in 1999. Somewhat of a hate figure for many Albion fans but in reality, he was 'One who got away'. Fast, direct, aggressive, two-footed but sometimes lacking in close control.

However, he more than made up for that with his amazing goalscoring exploits in the lower divisions. In 1987/88 he set a Wolves club record of 52 goals in a season. He added another 50 in 1988/89. In 504 league matches he scored 271 goals and was capped for England whilst playing in the Third Division. On 21 February 2008, Bull entered management with Stafford Rangers. He had previously worked as a coach with Hereford United in the 2000–01 season and had completed his UEFA Pro B coaching licence. He worked for local radio commentating on his former team Wolves, where he was also an ambassador & Vice President. Became a popular figure on the after- dinner circuit and assisted his wife in the running of her events company Steve Bull Events. Steve also fills his time playing the odd round of golf, walking the dog and going to the gym.

BURGESS Daryl

Centre back/defender 5'10½"
Born *24/1/1971 Birmingham*
Playing career: *West Bromwich Albion (359 +18 sub appearances 13 goals July 1989 – July 2001), Northampton Town, Rochdale, Kidderminster Harriers, Nuneaton Borough, Bromsgrove Rovers. (1989 – 2008)*

Burgess began his career at West Bromwich Albion, where he made his debut during the 1989/90 season. He was a regular in Albion's defence for a decade.

He started out as an orthodox right back, he subsequently starred in the middle of the back four and also as a sweeper. A strong tackling defender, he always maintained a steady level of performance and received a well-deserved testimonial match against Newcastle United before moving to Northampton Town. He spent 14 years at the Hawthorns, and played 377 first-team games for the Baggies. He was released by West Bromwich Albion in 2001, and then joined Northampton Town. He played 61 league games scoring twice for the Cobblers before moving in 2003, to join Rochdale on a free transfer. After two seasons at Rochdale playing 56 league games, he moved back to the West Midlands to join Kidderminster Harriers of the Conference. He left Kidderminster at the end of the 2005/06 season and signed for Nuneaton Borough, and later joined Bromsgrove in January 2008. In a 21-year playing career between 1987 and 2008, Daryl amassed a grand total of 507 senior appearances for his 3 football league clubs plus another 50 for Kidderminster and he also played in 120 reserve and intermediate games for West Bromwich Albion. In 2008, Burgess started his own soccer school 'Total Football Premier Coaching' with his ex WBA teammate Richard Sneekes and also DJs at various venues around the country. He was still living in Birmingham with his wife Catrina.

Daryl Burgess

BURNSIDE David 'Davy'

Inside forward/midfielder 5'10"

Born *10/12/1939 Kingswood, South Gloucestershire*
Died *17/10/2009 Bristol aged 69*

Playing career: *West Bromwich Albion (135 appearances 42 goals Feb 1957 – Sep 1962), Southampton, Crystal Palace, Wolverhampton Wanderers, Los Angeles Wolves(guest), Plymouth Argyle, Bristol City, Colchester United. (1957 – 1973) England Youth and U-23 International. Bath City player/manager Apr 1972 – Mar 1973,*

His father was so keen to see David develop his football skills that he installed floodlights in his back garden to enable his son to practice in the evening. He signed as a professional for Albion in Feb 1957. Dave soon acquired nationwide fame for his incredible ball-juggling abilities when, in October 1957, during the half-time in a televised friendly match against Russian team CDSA Moscow, he performed his tricks to entertain the crowd. He was offered a lucrative contract to appear regularly on shows all over the world but he turned the offer down to concentrate on playing football. Sadly, his footballing skills were often spasmodic, not matching up to his ball skills. In 5 seasons at the Hawthorns he played in 127 league games scoring 39 goals. He moved to Southampton for £17,000 in September 1962 and in two seasons he played 61 league games scoring 22 goals. Then in December 1964 he was transferred to Crystal Palace playing 58 league games scoring 8 goals. He returned to the Black Country in September 1966 joining Wolverhampton Wanderers. He was in their team that won promotion from the Second Division in 1966/67.

Dave was popular with some Wolves fans whereas others preferred the showmanship of his rival Peter Knowles. After 40 league games and 5 goals he moved to Plymouth Argyle playing 105 league games scoring 15 goals between 1968 and 1971. Dave also played for Bristol City, Colchester United and Bath City as player/manager hanging up his boots in 1973 after amassing 454 league appearances and scoring 90 goals. Burnside had spells at Walsall as assistant manager August-December 1973, Cadbury Heath Minehead 1974/75, Bridgewater Town as player/manager 1975-79, Taunton Town 1979/80. Dave started working for the FA in 1979 as a regional coach in the West Country. Later he became part of the International set up when appointed England Youth team manager June 1983, under England manager and ex-Albion team mate Bobby Robson. He left this position in Jan 1997 when he returned to Bristol City as Director of Youth Football, taking on the role of joint caretaker manager with Tony Fawthrop in Jan 2000 after the departure of Tony Pulis. They took the Robins to Wembley in the Auto Windscreens Shield Final losing 2-1 to Stoke City. After Leroy Rosenior was appointed manager in summer 2000 Burnside continued to assist City as technical advisor before moving to work with Bobby Gould as football co-ordinator at Cheltenham Town which ended in October 2003. Burnside died in October 2009 after suffering a heart attack aged 69. Shortly before his death, he had been accepted to contest a Bristol seat for the United Kingdom Independence Party (UKIP) in the 2010 general election.

BURROWS David

Fullback 5'10"

Born *25/10/1968 Dudley*

Playing career: *West Bromwich Albion (43+10 sub appearances 1 goal July 1985- June 1988), Liverpool, West Ham United, Everton, Coventry City, Birmingham City, Sheffield Wednesday. England U21 and B International (1985 – 2003)*

He did his footballing apprenticeship at Albion. In the shadow of Derek Statham then in competition with Barry Cowdrill for the number 3 shirt at left back. Having made 43 starts and 10 substitute appearances in 3 years at the Hawthorns, he signed for Liverpool for £500,000 aged 20.

He won Division One Title with Liverpool in 1990 and the Charity Shield. In both 1989 and 1990. Won the FA Cup in 1992. After a career taking in 7 clubs and almost 400 league appearances, he quit football after an injured collar bone and a hamstring problem in 2003. He moved to the South-West France with his wife and three children. He played amateur football in the Dordogne.

BUTLER Peter

Midfielder 5'9"

Born *27/8/1966 Halifax*

Playing career: *Huddersfield Town, Cambridge United (loan), Bury, Cambridge United, Southend United, Huddersfield Town (loan), West Ham United, Notts County, Grimsby Town (loan), West Bromwich Albion (loan then signed Cost £175,000 55 +11 sub appearances March 1996 – June 1998), Halifax Town, Sorrento FC. (Western Australia) Butler retired in 2000 whilst player-caretaker manager of Halifax Town. (1984 – 2000)*

He started his professional career at Huddersfield Town, had a loan spell at Cambridge United and a brief stint at Bury before signing for Cambridge United. Here he settled and scored 9 goals in 55 games between 1986 – 1988. Next stop was Southend for 4 years between 1988-1992 where he played 142 games scoring 9 goals. He had a short loan spell back at his first club Huddersfield. West Ham United paid around £125,000 and he played 70 league games scoring 3 goals for the Hammers. Notts County bought him for around £375.0000 but he only played 20 league games and was loaned out to Grimsby and West Bromwich Albion who eventually bought him for £175,000. A stocky, tough tackling player.

In two years at The Hawthorns he played 65 league games without scoring, often playing as a defensive midfielder. His final port of call in England was with Halifax Town where he played for two seasons notching up another 63 league games. Peter had a long professional career spanning 18 years and featured for 10 different teams playing 455 league games scoring 23 goals. He then moved to Australia where he managed Sorrento FC, before moving again this time to Singapore. He coached Singapore Armed Forces Football Club, then with Malaysian outfit Sabah FA and Indonesian club Persiba Balikpapan. He moved back to Malaysia in 2009 to coach Kelantan FA before joining Yangon United in Myanmar as a technical director. In September 2010 Butler became head coach of Thai Premier League team BEC Tero Sasana FC. He holds a UEFA Pro Licence Qualification. Moved to Indonesian Super League side Persiba Balikpapan 2012 but quickly moved again to take a head coach role at Terengganu FA in Malaysia. In Feb 2014 he was appointed manager of the Botswana national team in Southern Africa until 2017. Appointed head coach of Platinum Stars in South Africa's Premier Soccer League June – Sep 2017. Worked at Persipura and PSMS both in Indonesia in 2018. In 2019 he was appointed as manager of the Liberian national football team. He signed a one-year deal with a mandate to qualify for the 2021 Africa Cup of Nations and 2022 World Cup.

BUTLER (Philip) Anthony 'Tony'

Centre back 6'2"

Born *2879/1972 Stockport*

Playing career: *Gillingham, Blackpool, Port Vale, West Bromwich Albion (Cost £140,000 76 + 6 sub appearances 1 goal Mar 2000), Bristol City,, Blackpool, Forest Green Rovers, Newport County (loan), Hinckley United, Alfreton Town. (1991 – 2007)*

Tall, rangy, no-nonsense centre back. He began his career at Gillingham in 1991, helping the club to win promotion out of the Third Division in 1995/96. He was sold to Blackpool in August 1996 for £225,000, before he was moved on to Port Vale for a £115,000 fee in March 1999. He was one of four deadline-day signings made by manager Gary Megson for West Bromwich Albion in March 2000 for a £140,000 fee.

Butler featured seven times for the "Baggies" in 1999/2000, as Megson steered the club away from the relegation zone. He made 51 appearances in 2000/01, as Albion reached the Play-Offs, only to be defeated by Bolton Wanderers at the semi-final stage. He featured 23 times as the club won promotion as runners-up in 2001/02, finishing ten points behind champions Manchester City. He featured in the "Battle of Bramall Lane" on 16th March 2002, replacing Larus Sigurdsson 14 minutes before the match was abandoned. With the club now in the Premier League, he found himself surplus to requirements at The Hawthorns, and was loaned out to Bristol City, for whom he subsequently signed permanently. Moved on to Blackpool and Forest Green Rovers. In 16-years he made 475 appearances in league football scoring 13 goals.

CAMPBELL Kevin

Striker 6'2"

Born *4/2/1970 Lambeth, London*
Playing career: *Arsenal, Leyton Orient (loan), Leicester City (loan), Nottingham Forest, Trabzonspor, Everton (loan then signed), West Bromwich Albion (Free Transfer 36 + 13 sub appearances 6 goals Jan 2005 – Aug 2006), Cardiff City. England U21 and B International. (1988 – 2007)*

He won the First Division Title in 1990/91, the Charity Shield in 1991, shared, and the European Cup Winners' Cup in 1993/94 whilst with Arsenal. Signed by Bryan Robson for West Bromwich Albion on a free transfer in January 2005, Campbell was appointed captain helping in Albion's 'Great Escape' of 2004/05 when they avoided relegation from the Premiership on the final day, despite having been bottom of the Premier League at Christmas 2004. Tall, powerful good footballer, who could bring others into play with his skill at holding and shielding the ball. A leader on and off the pitch. He had lost a yard of pace by the time he joined Albion but his experience was invaluable. Albion were relegated the following season and in May 2006 Campbell moved to Cardiff City. He was released in May 2007 and announced his retirement. After football he was the co-owner of security company T1 Protection, specialising in supplying bodyguards to celebrities and other wealthy customers whilst travelling abroad.

Campbell also worked with Asia-based TEN Sports as a commentator for their Premier League and Champions League coverage. Campbell ran his own record label 2 Wikid. He has also worked as a commentator on Asian channel TEN Sports coverage of Premiership games and a summariser on BBC TV. His Son Tyrese Campbell was a professional player at Stoke City.

CANTELLO Leonard 'Len'

Midfielder/full back 5'10"

Born 11/9/1951 Manchester
Playing career: West Bromwich Albion (365+4 sub appearances 21 goals Oct 1968 – May 1979), Bolton Wanderers, Dallas Tornado (loan), Hereford United, Bury, SC Cambuur in Holland, Eastern AA in Hong Kong, Northwich Victoria (1968 – 1986) England Schoolboy, Youth and U-23 International.

Len carried out many duties for Albion during, donning 10 different shirts in the first XI, performing with style and artistry, mainly as a midfielder. Aged 18, Cantello was part of the Albion team that lost the 1970 League Cup Final at Wembley 2-1 to Manchester City after extra-time. He certainly had flair, and had an excellent understanding first with Asa Hartford, then with Bryan Robson and Tony Brown. As a defender, mainly lining up at left back, Len tackled with venom and was always eager and willing to join in the attack on the flank.

Len Cantello

Cantello scored ITV's goal of the season in December 1978, a brilliant team goal which Len scored at Old Trafford in a 5-3 victory for Albion. He appeared in 369 first team games scoring 21 goals. He moved to Bolton Wanderers for £350,000 at the end of the 1978/79 season. He moved to Bolton Wanderers in 1979 but he was awarded a testimonial match by West Bromwich Albion, a game that saw a team of white players play against a team of black players. In three seasons at Bolton he appeared in 90 league matches, scoring 3 times. After retiring from professional sport, Cantello became the UK managing Director of FieldTurf, then a Canadian-based brand of artificial turf playing surface. He lives in his home town of Manchester.

CARBON Matthew 'Matt'

Centre back 6'1½"

Born. *8/6/1975 Nottingham*

Playing career: *Lincoln City, Derby County, West Bromwich Albion (Cost £800,000 117 + 9 sub appearances 5 goals Jan 1998 – July 2001), Walsall, Lincoln City (loan), Barnsley, New Zealand Knights 2006-07, Milton Keynes Dons (1993 – 2008) England U-21 International*

Matt Carbon started his professional career at Lincoln City playing 69 league games, before signing for Derby County in 1996 for £385,000. However, in his two years there he only made 12 league starts and 9 substitute appearances, before moving to West Bromwich Albion for £800,000 in January 1998. Tall and powerful in the air, strong in the tackle, he was a good defensive organiser. Carbon became a regular during his time at The Hawthorns, making 117 + 9 substitute appearances in total before his free transfer move to Walsall in 2001. He made 55 league appearances for the Saddlers, before a free transfer to Barnsley where he notched up fifty league Carbon moved to the Australian A-League to play for New Zealand Knights but never played, spending only one game on the bench before being released. He signed for Milton Keynes on an initial two-month deal on 4 December 2007 before retiring. He now runs Matt Carbon Football Coaching offering the following: One 2 one coaching sessions, Group coaching sessions, Team coaching sessions.

CARR Franz

Right winger/forward 5'7"

Born *24/9/1966 Preston*

Playing career: *Blackburn Rovers, Nottingham Forest, Sheffield Wednesday (loan), West Ham United (loan), Newcastle United, Sheffield United, Leicester City (loan), Aston Villa, Reggiana (Italy), Bolton Wanderers (loan), West Bromwich Albion (1+3 sub appearances Feb – May 1998). Pittsburgh Riverhounds England U-21 International. (1984 – 1998).*

Carr was a speed merchant winger. Alas, there wasn't much more to his game. He was at Nottingham Forest who signed him for £25,000 rising to £100,000 in August 1984, staying for 7 years playing 131 league games scoring 17 goals between 1984 and 1991. After leaving the City Ground, he flitted from club to club on loan or being transferred never really settling at any club. His final club was West Bromwich Albion where Gary Megson signed him. He only made one start in a 1-1 draw at the Hawthorns against QPR in February 1998. He made 3 more substitute appearances but was released at the end of the season. Franz worked as a players' agent. Lived in Golden Valley, Derbyshire.

CARTER Geoffrey 'Geoff'

Left winger 5'10"

Born *14/2/1943 Northwich, Cheshire*

Died *19/3/2018 West Midlands aged 75*

Playing career: *West Bromwich Albion (25 appearances 3 goals Feb 1959- July 66), Bury, Bradford City, Darlaston Town. (1959 – 1967)*

Carter joined Albion in May 1959, signing professional terms in February 1960. Geoff was a stocky, ginger-haired left winger who made his Albion debut v Arsenal in April 1960, the same day as Bobby Hope. He had a fair turn of speed and a good powerful left foot, packing a fierce shot, but his final delivery was often lacking. Most of his career at the Hawthorns was spent in the reserve team. Carter made 25 league appearances for Albion scoring 3 goals in 7 years. He moved to Bury in 1966 and then Bradford City the following year but only for a month, playing one league game. In 1974 he was groundsman at Albion's Spring Road Training Ground staying for four years, later doing a similar job for Accles and Pollocks in Oldbury. He lived in Tipton, and died in March 2018 suffering from leukaemia, after a stroke.

CARTER Joseph 'Joe'

Inside right 5'11"

Born *27/7/1899 Aston, Birmingham*
Died *7/1/1977 Handsworth, Birmingham*
Playing career: *West Bromwich Albion (451 appearances 155 goals April 1921 – Feb 1936), Sheffield Wednesday for 6 days, West Bromwich Albion (Feb 1936 -May 1936), Tranmere Rovers, Walsall, Vono Sports (player/manager) retired 1942. 3 England International caps*

Joe Carter was a wonderfully balanced, upright player with a fine dribbling technique, great body swerve and exceptional positional sense. He won three England caps, scoring four goals including 2 in a 4-3 defeat May 1929 in Spain who were the first foreign team to beat England. Carter won an FA Cup winner's medal with West Bromwich Albion in 1931, also helping the team win promotion to Division One in the same season. In September 1931 he became the first ever Albion player to be sent off at The Hawthorns. He played in the 1935 FA Cup Final when Albion finished as runners-up to Sheffield Wednesday, when neither he nor Tom Glidden should really have played due to previous injury problems. He gave Albion 15 years loyal service as a quality inside forward making 451 appearances scoring 155 goals. He also scored 34 goals in 57 Central League games, gaining successive Championship medals in 1922/23 and 1923/24. Partnering his captain Tommy Glidden, they played together in more than 350 first team games for Albion. Joe left Albion for Sheffield Wednesday in February 1936 but returned to the Hawthorns 6 days later following a failed medical, after an accident at home earlier in the week. Transferred to Tranmere Rovers three months later, he didn't settle down in Birkenhead and quickly returned to the Midlands, joining Walsall After football he became a stamper before becoming the licensee of The Grove public house in Handsworth, Birmingham. He died of dehydration in 1977.

CHILDS Gary

Midfielder 5'7"

Born *19/4/1964 Kings Heath, Birmingham*
Playing career: *West Bromwich Albion (2+1 sub appearances Feb 1982 – Oct 1983), Walsall, Birmingham City, Grimsby Town, Wisbech Town, Boston United Childs dropped out of the professional game with Grimsby Town in 1997 and briefly became player-manager of Wisbech. After a brief playing return with Boston United, (1982 – 2000)*

A clever ball player who was restricted to just three outings for the Albion first team. He was transferred to Walsall for £15,000 after a loan period, playing 131 league games becoming a crowd favourite. In July 1987 he moved to Birmingham City for £21,500, playing 55 league games. After two seasons at St Andrews he moved on to Grimsby Town where he spent eight years and played 233 league games scoring 26 goals. He helped the Mariners to two successive promotions from the Fourth Division 1989/90 and from the Third Division the following season 1990/91. After eight years he was released by Grimsby and Childs was appointed player-manager of Wisbech Town, newly elected to the Southern League Midland Division. He led the club to fifth place in the league and the 2nd round of the FA Cup before poor form led to his dismissal. He then joined Boston United until the end of the 1999/2000 season. He is a qualified Coach. Childs returned to former club Grimsby Town in 2001 where he became the club's Sport in the Community coach. Gary was also Sports Development Manager at Grimsby Institute of Further & Higher Education.

CLARK Clive 'Chippy'

Left winger 5'7"

Born *12/12/1940 Leeds*
Died *1/5/2014 Scarborough*
Playing career: *Leeds United, QPR, West Bromwich Albion (Cost £17,000 351 a+2 sub appearances 98 goals Jan 1960 - June 1969), QPR, Preston North End, Southport, Washington Diplomats (USA). (1957 – 1974) England U-23 International.*

Nicknamed 'Chippy', Clive Clark was an accomplished left-winger, fast, direct, courageous and a supreme goal scorer. He was signed from Queens Park Rangers by Albion manager Gordon Clark in a deal worth £17,000. What a bargain that turned out to be. Although he represented the England U-23's he was very unlucky not to earn a full England call up. He took over the number 11 shirt from Derek Hogg and was virtually a permanent fixture in the team until the end of the 1967/68 season. He scored 10 or more league goals in 5 successive seasons from 1963/64 to 1967/68.

The 'Three Degrees'

THE CELEBRATION
BRENDON BATSON
LAURIE CUNNINGHAM
CYRILLE REGIS

Dennis Clarke

He was Albion's top scorer in 1966/67 season. Clive became the first player score in every game in the League Cup including both legs of the semi-final and two in the Final at Wembley 1967 losing 3-2 to his former club Queens Park Rangers. He was an FA Cup Winner with Albion in 1968. He was badly injured on a tour of East Africa shortly after the FA Cup win in 1968 and never really recovered his fitness and his lightning speed was gone. He returned to QPR briefly in 1969, before signing for Preston North End in 1969/70, making his debut against Bristol City on 24th January 1970. He made 83 appearances, including 2 as substitute, for the Deepdale club, scoring 12 goals. He won a Third Division championship medal in 1970/71. Clark moved to Southport in 1973, where he ended his career after just one season in the Third Division, playing eight league games and scoring once. Clive worked in the building trade in Filey. When he was in his 50's he suffered several family bereavements and his health suffered as a consequence. By the time he was 57 he was in a Nursing Home in Scarborough and remained in Nursing Homes until his death on 1st May 2014 aged 73. Clive's wife June passed away in June 2020. Her father had been a member of the Albion ground-staff during the early 1960's.
Personal note: *In my view, Clive was very unlucky not to be part of the England International squad that won the World Cup in 1966. He was fast, direct, courageous and regularly scored 10 or more goals a season from the left wing. Alf Ramsey did not even include Clive in the original 40 players, although John*

Kaye was named in that squad. John failed to make the final group of 22 players. He often played with his socks rolled down and without shin pads, almost 'asking' for a tackle, but he was too quick and clever for most tough tackling full backs. I had the great pleasure in meeting Clive for the final time at the Hawthorns in 2008 at the 40th year celebration of winning the FA Cup.

CLARKE Dennis
Full back/centre back 5'9½"
Born *18/1/1948 Stockton-on-Tees, County Durham*
Playing career: *WBA (25 +1 sub appearances Feb 1965 – Jan 1969) Huddersfield Town, Birmingham City. (1965 – 1975)*
He was a solid full back who could fill in at centre half. Most of his career at the Hawthorns was spent in the reserve team, playing in the Central League, although, Dennis played for Albion in the first League Cup Final at Wembley in 1967 and he was the first substitute used in a Wembley FA Cup Final replacing the injured John Kaye in extra-time as Albion beat Everton 1-0 in May 1968. He played over 200 league games in his career the majority being at Huddersfield after he left the Hawthorns. He had a building consultancy business in Huddersfield. He is an active supporter of Old Baggies the Former Players' Association.

CLEMENT Neil
Left back/centre back 6'0"
Born *3/10/1978 Reading*
Playing career: *Chelsea, Reading (loan), Preston North End (loan), Brentford (loan), West Bromwich Albion (loan then signed Cost £150,000 275+25 sub appearances 26 goals Mar 2000 – Dec 2009)), Hull City (loan) (1995 – 2009) Neil played for England U-16's and U-18's.*
Neill's father, Dave Clement, former QPR & England International, died aged 34 in March 1982 after suffering with depression, he committed suicide with weed-killer. Neil was three years old at the time. Neil was the only Albion player to win three Promotions to the Premiership 2002,2004 and 2008, until Chris Brunt also achieved this fete with his third Promotion in 2020, added to those from 2008 & 2010. He played left back, left wing back and centre half. Neil was signed on transfer deadline day in March 2000 initially on loan, then permanently for £150,000, as Albion successfully battled to avoid relegation to the third tier.

A tall, strong left footed defender who loved to maraud down the left side of the field. Later settled into the centre half role, becoming safe in the air, sound on the ground and strong in the tackle. He was a set-piece specialist scoring some cracking free-kicks and penalties. He was forced to retire from football with an on-going knee injury. Neil owned a racehorse but was to receive a 15-year ban after committing corrupt or fraudulent practice, placing a bet on a horse he owned and failure to provide phone records to the inquiry. He has since done some television work for Sky. Moved to live in Spain. Brother to football manager Paul Clement. His Step-Father is Mike Kelly, a former goalkeeper and an ex-Albion coach.

COLDICOTT Stacy

Midfielder 5'11"

Born *29/4/1974 Redditch*

Playing career: *West Bromwich Albion (79+46 sub appearances 8 goals July 1992- June 1998), Cardiff City (loan), Grimsby Town, Hereford United, Cambridge United (loan), Armthorpe Welfare, Feckenham, Grantham Town (1992 – 2007)*

Coldicott came through the youth ranks at West Bromwich Albion making his League debut in 1992/93. The central midfielder featured for Albion until 1998, playing 125 games in all competitions including 46 as a substitute.

Stacy Coldicott

He had a brief loan spell with Cardiff City, before signing for former West Bromwich Albion manager Alan Buckley at Grimsby Town for a fee of £125,000. He played regularly for the first team, combining well with players such as ex-Baggies Paul Groves and Kevin Donovan. He continued to feature and played in three divisions for The Mariners. After 221 league appearances, Coldicott was released in the summer of 2005. After playing non-league football, he retired from the game in 2007. Stacy is the former husband of Big Brother 4 contestant Steph Coldicott, the couple were going through a divorce during her appearance on the 2003 show. Since finishing playing football he has been working as a firefighter in Grantham, as well as co-founding a Non-League football scouting website.

COLLARD Ian

Midfielder/full back 5'7"

Born *31/8/1947 Easington Colliery, County Durham*

Playing career: *West Bromwich Albion (90+7 sub appearances 8 goals Nov 1964- May 1969), Ipswich Town, Portsmouth (loan) (1964 – 1975)*

A solid player who always put maximum effort into his performances. Started his career as an inside forward but did splendid work at left half and left back. He was a member of the WBA losing team in the 1967 League Cup Final at Wembley and the FA Cup winning team in 1968. After playing 97 games scoring 8 goals for Albion, he left for Ipswich in May 1969 for £55,000, in a deal which saw Danny Hegan move in the opposite direction. A hip injury forced him to retire from soccer in 1976, aged 29. Ian has since travelled extensively, coaching the Kuwait Sporting Club 1978/79 and was later employed in Australia as Manager/Head Coach to Sunshine George Cross. He also ran a leisure centre near Ipswich and a staunch supporter of the Old Baggies former Players' Association. Ian has long retired and still lives in Ipswich with his wife Sonia, enjoying spending months in Tenerife.

"DID YOU KNOW?"

"West Bromwich Albion's highest ever goal scorer in one league season is W.G. Richardson who scored 39 goals in Division One in 1935/36"

COLQUHOUN Edmund 'Eddie'

Centre back/full back 6'0"

Born *29/3/1945 Prestonpans, Scotland*

Playing career: *Bury, West Bromwich Albion (Cost £25,000 54 appearances 1 goal Feb 1967 - Oct 1968), Sheffield United, Detroit Express, Washington Diplomats (player/coach 1980/81). Scottish International at full level, U-23 and Youth. (1962 – 1981) 9 Scotland International Caps. Eddie was unlucky at Albion suffering a bad leg injury*

A tall rangy centre half who could fill in at right back. Deceptively quick, brave, strong in the tackle and a really good header of the ball. Eddie was unlucky at the Hawthorns in the 1967/68 season. He had only missed 3 games all season when he suffered a bad leg injury away at Newcastle in the run up to the FA Cup Semi-Final and eventually the FA Cup Final. Totalled 476 league appearances and scored 1 goal for the Baggies.

Eddie left for Sheffield United in October 1968 for £27,500. He became a legend at Bramall Lane playing over 350 games, earning a Testimonial in 1980 . The Scotsman then spent some time playing in the USA and later ran a Post Office in South Yorkshire.

Eddie Colquhoun

49

COOKSON James 'Jimmy'

Centre forward 5'8"
Born *6/12/1904 Manchester*
Died *Dec 1970 Warminster:*
Playing career: *Manchester City, Southport (loan), Chesterfield, WBA (Cost £2,500 131 appearances 110 goals June 1927- Aug 1933), Plymouth Argyle, Swindon Town. Went on FA tour of Canada 1931.*

Jimmy began his career as a wing half with South Salford Lad's Club. Having failed to make the break through into Manchester City's first team, he was loaned out to Southport for a trial period in 1924. Then he moved to Chesterfield in 1925. It was here, where he had played at right back for the reserves, before being converted into a powerful and most prolific goal-scoring centre forward. He had no pedigree as a forward, but this experiment became an immediate success. Jimmy had little understanding of the finer points of distribution, or of the role of the leading forward knitting the wing play together. He was a ready shot with either foot, and the ability to move into the right position came naturally to him. His quick control enabled him to take the ball in his stride, and his trademark was the straightness of his run to goal when in possession of the ball.

To a defender Cookson was a damned difficult player to force to one side of the goal or the other. His greatest strength, though, was his pace. He would be off the mark and away, leaving defenders vainly appealing for offside. Cookson was the leading goal scorer in the Third Division North for the 1925/26 season with 44 goals and scored he scored 85 overall in 74 league appearances for Chesterfield. In August 1927, he joined West Bromwich Albion for a £2,500 fee. He continued to score goals at his new club, just three months after signing scoring six goals in a 6-3 win over Blackpool in a second division match. He was a member of the 1930/31 squad that won promotion to the First Division and the FA Cup although his place at Wembley was taken by WG Richardson. Later in 1931, Cookson was selected for the Football Association tour of Canada. He helped Albion win the Central League title in 1932, when he was top scorer with 29 goals. He left Albion to join Plymouth Argyle for £1,500 in 1933. He played 46 league games and scored 37 goals in 3 years at Home Park. He moved to Swindon Town in 1936 to play two more seasons appearing in 50 league games and scoring 31 goals.

Barry Cowdrill

In a 15-year career he amassed 292 league games scoring 256 goals. A terrific scoring ratio. He retired in 1938 but still played amateur football in the Swindon area until 1952. As an Albion scout, he spotted the up and coming Ray Barlow in 1944. Jimmy's brother Sam enjoyed a long career with Manchester City and Bradford City. He was a publican. He eventually settled in the West Country, becoming the steward of a social club in Frome, and serving on the committee of Frome Town and Warminster Town.

COWDRILL Barry

Born *3/1/1957 Castle Vale, Birmingham*
Playing career: *Sutton Coldfield Town, West Bromwich Albion (Cost £5,000 143+5 sub appearances 1 goal Apr 1979 – Jun 1988), Rotherham United (loan), Bolton Wanderers*
Nicknamed 'Basil', Cowdrill was a gangly, almost awkward-looking, long-striding player but Barry was a very useful, skilful footballer. Signed by Ron Atkinson as a left winger, it was not long before he converted to the left back position. Always gave 100% and loved to overlap down the wing. He made his debut in March 1980 against Norwich away. Barry would have probably played more games but for the fact he was competing against Derek Statham for the left back position He scored just once, against Grimsby in the FA Cup. He left to join Bolton Wanderers in 1988 playing 119 league games in four years scoring 4 goals. He helped them win the Sherpa Van Trop at Wembley in May 1989 Barry lived in Bournemouth with his wife Rachel and worked at Littledown Leisure Centre as Food & Beverage Manager.

COX Frederick 'Freddie'

Outside right 5'7"
Born *1/11/1920 Reading*
Died *07/08/1973 Bournemouth*
Playing career: *Tottenham Hotspur, He joined the RAF and won the Distinguished Flying Cross as a fighter pilot and later Transport Command over 6.5 years. He guested for Fulham, Manchester City. Reading, and Swindon Town during WW2. Arsenal, West Bromwich Albion. (player/coach 4 appearances 1 goal July 1953 – Apr 1956),*
He signed for Tottenham, Hotspur in 1938 but his career was interrupted by WW2. Cox served as a fighter pilot in the Royal Air Force, switching to Transport Command.

He clocked up 2000 'flight' hours in the Far East. He was awarded the Distinguished Flying Cross after 6½ years in the RAF. At Spurs he played 99 league games scoring 15 goals before moving to Arsenal in 1949. He played 79 games for the Gunners scoring 9 goals. In his day Freddie he was a dashing forceful outside right with heaps of energy and a powerful shot. He won the FA Cup in 1949/50 with Arsenal and was also runner up with them in 1951/52. Cox only played four matches for West Bromwich Albion and at the end of the 1953–54 season he was appointed as first team coach by manager Vic Buckingham. He later went on to Bournemouth as coach, Portsmouth as Manager between 1958 and 1961, Gillingham as manager June 1962 – 1965. He returned to Bournemouth as Manager 1965. Eventually Fred retired from football, in Bournemouth to run his newsagent's shop until his death in 1973

CRAM Robert 'Bobby'

Right half / right back 5'10½"
Born *19/11/1939 Hetton-le-Hole, County Durham*
Died *14/4/2007 Vancouver, British Columbia, Canada*
Playing career: *West Bromwich Albion (163 appearances 26 goals Jan 1957 – Aug 1967), Vancouver Royals, Eintracht Vancouver, Colchester United, Bath City, Seattle Sounders, Bromsgrove Rovers (1957 – 1975)*
Bobby was an energetic, determined and versatile footballer. He played at right back, right half, inside forward and even centre forward during his Albion career. Cram was a League Cup winner with Albion in 1966 and a runner up at Wembley in 1967. He was one of the very few defenders to score a hat trick in a top-level match v. Stoke City Sept 18th 1965. In 1968, he went on loan with the Vancouver Royals in the North American Soccer League. After leaving the Hawthorns, he is perhaps most remembered for being the captain of the Colchester United team that beat Baggies at the Hawthorns in the Watney Cup in 1971 after extra time and penalty shoot-out. Although he also led Colchester to a famous victory against Leeds United in the 1971 FA Cup, one of the greatest shocks in the competition's history. Cram died in Canada of a heart attack, aged 68, in April 2007. Bobby Cram was also the uncle of athlete Steve Cram.

Campbell Crawford

CRAWFORD Campbell

Full back 5'7"

Born *1/1271943 Alexandria, Scotland*

Playing career: *West Bromwich Albion (14 appearances Feb 1960 – July 1967), Exeter City, Kidderminster Harriers, Wednesbury Athletic (1960 – 1977*

A Scottish schoolboy international, Crawford joined West Bromwich Albion as a junior in June 1959 and worked through the various teams to earn a full contract in February 1960. A small, boyish-looking full back who arrived at the Hawthorns in the summer of 1959 with fellow Scots Bobby Hope, Ken Foggo and Bobby Murray. Crawford made his debut at Manchester United in Division One 14th September 1963 in front of 51,000 fans, losing 1-0. He only made 10 league and 4 Cup appearances in 7 years at the Hawthorns playing mostly for the Reserves in the Central League. He moved to Exeter City in July 1967. It proved to be a good move for both club and player as Crawford went on to become one of the mainstays of the Grecians team, playing well over 250 league and cup games, right through until his final season at St James' Park in 1973/74. This included being voted the Exeter City Player of the Year for 1970/71. He left Exeter to sign for Kidderminster Harriers and remained with them as a player until 1976/77, whereupon he assisted Harriers in a coaching capacity. Upon retiring from playing Campbell made many appearances for the Albion All Stars whilst working in a Sales capacity within the Steel Industry. Campbell has spent much of his life living in Walsall with his wife Margaret. A staunch supporter of the Old Baggies Former Players' Association.

CRAWFORD Raymond 'Ray'

Centre forward 5'10"

Born *13/7/1936 Portsmouth:*

Playing career: *Portsmouth, Ipswich Town, Wolverhampton Wanderers, West Bromwich Albion (Cost £30,000 17 appearances 7 goals Feb 1956- Mar 1966), Ipswich Town, Charlton Athletic, Kettering Town, Colchester United, Durban City in South Africa (1957 – 1971). 2 England International caps, played for the Football League and an FA XI.*

Ray was a powerful goal scoring centre forward with the knack of turning half chances into important goals. He was one of the most prolific goal scorers of his day.

Crawford started his professional career at his home town club Portsmouth but only played 19 times scoring 9 goals before he moved to Ipswich Town in September 1958. Crawford helped Ipswich to win back-to-back titles, the Second Division in 1960/61 and the First Division in 1961/62. In the latter season, he was joint leading scorer in Division One – alongside Derek Kevan of West Bromwich Albion – with 33 goals. During this time, he won the first of his two England caps, becoming the first Ipswich Town player to be capped for England. In 5 years at Portman Road he played 197 league games scoring 143 goals. He moved to Wolverhampton Wanderers in September 1963, scoring 39 goals in 57 games before Jimmy Hagan bought him to West Bromwich Albion for £30,000 in February 1965. A strong, powerful player who had good ball control. He was good in the air and a terrific goalscorer, although he had lost a yard of pace, by the time he joined Albion. He always looked so suntanned compared to most of his pasty-looking team mates. He was in competition with Jeff Astle and John Kaye for the striker's positions. In 14 games he scored 6 times before being sold back to Ipswich Town for £15,000 in March 1966. He later had spells at Charlton Athletic, Kettering and Colchester United before a short spell in South Africa with Durban City in 1971. In his 14-year career Ray played 476 league games scoring 289 goals. Ray became youth coach at Brighton, briefly working under Brian Clough, and then held a similar post at Fratton Park and assistant manager to Jimmy Dickinson until 1979. He Managed Fareham Town and Winchester City for a short while before retiring in 1984. At the end of his football career he worked as a representative and merchandiser for Nurdin & Peacock, but is now enjoying a happy retirement in Porchester. His autobiography entitled "Curse of the Jungle Boy" was published in 2007. Worked as a summariser on Express FM commentaries on Portsmouth matches and occasionally on Radio Suffolk on Ipswich Town games. Wrote a weekly column for the Yellow Advertiser online newspaper discussing the fortunes of Colchester United. He has appeared regularly at charity events and played an active role within the community of Portsmouth.

CRICHTON Paul

Goalkeeper 6'2"

Born *3/10/1968 Pontefract*

Playing career: *Nottingham Forest, Notts County(loan), Darlington (loan), Peterborough United (loan), Swindon Town (loan), Rotherham United (loan), Torquay United (loan),Peterborough United, Doncaster Rovers, Grimsby Town, West Bromwich Albion (loan Sep 1996 + signed Cost £250,000 34 appearances in total Aug-Nov 1998), Aston Villa (loan), Burnley(two loan spells then signed), Norwich City, York City, Gainsborough Trinity, Stafford Rangers, Leigh RMI, Accrington Stanley, Gillingham, Cambridge United, Kings Lynn (loan at first), Brighton & Hove Albion, Sheffield United.*

Somewhat of a footballing nomad, Crichton had numerous loan spells before eventually settling at Grimsby Town where he played 133 league games between 1993-96. Initially signed on loan by manager Alan Buckley Crichton was one of a group of former Grimsby Town players that made their way to the Hawthorns. He eventually completed a transfer for £250,000. His time with Albion was rather disappointing and he was prone to simple errors. He was not very popular with the fans. After further loan spells at Aston Villa and Burnley, he signed for Burnley for £100,000 in November 1998. He made 84 league appearances at Turf Moor before continuing his travels. Between 1986 and 2011 he played 480 league games. Whilst with Gillingham in 2005/06, Crichton was given the role of player-goalkeeping coach which was a position he later took up with Cambridge United. Paul became Brighton & Hove goalkeeping coach 2008-09. He was later appointed as a full-time goalkeeper coach at Norwich City in February 2009, but left the club exactly a year later when he left to join Sheffield United 2010-2011 to coach, although also registered as an emergency player in his 1st season. In 2012 he took the goalkeeping coaching job at Huddersfield Town. 2014 returned to Grimsby Town as goalkeeping coach.

"DID YOU KNOW?"

" In 1882 Albion recorded their biggest ever victory thrashing Coseley 26-0 in a Birmingham Cup Tie and every outfield player scored"

After only a week of pre-season training, he left and joined Blackpool, then QPR until 2016. Moved to Port orange in Florida, USA as a coach for PSA Soccer Academy.

CROOKS Garth

Striker 5'8"

Born *10/3/1958 Stoke-on-Trent*

Playing career: *Stoke City, Tottenham Hotspur, Manchester United (loan), West Bromwich Albion (Cost £100,000 50 appearances 21 goals July 1985 – Feb 1987), Charlton Athletic. England U-21 International (1975-1991)*

A goalscorer of the highest quality, he scored 48 goals in 147 league games at his hometown club Stoke City. In July 1980 Tottenham Hotspur paid £600,000 to take him to White Hart Lane. He received FA Cup winning medals in 1981, scoring against Manchester City, and again in 1982. He was a League Cup runner-up in 1982 losing to Liverpool. After a loan spell at Manchester United, in July 1985 Johnny Giles Albion's manager signed him for £100,000, playing him alongside Imre Varadi. Albion were related at the end of that season 1985/86. Garth was top scorer in 1986/87 in Division Two, scoring 11 goals in 21 league appearances, alongside Bobby Williamson, even though Ron Saunders sold him to Charlton Athletic for f75,000 in March 1987. Garth played 56 league games at the Valley scoring 15 goals. He totalled 129 goals in 375 league games from 1976 -1990. Crooks became the first black chairman of the Professional Footballers' Association but gave up the role after retiring with knee problems in 1990. A pundit/reporter for BBC TV, In the late 1990s, Crooks became presenter of the political television show Despatch Box. In 1999, he was awarded an OBE in the Queen's Birthday Honours for his services to football punditry, specifically citing his ability to bring passion to football. He appeared regularly on Final Score as a pundit and on rare occasions appeared on Match of the Day as a replacement for regular pundits Alan Shearer and Danny Murphy. He was occasionally seen interviewing players for Football Focus. He was Chairman of the PFA in 1988. Garth became Chairman of the Institute of Professional Sport, and on the board of the North West London school Capital City Academy.

CROSS David

Centre forward 6'1"

Born *8/12/1950 Heywood, Lancashire*

Playing career: *Rochdale, Norwich City, Coventry City, West Bromwich Albion (Cost £150,000 1st spell Nov 1976-Dec 1977), West Ham United, Manchester City, Vancouver Whitecaps, Oldham Athletic, Vancouver Whitecaps, West Bromwich Albion (2nd spell Free Transfer Total in 2 spells 61+1 sub appearances 23 goals Oct 1984-June 1985), Bolton Wanderers, Bury, Aris Limassol, Blackpool (1969 – 1987).*

A tall, skilful striker who scored goals wherever he played. Cross played for Third Division club Rochdale, He moved to Norwich City, with whom he won the Second Division championship in 1972. He then joined Coventry City for £150,000, a club record. He joined West Bromwich Albion for £150,000 in November 1976, scoring 18 goals in 38 league games. Cross scored in a 3-0 victory over Everton at the Hawthorns on 27th November 1976 when a small Jack Russell dog ran on the pitch, as if to chase the ball. This distracted the Everton keeper, Dai Davies, and Cross ran past the keeper with the ball and rolled it into the net. West Ham United broke their club record for Cross when they paid for £200,000 for his services on 9th December 1977. He scored 78 times 179 league games for the Hammers. He moved to Manchester City for £125,000 and then Oldham Athletic for £20,000. Cross later spent the summers of 1983 and 1984 with Vancouver Whitecaps, making 46 appearances and scoring 29 goals. He returned to West Bromwich Albion on a free transfer in October 1984, staying for the rest of the 1984/85 season. Later he signed for Bolton Wanderers, but a fractured skull helped to end his professional career in England with a loan spell at Bury. He then had a brief stop at Aris Limassol of Cyprus, and finished his career at Blackpool. In a playing career 18 years he played over 700 games and scored over 250 goals. He later spent nine years in the insurance industry, has worked as a financial advisor for Allied Dunbar in Manchester and scouted for Watford, coached the reserves and youth team at Oldham, later becoming assistant manager to Iain Dowie. David has acted as a scout for West Ham and worked on opposition analysis for Blackburn. He was also a business man in Heywood Lancashire and is President of the local cricket club.

Nicky Cross

CROSS Nicholas 'Nicky'

Striker / forward 5'9"

Born *7/2/1961 Shirley, Birmingham*

Playing career: *West Bromwich Albion (79 + 40 sub appearances 19 goals February 1979 – August 1985), Walsall, Leicester City, Port Vale, Hereford United, Solihull Borough (1980 – 1996)*

Cross signed for First Division side West Bromwich Albion as an apprentice in July 1977. He turned professional in February 1979. He made his debut at Old Trafford in Division One coming on as a substitute in April 1981, as the club finished fourth in the league under Ron Atkinson in the 1980/81 season. Cross was a tenacious and intelligent forward who could hold the ball up well to make up for his lack of pace and dominance in the air. The club struggled under Ronnie Allen's stewardship in 1981/82, avoiding relegation by only two points. They went on to finish in mid-table in 1982/83 under Ron Wylie, before Wylie was replaced by Johnny Giles in February 1984. Nicknamed 'supersub' during his Albion days, sitting on the bench more than any other player. He never really became a regular in his eight years at the Hawthorns. At the end of the 1984/85 season, Cross left The Hawthorns to join Walsall, who paid a £48,000 transfer fee. He had played a total of 105 league games for West Bromwich Albion, scoring 15 goals.

In two seasons with the Saddlers he played 109 league games for Walsall, scoring 45 league goals, before he was sold on to Leicester City for a £80,000 fee in January 1988. Cross scored 15 goals in 58 league games for City. He was sold on to Port Vale for a £125,000 fee in June 1989, and would play a total of 176 games for the club in league and cup competitions, winning the Football League Trophy in 1993, and helping the club to promotion out of the Third Division in 1993/94. After this success he spent two years with Hereford United, before heading into non-league football with Solihull Borough in 1996. He scored 128 goals in 481 league games in a sixteen-year career in the Football League, playing for five different clubs. He later managed Redditch United and Studley KBL, before heading into the financial and pensions sector in 2004. Nicky lives in Solihull and is a staunch supporter of the Old Baggies Former Players' Association.

CUMBES James 'Jim'

Goalkeeper 6'2"
Born *4/5/1944 Manchester*
Playing career: *Tranmere Rovers, West Bromwich Albion (Cost £33,350 79 apps 1969 – 1971), Aston Villa, Portland Timbers, Runcorn, Southport, Worcester City, Kidderminster Harriers (1962 --1984).*
Nicknamed 'Jimbo' he was a tall, acrobatic goalkeeper who had a safe pair of hands but sometimes seemed to lack total concentration. In 1966/67 he helped Tranmere Rovers win promotion to Division Three. Signed in August 1969 by Alan Ashman, for £33,350, Cumbes vied with John Osborne for the keeper's position at the Hawthorns. He played in 79 games for Albion before moving to Aston Villa in November 1971 for £36,000. Whilst with Aston Villa, he won a Third Division Championship medal in 1971/72, a runners-up medal in Division Two in 1974/75 and won a League Cup tankard in 1975 at Wembley. In March 1976 Jim

Jim Cumbes

moved to Portland Timbers, then returned to the UK and played non-league football until retiring in 1984. He played First-Class cricket for four counties, Lancashire, Surrey, Worcestershire & Warwickshire as a right-arm fast-medium bowler and lower-order right-handed batsman. Cumbes won a County Championship winners medal and Gillette Cup winners' medals with Worcestershire. He went into business together with John Osborne in the sports outfitters trade. Jim was Commercial Manager at Warwickshire CCC and later chief executive at Lancashire CCC.

Personal note: *I saw Jim throw the ball well over the half way line in a 'bowling' action at Villa Park, when they were in the Third Division, in the days when you could go to watch any team locally, paying on the gate.*

CUNNINGHAM Laurie

Winger 5'11"

Born *8/3/1956 Archway, London*
Died *15/7/1989 Madrid, Spain aged 33*
Playing career: *Leyton Orient, West Bromwich Albion (Cost £110,000 102 + 8 sub appearances 28 goals Mar 1977- June 1979), Real Madrid in Spain, Manchester United (loan), Sporting Gijon in Spain (loan), Marseille in France, Leicester City, Rayo Vallecano in Spain, Charleroi in Belgium, Wimbledon, Rayo Vallecano. 6 caps full England International and 'B', and U-21 levels.*

Born in Archway, London, he was the son of a former Jamaican race-horse jockey. Cunningham was turned down by Arsenal before joining Leyton Orient in 1974, where he played in 75 league games scoring 15 goals. He joined West Bromwich Albion in March 1977 for £110,000. Under manager Johnny Giles, he teamed up with another black player, Cyrille Regis, and the following year, under manager Ron Atkinson, with Brendon Batson, Atkinson collectively referred to Cunningham, Batson and Regis as "The Three Degrees" after the U.S. girl singing trio. Laurie played in 86 league games for Albion, 114 games in all competitions, scoring 30 goals. Whilst a West Bromwich Albion player, he played in a benefit match for Len Cantello, that saw a team of white players play against a team of black players. In the summer of 1979, he made a historic move as the first British player to transfer to Real Madrid, who paid West Bromwich Albion a fee of £950,000.

He scored twice on his debut and helped Real win the league and cup double. He suffered with a broken toe but recovered in time for the 1981 European Cup Final against Liverpool in Paris, as Real Madrid lost 1–0. Cunningham played 44 league games for Real, scoring 13 goals, but he received some very harsh treatment from some of the opposing defenders. Laurie had a brief loan spell with Manchester United in 1983 playing 5 league games scoring once. He was then loaned to Sporting Gijon for the rest of the 1983/84 season playing in 30 league games scoring 3 goals. He moved to Marseille and in 1984/85 he played in 30 league games scoring 8 goals. Laurie returned to England joining Leicester City in for the 1985/86 season. He moved back to Spain with Rayo Vallecano in 1986/87 and made one appearance in the Belgian league for Charleroi in 1987 before joining the 'crazy gang' at Wimbledon in 1988. His career was blighted by injuries but he did manage to help Wimbledon beat Liverpool in the 1988 FA Cup Final. He headed back to Spain and Rayo Vallecano for the 1988/89 season, enjoying playing and scored the goal that secured their promotion to the Primera Liga. In a 15-year career he had played 348 league games scoring 67 goals. Laurie Cunningham was killed in a car crash in Madrid on the morning of 15 July 1989, at the age of 33.

Personal note: *If West Bromwich Albion had been more determined to hold on to Laurie Cunningham in 1979, I am convinced the team could have gone on to win the First Division Championship or certainly a major trophy. Alas the lure of Real Madrid and a fee of £995,000 was too much for the Albion Board and Laurie to turn down. He was called the 'Black Pearl' or in Spain the Madrid fans nicknamed him 'El Negrito' which means 'little black person' in English. This would certainly not be allowed nowadays. The racial discrimination and abuse that Cunningham, Regis and Batson suffered was disgusting but their way of dealing with it was by playing at their best on the pitch.*

"DID YOU KNOW?"

"West Bromwich Albion were the first Midlands team to appear in an FA Cup Final in 1886."

CUNNINGTON Shaun

Midfielder 5'9"

Born *4/1/1966 Bourne, Lincolnshire*

Playing career: *Wrexham, Grimsby Town, Sunderland, West Bromwich Albion (Cost £220,000 11+7 sub appearances Aug 1995 – Mar 1997), Notts County, Kidderminster Harriers, coach upon retiring in 2000 (1982 – 2000)*

Shaun made 198 league appearances for Wrexham, then moved to Grimsby Town for £65,000 in 1988. He played 182 league games for the Mariners. A £650,000 move to Sunderland followed but he only made 58 league appearances between 1992 – 1995. Alan Buckley signed him for £200,000 as one of a band of former Grimsby players that he brought to the Hawthorns. Shaun never really made the grade with Albion, poor form and injuries limited him to a total of 18 appearances before leaving for Notts County for £25,000. He finished his playing career at Kidderminster Harriers playing 35 league games between 1998-2000. Cunnington stayed on with his final team, Kidderminster Harriers working as a coach, and briefly taking caretaker charge in 2004 after Jan Molby resigned, but later reverted to Youth Team coach. He also managed Willenhall Town from May 2008 until November 2009. Managed Halesowen Town in January 2011 until Sept 2012. May 2013 was manager of Evesham United. Catering Sales Manager at Booker Wholesale Foods Ltd. For Hanbury, Hereford and Worcester. He lives in Droitwich Spa, Worcestershire.

CUTLER Reg

Left winger 5'7"

Born *17/2/1935 Rowley Regis, Blackheath*

Died *5/5/2012 Kidderminster*

Playing career: *West Bromwich Albion (5 appearances Feb 1952 - June 1956), Bournemouth, Portsmouth, Stockport County, Worcester City, Dudley Town, Bromsgrove Rovers (1951 – 1963)*

Reg joined Albion as an apprentice in May 1950, turning professional in February 1952. In the following four years between 1952 – 1956 Reg was reserve to George Lee at the Albion. He only appeared in 5 league games for the Baggies. He was transferred for £500 to Bournemouth. He made 96 league appearances for the Cherries between 1956 – 1958 scoring 21 goals During his time at Portsmouth he helped 'Pompey' win the Third Division championship in 1961/62

when another ex-Baggie Jimmy Campbell played on the opposite wing and Ron Saunders was centre forward. He made another 100 league appearances at Portsmouth scoring 13 goals between 1958-1962. This was followed by 34 league appearances at Stockport County in 1962/63 before returning to the Midlands and moving into non-league football. He worked in a factory in Wolverhampton and later worked for Oakvale Nurseries in Worcestershire before retiring in 2000. He lived in Wolverley near Kidderminster.

DARBY Julian

Midfielder 6'0"

Born *3/10/1967 Farnworth, Lancashire*

Playing career: *Bolton Wanderers, Coventry City, West Bromwich Albion (Cost £250,000 37 +7 sub appearances 1 goal Nov 1995 – July 1997), Preston North End, Rotherham United (loan), Carlisle United.*

Darby had a good career at Bolton Wanderer playing 270 league games between 1986 – 1993 scoring 36 goals. He scored for Bolton in the Associate Members Cup Final at Wembley in 1989 as Bolton beat Torquay United 4-1. He moved to Coventry City in 1993 and made 55 league appearances scoring 5 goals in two seasons. He was signed for Albion by manager Alan Buckley for £250,000 in November 1995. In two years at the Hawthorns he played 39 games scoring once. He moved on to Preston only making 36 appearances in three years. After a loan at Rotherham United he ended his playing career at Carlisle United featuring in 18 league games scoring once. Upon retirement Darby completed his coaching badges and was appointed as a first team coach at Preston North End alongside Billy Davies, before moving with Davies, to take up a similar role with Derby County in 2006. From 2009-2011 he was Nottingham Forest first team coach again working with manager Billy Davies. Also coached the Youth team at Bolton Wanderers and a short spell as assistant caretaker manager to Jimmy Phillips. In 2013 he returned for a second spell at Nottingham Forest as First Team coach until 2014. In 2005 he joined Uwe Rosler's Leeds United as first team coach. In August 2016 he coached the Bolton Wanderers U-16's and the following season 2017 took a full-time role at Bolton's academy.

DARTON Scott
Left back 5'11"
Born 27/3/1975 Ipswich, Suffolk
Playing career: *West Bromwich Albion (21 appearances Oct 1992 –Jan 1995), Blackpool, Kings Lynn, Chelmsford*

Tall, blonde, left back Darton began his career as a trainee with West Bromwich Albion, turning professional in October 1992. In September 1994 at the Hawthorns Scott Darton was getting booed at every turn on a cold weeknight when Albion were at the bottom end of the Second Division playing Portsmouth in a 2-0 defeat. Surely a player knows when he is not playing well. The crowd booing almost certainly led to Darton losing confidence and being removed from the first team, playing just 7 games that season. At the Albion, he made a total of 15 league appearances and played in 6 cup games. In January 1995 he joined Sam Allardyce's Blackpool for £7,500. In two years with the Seasiders he made 29 appearances and scored one goal, his only goal in the Football League. He joined Torquay United on trial on 3 October 1996 with a view to signing on loan. He played for Torquay's reserve side but was not signed. Darton moved into non-league football with King's Lynn in August 1997. He subsequently played for Ipswich Wanderers, Cambridge City, Heybridge Swifts, St Albans City and Chelmsford City in September 1998, from where he returned to Ipswich Wanderers in July 2001.

DAVIES Stanley 'Stan'
Centre forward/inside forward 5'10½
Born 24/4/1898 Chirk, Wales
Died 17/1/19772 Birmingham
Playing career: *Rochdale, Preston North End, Everton, WBA (Cost £3,300 159 appearances 83 goals Nov 1921 – Nov 1927), Birmingham City, Rotherham United as player/manager, Barnsley. 19 Welsh International caps. Toured Canada with Welsh FA in 1929 (1919 – 1930). Captained Wales twice.*

In World War 1 he distinguished himself with the Royal Welsh Fusiliers. Davies was wounded during the Battle of Cambrai and later transferred to the Army Signalling School and was awarded the Military Medal and the Croix de Guere. Stan was big and strong and possessed a cracking shot. He could head a ball hard and true and had lots of stamina.

Davies turned professional with Rochdale in January 1919 but just three months later joined Preston North End for £800. After two years with Preston, Davies moved to Everton on in January 1921 for a fee of £4000, a club record for Preston at the time. He played with the Toffees from February to November 1921 when he joined Albion for £3,000 when the centre forward position was becoming a problem position. He became a firm favourite with the fans during his six years at the Hawthorns. He averaged a goal every two games, totalling 159 appearances and 83 goals in all competitions. Later in his career he played for Birmingham, Cardiff City, Rotherham United as player/manager and Barnsley. He became Chelmsford City trainer and was later a publican at the Crown & Cushion in West Bromwich between 1931 and 1935.

DEEHAN John 'Dixie'
Striker/midfielder 6'0"
Born 6/8/1957 Solihull
Playing career: *Aston Villa, West Bromwich Albion (Cost 424,000 47 + 3 appearances 5 goals Sept 1979 - Dec 1981) Norwich City, Ipswich Town, Manchester City, Barnsley. England U-21 and Youth International. and became player/coach at Manchester City in July 1988 and switched to Barnsley in the same role in 1990 (1975 – 1991).*

Nicknamed 'Dixie', he won the Football League Cup with Aston Villa in 1977. When Albion signed Deehan in 1979 for £424,000, he was the first player from Aston to join the Baggies since George Harris in 1909. He never really hit it off alongside Cyrille Regis at the Hawthorns, as he was often asked to play wide or drop back into midfield, a role he was not used to. He was more accustomed to the striker's role, yet had little opportunity to play in that position for Albion. He played in 50 games scoring 5 goals before leaving after two years to join Norwich City for £175,000. He was a member of the Norwich City side which was promoted to Division One in 1981/82, won the 1985 Football League Cup and the Second Division championship in 1986. Deehan returned in 1992 to his old club Norwich as assistant manager and later succeed Mike Walker as manager in January 1994 until April, however he left after a string of poor results. Later managed Wigan 1995 – 1998.

John was assistant manager at Aston Villa July 1999 – January 2002 and had a short spell as joint caretaker manager at Villa Park with Stuart Gray in early 2002. He then became the Director of football at Northampton Town 2003-2006, Lincoln City Director of Football Oct 2007, shortly followed by a move to scouting for Bolton Wanderers in November 2007. In January 2009 he was appointed chief scout for Norwich City. December 2009 John moved to become assistant manager at Kettering Town but was sacked later that month. In March 2010 Grimsby Town appointed him as Head of Recruitment & Director of Football until May 2010. January 2012 Deehan was appointed Director of Football at Plymouth Argyle but left at the end of the season. In 2014 he joined the coaching staff at Sheffield Wednesday.

DIBBLE Andrew 'Andy'

Goalkeeper 6'3"
Born *8/5/1965 Cwmbran, Wales*
Playing career: *Cardiff City, Luton Town, Sunderland (loan), Huddersfield Town (loan), Manchester City, Aberdeen (loan), Middlesbrough (loan), West Bromwich Albion (loan 9 appearances Feb – June 1992), Sheffield United (loan), Rangers FC, Sheffield United, Luton Town, Middlesbrough, Altrincham, Barry Town, Hartlepool United, Carlisle United (loan), Stockport County, Wrexham, Accrington Stanley. Welsh International (1982 – 2006)*
Andy Dibble was something of a footballing nomad, tall and steady goalkeeper but not flashy. Played for 20 different team either transferring or on loan He started at Cardiff City making 61 league appearances between 1982-84. His longest spell was at Manchester City where he appeared in 166 league games but had 5 loan spells including one at the Hawthorns. He made 9 league appearances for Albion between February and April 1992 deputising for the injured Stuart Naylor. He had spells in Scotland and later in non-league football. Won the Football League Cup with Luton Town in 1987-88, Scottish Premier Division winner with Rangers in 1996/97. Dibble retired in 2006 whilst player-goalkeeping coach of Accrington Stanley. In a 24year playing career he made 397 league appearances. He went on to become goalkeeping coach for Accrington Stanley moving to Coventry City in November 2006 for only three months. In

March 2007 he joined Peterborough United as goalkeeping coach until October 2009 when he joined Rotherham United on Ronnie Moore's coaching staff, being appointed joint-caretaker manager in October 2016. In January 2017 he joined Cardiff City as goalkeeping coach.

DICHIO Daniele 'Danny'

Striker 6'3"
Born *19/10/74 Notting Hill, London*
Playing career: *QPR, Welling United (loan), Barnet (loan), Sampdoria, Lecce (loan), Sunderland, West Bromwich Albion (loan then signed Cost £1,250,000 59 + 17 sub appearances 18 goals July 2001 – Jan 2004) Derby County , Millwall, Preston North End, Toronto.*
Born in Hammersmith, London, to an English mother and an Italian father, Dichio began his career at Queens Park Rangers. Had a couple of loan spells followed by a season in Italy with Sampdoria only playing 2 league games scoring two goals before being loaned out to Lecce. Returned to England to play for Sunderland. He played 76 league games for the Black Cats scoring 17 goals. Nicknamed 'Deech'. Dichio went on loan to West Bromwich Albion at the start of the 2001/02 season which was a successful one, with Danny scoring on his debut away at Sheffield Wednesday on 25th August 2001 and again on his home debut in a 1–0 win against Gillingham two days later. He joined the Midlands side on loan and the Albion fans really took to him as he always gave 100% effort. However, he broke his foot in just his third Baggies outing. He signed permanently in November 2001 in a £1.25 million deal, and helped them to achieve promotion. In Albion's first Premiership campaign the following season, Dichio was their second highest scorer in the league with Scott Dobie, although with just five Premiership goals, that was not enough to prevent relegation. He finished as top scorer with 8 goals overall, by virtue of his FA Cup hat-trick against Bradford City. The following season saw Dichio move himself and his family up to the Midlands, having previously commuted from London. He was a member of the Albion promotion winning side of 2001/02. After loan spells at Derby County and Millwall, Danny signed for Millwall Dichio. He was unable to play in the 2004 Cup Final for Millwall due to suspension.

He moved to Preston in the summer of 2005, playing 63 league games, scoring 9 goals. In April 2007 he was released from his contract to let him join newly created MLS Toronto FC. In three season he scored 14 goals in 59 games. He became a permanent resident of Canada in 2009, where he worked as a coach at Toronto FC youth academy. In 2010 became assistant coach, then moved back to coach the Toronto FC academy, U-21's. Technical Director for Thornhill Soccer Club. In 2016 he applied for Canadian Citizenship. He is also a football analyst for Canada's largest sports network.

Personal note: *For my 50th birthday I was treated to a meal in an Executive Box in the East Stand for the home game against Watford on 5th March 2002, courtesy of my old friend and ex-Albion Director Clive Stapleton. We drew 1-1 with 'Deech' scoring Albion's goal.*

DOBIE (Robert) Scott

Striker 6'1"
Born *10/10/1978 Workington*
Playing career: *Carlisle United, Clydebank (loan), WBA (Cost £200,000 64 + 63 sub appearances 25 goals July 2001-2004), Millwall, Nottingham Forest, Carlisle United, St Johnstone, Bradford City (loan), York City. Full Scottish International 6 caps (1996 – 2011).*

Began his professional career with Carlisle United in May 1997 and it was his header that was parried into the path of Carlisle keeper Jimmy Glass to score with the last kick of the match in the final game of the 1998/99 season to preserve Carlisle's Football League status. After playing 136 league games scoring 26 goals, Dobie was transferred to West Bromwich Albion in July 2001 for an initial £150,000 fee, with another £50,000 being paid once he reached 25 appearances. He finished the 2001/02 season as the club's joint top scorer with 11 league goals, 13 in total. His performances helped Albion get promoted to the Premier League. In Albion's first Premiership campaign the following season, Dobie was their joint top scorer with Danny Dichio, though with just five goals, not enough to prevent relegation. He joined Millwall for the 2004/05 season playing 16 league games scoring 3 goals. He then joined Nottingham Forest in 2005 and in three years made 41 league appearances scoring 3 goals. Scott then re-joined Carlisle United in 2008 making 84 league appearances scoring 12 goals in two years.

A short spell with St. Johnstone and a loan spell with Bradford City followed. Scott took a 16-month sabbatical after leaving Bradford to start police training, then he signed a 3-month contract with York City, who had ex-Baggie Des Lyttle on the coaching staff, but he failed to make a league appearance. Dobie has worked as a police officer with the armed response team in Cumbria.

DOBSON Anthony 'Tony'

Defender 6'1"
Born *5.2.1969 Coventry*
Playing career: *Coventry City, Blackburn Rovers, Portsmouth, Oxford (loan), Peterborough (loan), West Bromwich Albion (Free transfer 8+7 sub appearances July 1997 – Sep 1998), Gillingham, Northampton Town, Forest Green Rovers (1986-2001)*

Dobson started his professional career at Coventry City signing professional in July 1986. He made 54 league appearances, scoring 1 goal, between 1986-1991. He was transferred for £275,000 to Blackburn Rovers in 1991, where he made 41 league appearances during his two-year stint. He was transferred to Portsmouth on 22 September 1993, for a transfer fee £150,000. There he made 53 league appearances, scoring 1 goal. He also had loan spells with Oxford United and Peterborough United. West Bromwich Albion were his next team signing in July 1997 on a free transfer. He was tall and strong. Dobson made 8 starts and 7 substitute appearances before moving on for a short spell at Gillingham. Then he went to Northampton Town for £25,000 from 1998-2000. He ended his playing career at Forest Green Rovers playing just two league games. In 2001, he became the manager of Rugby Town, then called Rugby United. In 2005, he left Rugby Town to become the manager of Solihull Borough. He left the post in 2006, but then began his second spell in charge of Rugby Town, signing a new contract on 16 September 2008 to October 2009. From time to time Tony has appeared for the Coventry City Sky Blues Legends XI in charity games.

"DID YOU KNOW?"

West Bromwich Albion first wore Navy Blue and White stripes in 1919."

DONOVAN Kevin
Right winger/midfielder 5'7"
Born *17/12/1971 Halifax, England*
Playing career: *Huddersfield Town, Halifax Town (loan), West Bromwich Albion (Cost £70,000 170 + 33 sub appearances 32 goals October 1992 – July 1997), Grimsby Town, Barnsley, Rochdale, York City, Alfreton Town (1989 – 2007).* Nicknamed 'Jason' after a certain Australian Soap Star. A fast, direct and skilful player who was always full of running and gave 100% in every game. He started his career at Huddersfield but only played 20 league games in a four-year spell. He moved to West Bromwich Albion when Ossie Ardiles signed him for £70,000 in October 1992. He made his Albion debut against Port Vale in the same month. Donovan scored in Albion's 3–0 win over Vale in the Division Two play-off final May at Wembley1993 as the club clinched promotion. He played 203 times for Albion scoring 32 goals. Alan Buckley took him to Grimsby for £300,000 where he spent four years playing a further 154 league games scoring 23 goals. Spells at Barnsley, Rochdale and York City followed before finishing playing at Alfreton Town in 2007. Living in West Yorkshire, he has since coached youngsters holding soccer classes at Brighouse Town in his native county of Yorkshire, where he also coached the youth side. Coach at Huddersfield Town Academy.

Has appeared as a guest pundit for BBC Radio Humberside whilst commentating on Grimsby Town games. He is a staunch supporter of Old Baggies Former Players' Association.

DUDLEY George
Inside forward / outside left 5'9½"
Born *Feb 1916 Gartcosh, Glasgow*
Died *December 1979*
Playing career: *West Bromwich Albion (25 appearances 5 goals Oct 1937 – Oct 1946), Banbury Spencer, Dudley Town, Netherton, Cradley Heath. He also guested for Walsall for 3 seasons during WW2 and for Leicester City, Oldham Athletic & Bromsgrove Rovers (1937- 1953)*
George was the first Scot to play for Albion since Tom Dilly in 1907. He was an inside forward who mainly relied on skill rather than strength and effort. Another player whose career was interrupted by WW2. George only played 6 league games scoring twice, although he did appear in 19 War Time League or cup games. Dudley left Albion to play non-league football with Banbury Spencer, Dudley Town, Netherton and Cradley Heath. He also played briefly for Accles & Pollock works side in mid-1950's and later became Aero Dept's V.E. Chief Planning Engineer at the Broadwell Works Depot. Brother of Jimmy.

Kevin Donovan

DUDLEY James 'Jimmy'

Wing half 5'10"

Born *24/8/1928 Gartcosh, Glasgow*
Died *25/4/2006 West Bromwich*
Playing career: *West Bromwich; WBA (320 appearances 11 goals Aug 1945 – Dec 1959), Walsall, Stourbridge, Arcadia United FC in Pretoria, South Africa. Scotland B International team (1945 – 1968)*

He did two years National Service with the RAF, serving mainly in Germany just after the War. Originally an inside forward, Jimmy moved to right half. Dudley made 166 successive appearances between 1952 and 1956, a club record that was surpassed by Ally Robertson in 1979. Scored a goal in the FA Cup Semi-Final victory over Port Vale at Villa Park. Then he won an FA Cup winner's with Albion in 3-2 victory over Preston North End at Wembley in 1954. Jim played in 320 First team games for Albion scoring 11 goals in 14 years. Dudley moved to Walsall in 1959 playing 167 league games and helping them win the 4th Division Championship in 1959/60. He worked at Guest Motors West Bromwich Ford dealer as a van parts salesman for over 20 years. Brother of George.

DUGDALE James 'Jim'

Centre half 5'10"

Born *15/1/1932 Liverpool*
Died *26/2/2008 Birmingham*
Playing career: *West Bromwich Albion (75 appearances July 1952 – Dec 1955), Aston Villa, QPR. FA Cup winner with WBA in 1954 and Aston Villa in 1957 (1952 – 1963).3 England 'B' caps.*

He served with the Army during his National Service, spending most of his time at Oswestry, playing for the Albion in the Birmingham Combination side until 'demob'. He signed full time for Albion in May 1952. Jimmy was an outstanding centre half who could control the heart of the defence with authority. He was a member of the 1954 FA Cup winning team at Wembley in 1954 beating Preston North End 3-2. Jim was a rival to Joe Kennedy for the number 5 shirt at the Hawthorns and eventually, after 63 league games for Albion, he opted to leave for Aston Villa who paid £25,000 for him in February 1956. He won a second FA Cup Winners medal with Aston Villa in 1957, beating Albion in the Semi-final after a replay on the way to beating Manchester United's Busby Babes in the Final.

He was also a League Cup Winner with them over two legs in 1961 when they beat Rotherham, at a time when most of the bigger clubs did not enter. He played 215 league games for Villa scoring 3 goals. He was a publican for 25 years, first in Perry Barr, Aston at the Villa Lions Club, later at Moseley Rugby Club Moseley, and then was licensee/steward at the Conservative Club, Hasbury near Halesowen. Jim had to have a leg amputated in the1990's. Died in 2008 after a long illness, aged 76.

DURNIN John

Striker/forward 5'10"

Born *18/8/1965 Bootle, Merseyside*
Playing career: *Liverpool, West Bromwich Albion (loan 5 appearances 2 goals Oct/Nov 1988), Oxford United, Portsmouth, Blackpool (loan), Carlisle United, Kidderminster Harriers, Rhyl, Port Vale, Accrington Stanley. (1986 – 2004)*

Nicknamed 'Johnny Lager' He began his career at Liverpool in 1986, but made just three minor cup appearances for the first team. Durnin played 5 games for Albion on loan from Liverpool in October - November 1988, scoring twice. I don't think Albion could afford to buy him so he joined Oxford United for a £225,000 fee in February 1989, playing 161 league games and scoring 44 goals. He was sold on to Portsmouth for £200,000 in 1993 making 181 league appearances scoring 31 goals. Pompey loaned him out to Blackpool, and then allowed him to leave permanently in 1999 to join Carlisle United. He signed with Kidderminster Harriers in 2000, before briefly entering the Welsh football circuit with Rhyl in 2001. Later that year he returned to the Football League with Port Vale, before he joined Conference side Accrington Stanley for a twelve-month spell in May 2003. He retired from the game in 2004 having played 477 league games scoring 99 goals in an 18year career. In July 2006, John joined the coaching staff of Southport but left in October of that year. Later coached at former club Port Vale and then spent four years at Bolton's Academy. The likeable Scouser eventually settled in Warrington, undertaking media work both in the local press and on radio whilst also being a regular for the Liverpool Masters team.

DYSON Paul

Centre half 6'1"

Born 27/12/1959 Kings Heath, Birmingham

Playing career: *Coventry City, Stoke City, West Bromwich Albion (Cost £60,000 69 appearances 5 goals March 1986 – March 1988), Darlington, Crewe Alexandra, Telford United, Solihull Borough England U-21 International. (1978 – 1990)*

Tall, solid no-nonsense centre back, strong in the air. Paul played 140 league games for Coventry City scoring 5 goals between 1978 - 1983. In the summer of 1983 joined First Division rivals Stoke City. In 1983/84 he played in 44 matches as Stoke avoided relegation by two points but the Potters then suffered an embarrassing relegation in 1984/85, going down with a record low points tally of 17. Paul joined West Bromwich Albion for £60,000 in March 1986 helping the Baggies avoid relegation and he spent the next two seasons at the Hawthorns appearing in 69 games in all competitions, scoring 5 goals. Later he had sport spells with Darlington and Crewe Alexandra before deciding to retire at the age of 30. He played non-league football with Telford United and Solihull Borough, managing Solihull Borough for a time in the late 1990's. After leaving football he worked as a prison officer for many years including some time at HMP Woodhill, Milton Keynes. Then later had a sports shop in Kings Heath.

EARNSHAW Robert 'Earnie'

Striker 5'8"

Born 6/4/1981 Mufulira, Zambia

Playing career: *Cardiff City, West Bromwich Albion (Cost £3,000,000 27+23 sub appearances 17 goals Aug 2004 – Jan 2006) Norwich City, Derby County, Nottingham Forest, Cardiff City, Maccabi Tel Aviv Israel (, Torronto FC Canada, Blackpool, Chicago Fire USA, Vancouver Whitecaps & Wales. (1997 – 2015)*

Born in Zambia and raised in South Wales, Earnshaw joined Cardiff City as a junior in 1997, and turned professional a year later. After making his debut at the age of sixteen, he spent a brief spell on loan with Greenock Morton before establishing himself in the first team. His prolific goalscoring saw him break several club records as he helped the club win promotion to the First Division in 2003. Scoring over 30 times in the First Division following promotion. In August 2004 Earnshaw was transferred from Cardiff to West Bromwich Albion for £3 million.

The fee that could have reached a maximum of £3.62 million with performance-related add-ons. His agent Mel Eves was fined 30,000 Swiss francs or about £12,250 by FIFA in July 2007 over his role in the transfer. Eves was found guilty of acting for both his client, Earnshaw, and the buying club, West Bromwich Albion, in the deal. His first and only Premier League hat-trick came against Charlton Athletic on 19 March 2005 after coming on as a substitute with 30 minutes remaining, scoring the first Premier League hat-trick scored by a West Bromwich Albion player. Earnshaw thus became the only player to have scored hat-tricks in all four professional divisions in England, the FA Cup, League Cup and in an international fixture. Manager Bryan Robson preferred to use him from the bench as an impact player rather than as a starter. Nevertheless, Earnshaw finished as Albion's top scorer for that season 2004/05 with 11 league goals and another 3 in the FA Cup. On transfer deadline day, 31st January 2006, Earnshaw signed a three-and-a-half-year contract for Norwich City for a fee of £2.75 million, rising to £3.5 million. He scored 27 goals in 45 league games for the Canaries. Newly promoted Premier League side Derby County broke their transfer record by signing Earnshaw for a fee of £3.5 million on 29th June 2007. In a torrid debut season, Earnshaw made just seven starts, with a further 17 appearances as substitute, scoring only one goal, with Derby County relegated. In May 2008, less than a year after signing for Derby, Earnshaw joined Nottingham Forest for £2.65m, signing a three-year deal. He played 98 league games for Forest and scored 35 goals. In July 2011, Earnshaw re-joined boyhood club Cardiff City on a free transfer. Spending most of his time on the bench he went on loan to Maccab Tel Aviv. On his return, Cardiff announced he was surplus to requirements and on 28th February 2013, Earnshaw confirmed he had left Cardiff City to join Canadian Major League Soccer club Toronto FC., followed by spells at Blackpool, Chicago Fire and Vancouver Whitecaps, Earnshaw finally announced his retirement on 28th January 2016. A UEFA licenced coach. Rob was head coach of the Vancouver U-14 Pre-Residency team. Assistant manager Fresno FC in California in the United Soccer League.

EASTOE Peter

Striker 5'9½"

Born *2/8/1953 Dordon, Tamworth*

Playing career: *Wolverhampton Wanderers, Swindon Town, QPR, Everton, West Bromwich Albion (Cost £250,00 including swap for Andy King 33 + 1 sub appearances 9 goals July 1984 – Sep 1984), Leicester City Loan), Huddersfield Town (loan), Walsal (loan) l, Leicester City (loan), Wolverhampton Wanderers (loan), Farense in Portugal, Louletano in Portugal, Atherstone United.(1971 – 1988)*

As a youngster he won 8 Youth caps for England. He started his professional football career with Wolverhampton Wanderers but only made 6 league appearances. He joined Swindon Town in March 1974 for a club record fee of £88,000 after a successful loan spell, scoring 43 goals in 91 league games. The striker was signed by Queens Park Rangers in March 1976 for £100,000 with Don Rogers returning to Swindon as part of the deal. He was transferred to Everton in March 1979 in a straight swap for Mickey Walsh. After three full seasons at Goodison Park, he joined West Bromwich Albion in August 1982, where he had a full season in 1982/83 scoring 8 times in 32 league appearances. He lost his form, and his place in the first team, the next season, and it was clear he was not part of the club's future plans and he spent periods on loan at Leicester City, Huddersfield Town, Walsall and Wolverhampton Wanderers. During the twilight of his career he played in the Portuguese league at Farense and Louletano, and returned to England with non-league Atherstone United. He had a spell as manager of Nuneaton Borough, then was appointed manager of Alvechurch in 1991. Peter has also worked at Solus Garden as a picker and as a delivery driver for a packaging company. Lived in Stourbridge.

EDWARDS Clifford 'Cliff'

Wing half/Defender 5'7½"

Born *8/3/1921 Chase Terrace near Cannock, Staffs*
Died *March 1989 Walsall, West Midlands.*

Playing career: *Cannock Town, (West Bromwich Albion 102 appearances 3 goals May 1939 – June 1948), Guested for Bath City, Blackpool and Carlisle United during WW2. Bristol City, Gravesend & Northfleet. (1938 – 1950)*

A short, thick-set half back of natural ability, quick in the tackle and eminently solid in defence, where he usually occupied the centre half or wing half berth.

Cliff was a reliable performer who always gave a good account of himself despite his lack of height. His career, like many of his peers, was disrupted by WW2 and National Service. When Albion recruited the services of the brilliant Irishman Jack Vernon, Cliff's days at the Hawthorns were numbered and he subsequently moved to Bristol City in July 1948 in an exchange deal involving Cyril Williams and £500.Cliff made 40 league appearances for Albion, 2 FA Cup ties and 60 war-time fixtures. He made a further 33 league appearances for Bristol City before moving into non-league football with Gravesend & Northfleet in 1950. He returned to West Bromwich Albion as a Director in 1971 and retired in 1986 aged 65. Tony Brown reminiscing about the 1978 trip to China "Going to see the Great Wall of China was the highlight of the trip for me, it was a quite incredible sight. The funniest thing that I remember about it was Cliff Edwards who was with us, he was a director at the time, and he was wearing a pair of brand-new shoes, so the soles were very slippery. We were walking up hill and he couldn't get any grip and as we were walking, he'd take three steps forward and then slip half a dozen back!"

EDWARDS Ian

Striker 6'1"

Born *30/1/1955 Rossett, Near Wrexham, Wales*
Playing career: *Rhyl Athletic, West Bromwich Albion (Cost £5,000 17+3 appearances 3 goals Feb 1973-Nov 1976), Chester City, Wrexham, Crystal Palace, Mold Alexandra, Porthmadog. (1971 – 1984) 4 Welsh caps.*

He joined Albion from Rhyl Athletic for £5,000 after he had finished 6th form. Starting on £35 a week on a two- year contract although his Father earned that as a draughtsman. He was a tall powerful blonde striker whose lack of mobility prevented him, initially, from succeeding in the higher grade. Started his Albion career in the reserve team. His league debut came on March 8th 1975 at the Hawthorns when he scored a goal in a 4-0 victory over Sheffield Wednesday. He played in 7 games towards the tail end of the 1974/75 season, deputising for Joe Mayo. Having won promotion in 1975/76 Albion were now in the First Division, so at 21 he had to go and negotiate, without an agent, with the Chairman and Manager for a pay rise but they refused.

He was travelling with the first team but being left on the bench so frequently that he was not getting game time. After just 17 games, plus three substitute appearances, scoring 3 goals, in November 1976 he moved to Chester for £20,000, doubling his salary. Within two months of moving to Chester he was involved in a collision with the Rotherham keeper, Tom McAllister, as he scored. The knee buckled backwards. He was never the same after that. They did not put you in plaster then and he spent 3 weeks running up and down stairs to strengthen it. He was 21 and had to retire at 28, after 5 operations on the same knee.

He moved to Wrexham, whilst still; injured and they had hoped it would clear up but it never did. For almost three years he did no training just playing games, taking pain killers to get him through. During the spells at Chester and Wrexham he made his four Welsh International appearances. He owned two milk rounds in Wrexham, sold them and purchased an old country house in Criccieth which he bought from former Albion player Joe Mayo, and he converted it into Plas Isa hotel. He has had a spell as manager of Porthmadog, being replaced by Mickey Thomas.

Ian Edwards

EDWARDS James 'Jimmy'

Left half/Inside left 5'8"

Born *11/12/1905 Tipton, Staffs*
Died *April 1982 West Bromwich aged 76*
Playing career: *Stourbridge, Great Bridge Celtic, Stourbridge, West Bromwich Albion (Cost £350 202 appearances 9 goals May 1926 – May 1937), Norwich City, Bilston, Kingswinford, Dudley Town (1926 – 1944)*

Nicknamed 'Iron', Edwards joined West Bromwich Albion for a £350 fee in May 1926 and made his league debut for the club in March 1928 in a 1-1 draw away against Hull City. He started his career as an aggressive, go-ahead inside left but was converted to left half by Albion. Jimmy developed massive tree trunk legs, solid hips and tackled hard and true. He was a member of the team that won the FA Cup in 1931 and promotion to the Football League First Division in the same year. He also played.in the 1935 FA Cup Final, losing 4-2 to Sheffield Wednesday. Jimmy Edwards and William Richardson, the centre half, were known as 'Iron' and 'Steel'. He served Albion for eleven years playing 202 games and scoring 9 goals. He represented the Football League side. In May 1937 he moved to Norwich City for £750. He died in a West Bromwich hospital in April 1982 after becoming ill at his house in Birmingham New Road, Dudley.

ELLIOTT William 'Billy'

Right winger 5'8"

Born *6/8/1919 Harrington, Cumberland*
Died *November 1966 at Hotel Las Vegas, Canary Islands.*
Playing career: *Carlisle United, Wolves, Bournemouth, West Bromwich Albion (Cost £4,000 330 appearances 157goals Dec 1938 – July 1951) 2 England Wartime appearances.*

Elliott was a brilliant outside right, fast and clever, with incredible close ball control and a powerful shot, especially with his right foot. One particular smart trick of Billy's was his knack of running at top speed down the flank and then drawing his foot over the top of the ball intending to stop but never really doing so, causing his opponent to check their stride pattern. He was a superb footballer. His career was ended by a serious achilles tendon injury when he was just 32. Billy made 170 League appearances 12 in the FA Cup and scored 40 goals.

He also notched up 148 War Time League and Cup games wartime appearances scoring 117 goals for Albion. Bill served with the South Staffordshire Regiment in the Army. He was a qualified FA coach and a member of the Player's Union Committee. Later became a publican in Handsworth at the Farcroft Inn. He died whilst in the Canary Islands in 1966 aged just 47.

EVANS Alun

Inside forward/wing half 5'7½"

Born *December 1922 Penrhycadery, South Wales*
Died *30/1/2008 Kidderminster*
Playing career: *West Bromwich Albion (29 appearances 2 goals May 1943 - May 1948)*

He was nicknamed 'Boyo' or 'Bungo'. Evans started as an aggressive inside forward, but was converted by Albion into a diligent, steady, footballing wing half, who passed fluently and tackled keenly, inspiring his fellow team-mates. He had the soccer world at his feet when sadly Alun's eyesight failed after he managed a mere 29 senior appearances for Albion and he was forced into earl retirement, receiving just £350 compensation. He took a blow to the head whilst playing and lost his sight completely. He spent two years trying to learn Braille before his vision came back enough for him to get around. He had already represented Wales in a wartime International in 1944 v the RAF and had played for his Regiment int the Army versus Indian selected sides. He remained blind in one eye and partially sighted in the other. Alun had been in the RAF and was a fully qualified PE Instructor & Drill Training Officer. He worked at Brintons in the dye house for 25 years following his partial eyesight recovery, organising the company's football teams. He was an avid player of Indoor bowls at the Franche Village Club. His Son, also called Alun Evans, was Britain's first £100,000 footballer when he left Wolves for Liverpool in 1968. Died in January 2008 of pneumonia after suffering for two years with Alzheimer's.

"DID YOU KNOW?"

"Albion's biggest ever League victory was in a 12-0 win over Darwen on 4 April 1892."

EVANS Michael 'Mickey'

Striker 6'0"

Born *1/1/1973 Plymouth*

Playing Career: *Plymouth Argyle, Blackburn Rovers (loan), Southampton, West Bromwich Albion (Cost £750,000 40+33 sub appearances 9 goals Oct 1997 – Aug 2000), Bristol Rovers (loan), Plymouth Argyle, Torquay United. Republic of Ireland 1 International cap (1990-2006)*

Tall, honest, hard-working striker, not blessed with pace but a trier. He made his Plymouth Argyle first team debut in December 1990 at the age of 17, and signed his first professional contract in March 1991. After scoring 38 goals in 163 league matches, in March 1997 he was signed by Graeme Souness at Southampton for £650,000. He played only 22 league games scoring 4 goals but his career at The Dell only lasted just over six months and in October 1997 he moved on to West Bromwich Albion for a fee of £750,000. Used mainly as a substitute during 1997/98. It took him 12 games to register his first goal for the club. Evans' time at the Hawthorns was frequently blighted by injury and illness. Evans made 40 starts plus a further 33 substitute appearances scoring 9 goals. He was loaned out to Bristol Rovers, a successful spell which led to a £250,000 permanent deal being struck in September 2000 After an unsuccessful spell at Bristol Rovers, Evans then returned to Plymouth Argyle as one of the first signings of Paul Sturrock, joining on transfer deadline day 2001 for £30,000. It wasn't until his return to Plymouth when it was discovered that Evans had an asthmatic-related complaint which had contributed to his lack of form and fitness. In May 2006, Evans signed on a free transfer for local rivals Torquay United.

Evans retired in November 2006 to set up a building company MJ Evans but the company filed for administration in July 2012. In 2007/2008 having retired from playing, he was involved in a series of testimonial events to raise money for a number of local charities.

FAIRFAX Raymond 'Ray'

Full back 5'9"

Born *13/1/1941 Smethwick*

Playing career: *West Bromwich Albion (90 + 2 sub appearances 2 goals Aug 1959- June 1968), Northampton Town.. (1959 - 1974)*

He joined the Albion as a Junior in 1959 before completing professional forms in August of the same year. Some stern tackling distinguished Ray's displays at full back for Albion. His kicking was strong and relatively safe. Fairfax had Stuart Williams, Graham Williams and Don Howe ahead of him and he constantly had to work hard to get a first XI game. He spent 9 years at The Hawthorns and made 92 appearances in total. Being a full-back he got on the score sheet just the once, a thunderous shot from outside the penalty area, against Bologna in the Fairs Cup match in March 1976. Ray was part of the 1966 League Cup Winning side. He left the Albion in June 1968 signing for Northampton Town. Once played in an FA Cup in game in 1970 at Northampton against Manchester United when he was supposed to be marking George Best. After returning from a six-week ban, Best ran riot scoring six goals as United beat the Cobblers 8-2. The closest Ray got to Best, was at the final whistle. He had 3 years with the Northampton before winding down his career and subsequent retirement in May 1974. He had a big win on the football pools. He returned to West Bromwich that same year as assistant to the Commercial Manager before becoming Assistant Secretary the following year. Ray spent 9 years in this role before joining Port Vale as Secretary in 1985 where he stayed for 2 years. It seems Ray's destiny was to always be in football in some capacity because in 1988 he joined our local rivals Aston Villa as Ticket Office Clerk before returning to the Hawthorns again as Ticket Office Administrator in 2003. Ray lives in Sutton Coldfield with his wife Val and is a very keen supporter of the Old Baggies Former Players Association.

Ray Fairfax

FENTON Graham
Midfielder/Forward 5'10"
Born *22/5/1974 Whitley Bay*
Playing career: *Aston Villa, West Bromwich Albion (loan 7 appearances 3 goals Jan/Feb 1994), Blackburn Rovers, Leicester City, Walsall (loan), Stoke City, St Mirren, Blackpool, Darlington (loan), Blyth Spartans, North Shields (1992-2010). England U-21*

He signed professional forms in February 1992 at Aston Villa. Before he had played a league game, he was loaned out to West Bromwich Albion in January 1994, making his league debut against Leicester City in the same month. His loan spell at Albion was very successful, producing three goals in seven games and contributing to Albion's eventual survival in Division One. On leaving many Albion fans were bitterly disappointed when he did not sign permanently. He instead returned to Villa, In March 1994, he played in Aston Villa's League Cup winning side that beat Manchester United 3-1 at Wembley. In. November 1995, having struggled to claim a regular place in the Villa Park first team, Fenton made a £1.5million move to reigning Premiership champions Blackburn but his first team opportunities were limited as he faced competition from Alan Shearer, Chris Sutton and Kevin Gallacher. In August 1997, he moved to Leicester City for a fee of £1.1million. He later joined Walsall on loan in March 2000. In August 2000 he joined Stoke City on a monthly contract and then St Mirren. In August 2001, Fenton joined Blackpool on a free transfer, but once more struggled to establish himself in the first team. He had a spell on loan with Darlington but returned to the North East of England to join Blyth Spartans. Blyth manager Paul Baker appointed Fenton as player-assistant manager in July 2004. Graham took over as caretaker-manager of Blyth when Baker left that September, returning to his player-assistant manager role in October 2004 after the appointment of Harry Dunn as manager. In the 2005/06 season he was part of the Spartans' side that gained promotion to the Conference North by winning the Northern Premier League. He was assistant manager and player at North Shields from 2009 until 2012, remaining as manager until September 2016. He then joined South Shields as manager. Later he was joint-manager with Lee Picton.

Wayne Fereday

FEREDAY Wayne
Winger 5'9"
Born *16/6/1963 Warley, West Midlands*
Playing career: *Queens Park Rangers, Newcastle United, Bournemouth, West Bromwich Albion (Cost 43 +10 sub appearances 3 goals Sept 1991 – Dec 1993), Cardiff City (1980 – 1995) England U-21 International*

A tricky and speedy winger, Wayne started his career at Queens Park Rangers between 1980 - 1989 appearing in 246 league games scoring 21 goals. He went to Newcastle United in 1989/90 and played 33 league games before moving on to Bournemouth. In 1990/91 he played 23 games for the Cherries. Born within sight of the Hawthorns, it was Bobby Gould who recalled him to God's country, signing him for Albion in the midst of the traumatic 1991/92 campaign. He made his debut in a 1-1 draw at Bradford City in December 1991 and for the next few months, he played on either flank as we tried to get out of Division Three. Albion were involved in a promotion battle from the old Division Three and a 2-1 defeat at the hands of Bournemouth did not please either Gould or the travelling support. So, the unorthodox Baggies boss hauled in a disgruntled punter to vent his spleen on the players. Fereday explains "I can't remember whether Bobby had given us a rollocking, but he left the dressing room pretty quickly. He returned with a supporter and told him to have his say.

He wasn't too bad to start with as he probably thought Bobby was messing around, but then he opened up a bit and said that we were letting the fans down. I was quite lucky because I had played reasonably well, but a few of the lads got a bit of earache!" Injuries to Simeon Hodson and then Paul Raven pushed him into right-back duties, ideal for the following season when Ossie Ardiles arrived and used his full-backs as additional wingers anyway. Injuries ruined that season for Fereday. Heading down to the Wembley Play-Off Final on a supporters' bus, still on crutches after a knee injury Wayne was not on the team bus, but was still desperate to be a part of it all as an Albion fan through and through. Those injures never really went away, a legacy of Fereday being so desperate to do well for his club that all too often, he rushed back into action too early. Wayne played in 43 games plus another 10 as a substitute for Albion scoring 3 goals. Ardiles moved on to pastures new in the summer and his replacement, Keith Burkinshaw, had different ideas so Fereday left at the end of the 1993/94 campaign, joining Cardiff City where he made 44 league appearances scoring 2 goals. Wayne who now works in the furniture trade in the West Midlands as well as for the Press Association on matchdays, reckons his career was cut short by his time at Loftus Road. Queens Park Rangers were the pioneers of a plastic pitch but, as Fereday admits, the surface was nothing like what is available today. "I spent seven years on that pitch," he said. "It was like playing on cement and if the ball bounced it took ages for it to come down. There would be a queue of players waiting for it to arrive and I think a lot of players from that time struggled with injuries to their joints."

"DID YOU KNOW?"

"There was a member of the Everiss family working for WBA between 1896 and 1999 as father Fred and son Alan held the following positions; office boy, assistant secretary, secretary, secretary/manager, director, life member."

FETTIS Alan
Goalkeeper 6'2"
Born *1/2/1971 Newtownards, County Down, Northern Ireland*
Playing career: *Ards, Hull City, West Bromwich Albion (loan 3 appearances Nov-Dec 1995), Nottingham Forest, Blackburn Rovers, Leicester City (loan), York City, Hull City, Sheffield United (loan), Grimsby Town (loan), Macclesfield Town, Bury. Northern Ireland International 25 caps, also played at U-16, U-17, U-18 and 'B'. (1988 - 2007)*

He was as a tall goalkeeper, maybe lacking in confidence at times. He notably played for Hull City 155 league appearances in two spells plus two goals when deployed as a striker, due to injuries at the club, and York City 125 league appearances. He also had spells with Glentoran, and Ards. Alan Buckley signed him for West Bromwich Albion on loan from Hull City as emergency cover for injured Stuart Naylor. Fettis let in 8 goals in three matches, all lost. He also played for Nottingham Forest, Blackburn Rovers, Leicester City on loan, Sheffield United, Grimsby Town, Macclesfield Town and Bury. Fettis retired in 2007 whilst with Bury. He firstly joined Derby County as an assistant goalkeeping coach before moving to Cheltenham Town where he was appointed as chief scout, as well as the club's goalkeeping coach. In July 2009 he was appointed Sunderland's goalkeeping coach. In 2011 he joined Manchester United as goalkeeping coach for the club's academy teams, playing once for United's Reserves. In 2019 Fettis stepped up temporarily to support Senior Goalkeeping Coach Richard Harris, returning to his academy role on the appointment of Craig Mawson from Burnley.

FINCH Abel Robert 'Bob'
Full back 5'8½"
Born *31/8/1908 Hednesford, Staffs*
Died *2000 aged 92*
Playing career: *Hednesford Town, West Bromwich Albion (234 appearances Apr 1925 – May 1939), Swansea Town. 1945/46 (1925 – 1946)*
Bob nicknamed 'Able' was a redoubtable full back, dour, zealous and wholehearted in his play. He joined Hednesford Town in 1923, nut after only a few first team appearances he was approached by West Bromwich Albion, signing professional forms for them in 1925.

He made his debut at home against Leicester in February 1926 at the age of 17. In 14 years of sterling service at the Hawthorns, he made 234 league games and 231 appearances for Albion reserves, many as Captain, winning the Central League Championship in 1926/27, 1932/33, 1933/34, 1934/35. He never scored a first team goal but did score four own-goals. He was a first-team regular for three seasons 1927-30 but lost his place to George Shaw. He played in two trials for England in 1927/28. He was an important squad member of the 1930/31 Albion team that won the FA Cup in 1931 and promotion in the same season, still the only team to achieve such a fate. He played for Albion against Arsenal in the 6th Round FA Cup game 6th March 1937 when Albion won 3-1 in front of 64,815 fans at the Hawthorns. He was transferred to Swansea in May 1939, Bob managed only one game before the outbreak of WW2 curtailed his career. He joined the Police Force in Hednesford serving as a constable until retiring in 1956. Bob loved his golf and lived in Hednesford.

FITTON (George) Arthur

Outside left 5'7"
Born *30/5/1902 Melton Mowbray*
Died *10/9/1984 Worcester aged 82*
Playing career: *Kidderminster Harriers, West Bromwich Albion (Cost £400 99 appearances 11 goals Oct 1922 – Mar 1932), Manchester United, Preston North End, Coventry City (1920 – 1939).*
His full name was George Arthur Fitton but was known as Arthur but nicknamed 'Mother' Fitton. During WW1 he worked in a factory which produced hand-grenades. He was a penetrative left winger who gave Albion great service on and off the field. A very popular character indeed, well respected and admired by all. He left Albion for Manchester United for £1,000 playing just 12 games and scoring 2 goals before joining Preston North End in 1932 and then ending his career with Coventry City in 1935. He retired from football in 1937 and took up a coaching role with Coventry's third team. He returned to the Hawthorns in October 1948 as assistant trainer/coach until 1950, then First team trainer 1951-56 including the 1954 Wembley FA Cup Final. Fitton was named trainer of the Football League representative side v League of

Ireland in Dublin in Sept 1954. He played cricket for Staffordshire between 1927 and 1934, in the Minor Counties Championship, as a left-hand batsman and occasional wicketkeeper, also appearing for West Bromwich Dartmouth. Later Arthur became game warden at Kinver National Trust Park

FLYNN Sean

Midfielder 5'8"
Born *13/3/1968 Birmingham*
Playing career: *Coventry City, Derby County, Stoke City (loan), West Bromwich Albion (Cost £260,000 110 + 12 sub appearances 9 goals Apr 1997 – July 2000), Tranmere Rovers, Kidderminster Harriers (1991-2003). Non-league with Evesham United 2003, Redditch United 2004, Evesham Town, Redditch United 2005-08, Bodmin Town 2008, Mullion, Falmouth Town, Penzance.*
A non-stop, dynamic midfielder. Flynn signed for Coventry City from Halesowen Town in December 1991. Played 97 league games scoring 9 goals. In August 1995, after being told by then-Coventry manager Ron Atkinson, that he was no longer required at the club. Flynn dropped a division to Division One to become one of Jim Smith's first signings at Derby County for a fee of £250,000, where he appeared in 59 league games scoring 3 times as well as having a 5-game loan spell at Stoke City. Flynn made the switch to his boyhood club West Bromwich Albion for a fee of £260,000 in August 1997. As a West Bromwich Albion fan, one of the highlights of his career was when he captained the team. He used to raise a smile amongst fans if he did a terrible pass or missed an easy goal scoring chance, he would drop to the floor and do press ups as a self-punishment. He played 110 games plus 12 as substitute and scored 8 goals for the Baggies. In July 2000, Flynn moved on a free transfer to Tranmere Rovers spending two years there playing 66 league games and scoring 6 goals. Sean signed for Kidderminster Harriers in August 2002 on a free transfer and made 51 appearances scoring two goals before leaving in the September 2003. He continued playing at an amateur level as player/manager of Mullion Town. He was player/assistant manager of Falmouth Town 2009 -2011. Joined Penzance in 2011 and returned to Falmouth as a player for a short period. Since retirement Flynn has run a caravan park in Cornwall.

FOGGO Kenneth 'Ken'

Right winger 5'6"

Born *7/11/1943 Perth, Scotland*

Playing career: *West Bromwich Albion (135+1 sub appearance 29 goals Nov 1960- Oct 1967), Norwich City, Portsmouth, Brentford (loan), Southend United, Chelmsford City, Brereton Social. (1960-1980) Scotland schoolboy International.*

A diminutive outside-right often treated roughly by the bigger defenders who tried to mark him. Ken was a clever footballer whose centres on the run were usually spot-on. He arrived at the Hawthorns with fellow Scots Bobby Hope, Campbell Crawford and Bobby Murray in August 1959, after all four had played for Scotland Schoolboys. Ken had earlier represented his country on the rugby field. Ken took over the number 7 shirt from Alec Jackson in 1963 playing 135 appearances+ 1 as substitute, scoring 29 goals. Ken was an unused substitute for Albion in the 1967 in League Cup Final at Wembley. After leaving the Hawthorns Ken played 201 games for Norwich City scoring 57 goals. Won the Second Division Championship with Norwich in 1972. Moved on to Portsmouth, and Southend, giving him a career record of 432 senior appearances and 100 goals.

He went on to set up a launderette with Bobby Kellard and when their partnership split-up he continued in the business running his own launderette and dry cleaners in Wanstead, East London.

Personal note: *I once score Ken score an incredible goal against Leeds United at the Hawthorns 12th April 1965 as we lost 2-1. The ball came high across from the left, Kenny running along the goal line, with his back towards the Birmingham Road End, leaped high and nodded the ball back across the goal and somehow the ball drifted over the head of keeper Gary Sprake, and into the net. I have never seen a goal like that before or since.*

FORD Anthony 'Tony' MBE

Midfielder/winger/full back 5'9"

Born *14/5/1959 Grimsby*

Playing career: *Grimsby Town, Sunderland, Stoke City, West Bromwich Albion (Cost £145,000 127 + 1 sub appearance 15 goals Mar 1989 – Oct 1991), Grimsby Town, Bradford City (loan), Scunthorpe United, Barrow, Mansfield Town, Rochdale (1977-2001) England 'B'.*

Through most of his playing days, Ford was a right winger or midfielder, but in the later years, he was converted to right back.

Ken Foggo

In a career that spanned 26 years, across four decades, Ford played no fewer than 931 league matches, which is the all-time record for matches played in the English league by an outfield player with not one game played in the top-flight division. Only goalkeeper Peter Shilton, 1005 matches, has played more. Ford is in fact only one of three outfield players to play in English football to have ever passed 1000 games in competitive matches league and cup. Ford began his career at his hometown club Grimsby Town, making his first-team debut as a 16-year-old in October 1975. He spent 11 years at Blundell Park, where he made his name as one of the most talented players outside the top division. In 1986, after 355 league games and 55 goals, he left Grimsby. He had a short loan spell at Sunderland March 1986, and later joined Stoke City in a permanent deal for £35,000 in July 1986.Ford spent two and a half years at Stoke playing 112 league games scoring 13 times. He appeared for Stoke in a league game at the Hawthorns on 18th December 1988 when Albion won 6-0 and Ford was sent off, a few months before being signed by player/manager Brian Talbot for West Bromwich Albion in March 1989 for £145,000. After three years at The Hawthorns, he re-joined Grimsby in late 1991. His second spell at Blundell Park lasted three seasons, and he left the club at the end of the 1993/94 season, having played 423 league games scoring 58 goals for the club. In 1994, Ford joined Grimsby's arch-rivals Scunthorpe, where he played two seasons. When he was released at the end of the 1995–96 season, after a short spell at non-league side Barrow, he was asked by Steve Parkin, who had recently been appointed manager at Mansfield to become his assistant. This allowed Ford to continue his playing career. Parkin took Ford with him in his 40's as player/assistant manager to Rochdale. Retired from playing in 2001 and they both linked up again at Barnsley but both were sacked after 11 months. Ford returned in August 2003 to Rochdale to become assistant manager to Alan Buckley. Ford kept his job when Parkin replaced Alan Buckley on 31 December 2003. They were both sacked three years later. He went on to work for former club Grimsby Town as a scout but was relieved of his duties in May 2011.

Adrian Foster

FOSTER Adrian
Striker 5'9"
Born *19/3/1971 Kidderminster*
Playing career: *West Bromwich Albion (14+19 sub appearances 2 goals July 1989 – June 1992), Torquay United, Gillingham, Exeter City, Hereford United, Rushden & Diamonds, Yeovil Town, Forest Green Rovers, Bath City, Fromm Town, Taunton Town, Street, Chard Town (1990 – 2006) He represented England at Semi-Professional level.*

At the Hawthorns from 1989 – 1992 Foster made 14 starts with a further 19 substitute appearances, scoring just 2 goals. Described by one Albion supporter as 'small and paceless', he once scored in a defeat at Wolverhampton Wanderers in March 1990. He spent two years at Torquay United playing 65 league games scoring 24 goals 1992-1994. At Gillingham he played 40 league games scoring 9 times 1994-1996. He had a short loan at Exeter City before moving on this time to Hereford United playing 43 games with 16 goals 1996-1997. Rushden & Diamonds were next where he played 55 league games scoring 25 goals 1997-1999. Spells at Yeovil Town, Bath City, Frome Town, Taunton Town, Chard Town followed before going into management. 2007 – 2013 he was manager of Gillingham. In December 2013 he was appointed manager of Frome Town, given a two -year contract in 2014.

Doug Fraser

FOX Ruel
Right winger 5'6"
Born *14/1/1968 Ipswich, Suffolk*
Playing career: *Norwich City, Newcastle United, Tottenham Hotspur, West Bromwich Albion (Cost £200,000 44+23 sub appearances Aug 2000 – June 2002) England 'B' International and 2 Full International Caps for Montserrat (1986-2002).*

Fox left Norwich on 2 February 1994 to join Newcastle United for a fee of £2,250,000. Newcastle manager Kevin Keegan described him as "the best player in his position in the country". The arrival of David Ginola in June 1995 left Fox facing a fight for regular first team action. He signed for Tottenham Hotspur in October 1995 in a deal worth £4.25million. His fee made him Tottenham's second most costly player at the time, behind Chris Armstrong whose £4.5million deal had been concluded just a few months earlier. He moved to West Bromwich Albion at the start of the 2000/01 season. Skilful, good close ball control, with bags of experience Ruel was very popular with the fans, although he had lost a yard of pace. He helped them to promotion in 2001/02, before being released at the end of the season. Ruel became Montserrat head coach in October 2004. He was head coach of Ipswich-based club Whitton United until 2008. He returned to his hometown Ipswich where he runs a restaurant and bar. Ruel is also a personal trainer. He is Chairman of Whitton United FC.

FRASER Douglas 'Doug
Midfielder/full back 5'8½"
Born *8/12/1941Busby, Scotland*
Playing career: *Aberdeen, West Bromwich Albion (Cost £23,000 323+3 sub appearances 12 goals Sept 1963 – Dec 1971), Nottingham Forest, Walsall. (1963-1974) Full Scottish International 2 caps.*

Doug signed as a professional at Aberdeen in December 1959, playing 64 league games and scoring 1 goal before he was snapped up by West Bromwich Albion for a bargain £23,000 in September 1963 by manager Jimmy Hagan. Doug was a fine compact wing half, fast in gathering the ball and feeding it to his forwards in one smooth flowing movement. He had a fine tackle, was stylish in his overall play and did studious work for Albion appearing in 323+3 games scoring 8 goals from 1963-1971. He played in the League Cup Finals of 1967 against Queens Park Rangers losing 3-2 and again in 1970 losing 2-1 after extra time to Manchester City, when he skippered the Albion team. Also picked up a winners' medals in the 1966 League Cup Final against West Ham in a two-legged affair and the 1968 FA Cup Final beating Everton 1-0 after extra time. He moved to Nottingham Forest for £35,000 in January 1971. Doug stayed for two seasons, appearing in 85 league games scoring twice. In 1973 he joined Walsall for £8,000 and made a 27 league appearances before taking over as manager in July 1974 until June 1977. Fraser retired from football in 1977 to become a warder at Nottingham Prison for nearly 20 years, playing for the Nottingham Prison Officers FC in 1981. Upon his retirement Doug remained in Nottingham where he lives with wife Marie.

FUDGE Michael 'Micky'
Forward 5'5"
Born *5/12/1945 Bristol*
Playing career: *West Bromwich Albion (16 appearances 5 goals Dec 1963 – June 1967) Exeter City, Wellington Town, Telford United. Kidderminster Harriers, Malvern Town. Brierley Hill, Brereton Town (player/manager) (1963-1980).*

Micky burst onto the scene with a hat-trick against Everton in only his tenth senior game. Unfortunately, he played just 16 first team games for Albion scoring 5 goals and spent the majority of his time in the Albion reserves. He gradually faded out of the big-time but made a name for himself in the non-League circles, winning two medals with Telford in the 1970 and 1971 FA Trophy Finals at Wembley, scoring the winning goal in the 1971 Final against Hillingdon Borough. After football he was a Licensee and with his wife Pat ran a few pubs in the Telford area including the Lord Hill Public House, Dawley. Retiring from the brewery trade, he is a supportive member of Old Baggies Former Players' Association.
Personal note: *I saw Mick score that hat-trick against Everton at the Hawthorns on 31st March 1964. It was a tremendous performance by an 18-year old forward. One goal was a terrific lob over the keeper. Breaking in to the first XI at around the same time as Tony Brown, it was sad that Fudge's Albion career was so short-lived. After such a promising start, his career failure at the Hawthorns was possibly one of the biggest disappointments for me as a fan.*

GAARDSOE Thomas 'Tommy'

Centre back 6'2"

Born *23/11/1979 Gassum, Denmark*

Playing career: *Aalborg Boldspilklub in Denmark, Ipswich Town, West Bromwich Albion (Cost £720,000 85 + 6 sub appearances 4 goals July 2003 –Dec 2006)*

Tom moved to Aalborg Boldspilklub in the Danish Superliga championship, and made his senior debut in June 1997. Despite good performances, he had a hard time forcing his way into the AaB starting line-up in his role as central midfielder. He made his AaB breakthrough in spring 2001, as a replacement for the injured central defender Torben Boye. He impressed in his new role at AaB. In the summer 2001, he was sold to English club Ipswich Town in the FA Premier League championship in a transfer deal worth £1.3 million. After his first season at the club, Ipswich suffered relegation into the English First Division. In the First Division, Gaardsøe became an important member for the squad, scoring six goals in all competitions of the 2002/2003 season. He was sold in the summer of 2003, to First Division rivals West Bromwich Albion for a reported £720,000, and his first appearance came in a 4–0 thrashing of Brentford in the Football League Cup in August 2003. He scored his first goal for Albion in a 4–1 victory over his former club

Ipswich, on 13th September 2003 and went on to be an ever-present in Albion's promotion winning team. Gaardsoe was calm, polished, and elegant When he arrived from Ipswich at the start of the 2003/04 season, it was with a healthy reputation as a member of Joe Royle's side, most notably playing in a three-man central defence. That made him the ideal candidate to slot into Gary Megson's team that was looking to bounce back to the Premier League at the first attempt where he played alongside the likes of Darren Moore, Phil Gilchrist and Sean Gregan as the central defence changed over the course of the season. Gaardsoe was very much the pivotal figure, his reading of the game exemplary as he often moved into position to snuff out danger before it had ever really materialised while he was equally adept at bringing the ball out from the back, playing as the spare man in something of a sweeper role. He was named "Player of the Year" by the supporters who, in turn, dressed up as Vikings in his honour for the away match at Reading on 1 May 2004. Playing in what turned out to be the 'Great Escape' season 2004/05, Gaardsoe was troubled by a couple of niggling injuries but also by a change in formation as they went to a back four which required him to be a more aggressive type of man to man marker.

Micky Fudge

Tommy Gaardsoe

He had previously excelled as a covering defender. Nonetheless, he made 31 appearances that season and played a full part in keeping Bryan Robson's team in the Premier League. That was the high watermark of his time with the Albion as the 2005/6 season degenerated into a nightmare as a persistent groin injury restricted him to only seven league games, his final Albion performance coming in the 6-1 thrashing at Craven Cottage. In the beginning of the 2006/2007 season, the continued injury problems made him consider a premature retirement from football. On 19 December 2006 Gaardsoe announced his retirement from the game, having been unable to regain full fitness from the groin operation in the summer. Two and a half year later he returned to football after having fully recovered from his injury. This time he signed for his childhood club Aalborg BK. Gaardsoe had not succeeded in establishing himself in the AaB squad and signed a contract with Danish superliga rivals Esbjerg in January 2010. Retired after his contract ended in the summer of 2012.

GARNER Simon

Striker 5'8"

Born 23/11/1959 Boston, Lincolnshire
Playing career: Blackburn Rovers, West Bromwich Albion (Cost £30,000 35+10 sub appearances 9 goals Aug 1992 – Feb 1994), Wycombe Wanderers, Torquay United (loan) (1978-1996).

He played 474 league games for Blackburn Rovers, in which he scored a club-record 168 league goals. After his long spell at Rovers, he moved to West Bromwich Albion for £30,000 in August 1992 and made 33 league appearances for the Baggies, scoring eight league goals and helping them win promotion from Division Two, coming on as a substitute in the Play Off final at Wembley in a 3-0 win over Port Vale. He was a popular, skilful smaller striker, lacking pace but very clever with his movement. He went to Wycombe Wanderers playing 66 league games scoring 15 goals. In 1996 Garner served a brief prison sentence in prison for contempt of court during his divorce, being released on appeal. He worked in mortgage sales and was a self-employed painter and decorator based in Berkshire, then worked as a postman, window cleaner and pundit. Does after-dinner speaking.

GILBERT David 'Dave'

Winger/midfielder 5'5"
Born *22/6/1963 Lincoln*
Playing career: *Lincoln City, Scunthorpe United, Boston United, Northampton Town, Grimsby Town, West Bromwich Albion (Cost £50,000 60 + 16 appearances 6 goals Aug 1995 – June 1998) York City (loan), Grimsby Town (loan), Grantham Town 1998/99, Spalding United 1999/2001, Grantham Town 2001/03, Lincoln United 2003/07, Grantham Town 2007/10 .(1981 – 2009)*

A short, stocky little player, skilful and clever. He started at Lincoln City but moved to non-league Boston United 1982-86. He was signed by Northampton Town, helping them win the Division Four Title in 1986/87. After playing 120 league games and scoring 21 goals for the Cobblers, he moved to Grimsby Town in 1989.At Blundell Park Gilbert spent seven seasons playing on the left wing. During his tenure, the Mariners were promoted twice and established themselves at the second-highest level of English football. In 1995, Alan Buckley signed him for West Bromwich Albion at a cost of £50,000 as part of an 'army' of ex-Grimsby players brought to the Hawthorns by Buckley. Gilbert was a regular at West Bromwich Albion until Buckley was sacked in early 1997. He then found himself in the reserves, and had loan spells at York City and Grimsby, before being released when his contract expired in 1998. He spent the following 10 years or so playing non-league football. He finally hung up his boots aged 46 whilst playing in his third spell with Grantham Town. retiring in September 2008. In December 2008 Gilbert was fined £560 plus costs for assaulting a 17-year old in Grantham in August 2008. He was also told he would not be able to work with youngsters again. In November 2009 he was appointed assistant manager of Lincoln United.

GILCHRIST Philip 'Phil'

Centre-back/Defender 6'0"
Born *25/8/1973 Stockton-on-Tees*
Playing career: *Nottingham Forest, Middlesbrough, Hartlepool United, Oxford United, Leicester City, West Bromwich Albion (Cost £500,000 102+3 sub appearances Mar 2001 – June 2004), Rotherham United (loan then signed), Oxford United (1990 – 2007)*

Started his career at Nottingham Forest and then Middlesbrough, without playing a first team league game. It was at Hartlepool United that he started his league career playing 82 games. He signed for Oxford United in February 1995 for £100,000 and formed a solid defensive partnership alongside Matt Elliott. After 177 league games for Oxford, he was transferred to Leicester City for £500,000 in 1999. He was an unused substitute for Leicester in the 2000 League Cup Final. He was signed by Gary Megson for West Bromwich Albion at a cost of £500,000 in March 2001. He was a regular during the 2001/02 season in a solid defence that kept a record 27 clean sheets, helping Albion gain promotion to the Premier League for the first time. He played 90 league games for Albion before being loaned out to, and then signed by, Rotherham United in March 2004. He returned to Oxford United in June 2006 finally retiring in December 2007. However, in May 2008 he was appointed as assistant-manager at Conference National club Woking, where he also registered as a player. Temporarily appointed to joint manager position with Andy Cook. In Sept 2008 he was confirmed as permanent manager until the end of the season but he was sacked on second of April 2009. Phil was later Head of Sport at Oakham School and Senior Housemaster and Co-Curricular Coordinator at Radcliffe College in Leicestershire. In this role, he is responsible for the annual intake of youngsters from Thailand who train at Leicester City's Academy.

GILES John

Midfielder/winger 5'7"
Born *6/11/1940 Dublin, Ireland*
Playing career: *Manchester United, Leeds United, West Bromwich Albion (Cost £35,000 player/manager 87+1 sub appearances 5 goals June 1975 – May 1977), Shamrock Rovers (player/manager), Philadelphia Fury USA (loan) (1957 – 1983) John was player/manager from 1973 – 1983, including 7 years as player/manager of Republic of Ireland (1973-80).*

What a little tough-tackling, ball-playing genius. Started out as a right winger with Manchester United but converted to a wonderful inside forward/midfielder alongside the great Billy Bremner at Leeds United. Giles won FA Cup, First Division

Phil Gilchrist

Title twice, Second Division Title, League Cup, Charity Shield, Fairs Cup twice and was a runner up in the European Cup Final with Leeds in 1975. He was instrumental in breathing new life into the Hawthorns in 1975/76 as player/manager when the team were promoted to the top division. The following year Albion finished 7th. Giles then left Albion to play in the USA with Philadelphia Fury. In 1977 he became player/manager at Shamrock Rovers, retiring from playing football in 1983. John was later manager in Canada with Vancouver Whitecaps. before returning to the Hawthorns for a less successful second spell as Manager during the 1983/84 season, with Norman Hunter and Nobby Stiles as part of his backroom staff. After selling Gary Thompson and Cyrille Regis, replacing them with Imre Varadi & Garth Crooks, proved unsuccessful. Giles resigned in October 1985. Nobby Stiles took over temporarily before Ron Saunders arrived and Albion were relegated at the end of that season. He returned to Ireland and settled into a career in journalism. Starting out as a pundit for RTE in 1986. He featured in Premier Soccer Saturday and its International and European soccer coverage. In 2008 Giles launched a non-profit organisation called the John Giles Foundation, aimed at helping Irish children to improve their health and fitness and keep them clear of petty crime. All proceeds from his Autobiography 'A Football Man' 2010 going to the foundation. He worked as a radio pundit in Ireland for RTE, particularly covering Republic of Ireland Internationals.

He covered the 2010 and 2014 World Cup Finals and the UEFA 2016 Euros leaving after the Final, having given 30-years of service to the broadcaster. He was a soccer analyst on Newstalk. He is a member of the Edgbaston Golf Club, a great supporter of the Old Baggies' Former Players Association and now lives in Harborne, Birmingham.

GLIDDEN Thomas 'Tommy'

Outside right 5'7"
Born *20/7/1902 Coxlodge, Newcastle-on-Tyne*
Died *10/7/1974 West Bromwich*
Playing career: *West Bromwich Albion Apr 1922 – May 1936) He played for England school boys*
Thomas Glidden was born in Coxlodge when it was a settlement consisting of a handful of terraces around a couple of collieries. He began kicking a football in earnest for local outfit Colliery Old Boys, before moving on to Boldon Villa and Sunderland West End. Moving up to the professional game, he spent his entire career thereafter in the Midlands at West Bromwich Albion. Extremely nimble, he was a fine ball player who was seemingly always on hand to score the opportunist goal from close-in. Tommy made his league debut on 25th November 1922, as Freddie Morris scored in a 1-0 win. At Everton. After a few games on the left wing he settled down on the right, forming a superb partnership with Joe Carter. He helped the club to a 2nd place finish in 1925, before they relegated in 1927. Tom captained the Albion to victory in the 1931 FA Cup Final win over Birmingham and a week later to Promotion from the

John Giles

Second Division. Albion being the first team to achieve such a feat in the same season. He was captain again in the 1935 FA Cp Final, losing 4-2 to Sheffield Wednesday. Glidden and Carter had injuries prior to the Final but both were deemed fit to play, yet Carter was injured early on and Glidden who had not played since December due to injury, later admitted that he should not have played. Arthur Gale was very unlucky to miss the Cup Final after playing in very round up until then. Glidden accrued 479 appearances and scored 140 goals. He also made 91 reserve team appearances scoring 17 goals, receiving championship medals in 1923 and 1924. Upon retirement he became a coach at the Hawthorns 1936—39. Tommy joined the board of directors in 1951, a position he held until his death in 1974. He had received a special award in 1972 celebrating 50 years association with West Bromwich Albion. His brother Sid Glidden, was an Albion reserve in the 1920's and later played for Halifax Town, Doncaster Rovers, York City Peterborough United, Newport County and Wigan Athletic. Tom died of a heart attack in 1974, aged 71.

Tony Godden

GODDEN Anthony 'Tony'

Goalkeeper 6'0½"

Born *2/8/1955 Gillingham*

Playing career: *Ashford Town, West Bromwich Albion (326 appearances July 1975 - May 1986), Luton Town (loan), Walsall (loan), Chelsea, Birmingham City, Atvidabergs FF in Sweden, Peterborough United. (1976-1990). In October 1981,*

Godden was a goalkeeper with a safe pair of hands and tremendous reflexes. He had excellent goal-line ability but was not quite so adept at taking high crosses. Tony set a club record by appearing in 228 consecutive first-team game. He then lost his place in the team to Mark Grew. He had a Testimonial Match at the Hawthorns in May 1986 He played 267 league games for Albion over 11 years. Godden had loan spells at Luton Town, Walsall and Chelsea, eventually joining the Stamford Bridge outfit permanently in 1986, playing 26 league matches. He moved back to the Midlands, joining Birmingham City for £35,000 in July 1987. Tony made 29 appearances for Blues, finishing his career at Peterborough United in 1990. He then served as coach to a number of League clubs including Rushden & Diamonds, taking on the caretaker manager role for a short period. He has also managed non-league Kings Lynn FC 1994/95, then managed Bury Town 1996-99. After his stint as goalkeeping coach at Rushden and Diamonds, he moved on to take up a similar role with Brighton & Hove Albion in 2009 replacing ex-Baggie Paul Crichton. Believed to be living in the Brighton area. Since 2013, Tony has been Cambridgeshire Outbase Supervisor for Oak Furniture Land, Whittlesey, near Peterborough.

GOODMAN Donald 'Don'

Striker 5'9"

Born *9/5/1966 Leeds*

Playing career: *Bradford City, West Bromwich Albion (Cost £50,000 163+18 sub appearances 63 goals March 1987 – Dec 1991), Sunderland, Wolverhampton Wanderers, Sanfrecce Hiroshima in Japan, Barnsley (loan), Motherwell, Walsall, Exeter City, Doncaster Rovers (loan), Stafford Rangers (1984 – 2006)*

Don was working as an electrician with Leeds City Council when he turned down an apprenticeship at Bradford but agreed a non-contract deal. He was still 'on the tools' when he made his debut at 17 in May 1984.

Don Goodman

Turned professional in that summer but the club allowed him to go to college one day a week. On May 11th 1985 he was playing for Bradford City, along with Martin Singleton, against Lincoln City, who had John Thomas on as an early substitute, on the day of the disastrous fire at Valley Parade, as the team won promotion as Third Division Champions. A lighted cigarette in the main stand led to the death of 56 people with 200 supporters carted off to hospital. Don lost one of his best friends and also his former girlfriend died in the fire. They were no longer going out together but Don had given her two tickets for the game. Don signed for Albion in March 1987 for £50,000, possibly the best thing Ron Saunders, then manager, ever did at the Hawthorns. He was top scorer for Albion in 1988/89 with 15 league goals and 1989/90 scoring 21 league goals. In an injury ravaged season that followed Albion were relegated to the third division for the first time, under Bobby Gould. Inexplicably the manager left Don out of the final league game after having scored in each of the previous three games, needing a win to stay up, the team drew 1-1 and were relegated. He scored 60 goals for Albion in 158 league games. He was sold to Sunderland for £900,000 in December 1991. He played 116 league games in total for the Black Cats and managed to score 40 goals.

Don moved to Wolverhampton Wanderers in 1994 for a fee above £1 million. He stayed with Wanderers until 1998. He suffered a depressed skull fracture playing for Wolves against Huddersfield in April 1996. Goodman made 125 appearances in the league, scoring 33 goals in the old gold and black. He had a spell in Japan, loan spells at Barnsley and Motherwell, eventually signing for the Scottish club in 1999. He returned to the Midlands in 2001 to play one season at Walsall before he moved to Exeter City for a year. He played a total of 586 league games scoring 162 goals in a 19-year career. He had his own company called Formula GFI Limited in 2003 and was a Fitness Instructor. He has his own company called Don Goodman Limited dealing with television programme production activities, 2010. Having done radio match summarising, he now works as a TV football pundit for Sky Sports.

GORDON Dennis 'Den'

Outside right 5'10"
Born *7/6/1924 Bilston, Wolverhampton*
Died *May 1998 Jersey*
Playing career: *Headington United 1939, Lincoln (guest), Oxford City 1945, West Bromwich Albion (30 appearances 10 goals Sept 1947- July 1952), Brighton & Hove Albion, Guilford City, Tunbridge Wells Rangers (1939 – 1966)*

Nicknamed 'Flash'. Den served in the RAF during WW2 as a Pilot-observer. He became a sergeant qualifying as a compass adjuster and teaming up with the 97th Bomber Squadron flying Halifax and Lancaster bombers. Her played regularly for the RAF groups overseas in India. He had a trial for England Amateur team. Den returned to Oxford where he took a job as an audit clerk in the Borough Treasurer's department. He was on the books of Tottenham Hotspur as an amateur, playing for their reserves. He signed as an amateur for Albion, just before Spurs wrote and offered him terms for the following season. He was in competition with Billy Elliott for the outside right position at the Hawthorns, only playing 27 league games plus 3 FA Cup appearances scoring 10 goals in 5 years. He signed for Brighton in July 1952 for £3,5000 and had a good career there, playing 277 league games scoring 62 goals between 1952 – 1961. He played non-league football for Guilford City and Tunbridge Wells. On retiring from football, he returned to local government working in the housing department of Brighton Corporation's Housing Department. until his retirement in 1982.

GOULD Robert 'Bobby'

Striker 5'10"
Born *12/6/1946 Coventry*
Playing career: *Coventry City, Arsenal, Wolverhampton Wanderers, West Bromwich Albion (Cost £66,666 60 goals 19 appearances Sept 1971 – Dec 1972), Bristol City, West Ham United, Wolverhampton Wanderers*

Gould really was a 'wanderer' as a footballer, playing for Coventry for 5 seasons scoring 40 goals in 82 league games. He moved to Arsenal in February 1968 for £90,000 but could not hold down a regular place in the Arsenal first team, although he did score a headed goal in the 1969 League Cup Final against Swindon Town, which Arsenal went on to lose 3–1. In June 1970 Gould was transferred to Wolves for a fee of £55,000. After just 15 months he was signed by West Bromwich Albion manager Don Howe for the unusual fee of £66,666 in September 1971. A willing runner, brave but he lacked close ball control. He covered for Jeff Astle during an injury hit season and went on to score 12 goals in his first season at the Hawthorns. In all he scored 19 goals in

60 appearances for Albion, but when his form began to wane, he was sold to Bristol City for £68,888 in December 1972. Gould joined West Ham United in November 1973 for an £80,000 fee, and picked up a winners' medal in the 1975 FA Cup Final as a non-playing substitute. He re-joined Wolves for £30,000 in December 1975 and helped them to win the Second Division title in 1976/77. Gould started his coaching whilst still a player with Bristol Rovers as player/coach in October 1977. He moved to Aalesunds FK in Norway as coach 1977/78. Later he joined Hereford United as a coach in September 1978, Charlton Athletic were his next stop off point, as coach in 1979. Gould was signed by Chelsea as assistant manager in October 1979 until June 1981. He returned briefly to play for Wimbledon as a non-contract player in August 1981.Aldershot appointed him as assistant manager/coach between September and October 1981. Gould joined Bristol Rovers as manager in October 1981. Bobby returned to one of his former clubs, Coventry City, as manager in May 1983 until December 1984. He had a second stint with Bristol Rovers as manager in May 1985. He joined Chairman Sam Haman at Wimbledon as manager in June 1987 until 1989, including an FA Cup Final win against Liverpool. QPR was Gould's next position as assistant manager in December 1990 until January 1991. He next moved to another former club, West Bromwich Albion, part of the darkest period in the history of the club, between February 1991, taking Albion down into Division Three for the first time in the club's history. He was sacked in May 1992 after failing to gain promotion, and at a time when some fans carried coffins at the Gay Meadow, Shrewsbury on the last day of the season. Coventry City came calling again appointing him as joint manager with Don Howe, then manager from June 1992 to October 1993. Incredulously, he was appointed as Wales' National Coach in June 1995, remaining in post until 1999. Gould returned to club management with Cardiff City from August 2000 until October 2000, then became General Manager in May 2001. Cheltenham Town appointed Gould as manager in February 2003 until October 2003. He then joined Peterborough United as coach in 2004/05. Gould moved to Hawkes Bay in New Zealand as assistant coach in

September 2006, helping his son Jonathan who was coach. He returned to the UK joining Weymouth as manager in April 2009 for the final 5 games of the season. Portishead Town called on Gould as assistant manager, his final position. Gould has worked on radio as a match summariser. Married to Marjorie since 1968, the couple have two sons Jonathan and Richard. Richard Gould was the Chief Executive of Surrey County Cricket Club and Jonathan Gould, is a former Coventry City and Celtic goalkeeper. Matt Gould, Bobby's grandson, was goalkeeper for Spennymoor Town.

GRANT Anthony 'Tony'

Midfielder 5'10"

Born *14/11/1974 Liverpool*

Playing career: *Everton, Swindon Town (loan), Tranmere Rovers (loan), Manchester City, West Bromwich Albion (loan 3+2 sub appearances Dec 2000), Burnley, Bristol City, Crewe Alexandra, Accrington Stanley, Chester City. (1993 – 2008)*

Started his professional career at Everton, playing 94 league games in six years. On Christmas Eve, December 1999, Tony Grant signed for Manchester City for a fee of £450,000. Gary Megson signed him on-loan for the Albion in December 2000. In an unremarkable time at the Hawthorns he started 3 league games and made two further substitute appearances. After playing 31 games for Manchester City he was sold to Burnley for £250,000 in October 2001. At Burnley he was most frequently played in the defensive-midfield role, which enabled him to display his range of passing and game-reading ability. He had spells at Crewe Alexandra, Accrington Stanley and Chester City. Tony became player coach at Crewe Alexander 2006/2007, working closely with Dario Gradi at Championship and League One level. Tony then moved on to Accrington Stanley and Chester City 2007-2009 as first team player coach at League Two level. Tony joined Blackburn Rovers U18 as coach in 2010 to 2012, here he brought new ideas to the club with the emphasis on development. Here they Won the Academy Elite league, finalists in the FA Youth Cup and also the Premiere League Cup. Tony then moved as First Team coach at Blackburn Rovers from 2012 to 2015. Grant returned to Everton as European scout in October 2016.

Named Blackpool's assistant manager on 14th March 2019. He was assistant coach to Robbie Fowler at Brisbane Roar in Australia 2019/20 until the Corona Virus pandemic, when he & Fowler returned to the UK.

GRAY Andrew 'Andy'

Striker 5'11"

Born *30/11/1955 Glasgow, Scotland*

Playing career: *Dundee United, Aston Villa, Wolverhampton Wanderers, Everton, Aston Villa, Notts County (loan), West Bromwich Albion (On loan Aug-Sep then signed 34 + 3 sub appearances 11 goals Oct 1987 – Sept 1988), Rangers Cheltenham Town (1973 - 1990) 20 caps for Scotland, also played schoolboy, Youth, & U-23 levels.*

A Scottish International whose determination and all-out effort made him one of the greatest strikers of his era. Started his career in Scotland with Dundee United, scoring 36 goals in 62 league games before Aston Villa bought him for £110,000 in October 1975. Won the League cup with Villa in 1977. He played in 113 league games for Villa before local rivals Wolverhampton Wanderers paid an English record transfer fee of £1.49 million in September 1979. He scored the winning goal for Wolves in the 1980 League Cup final and remained with the club through their relegation in 1982 and helped them win promotion a year later. He moved to Everton in November 1983 for £250,000. He spent two seasons with the Merseyside club, winning the FA Cup in May 1984. Gray scored in the final against Watford. A year later, he won the League Championship and European Cup Winners' Cup, also scoring in the final of the latter. He also reached another FA Cup final, but this time he was on the losing side as Everton were defeated by Manchester United. 10 July 1985 Gray returned to Aston Villa in a £150,000 deal. He scored five goals from 35 league games in 1985/86 as Villa narrowly avoided relegation to the Second Division, and the following season he failed to score a single goal from 19 league games as Villa fell into the Second Division. He began the 1987/88 season still with Villa, but was transferred to their local rivals West Bromwich Albion in September 1987 initially on loan but later signed a contract. He was popular with the Albion fans especially after scoring the winner against local rivals Birmingham City at the Hawthorns.

Andy played 37 games including substitute appearances scoring 11 goals. He was obviously past his peak, slower and less energetic than his earlier days but he brought a lot of enthusiasm and experience to the Hawthorns. Early in the 1988/89 season his beloved Glasgow Rangers tempted him back to Scotland, signing for £50,000 in September. He spent one season at Ibrox, helping them win the Scottish Premier Division title. He dropped into non-league football with Football Conference club Cheltenham Town. Gray became coach and assistant to Ron Atkinson at Aston Villa before focusing full time on his TV work on SKY. In 2011 Gray was forced to apologise for comments made about a female assistant referee. Believing the microphone to be turned off, Gray commented to his co-host Richard Keys, "Can you believe that? A female linesman. Women don't know the offside rule." Keys replied "Course they don't." Both had their contracts terminated. Gray later appeared on the Talk Sport show and with Richard Keys on TV on beIN Sports 2014. He also returned to commentating on BT Sport. Andy Gray has been married to Rachel Lewis, a former model who was previously married to his long-term friend and agent Michael Lewis.

'In the blood!'

GREALISH Anthony 'Tony'
Midfielder 5'7"
Born *21/9/1956 Paddington, London*
Died *23/4/2013 Ilfracombe, Devon*
Playing career: *Leyton Orient, Luton Town, Brighton & Hove Albion, West Bromwich Albion (Cost £80,000 65+11 sub appearances 5 goals 1984 – 1986), Manchester City, Rotherham United, Salgueros in Portugal (loan 1987), Walsall, Bromsgrove Rovers. (1974-1995) Republic of Ireland International 45 caps*
Started his professional career at Leyton Orient playing 171 league games between 1874 and 1979. Luton Town paid £150,000 to take him to Kenilworth Road in August 1979. He played 78 league games for the Hatters scoring twice before a £100,000 move to Brighton & Hove Albion in July 1981. He was captain of the Brighton side in the FA Cup Final draw at Wembley in 1983.He missed the replay. He was signed by John Giles for £80,000 at the same time as Steve Hunt joined. They formed a very useful midfield partnership. Tony played in 65 league games scoring 5 goals for Albion. In October 1986 he signed for Manchester City for £20,000 but soon moved again to Rotherham United where he stayed for three seasons appearing in 110 league games, scoring 7 times. He returned to the West Midlands signing for Walsall. He ended his career at Bromsgrove Rovers. In 19-years he played in 589 league games scoring 31 goals. He worked in the scrap metal business. Coached in West Brom's youth academy. Moved to Marbella and lived near to his close friend Derek Statham. Moved back to the UK. Tony died in April 2013, at the age of 56, after losing his battle against colon cancer.

GREENING Jonathan
Midfielder 5'11"
Born *2/1/1979 Scarborough*
Playing career: *York City, Manchester United, Middlesbrough, West Bromwich Albion (Cost £1.580,000 215+9 sub appearances 8 goals July 2004 – Aug 2009), Fulham (loan then signed), Nottingham Forest, Barnsley (loan), Tadcaster Albion, York City, Tadcaster Albion (1996-2017) He represented England U-18, U-21*
Greening began his career in 1996 with York City, but moved to Manchester United in 1998, with whom he won the 1998/99 UEFA Champions League as a non-playing substitute in the final.

However, he failed to make a breakthrough in the Manchester United first team and followed United assistant manager Steve McClaren to Middlesbrough in 2001. During his time at Middlesbrough, Greening earned his first call-up to the England national team, but he did not make an appearance. In 2004, he joined West Bromwich Albion for an initial fee of £1.25 million. Greening made his Albion debut in a 1–1 draw away to Blackburn Rovers on the opening day of the 2004/05 Premier League season, and quickly established himself as a key player in the Albion midfield, helping to secure their Premier League survival in his first season. He was named Albion's Player of the Year in 2005/06, in which he made 41 appearances and scored 2 goals as the club was relegated to the Championship. He captained Albion in the FA Cup semi-final, where they lost 1–0 to Portsmouth later led the team to promotion as winners of the Championship. Greening was named in the 2007/08 Championship PFA Team of the Year, alongside teammates Paul Robinson and Kevin Phillips. During the last two months of the season Greening suffered from a double hernia problem but played on until the end of the campaign, when he had an operation to rectify the injury. He amassed 215 +9 sub appearances scoring 8 goals for the Albion.

In August 2009, Greening joined Fulham on a season-long loan for 2009/10, with a view to a permanent move. He helped them to the 2010 UEFA Europa League Final, before signing permanently the following summer. He signed for Nottingham Forest in 2011 and had a three-year spell with the club. Played a few seasons in non-league football finally retiring in May 2017. During his 21year career he amassed 473 league games scoring 22 goals. He completed his UEFA B & A licences whilst at Forest. Jonathan was coach to Forest's U-21's before coaching at York City with their U-18's at their academy. He was coaching at the i2i International Soccer Academy in York with ex-Stoke City player Richard Creswell and ex-Blues player Bryan Hughes and ex-York goalkeeper Michael Ingram based in York, coaching gifted students from York St. John University. He was doing his pro-licence in 2019.

GREGORY Howard
Outside left 5'7"
Born *6/4/1893 Aston Manor, Birmingham*
Died *15/8/1954 Handsworth, Birmingham*
Playing career: *Birchfield T, West Bromwich Albion (181 appearances 45 goals Aug 1911 – May 1925)*
Howard was known as the 'Express Man' but his nickname was 'Greg'.

Jon Greening

He joined Albion from Birchfield Trinity in May 1911, making his Football League debut at Everton in April 1912. A quick-witted left winger, fast and plucky, who was always likely to produce something extraordinary. Like so many players of the time, his career was interrupted by WW1. In the four pre-war seasons, he scored 12 goals in 30 appearances for the first XI and also played over 100 games for the reserve team in the Birmingham & District League gaining a Championship medal in 1912/13, before the hostilities brought a suspension to football. In the first season back, Gregory won a League Championship medal with Albion in 1919/20 forming a terrific left flank partnership with Freddie Morris, scoring 49 of the 104 goals Albion scored that season. He took a little time to settle into Albion's style of play and to establish himself in the senior side. He did become a key player, clocking up 181 appearances scoring 45 goals. In one game against Wolves at Molineux, Howard hit the ball so hard that it burst in flight, the inside bladder went into the net and the ball casing went over the bar. No goal! Howard retired through injury and became licensee of the Woodman Inn, next to the Hawthorns from 1927-32. He remained in the beer trade until 1953.

GREW Mark

Goalkeeper 5'10"

Born *15/2/1958 Bilston, West Midlands*

Playing career: *West Bromwich Albion (Total in 2 spells 47 + 1 substitute appearances June 1974- June 1983), Wigan Athletic (loan), Notts County (loan), Leicester City, Oldham Athletic (loan), Ipswich Town, Fulham (loan), West Bromwich Albion (loan Jan-Feb 1986), Derby County (loan), Port Vale, Blackburn Rovers, Cardiff City, Hednesford Town (1976-1995).*

Grew lived in Bilston, where he attended the goalkeeping academy run by legendary Wolverhampton Wanderers goalkeeper Bert Williams after accepting that in his words, he "was probably too fat and lazy to play outfield". He joined Albion in 1973 as an apprentice and turned professional at West Bromwich Albion in the June 1976, having just starred in the FA Youth Cup final, which Albion won on 5–0 aggregate over two legs against Wolverhampton Wanderers. With Tony Godden entrenched as the number one keeper Grew went out on loan spells at Wigan Athletic and Notts County. He vied with Godden during the 1981/82 season for the number one jersey, playing 23 league games. Grew started the 1982/83 season as first choice keeper until October 1982 when Godden replaced him. In January 1983 manager Ron Wylie signed Paul Barron.

Msrk Grew

Having played 47 games plus 1 substitute appearance for Albion. Grew moved to Leicester in June 1983 for £40,000 playing 5 league games. After a brief loan spell at Oldham he signed for Ipswich Town for £60,000 in March 1984. He only played 6 league games for the Tractor Boys and had further loan spells at Fulham playing 4 games, West Bromwich Albion for 1 league game January-February 1986. He also went on loan to Derby County where he did not play a league game. In August 1986 he moved on a free transfer to Port Vale and really found a place where he felt wanted. In six seasons at Vale Park he made 184 league appearances. He had a short loan spell at Blackburn before moving to Cardiff City in May 1992. In March 2003 he was appointed as assistant manager at Stafford Rangers but quickly returned to coaching at Vale Park as a key member of the backroom staff including a role as Head of Youth. In December 2010, he was made joint caretaker manager at Vale, along with Geoff Horsfield, following the departure of Micky Adams. In March 2011, Mark was elevated to the position of caretaker-manager for the third time in twelve years. Upon Micky Adams' return as manager he reshuffled the club's coaching set-up, and in July 2011 Grew was made assistant manager. In July 2014 his role changed to that of goalkeeping coach and scouting co-ordinator. In May 2015 he decided to take time out from football and to undergo a back operation. He finally left Port Vale following his testimonial game to honour his 25 years of service to the club. He started an industrial cleaning business with his wife.

GRIFFIN Frank

Outside right 5'8"

Born 28/3/1928 Pendlebury, Manchester
Died 4/6/2007 Shrewsbury, Shropshire
Playing career: *Bolton Wanderers, Shrewsbury Town, West Bromwich Albion (Cost £9,5000 275 appearances 52 goals Apr 1951 – June 1959), Northampton Town, Wellington Town, GKN Sankey's (1950 – 1962)*
A fast and clever right winger, with an eye for goal. He played reserve team football aged 16 at Bolton Wanderers before an injury, in a game at Villa Park, left him lacking in confidence and he left for St. Augustine's Youth Club where the team won the League and Cup. Later signed for

Shrewsbury Town, where Frank played 37 league games, scoring 5 goals. Albion paid £9,5000 for his services in April 1951 as a replacement for Billy Elliot. Franks spent eight wonderful years at the Hawthorns appearing in 240 league games and 34 FA Cup ties scoring 52 goals and also played 42 Central League games scoring 5 goals. As a winger, he enjoyed hugging the touchline and keeping his full back occupied. He possessed good pace, had excellent ball control and delivered precise crosses, as well as packing a strong shot with his right foot. He was the scorer of Albion's 87th minute winning goal in the 1954 FA Cup Final 3-2 win over Preston North End. Albion also finished runners up to Wolves in the First Division. He scored a hat trick in a record 9-2 home league win over Manchester City in September 1957. Sadly Griffin, who was in line for an England call up, broke his right leg playing against Sheffield United in an FA Cup replay in February 1958. Although he did regain his fitness, he was never the same player he was before the injury. He moved to Northampton Town for £1,500 in the summer of 1959, going on to play just 16 league games, before dropping down to non-league football. Griffin was manager of Worthen United from 1962-65. He retired to live in Shrewsbury.

GROVES Paul

Midfielder/defender 5'11"

Born 28/2/1966 Derby
Playing career: *Burton Albion, Leicester City, Lincoln City (loan), Blackpool, Grimsby Town, West Bromwich Albion (Cost £600,000 30+2 sub appearances 5 goals July 1996 – Aug 1997), Grimsby Town, Scunthorpe United (loan), York City. (1987-2005).*
In an 18-year footballing career Groves played 699 league games scoring 109 goals. His longest spells were at Blackpool 1990-92 where he played 107 games and scored 21 goals. In August 1992 Groves signed for Grimsby Town for £150,000 who at the time were managed by Alan Buckley. Groves became very consistent as a player at Grimsby and was a first team regular who scored goals from midfield, in addition to being a good tackler. His next port of call was West Bromwich Albion, signed for £600,000 in 1996 once again by Alan Buckley. He was not very popular with the Albion fans considering his high transfer fee.

He was strong in the tackle but lacked creativity and real pace. He seemed out of place in midfield, too easily caught in possession. After one season with Albion, Buckley had moved back to Grimsby taking Groves with him for £250,000 as well as Kevin Donovan amongst others. Groves soon became captain, successfully winning the play-off final to gain promotion and the Football League Trophy in two Wembley Stadium wins. In the final game of the 2000/01 season, Groves scored a 25-yard goal to win 1–0 against already promoted Fulham, to secure Grimsby's place in Division One. Following the sacking of Lennie Lawrence in December 2001, Groves was appointed player-manager. He was sacked in 2004 but Groves remained as a player until he was released by the club's incoming new manager. He made at total of 454 league appearances in two spells at Blundell Park, scoring 71 goals He had a spell on loan at Scunthorpe but then signed for York City in June 2004 along with Kevin Donovan for a year. Then in the summer of 2005 Groves became player/assistant manager at Stafford Rangers. In July 2006 he joined the Portsmouth coaching staff. In July 2010 Groves became senior coach at West Ham United July 2010, following Avram Grant from Portsmouth. He left the Hammers in June 2011 and joined Bournemouth as youth team manager. Groves was reappointed youth team boss. He left Bournemouth in January 2014. He joined Crawley Town as first team coach in June 2014 until May 2015. Groves was appointed Academy Manager at Bristol City July 2015. In March 2017 he joined Northern Premier League side Mickleover Sports as Assistant Manager. Groves moved to join Birmingham City and Harry Redknapp April 2017 as first-team coach. He stayed with Steve Cotterill but left when Cotterill was sacked in March 2018. In July 2018 he was named as John Gregory's assistant for Indian Super League side Chennaiyin FC. Recently he was assistant coach at Maccabu Haifa FC in Israel.

HAAS Bernt

Defender 6'1"
Born *8/4/1978 Wien, Austria*
Playing career: *Grasshoppers Zurich in Switzerland, Sunderland, FC Basel (loan), West Bromwich Albion*

(Cost £500,000 51 + 1 sub appearances 3 goals July 2003 – Jan 2005), SC Bastia of Corsica in French League (loan then signed), 1.FC Koln in Germany, FC St. Gallen in Switzerland. Swiss International 36 caps
Haas was born in Vienna, Austria. He began his career at Grasshoppers Zurich, where he played for several seasons before moving to England to join Sunderland in August 2001. Despite making 27 appearances for the club in 2001/02, he was loaned out to FC Basel the following season. Bernt played against Albion in a pre-season friendly with Sunderland when he even outshone Kevin Phillips, scoring a quite glorious goal from 30 yards, an absolute screamer. Haas a former Armani model, joined West Bromwich Albion in 2003 for £500,000. At the Hawthorns, it didn't really get a lot better for him to be honest. Albion's Premier League preparations included a trip to Ashton Gate to take on Bristol City. Low key stuff you might think, a simple training exercise. Not exactly. Ten minutes in and Bernt had endured an absolute roasting from Leroy Lita. It's rare to see a player substituted after a few of minutes, even more so in a friendly, but Gary Megson was wont to use the odd punishment substitution and the Swiss player was beckoned back to the bench. Poor Bernt spent the half-time interval glued to said bench, head in his hands, not daring to venture back to the dressing room. He was a regular at right-back in 2003/04 as Albion were promoted back to the Premier League. He scored with a superb volley in the 2–0 League Cup win against Manchester United. He made 51 appearances for Albion scoring 3 goals. His Albion career came to a premature close amid a bizarre flurry of Christmas party shenanigans, Robin Hood costumes and misadventures with a webcam, a heady cocktail for the tabloid age, and one which it was hard to survive, Haas leaving The Hawthorns in January 2005 and thereby missing out on the 'Great Escape'. He left the club by mutual consent on 21st January 2005. The following day Haas signed for SC Bastia in France on a free transfer, prior to joining 1. FC Köln. After just one season at Cologne, he joined Swiss Super League club FC St. Gallen in 2007. Between 2015 – 2018 he managed FC Vaduz as Director of Football a Lichtenstein club that plays in the Swiss Football League.

HACKETT Gary

Winger 5'9"

Born *11/10/1962 Stourbridge*

Playing career: *Bromsgrove Rovers, Shrewsbury Town, Aberdeen, Stoke City, West Bromwich Albion (Cost £70,000 30+21 sub appearances 4 goals Mar 1990 – June 1993), Peterborough United, Chester City, Halesowen Town, Stourbridge (player coach) (1982-1997)*

Hackett was born in Stourbridge and began his career with non-league Bromsgrove Rovers before joining Football League side Shrewsbury Town. After playing 174 times scoring 20 goals for the Shrews, he joined Scottish Premier Division side Aberdeen in the summer of 1987. He moved back to England with Stoke City under the management of Mick Mills. Hackett was an ever-present in 1988/89. He was sold to West Bromwich Albion in March 1990 for £70,000, with Stoke destined for relegation to the Third Division A tricky winger who, although he was an Albion fan, was never able to establish himself with the Baggies. He made 51 appearances in four seasons with Albion suffering relegation to the Third Division for the first time in their history, although he only made 5 substitute appearances. He played 13 games and made 2 substitute appearances in the 1991/92 season.

He played 4 games and made 6 substitute appearances in 1992/93 season as Albion won promotion. He ended his career with a season each at Peterborough United and Chester City before entering non-league football with Halesowen Town. Bromsgrove Rovers (joint manager 2001 -2003), Stourbridge FC joint manager with John Ford 2003-2005, then Manager with Ford as his assistant 2005-2019. Stourbridge won promotion to the Southern League Premier Division with two promotions in three seasons under Hackett's management, as well as reaching the FA Cup proper rounds for the first time in the club's history. He resigned in May 2019, after 16 years following Stourbridge's defeat to Alvechurch in the Southern League play-off semi-final. Upon leaving Football, Gary joined a Company that Distributed Cleaning Chemicals to the food industry, in 2011 he started his own business Worcestershire Chemicals. in the same industry.

"DID YOU KNOW?"

"Players from 55 different countries have played for West Bromwich Albion."

Gary Hackett

Jack Haines

HAINES John 'Jack'

Inside forward 5'9"

Born *24/4/1920 Evesham, Worcestershire*
Died *13/3/1987 Worcester*
Playing career: *Liverpool, (WW2 guested for Wrexham, Doncaster Rovers, Notts County, Bradford Park Avenue, Lincoln City, Swansea Town. Leicester City, West Bromwich Albion (Swap deal involving Peter McKennan plus £6,000 62 appearances 23 goals Mar 1948-Dec 1949), Bradford Park Avenue, Rochdale, Chester. 1 England cap.*

Jack was football-mad at school and always wanted to be a footballer. He had a trial at Liverpool in 1938 but was signed by Swansea Town in 1939. Like so many footballers of his era, his career was interrupted by WW2. He played for Air Command and RAF teams during his National Service and also made guest appearances for Wrexham, Doncaster Rovers, Notts County, Bradford Park Avenue, Lincoln City. Back at Swansea in 1946/47 he played in 28 league games scoring 7 goals. Leicester City paid £10,000 for him in June 1947 and he went on to play 12 games for the Foxes, scoring 3 goals. In March 1948 he joined Albion in a deal worth £6,000 involving a swap with Peter McKenna. He was a highly skilled and mobile forward and during 1948/49 season he was a key player in Albion's promotion winning team, scoring 14 goals in 38 league matches. He won an England cap in 1948, scoring twice against Switzerland at Highbury.

At West Bromwich Albion Jack played 62 games scoring 23 goals. He moved on to Bradford Park Avenue for £10,000 in December 1949, scoring 34 goals in 136 games, before moving again to Rochdale and Chester. In a career thwarted by hostilities, he scored a total of 91 goals, playing 342 league games in peace time.

HALL Paul

Winger/midfielder 5'8"

Born *3/7/1972 Manchester*
Playing career: *Torquay United, Portsmouth, Coventry City, Bury (loan), Sheffield United (loan), West Bromwich Albion (loan 4 appearances Feb – March 2000), Walsall (loan then signed), Rushden & Diamonds, Tranmere Rovers, Chesterfield, Walsall, Wrexham (loan), Newport County, Stratford Town, Spalding United, Mansfield Town (1990-2011). Jamaican International 48 caps.*

In a 20-year career Hall made 685 league appearance scoring 138 goals. At his first club Torquay United he played 93 league games scoring 16 goals before moving to Portsmouth where between 1993-98 he played 188 league games scoring 37 goals. He had 5 different loan spells, one at West Bromwich Albion in February - March 2000 where he played 4 games at outside right, including a 6-0 thrashing away at Sheffield United. He had two spells with Walsall as well as appearing for Rusden & Diamonds 2001-2004, Tranmere Rovers 2004/05, Chesterfield 2005-07. His final port of call was at Mansfield Town in 2011 where he made three league appearances. He became a football instructor at Solihull College and in July 2010 he joined Conference side Mansfield Town as their Head of Youth but left just 2 months later when financial difficulties forced the club to shut down their youth team. He joined Spalding United as a player in 2010. He coached at Soleil College in 2009. Returned to Mansfield in Nov 2010 as assistant manager to Duncan Russell, registered as a player to ease injury crisis in 2011. Left this role in June 2011. Hall joined Marcus Law at Conference National side Tamworth, helping with coaching, as he lived locally in Tamworth. He holds a UEFA 'A' licence. Hall studied at Staffordshire University for a degree in Sports Journalism, graduating in 2015.Went to QPR as U-23's head coach/Senior Professional Development Coach in 2015.

HAMILTON Ian

Midfielder 5'9"

Born *14/12/1967Stevenage*

Playing career: *Southampton, Cambridge United, Scunthorpe United, West Bromwich Albion (Cost £160,000 266+16 sub appearances 28 goals June 1992 – Mar 1998), Sheffield United, Grimsby Town, Notts County, Lincoln City, Woking.*

Hamilton signed his first professional contract with Southampton on his 18th birthday in December 1985. He remained at The Dell for a further two years, playing in the reserves but failing to break into the first team leaving on a free transfer to Cambridge United in March 1988. He remained with the club until December of that year when he made a move to Scunthorpe United on a free transfer. He played 145 league games scoring 18 goals for Scunthorpe before his performances earned him a move to West Bromwich Albion in 1992 for £160,000. In his first season he was an ever-present, playing all 55 games including the Play Off Final at Wembley beating Port Vale 3-0. A reliable, consistent performer, he had six years at the Hawthorns playing 240 league matches scoring 23 goals. In 1998 Albion sold Hamilton to Sheffield United for £325,000 and he would remain at Bramall Lane for the next two seasons. While at United, he was re-signed by Alan Buckley at fellow First division side Grimsby Town.

Hamilton played six times for the Mariners, scoring once in his one-month loan spell. At the end of the 1999/00 campaign, following his release from United, Hamilton finished his playing career at Woking 2002/03. In an 18year career he played 539 league games scoring 46 goals. Hamilton retired in 2003 aged 35. He lives in Sutton Coldfield and has had a number of sales roles and worked as an IT Business development manager. He still plays in charity football matches and can been seen at many Albion home games. He is a staunch supporter of the Old Baggies Former Players' Association.

HARBEY Graham

Left back 5'8"

Born *29/8/1964 Chesterfield, Derbyshire*

Playing career: *Derby County, Ipswich Town, West Bromwich Albion (Cost £80,000 113 appearances 2 goals Nov 1989 – July 1992), Stoke City, Gresley Rovers*

A solid, tough tackling full back. At Derby County, Harbey made his debut in 1983/84. He played 21 times for the Rams in that season as they suffered relegation from the Second Division. He only played another 19 times before Ipswich paid £65,000 in 1987. He stayed for two years playing 59 league games. Albion signed him for £80,000 in November 1989.

Ian Hamilton

Asa Hartford

He was an ever present in 1991/92 and eventually played 97 league games scoring 2 goals in three seasons for the Baggies. He joined Stoke City in the Summer of 1992 and was part of the team that won the Third Division title in 1992-93, ironically Albion being promoted too, after the Play-Off Final at Wembley. He lived in Ashbourne, Derbyshire. Harbey was employed as a sponsorship manager. Later he was a lorry driver in 2013 in Hulland Ward, Derbyshire.

HARTFORD Richard Asa
Midfielder 5'7"

Born *24/10/1950 Clydebank, Scotland*
Playing career: *West Bromwich Albion (266 + 8 sub appearances 26 goals Oct 1967 – Aug 1974), Manchester City, Nottingham Forest, Everton, Manchester City, Fort Lauderdale Sun, Norwich City, Bolton Wanderers, Stockport County, Oldham Athletic, Shrewsbury Town. (1967 – 1991) 59 Full Scotland International caps and 5 U-23 caps.*

Known as Asa, he began his professional career at West Bromwich Albion in 1967. The team won the 1968 FA Cup Final, although in the squad, he did not play in the final. In 1969 Albion were beaten in the FA Cup Semi-Final by Leicester City and Hartford played as outside left. Asa was also part of the Albion team that lost 2-1 after extra time against Manchester City in the 1970 League Cup Final at Wembley, being replaced by substitute Dick Krzywicki. A proposed £175,000 transfer to Don Revie's Leeds United in November 1971 was cancelled, when the Leeds doctor found that Hartford had a hole in-the-heart condition during a pre-transfer medical examination. He returned to the Hawthorns and continued to play, appearing in a total of 274 matches until April 1974. Hartford moved on to Manchester City for £225,000, making his debut for City in a 4–0 victory against West Ham. He helped City win the 1976 League Cup Final. At the beginning of the 1979/80 season he was transferred to Brian Clough's Nottingham Forest for £450,000, only to be sold on to Everton for £400,000 after just three games with Forest. In October 1981 John Bond brought him back to Manchester City for £350,000. His second stint with City was less successful, as he suffered an ankle injury and the club were relegated in 1983. Hartford left City in 1984 and signed for American club Fort Lauderdale Sun.

He returned to English football soon afterwards with Norwich City. In the 1985 League Cup Final, Hartford's shot was deflected by Sunderland's Gordon Chisholm for the only goal of the match. They were relegated in the same season. He then had stints with Bolton Wanderers and Oldham Athletic. Hartford served Stockport County between 1987 and 1989, and Shrewsbury Town 1990/91 as a player/manager before his retirement as a player. He subsequently joined ex-international teammates Kenny Dalglish at Blackburn Rovers, Joe Jordan and Lou Macari at Stoke City, where he spent four matches as caretaker manager. He became assistant manager at Manchester City in 1995, working with Alan Ball and then caretaker manager in September 1996, after Ball left, but he did not express any interest in becoming manager on a permanent basis. He stayed with City for several years as their reserve team coach, until Stuart Pearce brought in his own team in May 2005. Hartford became a first team coach with Blackpool in December 2005, but left the club in May 2006. In June 2007 it was announced that Hartford had been appointed assistant manager at Macclesfield Town but both he and Ian Brightwell were sacked in February 2008 to be replaced by Keith Alexander. In April 2008 he was given a role with Accrington Stanley coaching the juniors and the reserves, but was made redundant in October 2011. He subsequently worked for Birmingham City as a scout.

HEATH Norman

Goalkeeper 5'11"
Born *31/11/1924 Wolverhampton*
Died *November 1983 Birmingham*
Playing career: *West Bromwich Albion (134 appearances Oct 1943 – June 1955)*
Norman signed for Albion in May 1942, turning professional in October 1943. Heath made his Albion debut in a Wartime League match against Wolverhampton Wanderers at the Hawthorns in September 1943. He did his National Service in the Army from 1944-1947, training in Oswestry before teaming up with the King's Shropshire Light Infantry at Llandrindod Wells, moving overseas where he was a storekeeper rising to the rank off C.Q.M.S in Poona, India with the 2nd Leicestershire Regiment.

He represented the platoon, company and battalion, and brigade team, also playing for the Combined Services XI on several occasions. He was a fine, courageous goalkeeper whose agility and brilliant reflexes were key features of his splendid displays for Albion. More solid than showy, his instinctive positional play helped him be in the right place at the right time. He was in competition with Jim Sanders for the number 1 spot. He made his league debut at Sheffield Wednesday in December 1947 in a 2-1 win but suffered a sickening neck injury whilst playing for Albion at Sunderland in March 1954, colliding with Sunderland's centre forward. This forced Norman to miss the 1954 FA Cup Final win over Preston at Wembley the following month. His place ironically went to Jim Sanders. He was later awarded a winner's medal along with Stan Rickaby who also missed the Final through injury. He had a testimonial at the Hawthorns in 1955, when 55,000 supporters turned out. He never played again, being forced to retire, his mobility forever impaired until his death at just 59 in 1983.

HEGAN Daniel 'Danny'

Midfielder 5'8"
Born *14/6/1943 Coatbridge, Scotland*
Died *6/8/2015 Birmingham aged 72*
Playing career: *Bellshill Athletic, Albion Rovers, Sunderland, Ipswich Town, West Bromwich Albion (Cost £88,000 plus swap Ian Collard May 1969 – May 1970), Wolverhampton Wanderers, Sunderland, Highlands Park, Partick Thistle (loan), Coleshill Town (1959-1978). He had one cap for Northern Ireland*
Born in Scotland he started his football career at Albion Rovers, playing 25 league games. He moved to Sunderland for £6,000 but in two years there he never played a league game. Ipswich Town signed him and between 1963-1969 he played 207 league games scoring 34 times. In May 1969 Alan Ashman signed Colin Suggett for £100,000 Allan Glover in a £70,000 deal involving Chippy Clark and Danny Hegan for the fee of £88,000 plus Ian Collard who moved to Ipswich Town. He only made 17 starts plus 1 as a substitute for Albion scoring 22 goals. His arrival was supposed to herald a brave new world for the Albion, part of a spending spree that was going to transform our reputation as a cup fighting team to a unit that could have a realistic go for the title.

He was great, if you could get him out the pub! A flair player, someone willing to play with the ball at his feet and willing to try to take it past his opponents. Playing with something of a swagger, Hegan was also the target for defenders who got a little tired of that style and in the days where the tackle from behind was not only legal but pretty much compulsory, he took his share of stick, which he then liked to give back, when the red mist descended. As Albion careers go, Danny Hegan did not go on to enjoy the most stellar of stays here at The Hawthorns. It lasted just twelve months, from the moment he arrived in May 1969 in return to the day. He left for Wolverhampton in May 1970, Albion collecting a mere £27,500, having bought him for £88,000. The disparity between the two price tags underlines just how badly wrong Hegan's move to the Black Country went and how delighted the Throstles were to see him go in the finish. Hegan was sued for libel by Billy Bremner inJanuary 1982 and the former Leeds United skipper was awarded £100,000 damages. Danny spent 11 seasons

coaching football at Butlins, Eight at Clacton and three at Minehead. Colin Bell headed up the operation and Jimmy Greenhoff and Martin Peters also coached there, as did Bobby Moore as a guest. Danny worked as a labourer for a plumber before working in the industrial cleaning business in Corby, using cleaning machines, painting or hoovering. Returned to Birmingham in 1991 where he did more labouring and cleaning. Also worked back stage in the Night Out in Birmingham, as well as three years doing odd jobs at Edgbaston Test Matches and the women's tennis tournament. Suffered with Asthma since 1997 although he still enjoyed a cigarette. He died from cancer in a Birmingham Hospice in 2015 aged 72.

In his own words: *"Wolves fans will be pleased that they saw a better side of me than the Albion fans had just before. I had problems finding a house at one point, lived in a hotel in West Bromwich and needed a kick up the arse every now and again. I don't have any regrets other than joining Albion. It was the wrong time for me to go there and the wrong time for them to sign me, and it just didn't work out."*

HERBERT Craig

Central defender 5'11"

Born *9/11/1975 Coventry*

Playing career: *Torquay United, West Bromwich Albion (Cost £10,000 8 appearances Mar 1994 – June 1997), Shrewsbury Town, Rugby United, Hayes, Rugby United, Moor Green, Rugby United, Solihull Borough, Rugby Town, Barwell (1994 – 2010)*

Herbert began his career as an apprentice with Torquay United, but was one of five trainees who left Plainmoor under a cloud in February 1994. The following month he signed for West Bromwich Albion, the Baggies paying Torquay a fee of £10,000 with another £6,000 due after 20 first team appearances and 15% of any future sell-on fee, even though he had never appeared in the Gulls first team. However, the additional fees never transpired as he played just eight league games for Albion and was released on a free transfer at the end of the 1996/97 season.

In July 1997 he joined Shrewsbury Town, but, due to injury, played just 41 times in total before being released in May 2000> spells ar Rugby and Hayes followed. He played for Hayes against Yeovil in the first-ever live televised Conference game. However, he was released the following month and re-joined Rugby United where he was appointed club captain for the following season. Craig remained with Rugby until August 2002 when he joined Moor Green. He then re-joined Rugby and stayed until the end of 2004/05 when he followed manager Tony Dobson to Solihull Borough. However, in October 2005 he returned again to Rugby Town. Herbert was appointed Rugby's caretaker manager in December 2007 following Billy Jeffrey's resignation and secured two wins and a draw before Rod Brown took over in January 2008. He was again appointed as caretaker manager in September 2008 after Brown left.

Craig Herbert

Frank Hodgetts

HODGETTS Frank

Outside left 5'7"

Born *30/9/1924 Dudley*

Died *27/3/2018 aged 93*

Playing career: *West Bromwich Albion (178 appearances 33 goals Sept 1939 – May 1949), Millwall, Worcester City (1940- 1957)*

He was the youngest player to play for Albion, making his debut at the age of 16 years 26 days v Notts County 26th October 1940. He went on to help Albion win the Midland Cup in 1944. As organised football began to resume after the war, Frank made his Wartime FA Cup debut in Albion's third round second leg game against Cardiff at The Hawthorns as Albion won 4-0 on January 9 1946. When the Football League resumed later that year, Frank was in the team and on the scoresheet in our first game, a 3-2 win away at Swansea Town's Vetch Field on August 31st 1946, the great Ray Barlow scoring the other two. Frank clocked up 70 post-war league and cup games for the Albion scoring 11 goals, totalling 178 first team outings, including war-time games. before moving on to Millwall for the princely sum of £6,000 in May 1949. He was a good old-fashioned outside left, although he could pop up anywhere in the forward line and he frequently did just that, to the annoyance of his opponents and sometimes his teammates. Frank had a cannonball of a shot. Frank retired from football after snapping an achilles tendon. He returned to Albion as a coach between 1958 and 1962, working mainly with the club's youngsters. Frank was Executive Director at Tube Investments, Oldbury. Chairman of the Herefordshire & Worcestershire County Tennis Association and Chief Organiser of Coaching. He was at the unveiling of the Tony Brown statue at the Hawthorns in 2014.

HODSON Simeon

Right back/defender 5'9"

Born *5/3/1966 Lincoln*

Playing career: *Notts County, Charlton Athletic, Lincoln United, Lincoln City, Newport County, West Bromwich Albion (Cost £5,000 89 + 5 sub appearances Mar 1988 – June 1992), Doncaster Rovers, Kidderminster Harriers, Mansfield Town, Kidderminster Harriers, Rushden & Diamonds, Telford United, Altrincham, Sutton Coldfield Town. (1983 – 2001) 3 England 'C' International caps*

Hodson made 237 appearances in the Football League starting at Notts County where he made 30 appearances. He made another 66 appearances for Lincoln. He was at Newport County where he had played 42 games before West Bromwich Albion signed him for £5,000 in March 1988. He was a utility defender, quick in recovery, who could also adopt to a midfield role.

Simeon Hodson

He made 94 appearances in total for Albion before moving onto Doncaster Rovers in the summer of 1992. Hodson also played for Kidderminster Harriers 1992, Mansfield Town 1992/93, Kidderminster Harriers 1993-97 where he had two spells playing 131 league games. Further spells followed at Rushden & Diamonds, Telford United, Altrincham and Sutton Coldfield Town 2001. A knee injury forced him to retire in August 2001, aged 35. He worked as a watchmaker and in distribution. In October 2006 Simeon joined Warwickshire Police as a Police Support Officer for Ansley Common, Ansley Village, Whitacre, and Arley. He was later responsible for Baddesley, Ensor and Dordon area. He lived in Glascote when in 2008, along with a 16-year old boy, he saved the life of a woman who had fallen into a canal in Fazeley. He was off duty at the time and passed the scene whilst jogging with his daughter. He was a PCSO associated with North Warwickshire Neighbourhood Watch association in 2018.

In his own words: *"The only sport played now is golf which I appear to be getting worse at, but enjoy the banter."*

HOGG Derek

Outside left 5'10"

Born *4/11/1930 Stockton-on-Tees*
Died *4/11/2014 On his 84th birthday*
Playing career: *Leicester City, West Bromwich Albion (Cost £20,000 87 appearances 12 goals July 1958 – October 1960), Cardiff City. (1952 – 1965), Kettering Town. He represented the Football League and an FA XI.*
He served early notice of his thrilling ability during a trial as a teenager with Preston North End, a period split by National Service commitments in Egypt. However, he didn't impress enough to earn a professional contract at Deepdale and had dropped into the Lancashire Combination with Chorley. He was signed by Leicester in the autumn of 1952. A right winger at that point, he made his senior entrance in a 3-3 draw with Leeds United, but barely featured as City won the Second Division title in 1953/54 and it was not until he switched to the left touchline during the following season, which ended in relegation from the top flight, that he made much impact. He quickly struck up a fruitful partnership with Arthur Rowley, who was destined to become the most prolific marksman in the history of English football.

A hint of an international future arrived in October 1955, when he was employed alongside top talents Johnny Haynes, Nat Lofthouse and Tom Finney in the Football League's 4-2 victory over the Scottish League at Hillsborough, but he never made the next step. Back at Leicester in 1956/57, Hogg was a regular provider as Rowley's 44 strikes were the key factor in City's second-tier championship triumph. However, he still retained England ambitions – and to further them he joined West Bromwich Albion for £20,000 in April 1958. Nicknamed 'Hoggy', he was an ingenious and fleet-footed outside left but had the tendency to hold on to the ball much too long. He arrived at the Hawthorns to replace George Lee and Roy Horobin and was flown out to join his new team mates in Spain for a friendly against Athletic Bilbao before settling into Albion's league side for the start of the 1958/59 season. During his time at the Hawthorns, meshing neatly with the well-balanced inside trio of Bobby Robson, Ronnie Allen and Derek Kevan, Albion finished fifth and fourth in the title race. But after that they fell away. Hogg left the club in October 1960 to join Cardiff City for £12,500. Still capable of dazzling thrusts, Hogg lit up Ninian Park in March that term when the mighty Tottenham Hotspur, who two months later would become the first club in the 20th century to win the League and FA Cup double, were the visitors. Taking possession well inside his own half, he sprinted half the length of the pitch before beating Scottish international Bill Brown with a rasping shot. The Bluebirds won 3-2. In 1961/62 Cardiff were relegated and at season's end the rangy 31-year-old outside-left, who had contributed 44 goals in his 283 League appearances for his three clubs, stepped down to join Kettering Town of the Southern League. He became a Leicester Publican

Personal note: *Derek was one of the first players I remember joining and leaving the Hawthorns. He was only 27 when he joined Albion but with his slicked back receding hairstyle, he looked about 20 years older. He was thin and gangly and slightly taller than many wingers of the day. He returned to the Hawthorns just a few weeks after joining Cardiff City appearing in the unusual red shirts of the away team, in a 1-1 draw on 27th December 1960, having beaten Albion 3-1 just the day before.*

HOGG Graeme
Centre back 6'1"
Born *17/6/1964 Aberdeen, Scotland*
Playing career: *Manchester United, West Bromwich Albion (loan 8 appearances Nov-Dec 1987), Portsmouth, Heart of Midlothian, Notts County, Brentford (1984-1998) Scotland U-21 International.*

He began his career with Manchester United in 1984 and went on to play 83 league games for the club before joining Portsmouth in 1988. During his time at Old Trafford, United were FA Cup winners in 1985, but Hogg was not part of the squad that beat Everton 1–0 at Wembley. When he played for Heart of Midlothian, his nose was broken when team captain Craig Levein punched him after an on-field dispute during a pre-season friendly match. He also played for West Bromwich Albion on loan, linking up with his ex-Manchester United boss Ron Atkinson. He played 7 league games November-December 1987, as cover for injured Martyn Bennett.

He was a solid centre back who played alongside unlikely partners in the form of Carlton Palmer or George Reilly, normally a centre forward. He returned to United before signing for Portsmouth in 1988 for £190,000. In three years, he played 100 league games for Pompey. He was transferred to Heart of Midlothian in 1995 for £270,000. In four injury-stricken years he only played 57 league games for Hearts. He then moved to Notts County, in 1995 for £99,000, where he won the Anglo Italian Cup, making 66 league appearances. His final club was Brentford where he played 25 games before retiring in.1998. Returned to live in his native Scotland and worked as a television engineer.

HOPE Robert 'Bobby'
Inside forward/midfielder 5'7½"
Born *28/9/1943 Bridge of Allan, Stirlingshire*
Playing career: *West Bromwich Albion (398 + 5 sub appearances 42 goals Aug 1959 – May 1972), Birmingham City, Philadelphia Atoms USA (loan 1975), Dallas Tornado USA (loan 1976), Sheffield Wednesday, Dallas Tornado USA (loans 1977 & 1978), Bromsgrove Rovers (1960 – 1983) He played for Scotland at Schoolboy, U-23 and won 2 full caps.*

Born in Bridge of Allan, Stirlingshire, Hope joined West Bromwich Albion in August 1959 signing professional in September 1960. A Glasgow Rangers supporter he was persuaded that a career south of the border would be a better option. Bobby was a player who displayed masterly control in midfield. His splendid ball skills and telling passes were highlights of a wonderful association with Albion. Together with Clive Clark on the wing, Hope provided the ammunition for players like Tony Brown and Jeff Astle. Hope enjoyed success during this period, winning the League Cup in 1966 and FA Cup in 1968 plus a runner up in two Wembley League Cup Finals in 1967 and 1970 whilst at the Hawthorns. In April 1971, Hope was awarded a testimonial match against Athletic Bilbao, then managed by Ronnie Allen. He moved to Birmingham City in 1972 for £66.666, spending time on loan in the NASL with Philadelphia Atoms and Dallas Tornado. He later played for Sheffield Wednesday between 1976 and 1978 and then joined Bromsgrove Rovers in August 1979 as player/coach appointed as manager May 1983.

Bobby Hope

He went on to manage Burton Albion August – October 1988. He returned to Bromsgrove Rovers as manager again in June 1989 leading them into the Conference. He had a Post Office in College Road, Handsworth Wood as well as coaching at Bromsgrove. Bobby re-joined Albion in July 1998 as Youth Development Officer becoming Chief Scout in 2001. It was only illness that made him retire in 2014 but he has made an excellent recovery and can now be seen watching the team he joined over 60 years ago along with his sons Adam & Jamie. Married to Carol they spend many happy hours together looking after the grandchildren or holidaying in North Wales. Bobby is a regular supporter of the Old Baggies Former Players' Association.

Personal note: *What a tremendously skilful footballer Bobby was. I recall him, taking the ball towards the right side of the field and in a twisting movement he sprayed a 40-yard pass to the opposite side of the pitch for the fleet-footed Clive Clark to run onto, without even looking. He knew where the players would be. Incredible. insight and vision. He once scored a goal against Ipswich at the Hawthorns where they had all 11 players on the goal line. Albion had been awarded an indirect free kick in the penalty area. The ball was touched to Bobby and he smashed it into the roof of the net. What a masterly ball player so thrilling to watch.*

HOPKINS Robert

Winger/midfielder 5'7"

Born *25/10/1961 Small Heath, Birmingham*

Playing career: *Aston Villa, Birmingham City, Manchester City, West Bromwich Albion (Swap deal involving Imre Varadi 90 + 2 sub appearances 11 goals July 1987 – June 1989), Birmingham City, Shrewsbury Town, Instant-Dict in Hong Kong, Colchester United, Solihull Borough, Bromsgrove Rovers (1979-1999).*

Nicknamed 'Hoppy'. Hopkins was born in the Hall Green district of Birmingham, and he supported Blues as a lad. He started his playing career at Aston Villa with whom he won the FA Youth Cup in 1980. For Aston Villa he made 3 league appearances, but he always wore a blues badge under his Villa shirt. He moved on a free transfer to Birmingham City playing 173 league games scoring 29 goals in two spells. Manchester City paid £135,000 for him in 1986/87 but he only played 7 league games

He was there for less than a year as the manager who signed him, Billy McNeil, left to take over at Aston Villa. His replacement, Jimmy Frizzell, wanted to bring in Imre Varadi from West Bromwich Albion and Ron Saunders would only agree to a deal if Hopkins went the other way. The two were reunited once more shortly after the start of the 1987/88 season. Robert's direct wing play, allied to fine crossing, good distribution and an aggressive, competitive attitude, made him a real handful. His temper sometimes got him in trouble with referees. He played 83 league games for Albion scoring 11 goals between 1987-89. Later he moved back to Blues in March 1989, then on to Shrewsbury Town and Colchester United. He also played in Hong Kong for Instant-Dict and for non-League clubs Solihull Borough and Bromsgrove Rovers. While at Birmingham, the club he has supported since childhood, he helped the club to win promotion to the First Division in 1985 during his first spell, and the Associate Members' Cup in 1991 during his second spell. He was living in Solihull and worked as a delivery driver has also written a column for a local newspaper Birmingham Mail.

In his own words: *"I loved Ron Saunders. He knew what I was all about. He signed me three times – for Villa, Blues and Albion. He used to try to give me advice but as a kid I wouldn't take any notice. You could see he cared though. He came across as a hard sergeant major type bloke, but you could see he cared about people".*

HORSFIELD Geoff

Striker 5'10"

Born *1/11/1973 Barnsley*

Playing career: *Halifax Town, Fulham, Birmingham City, Wigan Athletic. West Bromwich Albion (Coat £1,000,000 52+21 sub appearances 15 goals Dec 2003 – Feb 2006), Sheffield United, Leeds United (loan), Leicester City (loan), Scunthorpe United, Lincoln City, Port Vale, Alvechurch (1997 – 2010)*

He was a "strong and forceful" player, able to hold the ball up in order to bring other players into the game. Horsfield made his Football League debut with Scarborough as a teenager. Released by the club, he returned to part-time football with Halifax Town, Guiseley and Witton Albion, before a second spell at Halifax saw him help the club regain their Football League status.

He moved on to Fulham for £405,000, with whom he achieved promotion to the First Division, before joining Birmingham City for a club record fee £3 million. He played in the final of the 2001 League Cup with Birmingham, and the following season helped them reach the Premier League. After a short period at Wigan Athletic, who had paid £500,000 rising to £1 million if he had played enough games, but he left after just 16 league appearances, in December 2003, joining West Bromwich Albion for £1 million and he again won promotion to the Premier League in his first season under Gary Megson. In 2004/05 he was an important part of the squad now managed by Bryan Robson, who pulled off the Great Escape, avoiding relegation on the final day of the season, having been bottom of the table at Christmas. He made 18 league starts plus 11 as a substitute scoring just three goals, perhaps the most important being the opening goal in the final game of the season at home against Portsmouth, Albion winning 2-0 to stay up. In 2005/06 he made 10 league starts and 8 as a substitute scoring 4 goals as Albion were relegated. Geoff left in 2006 when he moved to Sheffield United for £1.62 Million, but much of his time there was spent on loan to other clubs, namely Leeds United, Leicester City and Scunthorpe United. Horsfield announced his retirement from football in 2008 after being diagnosed with testicular cancer, but after successful surgery he resumed his career, signing a six-month contract for Lincoln City in January 2009. He did his coaching badges. In July 2009 he was appointed player-assistant manager at Port Vale under Micky Adams, and the following summer he took up coaching full-time, before leaving the game completely in May 2012. In March 2013 he returned to playing football for Alvechurch until the end of the season. Geoff did not really enjoy coaching. Geoff was a builder before playing football and returned to this, renovating property as part of his charity work helping homeless and vulnerable communities in the Midlands. Helping others, through the 'Geoff Horsfield Foundation', is now all-consuming. Geoff is helped in that mission by foundation lynchpins Debbie Green and Andrew Griffiths, boss of a successful haulage company. "Debbie's my rock," says Geoff,

"and if it all ended tomorrow, I'd still count Andy as one of my best friends." Through linked body GH9 Housing, Geoff provides bricks and mortar as well as warmth and sustenance to the needy. Six homes in Erdington now provide accommodation for street people. He became charity partner of Birmingham City FC. He has even bought a caravan on Brean Sands in Somerset, offering mini-breaks to families with sick children.

HOULT Russell

Goalkeeper 6'3"

Born 22/11/1972 Ashby-de-la-Zouch

Playing career: *Leicester City, Lincoln City (loan), Blackpool (loan), Cheltenham Town (loan), Kettering Town (loan), Bolton Wanderers (Loan), Lincoln City (loan), Derby County loan then signed), Portsmouth (loan then signed), West Bromwich Albion (Cost £450,000 212+1 sub appearance Jan 2001 – Jan 2007), Nottingham Forest (loan), Stoke City, Notts County (loan then signed), Darlington (loan), Hereford United, (1991-2012).*

He started his professional career at Leicester City in 1991 and had loans spells at seven different clubs including Derby County who eventually signed him, in 1995. In 2000 he was fined £300 for kerb crawling. After 5 years and 108 league games for the Rams he was loaned out, then sold to Portsmouth. In January 2001 he left to join West Bromwich Albion for whom Gary Megson paid £450,000. Russell was tall, had a safe pair of hands, was great in the air collecting crosses and was sound with his distribution. An excellent shot-stopper. Hoult played a key role in helping Albion win promotion to the Premiership in 2001/02, keeping a club record number of clean sheets and being named in the PFA Division One team of the year. Following Albion's relegation, Hoult remained a fixture in the side for the following season, as the club were promoted to the Premiership at the first attempt. In 2004, he was named as one of West Bromwich Albion's 16 greatest players, in a poll organised as part of the club's 125th anniversary celebrations. He played for the majority of the 2004/05 season, as West Bromwich Albion escaped relegation. However, after being a regular in goal for the Baggies for several seasons, Hoult lost his place at the start of the 2005/06 season due to a groin injury.

Russell Hoult

In July 2008, Hoult returned to Notts County on a permanent basis, signing a two-year contract with the club. He played the first 3 games of the 2009/10 season, before being replaced by new signing Kasper Schmeichel. In September 2009, Darlington manager Colin Todd signed Hoult on loan for a month. Todd was sacked during Hoult's loan and he was recalled by Notts County at the end of his month spell. In May 2010 he was released by Notts County. He was goalkeeping coach at Hereford in August 2010, becoming assistant manager in October. Registered as a player for Hereford United as a back-up keeper in March 2012. Hoult signed for Thringstone Miners Welfare as player/manager and club president. He has a UEFA B coaching licence. Russel ran 'just4keepers' in Leicestershire for 5 years. Director of RH goalkeeping from 2017.

HUCKER Peter

Goalkeeper 6'2"

Born 28/10/1959 Hampstead, London

Playing career: *QPR, Oxford United, West Bromwich Albion (loan 7 appearances Jan-Mar 1988), Manchester United (loan), Millwall, Aldershot (1980-1991).*

Spent six years and made 160 league appearances for Queens Park Rangers. He played in the 1982 FA Cup Semi Final against Albion at Highbury when a 'fluke' Clive Allen goal, a rebound after an Ally Robertson clearance, took Rangers to Wembley. Hucker moved to Oxford United for three years, and had a loan spell at West Bromwich Albion in January – March 1988 playing just 7 league games keeping 4 clean sheets, whilst covering for Stuart Naylor. He had two loans spells at Manchester United but did not play a league game, before moving to Millwall, Aldershot and then non-league Farnborough Town. He gave up a milk round franchise to open Peter Hucker soccer schools in East London which he has run for over 25 years. He also coached the keepers at Spurs academy.

"DID YOU KNOW?"

"West Bromwich Albion have now been promoted to the Premier League five times."

Second choice to Chris Kirkland, who manager Bryan Robson had signed on a 12-month loan from Liverpool, Hoult was loaned to Nottingham Forest in September 2005. However, he was recalled during his second month with the club after Kirkland sustained a rib injury. Following the club's relegation and Kirkland's return to Liverpool goalkeeping duties for the 2006/07 season were shared between Hoult and Pascal Zuberbühler until reports about Hoult's personal life surfaced in national newspapers. In Jan 2007 he was suspended by West Bromwich Albion after footage of him involved in an orgy was leaked onto the internet. On 31st January 2007, Hoult was transferred to Stoke City on a free transfer after being sacked by West Bromwich Albion. In February 2008 Hoult joined Notts County on loan until the end of the season, following an injury to regular keeper Kevin Pilkington. He made 14 appearances for the club, keeping seven clean sheets and helping the club to avoid relegation. He was released at the end of the 2007–08 season.

HUGHES Lee

Striker 6'0"

Born *22/5/1976 Smethwick*

Playing career: *Kidderminster Harriers, West Bromwich Albion (Cost 200,000,rising to £380,000 July 1997 – June 2004) Coventry City, West Bromwich Albion (Cost £2.5 million Total 192 + 45 substitute appearances 98 goals in two spells Aug 2002 – Aug 2004), He had a 3 year break from football in HMP then returned to Oldham Athletic, Blackpool (loan), Notts County, Port Vale, Forest Green Rovers, Kidderminster Harriers, Ilkeston, Worcester City, AFC Telford, Worcester City, Halesowen Town, Mickleover Sports, Grantham Town. England 'C' International*

He was a roofer, working with his dad prior to playing professional football. Hughes spent four years at West Bromwich Albion as a schoolboy from ages 11 to 15, though was not offered a youth team contract. He started his career playing semi-professionally Kidderminster Harriers and was called up to the England 'C' amateur team. In total, Hughes scored 70 goals in 139 games for Kidderminster in all competitions Hughes was sold to West Bromwich Albion for an initial £200,000 – incentives later took the final sum up to £380,000 – in August 1997. Fans nicknamed him the 'Ginger Ninja'. Hughes was once described having red hair, tattoos of a Tasmanian devil and a British bulldog on his forearms, dynamite in his boots and Albion in his blood. He quickly became a fans favourite. He finished his debut season as the club's top-scorer with 14 goals in 41 appearances. He started the 1998/99 season in fine form, and claimed his first ever hat-trick in a 3–0 win over Port Vale at Vale Park on 22 August. He claimed further hat-tricks against Crystal Palace and Huddersfield Town, and finished the season with 32 goals in 45 games. This tally left him as the country's top-scorer. He was named on the PFA Team of the Year for the First Division. He then submitted a written transfer request, and his spokesman told the press that there have "been a number of things going on behind the scenes which have unsettled him recently" including his £1,400 a week salary compared with the £5,000 a week salary of under-performing teammate Fabian de Freitas.

Lee Hughes

He remained at the club for the 1999/2000 season, and scored 17 goals in 43 appearances. Albion struggled in the First Division under new manager Brian Little, though improved after Gary Megson replaced Little as manager in March 2000 and avoided relegation despite Hughes missing the final five matches of the season due to a knee injury. He was partnered with Jason Roberts for the 2000/01 season; the pair went on to score 40 goals between them to help secure the Albion a Play-Off place. With 23 goals to his name, he again attracted interest from other clubs. He scored two hat-tricks in seven days against Gillingham and Preston North End. Hughes converted a penalty in a 2–2 draw with Bolton Wanderers in the first leg of the play-off semi-final, before a 3–0 defeat at the Reebok Stadium ended Albion's play-off hopes. He refused to sign a new contract in July 2001, and was placed on the transfer list. Hughes was sold to Gordon Strachan's Coventry City for a club record transfer fee of £5,000,001, the unusual figure was because any offer exceeding £5 million would trigger an escape clause in his West Brom contract, in August 2001. His wages at Highfield Road were reported to be £15,000 a week. Hughes scored 14 goals in 40 games, including a hat-trick in a 6–1 win at Crewe Alexandra, and finished the 2001/02 season as the club's top-scorer. In August 2002, Hughes returned to West Bromwich Albion for a club record £2.5 million, half the fee Albion had received for him a year earlier, signing a four-year deal with the club. Despite being a regular in the first team, in the 2002//03 season, Hughes failed to score a single Premier League goal making 14 starts and 9 substitute league appearances. Albion were relegated in 19th place with just six wins and 26 points from 38 matches. He rediscovered his form back in the First Division, scoring 12 goals in 36 games in 2003/04 as West Brom secured promotion with a second-place finish. In August 2004, Hughes' contract at West Bromwich Albion was immediately terminated, as he was sentenced to six years' imprisonment for causing death by dangerous driving following a fatal crash on 23 November 2003. He spent the next three years in prison, serving half of his six-year sentence. Upon his release from prison on 20 August 2007, Hughes signed a two-year

contract with League One club Oldham Athletic. The club asked supporters "not to pass moral judgement". He signed for Notts County in July 2009, and was named on the PFA Team of the Year after scoring 30 league goals as the club won the League Two title in 2009/10. He left Notts County to sign for Port Vale in January 2013, and helped the club to secure promotion out of League Two in 2012/13. In January 2014, he signed for Forest Green Rovers. In January 2015, he returned to Kidderminster Harriers, and moved on to Ilkeston and then Worcester City in the summer. He continued to be a prolific goalscorer into his 40s, and signed with AFC Telford United in February 2017. He began his management career as joint-manager of Worcester City, alongside John Snape, in May 2017. In March 2018, he was declared bankrupt before he joined Halesowen Town as a player, where he remained until moving on to Mickleover Sports in August 2019. He joined Grantham Town in January 2020 and retired two months later at the age of 43. In March 2020 it was rumoured that Nuneaton Borough manager Jimmy Ginnelly was keen to take Hughes as they prepared for the run-in to the end of the season, however the Covid-19 pandemic put an end to that.

HUGHES Lyndon

Right back/Midfielder 5'9½"
Born 16/91950 Smethwick, Staffs
Playing career: *West Bromwich Albion (118+9 4 goals Jan 1968 – May 1975), Peterborough United, Bromsgrove Rovers. (1968-1977) England schoolboy and Youth International*

A powerful inside forward or wing half who made his debut as a substitute on 5th October 1968 in a 3-1 win over Queens Park Rangers. His first full league game was against Arsenal on 19th October when he lined up next to Jeff Astle as inside right in a 1-0 win with Tony Brown scoring the only goal of the game. Later, Lyndon converted to a sold right back. He played in 127 games including substitute appearances, scoring 4 goals. He had a kidney removed but continued to play. He left Albion for Peterborough United in 1975. A cruciate knee ligament injury finished his career so he went straight into the wine business and was 25 years as Area Manager for Wine Rack.

He then became a Consultant for a German Wine Company, finally retiring in 2015. Lyndon now lives in Evesham and spends his retirement walking, reading, watching all sports and consuming the odd glass of what he sold!

Personal note: *I went to the same senior school as Lyndon, Holly Lodge Grammar School in Smethwick and was a year below him. I played in the same team as him for one year as we won the Birmingham Schools' Cup. I saw him play for England Schoolboys at Wembley and at Luton. I was disappointed he didn't play many more games for Albion. He had a powerful shot but was often played as a full back.*

HUGHES Byron 'Wayne'
Midfielder/utility player 6'0"
Born *8/3/1958 Port Talbot, South Wales*
Playing career: *West Bromwich Albion (3 + 5 sub appearances 2 goals Mar 1976 – Oct 1979), Tulsa Roughnecks in USA, Cardiff City, Bath City, Paulton Rovers, Yeovil Town. (1976 – 1985) 3 Welsh U-21 International caps*

Hughes began his career with West Bromwich Albion, joining the club's youth system as an apprentice in 1974. He went on to captain the Baggies youth side and was part of the team that won the 1976 FA Youth Cup final against Wolverhampton Wanderers.

Wayne Hughes

He signed his first professional contract with West Brom in March 1976 made his debut in May 1977, in the final match of the 1976/77 season, a 4–0 defeat against Aston Villa. However, he struggled to establish himself in the first-team and made eight appearances during his time with the club. He joined the Tulsa Roughnecks in the North American Soccer League in January 1979 and scored 12 times during his only season at the club. In October 1979, Cardiff City manager Richie Morgan paid £70,000 to bring Hughes to the club, making his debut for the club in October 1979 in a 2–1 victory over Luton Town. He remained with the club for three seasons as they struggled in the Second Division and was released at the end of the 1981/82 season after they suffered relegation to Division Three. Following his release, he joined Bath City but retired from football after a single season. He later decided to return to football after eight months, playing for Bath for a second time and later had spells with Paulton Rovers and Yeovil Town. After finally retiring from football, Hughes worked as a pub landlord in Swansea before becoming a hotelier in Blackpool. Wayne then played Sunday football for the famous Mammas FC in Blackpool winning back to back Lancashire Sunday titles in 1993 and 1994 as well as being the only team to win the "Grand Slam" of four trophies in 1993.

HULSE Rob
Striker 6'2"
Born *25/10/1979 Crewe*
Playing career: *Crewe Alexandra, Hyde United (loan), West Bromwich Albion (Cost £750,000 35+11 sub appearances 13 goals July 2003 –Feb 2005), Leeds United (loan then signed), Sheffield United, Derby County, Queens Park Rangers, Charlton Athletic (loan), Millwall (loan) (1998 – 2013)*

Hulse began his career at Crewe Alexandra. A sudden spurt in height during his late teens left Hulse with a serious back injury, sidelining him for 12 months. When he returned to fitness, he went on a two-month loan to Northern Premier League side Hyde United, where he scored 9 goals in 11 appearances during 1999/2000. Hulse quickly became a fans' favourite on returning to Crewe, thanks to his high work-rate and finishing the 2000/01 and 2001/02 seasons as the club's top goalscorer with 11 and 12 goals respectively.

Rob Hulse

Crewe were relegated at the end of the 2001/02 season. In 2002/03. Hulse finished as the club's top goalscorer for the third season in succession, scoring 23 goals. His performances during the season earned him the club's Player of the Year award, as well as appearing in the PFA Division Two Team of the Year. West Bromwich Albion secured the signing of Hulse for a fee of £750,000. Hulse was a tall, blonde skilful striker, maybe lacking that short burst of pace, but he was always a willing runner. He scored his first goal for the club in the 4–0 home win over Brentford. Hulse played a key role in the club's promotion challenge prior to having a stomach injury during the Christmas period. After recovering from this injury, Hulse made a further 19 appearances, finishing the club's joint top scorer with Jason Koumas both on 10 league goals, although Hulse did also score three goals in the League Cup. Hulse was given little chance to prove himself in the top flight because of the summer signings of Robert Earnshaw, Geoff Horsfield and Nwankwo Kanu. Hulse only played seven games for West Brom during the 2004/05 season, without scoring. After a loan spell, he left for £1.1 million being transferred to Leeds United. He scored 18 goals in 52 league games for Leeds. In July 2006, Leeds accepted a bid of £2.2 million from Sheffield United where he played 50 league games, scoring 8 goals. The fee could have risen to £3 million. On 17 March, Hulse and Chelsea goalkeeper Petr Cech challenged for the ball in a league game at Stamford Bridge, resulting in a horrific injury. Hulse had fractured his left leg in two places, for which he underwent surgery. He was out for 9 months. In July 2008 Derby County completed a move for him for £1.75 million. He slowly returned to fitness, scoring 28 goals in 82 league games for the Rams. In September 2010 he joined Queens Park Rangers for an undisclosed fee in the region of £500,000. Only scoring 2 goals in 23 league games resulted in him joining fellow London side Charlton Athletic in October 2012 on a three-month loan. Hulse played 15 league games for Charlton, with 10 starts and 3 goals. He then joined Millwall until the end of the season but his loan at the New Den was cut short on 26 April after 11 league appearances without scoring.

Hulse announced his retirement from football in October 2013, with the intention to move into physiotherapy. In a 15year career he played 395 league games scoring 123 goals. He studied for a physiotherapy degree at the University of Salford, graduating in the Summer of 2017. Works at Russells Hall Hospital, Dudley Group NHS Foundation Trust as a physiotherapist

HUNT Andrew 'Andy'
Striker 6'0"
Born *9/6/1970 West Thurrock, Essex*
Playing career: *Kettering Town, Newcastle United, West Bromwich Albion (loan then signed Cost £110,000 228 + 12 sub appearances 85 goals March 1993 – June 1998) Charlton Athletic (1990 – 2001)*

Born in West Thurrock, Essex, Hunt started his career in non-league football, whilst training in business and tourism management, with King's Lynn and Kettering Town before being signed by then manager Jim Smith for Newcastle United in early 1991. Smith was replaced by Ossie Ardiles and the following year he himself was replaced by Kevin Keegan as Newcastle manager. David Kelly and Micky Quinn were his first choice attacking force. Hunt was on the sidelines for much of the next 12 months before departing at first on loan, to West Bromwich Albion, where Ardiles was now the manager. Andy Hunt was a leggy striker who always gave 100% effort. He signed for a fee of £110,000. Hunt scored a hat-trick on his home debut for Albion in March 1993 against Brighton. He scored the first goal in the Second Division Play-Off Final in 1993 at Wembley as West Bromwich Albion beat Port Vale 3–0 to gain promotion. Hunt was a regular over the next five seasons, creating an effective partnership with Bob Taylor, making 228 league appearances plus 12 as a substitute scoring 85 goals for the Baggies. Hunt joined Charlton Athletic on a free transfer in 1998 and they were relegated in 1998//99. In the following season Andy scored 24 goals as Charlton won the Division One title to gain promotion back to the premier League. He played 86 league games scoring 35 goals. He retired early in the 2000/01 season due to chronic fatigue syndrome. Returned to Charlton briefly in 2003 to try and earn another contract playing 3 reserves games but was not offered a contract.

The Hunts in 2001 sold their Greenwich home for £525,000 and bought a property for £140,000 in virgin forest in Belize. Andy and his wife Simone, a former MTV presenter, are running a jungle lodge in Belize called Belize Jungle Dome, Belmopan Hotel in the Cayo District of Belize. Alongside their hotel, their Green Dragon Adventure Travel business gives guests plenty to do. You can go jungle horseback riding, explore caves and temples, kayaking, abseiling, biking or try a zip line for thrills. There is also yoga on site. He also runs Rising Stars, Football Coaching in Belmopan, Belize.
In his own words: *This is what I do now: www.belizejungledome.com and this is my involvement with footy: https://www.facebook.com/groups/2155815217803126*

HUNT Stephen 'Steve'
Midfielder 5'7"
Born *4/8/1956 Witton, Birmingham*
Playing career: *Aston Villa, New York Cosmos, Coventry City, New York Cosmos, Coventry City, West Bromwich Albion (Cost £80,000 84 appearances 20 goals Mar 1984 – Feb 1986), Aston Villa (1974-1988) 2 England International caps*
Originally a left winger who became a left sided midfielder. He began his career with Aston Villa January 1974 - February 1977 only making 7 league appearances before moving for £50,000 to play for New York Cosmos in USA. He played alongside and against some of the greatest players in the world, including Pele. In September 1978 Coventry paid £40,000 to bring him back to the Midlands. He spent six years with Coventry City, playing 185 league games, scoring 27 goals. Played three times for an England XI whilst at Highfield Road. He returned to New York Cosmos between May-August 1982. In two spells with the Cosmos he played 70 games scoring 29 goals. He returned to Coventry in August 1982 before moving to West Bromwich Albion in March 1984 for £80,000 where he played alongside Tony Grealish and stayed for two years winning two England caps, playing on the left side of midfield. He played 68 league games for Albion scoring 15 goals. Hunt didn't see eye to eye with Albion Boss Ron Saunders and he returned to Villa Park in March 1986 in a £90,000 deal involving Darren Bradley moving to the Hawthorns. Hunt retired through injury in late 1987.

He was player/manager of Southern League side Willenhall Town, then youth team coach at Port Vale and Leicester City. He moved to the Isle of Wight and had a role with AFC Bournemouth's Community Sports Trust. He spent part of 1996 as co-manager at VS Rugby. In April 2017 he was appointed manager at Wessex League club Cowes Sports. Resigned in August 2018, wishing to take a break from the game.

INAMOTO Junichi
Midfielder 5'11"
Born *18/9/1979 Yusui, Kagoshima, Japan*
Playing career: *Gamba Osaka in Japan, Arsenal (loan), Fulham (loan), West Bromwich Albion (Cost £200,000 20 +12 sub appearances 1 goal July 2004 – August 2006), Cardiff City (loan), Galatasaray in Turkey, Eintracht Frankfurt in Germany, Stade Rennes in France, Kawasaki Ferontale in Japan, Hokkaido Consadole Sapporo, SC Sagamihara (1997 - -2019) 82 caps for Japan, plus U-17, U-20, U-23 International.*
He played for Japanese club Gamba Osaka during his last year of high school, signing with the club in 1997. In April when at the age of 17, he debuted in the 1997 season, which, made him the youngest player to play in the J.League at that time.

Steve Hunt

Junichi Inamoto

He stayed at Gamba until summer 2001 and played 118 matches in J1 League. Signed on loan for Arsenal in the Premier League. Inamoto scored two goals for the Japanese national team at the 2002 World Cup, but had already been released by Arsenal before the tournament began. He then signed for Fulham on a long-term loan deal from Gamba Osaka. He sustained a fractured tibia in an international friendly against England, and returned to Gamba Osaka to do promotional work. Inamoto signed with West Bromwich Albion for a decidedly small £200,000 transfer fee. However, Gary Megson departed as West Bromwich Albion manager shortly afterwards, and successor Bryan Robson was unsure of the player. Inamoto was loaned to Cardiff City for the latter part of the 2004/05 season where he impressed, being recalled to play a role in Albion's survival campaign in the Premiership. In 2005/06 he played 16 league games plus 6 substitute appearances in a struggling West Bromwich Albion side who were relegated at the end of the season. He was called up to the Japan squad for the 2006 FIFA World Cup, the first Albion player to play in the tournament for 20 years. In 31st August 2006, he signed for Galatasaray. On 29th May 2007, it was revealed that he signed a two-year contract with German club Eintracht Frankfurt, joining on a free transfer. Inamoto was released on 30th May 2009. After spell a with French Ligue 1 side Rennes, he moved back to his homeland, where he played for Kawasaki Frodntale, Consadole Sapporo, and later Hokkaido Consadole Sapporo, in J2 League. Consadole won the 2016 season and was promoted to J1. He resigned at the end of the 2018 season. In 2019, he signed with J3 League club SC Sagamihara.

Personal note: *I recall both Inamoto and Jason Koumas being singled out by Manager Bryan Robson, as having weaknesses in their games, producing videos for each player to study. This resulted in both players spending loan periods ironically with the same side, Cardiff City. I saw the best and worst of Junichi Inamoto, as he scored a thunderous goal from 20 yards for Albion in a League Cup game at Craven Cottage in a 3-1 win against his former Fulham in October 2005, with the fans urging manager Bryan Robson to play him every week. However, I also saw him in a league game at the same venue just a few months later in February 2006, when he looked a shadow of the same player, Albion were thrashed 6-1.*

JACKMAN Clive
Goalkeeper 5'11"
Born *21/2/1936 Aldershot*
Playing career: *Aldershot, West Bromwich Albion (Cost £1,000 21 appearances June 1957 – Dec 1958). (1953 – 1958) Retired early due to back injury. aged 24.*
Aldershot born Clive signed as an amateur for the 'Shots' at 15 whilst still at Farnborough Grammar School and played in the "A" team with occasional games for the Combination side. In the 1952/53 season, he twice turned out for the first team but a double fracture of the jaw sustained against Leicester reserves on Christmas eve that year prevented further opportunities for the top goalkeeping place. Signed professional for Aldershot in May 1953. He became the first choice 'keeper for Aldershot playing 38 league matches, until he was also transferred to WBA in June 1957 for a fee of £1,000. Clive was a fine keeper, ideally built an he was often brilliant in reserve team fixtures. He played 21 consecutive league games for Albion from March 1958 through to October 11th 1958 the following season. On that day, in the game at Villa Park, he suffered a bad spinal injury that was to end his career aged 24, just when it seemed as if he was establishing himself amongst the top 'keepers in the First Division. Albion won the game 4-1, in a season that would see Villa relegated, ironically, at the Hawthorns in April 1959 when Ronnie Allen scored to equalise 1-1 when Villa needed a win to stay up. Latterly, he settled in Christchurch, Dorset and was employed in the clock & watch trade.

Alec Jackson

JACKSON Alec

Right winger 5'7"
Born *29/5/1937 Tipton*

Playing career: *West Bromwich Albion (208 appearances 52 goals July 1954 – June 1964), Birmingham City, Walsall, Nuneaton Borough, Kidderminster Harriers, Warley, Oldbury Darlaston, Blackenhall, Lower Gornal, Rushall Olympic, Bush Rangers (1954-1985) He played for the Football League v Scottish League at Villa Park in in Longbridge.*

Nicknamed 'Jacko'. An exciting, plucky little utility forward, fleet of foot and able to perform in any forward position with a great deal of success, although his best position was probably on the right wing. He was a brilliant dribbler at times and he had a pretty useful shot. He made his Albion debut aged 17, in November 1954 in a 3-1 victory against Charlton Athletic. In 1958, Alec broke his leg playing at White Hart Lane against Tottenham Hotspur.

He made a full recovery and became a permanent fixture in Albion's senior side in 1959/60 and he was an ever present in 1961/62. Alec averaged a goal every four games for Albion. He played for the Football League against the Scottish League at Villa Park in 1962. Alec played 208 games for Albion scoring 52 goals. Birmingham City signed Alec in the summer of 1964 for £12,500 and he went on to make 78 league appearances for Blues, scoring 11 goals. In February 1967 he moved to Walsall laying 38 games scoring 7 goals between 1967-68. He later dropped down into non-league football, playing for Nuneaton Borough, Kidderminster Harriers, Warley, Oldbury Town, Warley County Borough, Darlaston, Blakenall, Lower Gornal, Rushall Olympic and Bush Rangers. When he retired Alec went into a mill, later went to work on the track, making cars at the Austin works in Longbridge. He had various other jobs, sometimes working up to 18 hours a day. Born in 1937, when he was growing up the population's sense of self-sufficiency was reflected in the numbers who produced their own food on allotments, plots of land made available for non-commercial gardening. There were more than a million of these in Britain after the Second World War. This number has dwindled to fewer than 300,000, one of them in the possession of Alec Jackson who had his allotment for over 35 years. He still had this in 2018 and a friend shared it, one half each. He still enjoys fishing too.

JARA Gonzalo

Defender 5'10"
Born *29/8/1985 Santiago, Chile*

Playing career: *Huachipato in Chile, Colo-colo in Chile, West Bromwich Albion (Cost £1.4 million 54 + 13 sub appearances 2 goals Aug 2009 – Jan 2013), Brighton & Hove Albion (2 loan spells), Nottingham Forest (loan then signed), Mainz 05 in Germany, Universidad de Chile, Estudiantes de la Plata in Argentina, Morelia in Mexico, Mazatian in Mexico (2003 – 2020) 155 caps for Chile and U-20 international.*

Jara made his professional debut in 2003 for Huachipato, where he played 69 games, until his 2007 transfer to Colo-Colo. He played another 64 games. Colo-Colo agreed to transfer him to English Championship club West Bromwich Albion.

Jara signed for Albion for a fee of £1.4 million on a three-year contract on 25 August 2009. Strong and competitive but sometimes outpaced by a sprightly winger. Although primarily a defender, usually a right back, he appeared in four different shirts in his first season playing 20 league games plus 2 substitute appearances. In 2010/11 he started the season as right back, playing 24 league games and another 5 as a substitute. In 2011/12 he only made one league start and 2 substitute appearances, going out on loan for two spells at Brighton & Hove Albion appearing in 26 league games. He joined Nottingham Forest in January 2013 initially on loan, then signed on a free transfer in June. He played 32 league games for Forest, leaving in July 2014 when he signed for German team FSV Mainz 05. In 2016 he returned to play for Universidad de Chile 2016-2018 making 58 appearances. He then played 15 games for Argentine club Estudiantes de La Plata. Early in 2020 he had played for Morelia and Mazatian in Mexico.

JENSEN Brian

Goalkeeper 6'5"

Born *8/6/1975 Copenhagen, Denmark*
Playing career: *B.93 Kabenhaven in Denamrk, AZ Alkmaar in Holland, Hvidovre IF in Denmark (loan), West Bromwich Albion (Cost £80,000 Mar 2000 – June 2003), Burnley, Bury, Crawley Town, Mansfield Town, Crusaders in Northern Ireland (1993 – 2018)*

Jensen began playing football as a defender in the youth team of B 93 in Denmark. His goalkeeping talent caught the attention of Dutch outfit AZ when he was named best goalkeeper at a youth tournament in the Netherlands. He was loaned out from Alkmaar to Danish club Hvidovre IF for eight months, while finishing his electrician education, before going to play as a full-time professional for Alkmaar in February 1998. Jensen managed one appearance in the Eredivisie championship in his time at Alkmaar. While waiting for his Alkmaar contract to run out, Jensen trained with Division One side West Bromwich Albion, where his imposing stature earned him the nickname "The Beast". Jensen moved to West Brom for a fee of £80,000 in March 2000. He made his Albion debut on 7th March 2000 and kept a clean sheet in a 2–0 victory over Tranmere Rovers. He stayed at West Brom for three years, playing a total of 50 games. He helped the club survive in Division One in 1999/2000, and was a regular for much of the following season, until the arrival of Russell Hoult saw the end of Jensen's playing time for West Bromwich Albion in February 2001. Jensen never re-gained a regular place, playing only one match in Albion's promotion season of 2001/02. He joined Burnley on 30th June 2003 on a free transfer after West Brom were relegated, finishing 19th in the Premier League. After 10 years and 271 league games, Jensen moved to Bury & Crawley Town for one season each. In 2015 he signed for Mansfield Town playing 28 league games. In 2017 He signed for Northern Irish team Crusaders playing 30 games. After a fruitful playing career spanning over 25 years, Jensen launched a new GK Icon youth goalkeeping academy in Sandbach, Cheshire on 31st May 2016. On In June 2018, it was announced that he had returned to Bury on a two-year contract as the first team goalkeeping coach. On 21st June 2019, Jensen joined the backroom staff as goalkeeping coach at League One side Shrewsbury Town.

JOHNSON Andrew 'Andy'

Midfielder 6'0"

Born *2/5/1974 Bristol*
Playing career: *Norwich City, Nottingham Forest, West Bromwich Albion (Cost £200,000 132 + 12 sub appearances 8 goals Sep 2001 – June 2006), Leicester City, Barnsley, Kings Lynn (1992 – 2009) 15 Welsh International caps.*

Nicknamed 'AJ', he began his career at Norwich City playing 66 league games scoring 14 goals, before joining Nottingham Forest in 1997 for £2.2m. Having made 119 league appearances for Forest, he moved on to West Bromwich Albion for £200,000 due to his contract expiring at the end of the season. Part of Albion's Promotion teams in 2002 and 2004. He was a fans favourite at The Hawthorns. He was involved in the 'Battle of Bramall Lane' when Albion beat Sheffield United and a certain Gorge Santos tried to seek revenge for an injury he had sustained at the hands, or elbow, of Johnson, whilst Andy was playing for Notts Forest. Santos was sent off with the game eventually being abandoned. Albion were awarded all three points. Johnson joined Leicester City in June 2006 playing 22 league games.

Andy Johnson

Johnson was signed by Barnsley on 8 June 2007 only playing 4 times before he joined non-league King's Lynn in 2009. He is a qualified electrician. Commentates on Albion games on Albion Radio. In 2020 he was part of a group of present and former players who sent messages or made phone calls to senior season ticket holders during the Corona Virus pandemic.

In his own words: "We went on pre-season to Portugal once where we had these little 'houses', rather than hotel rooms. I ended up sharing with Jono Greening, with Paul Robinson and Geoff Horsfield next door. One night we played Scrabble, as we weren't allowed out, and Jono got all excited with his letters. Anyway, it got to his turn and he laid down the tiles 'F...U...G'. We were all looking at him, waiting for the rest of the letters. But he was done with it. He thought he was putting down 'THUG'. That was Jono for you. That was the same trip where Jono reckoned there were two suns - one in England, one abroad, because it was so hot. Bless him."

JOHNSON Joseph 'Joe'
Outside left 5'6½"
Born *4/11/1911 Grimsby, Lincolnshire*
Died *8/8/1983 West Bromwich*
Playing career: *Scunthorpe and Lindsey United, Bristol City, Stoke City, West Bromwich Albion (Cost £6,5000 145 appearances 47 goals Nov 1937 – May 1946) 145 appearances 47 goals Nov 1937 – May 1946), Hereford United, Northwich Victoria, Hereford United. (1929 – 1950) 5 England International caps. He guested for Crewe Alexandra, Leicester City & Notts County in WW2.*

Joe Johnson was an excellent left winger, who received much praise for some quite superb displays in the Stoke side of the 1930's. With Stanley Matthews on the opposite wing, they helped steer Stoke City to the Second Division Championship in 1933. In 184 league games for the potters he scored 54 goals between 1931-1937. Johnson made 5 England International appearances between November 1936 and May 1937. Joe was part of the Stoke City team that beat Albion 10-3 in Feb 1937 and he scored four goals. He was signed up in November of that year for £6,500.

Johnson spent 9 years with the Baggies, in a career interrupted by WW2. He played in 57 league games scoring 22 goals. During the war years he made a further 88 appearances in Wartime League or Cup games, scoring 25 goals. In the 1939 register, Joe is listed as 'making aircraft strip'. He lived in Lyndhurst Road, West Bromwich. He guested for Crewe Alexandra, Leicester City and Notts County. Joe ran the refreshment room, which he rented, in Dartmouth Park West Bromwich from 1945 until he retired in 1976. He died in 1983 the same year that a fire destroyed the café. Johnson's daughter, Shirley Flood, now 76, worked in the Victorian cafe from the age of 10 and was helped by her two brothers, sister and mother Flo, who died in 1960.

In 2012 Joe's daughter cut the ribbon at the official opening of the new "Joe Johnson Snack Bar" part of a new £900,000 pavilion. The pavilion was been paid for by lottery money and Sandwell Council and the snack bar, which opens during weekends and school holidays, was named in his honour thanks to the Friends of Dartmouth Park.

JOHNSTON William 'Willie'
Left Winger/attacker 5'7"
Born *19/12/1948 Maryhill, Glasgow*
Playing career: *Rangers, West Bromwich Albion (Cost £138,000 251+5 sub appearances 28 goals Dec 1972 – Mar 1979), Vancouver Whitecaps, Birmingham City (loan), Rangers, Vancouver Whitecaps, Heart of Midlothian, South China AA (loan), East Fife. Scottish International.*

Willie Johnson

Willie worked as a miner in the Cardenden area of Glasgow prior to becoming a professional footballer. Johnston began his career at local Junior club Lochore Welfare, also signing schoolboy forms with Rangers. He joined the Gers full-time in 1964 aged 17. Having won numerous trophies at Rangers, playing 211 league games scoring 89 goals, his short temper had earned him a 2-month long ban in Scotland for punching an opponent, so he moved to England, where his ban did not count, joining Albion, managed by Don Howe, in December 1972. Albion paid a club record £138,000 to bring him to The Hawthorns. Albion were relegated at the end of the 1972/73 season. It took him a couple of seasons to adjust to the style of play in the second division under Don Howe. After the arrival of John Giles and Promotion in 1975/76 Johnston really started to put in stellar performances. Ron Atkinson encouraged him to express himself more in games, and his performances in 1977/78 season leading up to the World Cup in 1978, were quite exceptional. He became an Albion legend with his terrific pace, mazy runs and accurate crosses. He was real joker and an entertainer. He was sent off over 20 times in his career. Once at West Bromwich for aiming a kick at a referee, behind his back, but seen by a linesman. He is alleged to have agreed to purchase a greenhouse from a fan as he was about to take a corner at the Hawthorns. He was part of the Scotland World Cup Squad of 1978 but had to return home early after failing a drugs test. He left the Hawthorns joining Vancouver Whitecaps. Johnston once 'mooned' the Seattle Sounders bench whilst playing for Vancouver Whitecaps following a goal. after a loan spell with Birmingham, he re-joined Vancouver Whitecaps. He played for Hearts in Scotland, had a short spell in China, before ending his playing career at East Fife. After retiring from playing football he was head coach at Hearts, coach at East Fife and then Raith Rovers and Falkirk. He was licensee of the Port Brae Bar pub in the town which was run by his son Dean until a dispute with the Belhaven Brewery led to the pub being boarded up, locking Johnston's collection of memorabilia inside.

JOL Martin
Midfielder 6'2"
Born *16/1/1956 The Hague, Netherlands*
Playing career: *ADO Den Haag, Bayern Munich in Germany, Twente in Holland, West Bromwich Albion (Coast £250,000 78 +1 sub appearances 4 goals Oct 1981 – June 1984), Coventry City, ADO Den Haag. 3 International caps for the Netherlands Schoolboy, U-21, U-23 and 'B' International*

He turned professional with Den Haag in 1973. He won the 1975 Dutch Cup. In five seasons he played 132 league games scoring 9 goals. He played 9 games in the Bundesliga for the 1978/79 season with Bayern Munich before returning to the Dutch Eredivisie to play for Twente in 1979. While with Twente, he won his first cap for the Dutch national football team in 1980. Jol moved to England in October 1981, joining West Bromwich Albion for £250,000. The fans loved him and he was a great asset to the team, tackling tigerishly and spraying out passes in all directions. He was later joined by compatriot Romeo Zondervan. He appeared in the losing semi-finals of both domestic cup competitions in 1981/82. Jol played 63 league games for Albion, scoring 4 goals. His form dropped considerably after a couple of good seasons. thern after playing just 15 games for Coventry City, Jol returned to Den Haag in 1985. There he won the 1985 Dutch Footballer of the Year award. He played until 1989 appearing in 135 more league games scoring 6 goals. Jol's coaching career began in 1991 when he took over at the amateur side ADO Den Haag and took them to the highest local amateur division. Jol then moved to the leading local amateur side SVV Scheveningen for one season, where he won the national non-league championship. Jol then spent two years as manager at the professional Eredivisie side Roda JC from the town of Kerkrade, during which time he won the Dutch Cup in 1997, Roda's first trophy for 30 years. Between 1998 and 2004, Jol managed the Dutch professional team RKC Waalwijk. He started there in November with only three points at the bottom of the table. He saved them from relegation in their first year and was in contention for European football in the years after. He was honoured with the Dutch Football Writers Coach of the Year 2001 and with the Dutch Players and Coaches Coach of the Year 2002 awards.

Stan Jones

In June 2004 he became assistant manager of Tottenham Hotspur under Spurs' new coach, Jacques Santini. Santini resigned after just 13 games, and on 8 November 2004, Jol was confirmed as his replacement. He was replaced at Spurs by Juande Ramos. From the 2008/09 season, Jol began coaching German Bundesliga club Hamburger SV. Hamburg ended up finishing in fifth place, qualifying for the Europa League for the following season. They also reached the semi-finals of the UEFA Cup and the German League Cup, which were both lost against Werder Bremen. On 26 May 2009, it was announced that Jol was to be the new head coach of AFC Ajax, taking over from Marco van Basten. On 7th June 2011, it was announced that Jol had signed a two-year contract to take up the vacant post at Premier League side Fulham, after Mark Hughes' departure. On 24th February 2016, Jol was appointed as the new coach of the Egyptian Premier League club, Al-Ahly. On 19th August 2016, Jol was sacked because of his bad performance in the 2016 CAF Champions League competition. On 20th August 2016, Ahly SC made a farewell party to thank Martin and to celebrate the premier league achievement. Jol said that Al-Ahly the Egyptian team, is probably the biggest club in the world as they've got 17 million fans. Since leaving Cairo, the 64-year-old hasn't had a managerial role at any of his new clubs as he was appointed as an advisor and technical director at SW Scheveningen and Eredivisie side ADO Den Haag respectively.

JONES Stanley 'Stan'
Centre half 6'1"
Born *16/11/1938 Highley, Shropshire*
Playing career: *Walsall, West Bromwich Albion (Cost £7,000 267 appearances 3 goals May 1960 – March 1968), Walsall, Burton Albion, Kidderminster Harriers (player/manager), Hednesford Town (1957-1976).*
A colossus of a centre half who started his career at local neighbours Walsall. Stanley Jones joined the Albion in 1960 for a fee of £7,000 having spent 5 years at the Saddlers. That same day Albion made a double signing from Fellows Park because Peter Billingham another centre half joined as well. Stan was strong in the air, hard in the tackle and a player who hardly ever made a mistake. The only blemish being he scored 3 own goals over a period of 5 consecutive matches. Stan was an intelligent footballer who played 267 times for the Albion scoring just 3 times. He made his debut in 1960 against Birmingham City away. Stan was injured for the 1966 League Cup Final but the following year Jimmy Hagan dropped him for the final against QPR. In March 1968 Stan re-joined Walsall on a free transfer and spent another 5 years there before playing non-league for Burton, Kidderminster and a few other local clubs. Stan then spent seven years between 1980 and 1987 as a Trainer at Walsall followed by two years in at Burton Albion. Stan played many years for the Albion All Stars and could always be relied upon to pull on the No 5 shirt again. A great communicator whose views on the game of football are well worth a listen. Upon his retirement Stan involved himself in many aspects of the buildiong industry but his main interest was still sport and he ran a sports equipment business until his retirement. Stan still resides in Walsall with his wife Cherry and can be seen at many a home match and a regular supporter of the Old Baggies Former Players' Association.

JORDAO Adelino José Martins Batista
Midfielder 6'2"
Born *30/8/1971 Malanje, Angola*
Playing career: *Estrela Amadora in Portugal, Campomaiorense in Portugal (loan), Leca in Portugal (loan), Benfica, Braga, West Bromwich Albion (Cost £350,000 52 + 19 sub appearances 8 goals Aug 2000 – June 2003), Estrela Amadora (1990 – 2007) 1 appearance for Portugal U-21's*

His full name was Adelino José Martins Batista yet he was always known as 'Jordao'. He made his professional debut in 1990 for Lisbon-based C.F. Estrela da Amadora, but it took several years for him to become an important first-team member, also being loaned twice, to S.C. Campomaiorense and Leça FC, both in the second division. After two solid seasons at Estrela, Jordao joined Primeira Liga club S.L. Benfica, but was soon deemed surplus to requirements following the arrival of Graeme Souness as manager, and moved to fellow league team S.C. Braga in January 1998, where he would spend an additional two campaigns. In August 2000, having already played one league match for Braga, Jordao joined English side West Bromwich Albion for a transfer fee of £350,000, and made his debut in the same month against Barnsley. In 2001/02, he scored one of his five league goals in the Black Country derby win against Wolverhampton Wanderers at Molineux Stadium, helping Albion to achieve automatic promotion to the Premier League. After 71 appearances across all competitions, only three in the top flight, and eight goals for WBA, Jordao was released in the summer of 2003, re-joining Estrela da Amadora in January of the following year and playing sparingly making 38 league appearances in 3 years until his retirement three years later in 2007.

Personal note: *My youngest Son Matthew, then aged 14, was chosen to be Albion's mascot for the big local derby on December 2nd 2001, Wolverhampton Wanderers v West Bromwich Albion. I went into the ground with him and we were allowed to enter the Albion dressing room, with the music pounding from a ghetto blaster. I chatted briefly with manager Gary Megson about the nasty injury to Michael Appleton, but he would not talk about anything 'negative', and was just focussed on the game. Matthew was introduced to the Wolves players too, but I refused to go into their dressing room. As Matthew led the Albion team out onto the pitch, he looked like a new signing, as he was almost as tall as Derek McInnes. I was so proud prior to kick off. We were sat right behind Jordao as he hit the ball hard and true, almost lobbing it into the Wolves net to score the only goal of the game. He was an instant hero with all Albion fans, from that point.*

KAYE John

Centre back/striker 5'10"
Born *3/3/1940 Goole, England*

Playing career: *Goole Town, Scunthorpe United, West Bromwich Albion (Cost £44,750 May 358+3 sub appearances 54 goals 1963 – Nov 1971), Hull City (1960-1973).He played for the Football League and was a member of the original 40 players named for the 1966 World Cup Finals but was left out of the final squad. Kaye was voted Midlands Footballer of the Year in 1966 and 1970.*

John Kaye

Nicknamed 'Yorky'. John Kaye signed for Albion from Scunthorpe United in May 1963, following the departure of Derek Kevan, snapped up by new manager Jimmy Hagan, for the princely sum of £44,750, making his debut against Leicester City at The Hawthorns in August of that year. In those days John was a prolific goal scoring centre forward, and would soon team up with Jeff Astle and compete later with Ray Crawford. He was in the League Cup winning side of 1966, and was called up to Alf Ramsey's original 1966 World Cup squad of 40 players but did not make the final squad. He was in Albion's losing League Cup Final teams at Wembley in 1967 and 1970. In 1968, 'Yorky' heeded the call of then manager Alan Ashman, and successfully converted to a dominant, highly efficient and resourceful wing-half or centre back, becoming a member of the history making Albion side that lifted the cup at Wembley that year where injury forced him off for the extra time period, being replaced by Dennis Clarke. In all John amassed 361 appearances for Albion scoring 54 goals for the club. He was voted Midland Footballer of the Year. In 1971, He was transferred to Hull City for £28,000 in November 1971 as a player then coach and later manager between Aug 1974 -1977. He was assistant manager at Scunthorpe United Oct 1977 – Feb 1981. Later he managed Goole Town 1982 and Brigg Town. John went into the Hotel Business, later living in Hull he became a welder, working on gas rigs both onshore and offshore. He was also was a welder at Immingham Power station. 'Yorky' is now happily retired and living in

Kirkella, in Hull with wife Angela. In 2020 he was part of a group of present and former players who sent messages or made phone calls to senior season ticket holders during the Corona Virus pandemic.

KENNEDY Joseph 'Joe'

Centre Half/full back 6'0"
Born 15/11/ 1925 Cleator Moor, Near Whitehaven
Died 17/9/1986 West Bromwich
Playing career: *Altrincham, West Bromwich Albion (Cost £750 397 appearances 4 goals Dec 1948 – June 1961), Chester-City. (1948-1961). Player/manager Stourbridge, Brochkhouse Works (1946 -1966) Played for the England 'B' team and the FA XI.*

Former Albion player Arthur Gale, wrote to the Albion and recommended that they sign Joe, which they duly did in December 1948 for £750 from Altrrincham. Joe began his playing career as an inside-right, then had a good spell at right half but thereafter performed brilliantly as a centre half, being steady, reliable, consistent, superb in the air, sure and sound on the ground. A wonderful player, one of Albion's best post war pivots certainly since Jack Vernon. Raven haired Joe seemed destined for International honours with England after being seemingly a permanent reserve during the early 50's but injury forced him out of the reckoning at crucial times and the only representative calls he received were to skipper England 'B' on three occasions and play for the FA XI. Joe was drafted in at right-back to replace injured Stan Rickaby in the 1954 FA Cup win over Preston North End at Wembley in 1954. Joe had been out of the team himself, injured from January when Jimmy Dugdale took his place a number 5. He played 364 league games for Albion scoring 3 goals. He joined Chester on a free transfer in June 1961. He made 35 appearances but also played during the season in two league games against Accrington Stanley that were deleted from the records when Accrington resigned from the Football League during the season, leaving him on a total of 399 league appearances instead of 401. Kennedy joined Stourbridge as player-manager in August 1962 and later turned out for his works team, Brockhouse Works F.C. He retired from playing in 1966 at the age of 40. He continued to work at Brockhouse until the age of 60, when he collapsed and died there in September 1986.

KENT Kevin

Midfielder 5'11"

Born *19/3/1985 Stoke-on-Trent*

Playing career: *West Bromwich Albion (1+1 sub appearances July 1983 – June 1984), Newport County, Mansfield Town, Port Vale. (1983-1996).*

Starting his career as a winger at West Bromwich Albion in 1983 making just 1 start and 1 substitute appearance. He moved to regular football with Newport County the following year on a free transfer. Kevin played 33 games scoring 1 goal. He then made his name playing for Mansfield Town after a free transfer, helping the 'Stags' win promotion out of the Fourth Division in 1985/86. Over a six-year period from 1985 to 1991 he appeared in 229 league games scoring 37 goals. He then transferred to Port Vale, where he finished his career following a five-year spell, playing 115 league games scoring 7 goals. Over a thirteen-year professional career he played 454 games in all competitions, scoring 57. He won the Football League Trophy both with Mansfield in 1987 and with Port Vale in 1993. He was in the Vale Play Off Final team of 1992/93.

Kevin Kent

West Bromwich Albion won 3-0! Despite the dsappointment, he then helped the "Valiants" to win promotion out of the Second Division in 1993/94. Kevin joined Vale's back room staff at the club's Centre of Excellence from 1993 to 1996 and again 2004 to 2006. From 2005 to 2007 he worked at Stoke City's academy. He had a short coaching stint at Manchester United after obtaining his UEFA A Licence Between 2009 and 2011 he worked as the Indonesian Football Association's National Academy Director. He also worked as a manager at Barclays Bank Sports Facilities and Events department between 1997 and 2009 and a match summariser for BBC Radio Stoke.

In his own words: *"I have been a Sports Manager for Barclays Bank staff using my sports management degree. I have done football coaching at Stoke City FC and Manchester United FC. Currently working as a part-time coach for my son in grass roots football. He is training at Stoke City FC and Manchester City FC. I work full time in renewable energy for Project Better Energy as a divisional manager. I coach rugby as well at Knutsford Rugby Club. I live in Knutsford, Cheshire."*

KEVAN Derek

Centre forward/striker 6'0"

Born *6/3/1935 Ripon, West Riding of Yorkshire*
Died *4/1/2013 Birmingham*
Playing career: *Bradford Park Avenue, West Bromwich Albion (Cost £3,000 291 appearances 173 goals July 1953 – March 1963), Chelsea, Manchester City, Crystal Palace, Peterborough, Luton Town, Stockport County, Macclesfield Town, Boston United, Stourbridge. (1952-1975). 14 Full England caps; which included taking part in the 1958 World Cup Finals.*

Derek started his career in his native Yorkshire with Bradford Park Avenue. Kevan was the first signing made by Vic Buckingham after he had taken over from Jesse Carver as manager of West Bromwich Albion in February 1953. Signed for £3,000, Kevan completed his National Service in the Army before establishing himself full-time at the Hawthorns. Tall, muscular and afraid of no one. Coached by the club's former striker W.G. Richardson, Kevan had to wait until August 1955 to make his West Bromwich Albion League debut, a 2–0 home win over Everton in which he scored twice after being selected in place of the injured Ronnie Allen.

He became a regular in the first team during the 1956/57 season, and his committed and powerful style of play, big heart, heaps of stamina a lust for goals, earned him the nickname "The Tank" . Kevan scored 20 goals in the 1956/57 season, which included a run to the FA Cup semi-finals where Albion lost to Aston Villa. He scored 80 goals over the next three seasons – 23 in 1957/58, 28 in 1958/59 and 29 in 1959/60, including five in a 6–2 home League win over Everton. He added 18 in 1960/61 and then claimed 33 League goals the following season, when he finished joint top scorer in the First Division with Ipswich Town's Ray Crawford. In March 1963, after scoring 16 goals in 28 appearances that season, including four against Fulham, Kevan was transferred to Chelsea for £50,000. In a decade at Albion, he had scored 173 goals in 291 games. Derek had developed into one of the greatest strikers the club has ever seen. His spell at Stamford Bridge under Tommy Docherty was short and unsuccessful, and in the close season of the same year he moved to Second Division Manchester City for £35,000. Kevan finished the season as the club's leading goalscorer with 36 goals, 30 of them in the league. On 29th July 1965 he moved to Crystal Palace. making 21 League appearances and scoring five goals before moving to Peterborough United in March 1966, and then Luton Town. In March 1967, Kevan joined Stockport County, in an exchange deal involving Keith Allen. At Stockport, Kevan gained the first medal of his career, the Fourth Division title in 1967.

He was the landlord of the Moss Rose pub, adjacent to Macclesfield Town's ground. He also worked as a delivery driver before returning to the Hawthorns in 1983 to work as a lottery agent as well as playing for the Albion All Stars charity team, which he later managed. Derek worked for ASG Sign Company in Leamington Spa. Later he delivered ceramic tiles as a van driver.

Personal note: *I was at the Hawthorns as a young boy on 19th March 1960 when Albion played Everton. Trailing 2-1 at half time, the second half was explosive with Derek, who already had scored one in the first half, went on to score 4 more. One was really remarkable as the ball was lofted forward, he headed the ball down, ran about 20 yards before smashing it from outside the penalty area into the roof of the net. What a goal! Derek lived in an Albion club house in Hugh Road, Smethwick in the late 1950's and early 60's. On a Saturday night after a home game, I often saw Derek in my local newsagent's shop, Denning's in Devonshire Road, Smethwick queueing up for the delivery of the pink Sports Argus, to read about the game in which he had just played. I was starstruck just standing next to him. The newspapers were printed in Birmingham and rushed out in vans to be delivered to the various newsagents. The driver would throw down a bundle of papers tied up with string, outside the shop, at around 6.30pm. I was asked to record a short clip for the Albion History DVD called 'Full Throstle' and on the day I went to the East Stand to do the recording, Derek Kevan was there too. We spent about 10 minutes together just talking about the old days at the Hawthorns. A wonderful man.*

KING Andy
Midfielder 5'9"

Born 14/8/1956 Luton, Bedfordshire
Died 27/5/2015 Luton, Bedfordshire aged 58
Playing career: Luton Town, Everton, QPR, West Bromwich Albion (Cost £400,000 33+5 sub appearances 6 goals Sept 1981 – July 1982), Everton, SC Cambuur Leeuwarden in Holland, Orebro SK in Sweden, Wolverhampton Wanderers, Luton Town, Aldershot, Aylesbury, Waterford player/manager (Jan 1989) England U-21 International

He started at Luton Town, turning professional in July 1974, making 33 league appearances. He left to join Everton in April 1976 for a fee of £35,000 and became a crowd favourite with his tremendous skills in midfield and a knack for scoring goals.

He played 151 league games for the Toffees scoring 38 goals. He joined Queens Park Rangers in September 1980 for a £425,000 fee. In one season he scored 9 goals in 30 league games before he was transferred to West Bromwich Albion in September 1981 for £400,000. He played in both the League Cup and FA Cup Semi Finals which Albion lost. He was an attacking midfielder, occasionally asked to take on a strikers' role. After only one season and 25 league appearances, he moved back to Everton in July 1982 in a £250,000 deal involving a swap for Peter Eastoe. He stayed for two seasons, subsequently playing for Dutch side Cambuur Leeuwarden then Swedish team Örebro SK, before joining Wolverhampton Wanderers in January 1985. He returned to Luton Town in December the same year, but made just three league appearances before moving to Aldershot in August 1986. He retired from the professional game at the end of the following season in May 1987, playing non-league football with Aylesbury United and a trip to Ireland to play for Waterford United as player/coach & Cobh Ramblers, KePS in Finland and Southport. In August 1993 he was appointed manager of Mansfield Town. Andy left in 1996. He worked as a coach and scout, scouting for Sunderland. He joined Swindon Town in 2000 as assistant manager to Colin Todd, taking over as manager when Todd left for Derby in November. Andy was replaced by Roy Evans in June 2001 but re-appointed Swindon Town manager in December 2001, under new owners. He was eventually dismissed by Swindon in September 2005. He worked as a scout before being appointed manager of Conference National side Grays Athletic in November 2006, surprisingly resigning for personal reasons in Jan 2007. King was scout for Everton, then was Chief Scout at Plymouth Argyle. Later he became Head Scout at Colchester United in 2010. In November 2011 Andy was appointed as Assistant Manager to Aidy Boothroyd at Northampton Town. He became Caretaker-manager for a short while after Boothroyd's dismissal. Andy moved to Scouting for MK Dons in Feb 2014. Sadly, King died at his home on 27 May 2015 following a heart attack aged 58. He had previously suffered a heart attack in 2009.

KRZYWICKI Ryzsard 'Dick'

Right winger/forward 5'10"

Born *2/2/1947 Penly, Flint, North Wales*
Playing career: *West Bromwich Albion (60+11 sub appearances 12 goals Feb 1965 – Mar 1970), Huddersfield Town, Scunthorpe United (loan) Northampton Town, Lincoln City. (1964-1976) Welsh International at U-23 and Full level 8 caps.*

Dick was a speed merchant, exceptionally fast over 20-25 yards, but could not command a regular first team place at the Hawthorns. He was the first West Bromwich Albion substitute to enter the field in a League Cup match when he replaced Doug Fraser against Manchester City in October 1966. He went on to score a goal as Albion progressed winning 4–2. Krzywicki became the first Albion player to be substituted in an FA Cup game when he made way for Graham Lovett against Colchester United in January 1968. He was a member of the 1968 FA Cup winning squad but was not selected for the Final. He was a substitute in the 1970 League Cup Final, replacing Asa Hartford, losing 2-1 against Manchester City. He made 57 league appearances for Albion scoring 9 goals between 1964 and 1970.

He was transferred to Huddersfield Town for £45,000 in March 1970 where he played 47 games scoring 7 goals before leaving, after loan spells at Scunthorpe United, and Northampton Town, in July 1974. He made 68 league appearances for Lincoln City between 1974-76. He worked in the engineering industry in Batley, Yorkshire before joining Huddersfield Community Scheme then became one of three regional directors for the Football in the Community Scheme. He ran Moorlands Youth Club in Dewsbury.

LANGE Anthony 'Tony'

Goalkeeper 6"0"

Born *10/12/1964 West Ham, London*
Playing career: *Charlton Athletic, Aldershot (loan then signed), Wolverhampton Wanderers, Aldershot (loan), Torquay United (loan), Portsmouth (loan), West Bromwich Albion (Free 56+3 sub appearances 1992 – 1995), Fulham. (1983-1997).*

Lange signed for Charlton Athletic, turning professional in 1983, playing just 12 league games. He later played for Aldershot after a short loan spell, appearing in 132 league matches.

Peter Latchford

124

He was the 'Shots' Player of the Year in both the 1986/87 and 1987/88 seasons. He also won promotion to the Third Division with the club in the 1986/87 season. Lange was transferred to Wolverhampton Wanderers £150,000 and stayed there between 1988 – 1992 only making 8 league starts. He had loan spells at Aldershot, Torquay United and Portsmouth before moving to Black Country rivals West Bromwich Albion on a free transfer in August 1992. Albion won promotion via the Play-Offs in the 1992/93 season, with Lange appearing in the Final at Wembley, having replaced Stuart Naylor. Whilst at the club, he was nicknamed 'Freddie' due to his appearance being similar to Freddie Mercury and played 48 games. He moved to Fulham for £5,000 in 1995. Lange was a member of the Fulham team which were runners-up in Division Three in the 1996/97 season. He finished his playing career at St. Leonards Stamcroft. Lange worked as a landscape gardener and for Southern Railway .and then became a revenue protection officer for Southern Railways. Tony has remained in the South and currently lives in Orpington, Kent.

LATCHFORD Peter
Goalkeeper 6'0"
Born *27/9/1952 Kings Heath, Birmingham*
Playing career: *Redditch Town, Sutton Coldfield Town, West Bromwich Albion (104 appearances 1969 – 1975), Celtic (loan then signed), Clyde (1969 -1989). Played for England at U-23 level.*
Peter Latchford started his career at West Bromwich Albion. By early 1975 Latchford had played over 80 league games, however at this time he was dropped from the first-team and was playing with the youth side. Having expressed his frustration at lack of first-team football to manager Don Howe, a loan deal with Celtic was arranged and Latchford made his debut for The Bhoys on 22 February 1975 in a 2–1 league defeat against Hibernian at Easter Road. Latchford played 13 more league and Scottish Cup games that season for Celtic, culminating in his first winner's medal as Celtic defeated Airdrie 3–1 in the 1975 Scottish Cup Final. Latchford had impressed sufficiently at Celtic for the loan deal to be made permanent, and in July 1975 Celtic paid a transfer fee of £25,000 to West Bromwich Albion.

He made over 270 appearances for Celtic in the late 1970s and early 1980s, winning 2 League Championships and 3 Scottish Cups. These successes included a league and cup double in 1976/77, the 4–2 win over Rangers in the famous '10 men win the league' game in 1979 and the infamous 1980 Cup Final riot (Celtic beat Rangers 1–0 after Extra Time) the following season. Latchford's most memorable European game though was on 5th March 1980 when Celtic played Real Madrid at Parkhead in the first leg of a European cup quarter-final tie. His saves from England striker Laurie Cunningham and Spanish star Santillana helped Celtic to a 2–0 win on the night, although Celtic lost the return leg in Spain 0–3 to go out on aggregate. Latchford sustained a hand injury in the summer of 1980 and lost his place in the team to Pat Bonner. From then on Latchford featured rarely for Celtic, but he remained loyal to the club – to the probable detriment of his career. He did, however, get a brief run of first-team action during early 1986 when Bonner was out injured. He finally left in Celtic in the summer of 1987 after having made 272 competitive appearances for the club. Latchford joined Clyde on a one-year deal, where after a season he finally retired. He is now a goalkeeping coach and has worked in this capacity for Forfar Athletic, Clyde, Hearts and Motherwell. For a few years he combined goalkeeping coach duties at Dumfries club Queen of the South with coaching the youth goalkeepers at Celtic. Latchford's spell at Queens included the 2007/08 season run to the final of the Scottish Cup, where they lost narrowly (3–2) to Rangers. Peter had two footballing brothers Dave and Bob. He lived on a farm in Mauchline, has worked on Celtic TV.

LEE George
Left winger 5'9"
Born *4/6/1919 York*
Died *1/4/1991 Norwich*
Playing career: *York City, Nottingham Forest, West Bromwich Albion (Cost £12,000 295 appearances 65 goals July 1949 – June 1958), Lockheed Leamington, Vauxhall Motors. Guested for Bradford Park Avenue, Lincoln City and Chester City (1937 – 1958)*
Starting his career at York City in 1936, like so many players of his era, WW2 interrupted his footballing life.

His career at York City blossomed during the war when he was York's leading scorer for four consecutive seasons. In April 1943 Lee became the first player to score 100 goals for York City. He guested for various clubs and appeared for B.A.O.R. - British Army on the Rhine, in European Championships in 1946. He played a total of 37 league game for York City before moving to Nottingham Forest in August 1947 for £7,500. He made 78 league appearances for Forest scoring 20 goals. Nicknamed 'Ada', he was a wholehearted left winger who varied his game and style judiciously. Strongly built, he had powerful legs, a useful turn of speed and a cracking left foot shot. He arrived at Albion, for £12,000 in July 1949 when the number 11 shirt was a problem position. He filled that position for seven seasons. Injuries cropped up occasionally but generally George was the guy lined up at number 11. He made 295 appearances in all competitions scoring 65 goals. He gained an FA Cup winners' medal in 1954 laying on the first goal for Ronnie Allen to score. Lee joined non-league Lockheed Leamington on a free transfer in June 1958, before a short period at Vauxhall Motors. After retiring as a player, Lee returned to West Bromwich Albion as a coach/trainer in 1959. He became a coach at Norwich City in 1963, later as assistant trainer to the reserve side, serving the East Anglia club for 25 years.

LILWALL Steve

Left back 5'10"

Born *15/2/1970 Solihull, Birmingham*
Playing career: *Moor Green, Kidderminster Harriers, West Bromwich Albion (Cost £70,000 84 +2 sub appearances Aug .1992 – 1995), Rushden & Diamonds, Kidderminster Harriers, Moor Green*

Lilwall was born in Solihull. His uncle, Denis Thwaites, and his wife Elaine, plus another 36 tourists, were shot dead by an 'extremist' whilst on holiday in Sousse, Tunisia, in June 2015. Dennis was a former Birmingham City forward in the 1960s. Lilwall joined Moor Green during the 1985/86 season. In 1987, he moved on to Kidderminster Harriers. Steve made his Conference debut in the 1989/90 season, and became a first-team regular during the following campaign. He helped Kidderminster reach the final of the 1990/91 FA Trophy, which Kidderminster lost 2–1. Lilwall remained with Kidderminster for a

further season, taking his Conference appearance total to 65, and then became Osvaldo Ardiles' first signing as manager of third-tier club, West Bromwich Albion, for a fee of around £70,000. A bandy legged but enthusiastic left back, became a crowd favourite especially after stories of his having a tortoise that kept escaping. He went straight into the Albion first team, and by September 1992 Premier League club Liverpool were reported to be "monitoring his progress". He was ever-present during his first season, and was a member of the team that gained promotion to the First Division via the play-offs, beating Port Vale 3–0 in the final after Vale had a man sent off. Keith Burkinshaw was replaced by Alan Buckley and Lilwall fell victim to a succession of injuries, he drifted out of first-team consideration. He left Albion at the end of the 1994/95 season, having made 86 appearances in all competitions, and signed for Rushden & Diamonds of the Southern League. Injury also disrupted his time with Rushden & Diamonds. He contributed only seven Southern League games as his team won the 1995/96 Southern League title, and the following season played just four times in the 1996/97 Conference. In 1997, he re-joined Kidderminster Harriers, but appeared only infrequently for the first team, and ended his senior career back at Moor Green. Steve ended his career in 2000, largely due to persistent hip injuries, which resulted in a couple operations. Ljilwall took a degree in Physical Education and Social Psychology at Coventry University, and also earned a His studies helped him to a BA/BSc and he also gained UEFA Coaching awards, Sports Coacching certificates and a diploma in Sports Psychology. He passed his teacher qualifications in 2015, and taught physical education at Ninestiles School in Acocks Green, Birmingham. Steve was also running 'Soccer Start Coaching Academy' in the Solihull area.

LOVATT John 'Jack'

Centre forward 6'2"
Born *23/8/1941 Burton-on-Trent, Staffs*
Playing career: *West Bromwich Albion (18 appearances 5 goals Jan 1958-Nov 1963), Nuneaton Borough, Worcester City, Banbury Spencer (1958 – 1968)*

Steve Lilwall

Known as Jack but Nicknamed 'Shack', he was a tall, lanky striker who had good skills, a fair bit of energy and will-power but lacked that extra bit of snap and pace. John Lovatt had Derek Kevan and Keith Smith ahead of him, thus he only played 18 first team games scoring 5 goals. "Shack" joined the Albion as an amateur in January 1956 signing professional forms two years later in December 1958. He made his debut versus West Ham away in March 1961, scoring in a 2-1 win. John left the Hawthorns in November 1963 when he signed on a free transfer for Nuneaton Borough, 3 years later he joined Worcester City followed by Banbury Spencer before retiring in May 1968. He was a businessman in Willenhall. John is a regular supporter at the Old Baggies Former Players' Association and its functions including any Golf days. John has not moved far from his place of birth, he was residing in Swadlincote with his wife Sue.

LOVETT Graham

Wing half 5'10"
Born *5/8/1947 Sheldon, Birmingham*
Died *10/5/2018 England*
Playing career: *West Bromwich Albion (141+15 sub appearances 9 goals Nov 1964 – June 1972), Southampton (loan), Worcester City, Solihull Borough, Greaves FC. (1964-1976).*

Lovett signed as a professional in November 1964 and made his first team debut within three weeks as Albion lost 2–0 at home to Chelsea. He had a nickname 'Shuv' as he owned an 8-year old car that cost him £150 and kept breaking down and regularly needed a 'shove'. Lovett soon established himself in the first team and in March 1966 played in the first leg of the League Cup Final against West Ham United. Although Albion lost 2–1, they won the second leg, with Lovett replaced by Bobby Hope, 4–1 to take the cup on aggregate. Lovett, with his great strength and ability to pass the ball long or short, was becoming an important part of Albion's plans, but his career was interrupted when, on Christmas Eve 1966, his car suffered a tyre 'blow out' on the M1 motorway and ran off the road into a ditch. Lovett suffered a broken neck but an operation involving bone grafts enabled him to start to rebuild his football career. By the end of 1967, he was back in training and returned to the first team in January 1968.

Graham Lovett

On 27th January, he became the first Albion player to come on as a substitute in an FA Cup match when he replaced Dick Krzywicki at Colchester United. Lovett's return to the side added a new precision to the team who went on to defeat Colchester United 4–0 in the replay, in which Lovett made his first start in just over a year. In the fourth round of the FA Cup, Albion met Southampton who held them to a 1–1 draw at The Hawthorns. In the replay at The Dell, goalkeeper John Osborne had to be taken by ambulance to the local hospital at half-time with concussion. Captain Graham Williams went in goal, which left a space for Lovett to come on as substitute. Hugh Fisher then scored for the "Saints" to bring the scores level at 2–2 before, with two minutes remaining, Lovett ran through the midfield unchecked. His shot hit the post and rebounded to Clive Clark who passed to the unmarked Jeff Astle to score and put Albion through to the next round. After defeating another south coast club, Portsmouth in Round Five, Albion had a long, drawn-out tie against Liverpool, which went to a second replay, before defeating local rivals Birmingham City in the Semi-Final to set up a final at Wembley against Everton. In the final on 18th May 1968, Lovett was selected at outside right and had an early opportunity to score but was just sa little bit too slow to make the most of his chance. There was no score until the ever reliable Astle scored the only goal of the match in the first half of extra time, enabling Albion to win the cup. By the end of the 1968–69 season, Lovett had become an established fixture in the Albion side. On 31st May 1969, following an international tournament in Palo Alto, California, Lovett was driving home from the airport when a bus, which had rounded a corner on the wrong side of the road in Quinton, collided with his car. In the accident, Lovett broke his thighbone, suffered a collapsed lung and broken ribs. As a result of the accident, Lovett was out of action for nearly two years and was never able to successfully return to first-team football. Over two years later, in an attempt to rebuild his career, West Bromwich Albion loaned him to Southampton for a month in November 1971 with a view to a possible permanent transfer.

Lovett made three appearances but the trial was not considered a success by the Southampton management and he returned to West Bromwich Albion. Lovett was released from his contract in 1972 and played non-league football for Worcester City and Solihull Borough before retiring completely at the early age of 26. In 1973, in Birmingham Crown Court, he was awarded £14,000 damages against the West Midlands Transport Executive. On leaving football, he worked in advertising for the Express & Star newspaper in the West Midlands before emigrating to southern Spain. He later settled in Thailand. In March 2008, he flew to England to join in the celebrations of the 40th anniversary of the FA Cup victory. In 2017 he settled back in England with his wife Kate whom he married in 2016. Kate & Graham first met over 30 years ago but re-kindled the love affair in the middle of 2015. Graham died in 2018 after a short illness age 70.

In his own words: *After he was compared as a youngster by his manager, Jimmy Hagan, to Duncan Edwards, the Manchester United and England player who had died in the Munich air disaster in 1958 and ex-Albion stalwart Ray Barlow, Graham responded "It's great to be in the first team and playing with the big names against the big names, but there is a nagging feeling which makes me wonder whether you deserve the praise, and whether it's going to last. And I am really lost when they start talking about Duncan Edwards or Ray Barlow, neither of whom I ever saw play. But once the game starts, it's all different. The stars often seem quite ordinary when it's under way. I never have time to worry about the reputations of the opposition."*

Personal note: *Graham was a terrific footballer when fully fit. He broke into the Albion side aged 18 and looked every bit a man. He had close control, could run powerfully with the ball, had great vision and was strong in the tackle as well as in the air, with a powerful shot. After his first car accident, he managed to get fit again, appearing in the FA Cup Final of 1968 and in 1968/69 he seemed to be playing as well as ever, although his movement was slightly restricted. Then came that horrific second crash with a bus in Quinton. He never fully gained full mobility after that. In my opinion he could have become Albion's greatest ever player.*

Steve Lynex

LYNEX Steven 'Steve'

Right winger/midfielder 5'9"
Born *23/1/1958 West Bromwich*
Playing career: *West Bromwich Albion (Jan – May 1977), Shamrock Rovers, Birmingham City, Leicester City, Birmingham City (loan), West Bromwich Albion (Cost £5,000 28+5 sub appearances 5 goals Mar 1987 – June 1988), Cardiff City, Telford United (1977-1991).*
Lynex joined West Bromwich Albion in 1974 as an apprentice. In 1976, he was captain of the Albion side that won the FA Youth Cup, and in January 1977 manager Johnny Giles gave him his first professional contract. In July of the same year, without having appeared for Albion's first team, Lynex tried his luck in Ireland. After a trial with Sligo Rovers, he followed Giles to Shamrock Rovers on a free transfer. He left Rovers in December 1978. and after a trial at Queens Park Rangers he joined Birmingham City in April 1979. After three years with Birmingham playing 46 league games scoring 10 goals, Lynex moved to Leicester City for £60,000, where he is remembered for his prolific scoring for a winger as well as for creating chances for Gary Lineker and Alan Smith.

He reached double figures of goals scored in three of his five full seasons at the club. He also occasionally appeared as a stand-in goalkeeper, in the days when the League only allowed one substitute to be selected. He made 213 league appearances for the Foxes and scored 57 goals. After a loan spell at one former club Birmingham City, he went to re-join another, West Bromwich Albion, for £5,000, appearing in 33 games, scoring 5 goals in all competitions. He moved to Cardiff City on a free transfer in July 1988 scoring twice in 62 league games. He played his last Football League game in 1990 and then moved into non-league football with Telford United and Trafford Park. He turned out for Mitchells & Butlers football team and later ran the Red Lion pub in West Bromwich which sadly hit the headlines in 1994, due to a fatal bonfire night accident and later, the Hunting Tree pub in Hasbury, Halesowen.

LYTTLE Des

Full back/defender 5'9"
Born *24/9/1971 Wolverhampton, Staffs*
Playing career: *Leicester City, Worcester City, Swansea City, Nottingham Forest, Port Vale (loan), Watford, West Bromwich Albion (loan then signed 73 + 16 sub appearances 1 goal Mar 2000 – May 2003), Stourport Swifts, Northampton Town, Forest Green Rovers, Worcester City, Tamworth. (1990 – 2011)*
He started his career with Leicester City, but never made a league appearance and dropped into non-League football with Worcester City in 1991. A good season earned him a move to Welsh side Swansea City, and after 46 league appearances he moved to Nottingham Forest in 1993. After six years and 185 league appearances with the club, including a spell in the Premier League, he signed with Watford. After only playing 11 league games in season 1999/2000, he was loaned to West Bromwich Albion in March 2000 and signed permanently in June. After helping Albion reach the Premier League for the first time in 2001/02 appearing in 23 league games, 10 as a substitute. Sometimes used as a wing back, he preferred the right back position. He only appeared 3 times as a substitute in the Premier League in 2002/03, as Albion were relegated. After making 89 appearances, 16 as a substitute, scoring one goal, at the end of the season he joined Northampton Town.

A year later he left the Football League for the second and final time, signing with Forest Green Rovers. He was transferred to Worcester City in 2005, before joining Tamworth in 2007. In 2010, he was appointed caretaker manager at Tamworth, before being made player-manager on a full-time basis. He resigned the following year, claiming he was being undermined by the club's directors. He was appointed manager of Hucknall Town in October 2011, before departing seven months later. He later had a spell as first team coach at York City. Des Lyttle was head football coach at Thomas Telford School academy in 2014 in Shropshire, now in 2017 director of football.

MacKENZIE Steve

Midfielder 5'10"

Born *23/11/1961 Romford, Essex*

Playing career: *Crystal Palace, Manchester City, West Bromwich Albion (Cost £650,000 179+5 sub appearances 25 goals July 1981 – June 1987), Charlton Athletic, Sheffield Wednesday, Shrewsbury Town, Willenhall Town. (1979-1994) England Youth, U-21 & 'B' International*

He began his career at Crystal Palace but before playing a senior league or cup game, Malcolm Allison signed him for £250,000.

He had been a key member of the Palace Youth Cup teams of 1977 and 1978. At Manchester City, he played 58 league games scoring 8 goals. He moved to Albion in July 1981, shortly after scoring a spectacular goal in the 1981 FA Cup Final for City against Spurs. The fee was £650,000 and it proved to be money well spent despite having to miss out on virtually all of the 1982/83 season because of a serious pelvic injury. He played 156 league games scoring 23 goals for Albion between 1981-87. Steve was a popular player, energetic and could pick a good forward pass. He moved on to Charlton Athletic in June 1987 for £200,000, playing 100 league games scoring 7 goals. He had further spells at Sheffield Wednesday 1990-92, Shrewsbury Town 1992-94 before moving to non-league football with Willenhall Town and Gresley Rovers. Had a spell managing Atherstone United 2000-2002. He is the cousin of former Arsenal & England captain, Tony Adams. In recent years, Steve has run his own web design company, coached at West Brom's Academy and provided statistics for PA Sport. Unfortunately, he suffered a stroke in 2017 whilst working on an IT project at a University in Leicester.

Des Lytttle and son

Paul Mardon

MacLAREN Stewart
Right back/ central defender 5'10"
Born 6/4/1953 Larkhall, Scotland
Playing career: West Bromwich Albion (1969 – 1974), Motherwell, Dundee, Heart of Midlothian
When only sixteen years old, Stewart signed for top ranking English side West Bromwich Albion in 1969. Despite doing well in the youth and reserve sides, which he captained he never made the breakthrough in the senior squad, with Ally Robertson and John Wile ahead of him. He moved back to Scotland and signed for Motherwell making 123 league appearances scoring 5 goals between 1974 - 1978. His nicknames included 'Chopper'and 'Gonzo'. He was transferred to Dundee for £30,000 where ex-Celtic star Tommy Gemmell was manager and made a further 80 appearances in the league scoring 7 goals between 1978-1981. Stewart's final move was to Heart of Midlothian where he played 67 league games between 1981–1985, A recurring pelvic injury allied to back problems eventually ended his career. He then pursued a career in the motor trade.

MADDEN Craig
Striker 5'8"
Born 23/9/1958 Manchester
Playing career: Bury, West Bromwich Albion (Cost £50,000 11+2 sub appearances 3 goals Mar 1986 – Feb 1987), Blackpool, Wrexham (loan), York City, Fleetwood Town. (1977-1991).
Madden began his professional career at Bury in 1977. He spent nine years at Gigg Lane, making almost 300 league appearances and scoring 129 goals. Had a short spell at West Bromwich Albion, who paid £50,000 in March 1988 when Garth Crooks was injured. He played in just 11 league games scoring 3 goals. A highly successful marksman with Bury, scoring a record 152 goals. Craig never struck the same lethal form during his brief association with Albion, although he was never really given a long enough run in the team. He joined Blackpool, in February 1987 for £50,000. In 1989/90 he had a loan spell at Wrexham, then a short period at York City before he moved to non-league Fleetwood Town, where he found his scoring touch again and continued to enjoy the game.
In April 1991 he became community officer at Blackpool.

Ran summer soccer schools for children in the holidays. He was youth team coach at Stockport County, taking a caretaker-manager role before reverting to coaching the youth team. In 2010 Madden was appointed assistant manager at Fleetwood Town along with Manager Micky Mellon. Recently he was academy coach at Burnley. He also took an apprenticeship focused on Plastering at Manchester College of Construction.

MARDON Paul
Midfielder 5'9"
Born 14/9/1969 Bristol
Playing career: Bristol City, Doncaster Rovers (loan), Birmingham City, West Bromwich Albion (Cost £450,000 140 plus 14 sub appearances Nov 1993 – Jan 2001), Oldham Athletic (loan), Plymouth Argyle (loan), Wrexham (loan). Retired through injury (1987-2001) 1 Welsh International cap
Paul started his footballing career with hometown club Bristol City, making 42 league appearances between 1987 – 1991 but did havea short loan spell at Doncaster Rovers in 1990. Mardon joined Birmingham City in 1991, making 64 league appearances scoring once. Good on the ball and powerful in the air, he was popular with Blues fans. He was rumoured to be on the verge of a trial with Liverpool but injury curtailed that. West Bromwich Albion signed him in November 1993 for £450,000. Paul was a tough tackling, strong and powerful centre back, a good header of the ball and careful with his distribution. Nicknamed "Mards", Paul was made Albion captain, appearing in 154 appearances including 14 as a substitute, scoring on 3 occasions. The Bristolian played the majority of games for the Baggies in a strong partnership alongside Paul Raven. In October 1995 he made his debut for Wales against Germany Unfortunately a knee ligament injury shortened his career and he retired in January 2001 having had loan spells at Oldham, Plymouth & Wrexham. After retiring from football, Paul was a Gym Manager for Virgin Active 2001-03. He then became Area sales manager for Pendragon Furniture. Later he was a sub-agent for Habufa Meubelen BV furniture wholesalers. Then Paul was Midlands agent for Mark Webster Designs 2008-15. He was owner of PJM Furniture Ltd. from 2008 & Sales Agent at Carlton & Vintage Furniture, Dorridge.

MARTIN Dennis

Midfielder/winger 5'11"

Born *27/10/1947 Edinburgh, Scotland.*

Playing career: *Kettering Town, West Bromwich Albion (Cost £5,000 20+5 sub appearances 2 goals July 1967 – June 1970) Carlisle United, Newcastle United, Mansfield Town, Fremadamager in Denmark, Kettering Town. (1967-1980)*

Signed by Albion in June 1967 for £5,000 from Kettering Town. Tall rangy winger who had to try and fill the boots of Albion legend Clive Clark, rather unsuccessfully. He only played 20 games plus 5 substitute appearances scoring 2 goals He played in the 1969 FA Cup Semi Final at Hillsborough when Leicester beat the Albion 1-0. In 1970 he moved to Carlisle United for £22,222 and in 7 years he played 275 league games scoring 48 goals. He went to Newcastle in October 1977 making 11 appearances in the league before moving to Mansfield Town in March 1978, playing 46 league games. He finally returned to his former club Kettering Town. He worked in the Insurance industry before moving to Spain in 2004.

MARTIN Mick

Midfielder 5'9"

Born *9/7/1951 Dublin, Ireland*

Playing career: *Bohemians, Manchester United, West Bromwich Albion (on loan then signed Cost £30,000 105+6 sub appearances 15 goals 1975 – 1978) Newcastle United, Vancouver Whitecaps, Willington, Cardiff City, Peterborough United, Rotherham United, Preston. (1968 - 1987). Republic of Ireland 51 caps.*

Nicknamed 'Zico'. Started at Bohemians in 1968. He spent a year learning his trade in the youth team and 'B' team before progressing to the first team. When Martin excelled in a league match against Shelbourne in January 1973, the watching Manchester United manager Tommy Docherty liked what he saw and within 48 hours, Martin was on his way to Old Trafford. He spent two years at United playing 40 league games, before Johnny Giles took him to West Bromwich Albion in October 1975 initially on loan, signing him for £30,000 in December. Mick was a versatile player appearing in midfield, full back or even the centre of defence.

Mick Martin

Joe Mayo

He was a classy player, who helped Albion gain promotion to Division One in 1976. He stayed at the Hawthorns for 3 years playing 89 league games. In December 1978 Martin moved to Newcastle United for £100,000 and spent five years at the club, making 147 league appearances and scoring five goals. He had spells at Vancouver Whitecaps, non-league Willington, Cardiff City, Peterborough United, Rotherham United and Preston North End. He coached both Newcastle and Celtic. Martin has lived in the Wickham area of Newcastle for over 20 years. He opened a bookmakers' shop in 1987 and a sports shop, 'Zico', soon after. Since 1993, he has worked as a summariser on Newcastle games for Metro FM and is currently building up his own promotional company, Mick Martin Sports Management. His father was Con Martin who played for Aston Villa & Republic of Ireland.

MAYO Joe

Centre forward/full back/centre half 6'1"
Born *25/5/1951 Tipton*
Playing career: *Walsall, West Bromwich Albion (Cost £17,000 84+6 sub appearances 20 goals Feb 1973 – Mar 1977), Leyton Orient, Cambridge United, Blackpool (loan), Happy Valley United in Hong Kong, Caernarfon Town (1972-1987).*
His football career at Dudley Town before joining Walsall in September 1972.

Joe signed for the Albion in February 1973 for £17,000. He made 90 appearances scoring 20 goals. Joe made his debut versus Hull in September 1973 coming on as a sub. Mayo played in various positions including left back, but he preferred the striker's role. The "Big Man" was part of the successful promotion side season 1975/76. Mayo left in March 1977 as part of the deal that brought Laurie Cunningham to the Hawthorns from Leyton Orient. Four years at Orient saw Joe appear in the 1978 FA Cup Semi Final, unfortunately that year both Albion & Orient lost at the same stage. A move to Cambridge for £100,000 in September 1981 was followed by a stint in Hong Kong in the summer of 1983. Mayo became a hotelier in Crriccieth, North Wales running the 'Plas Isa', which he later sold to his friend and former Baggie, Ian Edwards. Joe became a rep for Imperial Tobacco. He appeared in series 12 of the reality TV show Coach Trip, being named winner in the final and appeared on ITV's 'The Chase'. Living in the North Midlands, now retired, he likes a game of golf and is a keen follower of horse racing. A regular supporter of the Old Baggies Former Players' Association. In 2020 he was part of a group of players who sent messages or made phone calls to senior season ticket holders during the Corona Virus pandemic.

McNAB Alex 'Sandy'

Left half 5'7"

Born *27/12/1911 Glasgow, Scotland*

Died *September* 1962 aged 50

Playing career: *Sunderland, West Bromwich Albion (Cost £6,750 186 appearances 4 goals March 1938 – April 1946), Newport County, Dudley Town, Northwich Victoria as player then player/manager 1948-51. Guested for Newport County, Nottingham Forest, Northampton Town & Walsall during WW2 (1932 – 1952) 2 Scottish International caps, also represented the Football League. Toured Canada & USA with the Scottish FA in 1939.*

Alex McNab nicknamed 'Sandy' because of his red hair. He played a leading role in two of Sunderland's greatest successes. He was on the pitch for the league championship clincher in 1936, and replaced injured captain Alex Hastings in the 1937 FA Cup Final. He played 97 league games for Sunderland scoring 6 goals. In 1938, McNab joined West Bromwich Albion for a fee of £7,000. He was a marvellous pint-sized left half whose tackling was done judiciously without him losing his poise. He was brave and seemingly tireless on the pitch. He toured Canada & USA with the Scottish FA in 1939. WW2 intervened and he went to various clubs on loan including Nottingham Forest, Northampton Town and Walsall. He made 52 league appearances plus 3 FA Cup matches for Albion scoring twice. McNab was Albion's skipper during wartime playing 132 games in the Wartime League and Cup competitions.

Bernie McNally

He led Albion to the Midland War Cup win over Nottingham Forest in 1944. He eventually signed for Newport County in 1946 for £1,000. McNab later played non-league football for Dudley Town and Northwich Victoria, becoming player/manager from 1948-51. He had been a grocer but became a licensee in West Bromwich early in the 1950's.

McNALLY Bernard 'Bernie'
Midfielder 5'7"
Born *17/2/1963 Shrewsbury*
Playing career: *Shrewsbury Town, West Bromwich Albion (Cost £385,000 168 apps + 21 sub 14 goals July 1989 – June 1995), Hednesford Town, Telford United (1980 – 1998) 5 caps for Northern Ireland*

A skilful midfield player McNally made 168 appearances scoring 14 goals for his hometown club Shrewsbury Town. Bernard joined the Albion from his home town club for a fee of £385,000 in July 1989. He made his debut against Sheffield United in August 1989. He was a small, reliable, energetic, clever footballer. Bernie was part of the promotion winning side at Wembley in 1993, Bernard played 5 times for Northern Ireland. McNally played 189 games for Albion scoring 14 goals in all competitions. Bernie saw his career wind down with spells at Hednesford, Telford and Rushall Olympic before returning to the Hawthorns as a youth development coach. Further football roles saw Bernie become Manager at Telford followed by roles at Hednesford, Newtown, Shrewsbury, Port Talbot and even a few months Managing in India. Bernie currently employed in the building trade and lives in Sutton Coldfield with his wife Caron.
In his own words *"I have done management and coaching at lower league level and managed in the Welsh Premier League for about two years. I also managed in India and Romania for four months each. Now I work on a construction site and live in the Sutton Coldfield area."*

"DID YOU KNOW?"

"Kevin Kilbane was the first player to sign for West Bromwich Albion for a fee above £1 million, actually costing £1.25 million from Preston in June 1997."

McNAUGHT Ken
Centre back 5'11"
Born *11/1/1955 Kirkcaldy, Scotland*
Playing career: *Everton, Aston Villa, West Bromwich Albion (Cost £125,000 50 appearances 1 goal Aug 1983 – June 1985), Sheffield United. (1974-1985).*

Ken McNaught was signed by Everton as an apprentice. His league debut came in 1974/75 and he went to make 66 league appearances for the Toffees over the next three seasons. He played for Everton against Aston Villa in the 1977 League Cup Final, a contest that went to two replays. McNaught played in all three games and collected a runners-up tankard. After impressing in the final he was signed by Aston Villa in the 1977 close-season. He was 22 at the time. He was a League Champion, European Cup winner and European Super Cup winner whilst at Aston Villa. McNaught spent the 1983/84 season at West Bromwich Albion costing £125,000, where he was a first team regular playing in 42 league games scoring once. He was a hard, physical and commanding centre half. His last season was with Sheffield United where he played 34 league games. He was then forced to retire early. McNaught was coach at Dunfermline Athletic 1987/88. He worked in the Pro Shop at the famous Gleneagles Golf Course and then worked as a general manager in a gold mine in Western Australia. Having returned from 'Oz' He was involved with corporate hospitality on match days at Villa Park and worked on local radio. McNaught lived in Dickens Heath, Solihull. Diagnosed with a severe heart issue in 2015, needing surgery to replace an aortic heart valve, but he had issues with the PFA refusing to fully fund the surgery in 2016. He did have the operation at the Queen Elizabeth Hospital, Birmingham and was home after a week, making a good recovery.

R. M'NEALL, West Bromwich Albion.
(Photo by A. Wilkes, West Bromwich)

McNEAL Robert 'Bobby'

Left half 5'6"
Born *15/1/1891 Stanley, County Durham*
Died *12/5/1956 West Bromwich age 65*
Playing career: *West Bromwich Albion (403 appearances 10 goals June 1910 – May 1925) Retired through injury becoming Albion coach 1926/27. Guested for Fulham, Middlesbrough, Notts County, Port Vale during WW1. 2 England International caps & represented the Football League 5 times*

McNeal was a stylish left half with a footballing brain. He distributed the ball accurately and defended with commendable steadiness and reliability. He was something of a penalty expert and often would fire a free kick from fully 25 yards, usually hitting the target. He turned professional with West Bromwich Albion in June 1910. In his first full season he helped the club to the Second Division title. The Albion then finished ninth in the First Division in 1911/12. He also won a runners-up medal in the 1912 FA Cup Final when Albion lost 1–0 to Barnsley in a replay at Bramall Lane. Albion went on to post top ten finishes in the league in 1912/13, 1913/14, and 1914/15, before the Football League was suspended due to World War I. During the war he appeared as a guest player for Fulham, Middlesbrough, Notts County and Port Vale. McNeal was part of West Bromwich Albion's league championship-winning side of 1919/20. The team also won the 1920 Charity Shield with a 2–0 victory over Tottenham Hotspur at White Hart Lane. Albion then dropped to 14th and 13th-place finishes in 1920–21 and 1921/22. They finished seventh in 1922/23 and 16th in 1923/24, before posting a second-place finish in 1924–25 – they ended the

campaign just two points behind champions Huddersfield Town. A grand clubman who made 403 appearances for Albion scoring 9 goals between 1910 and 1925. In May 1925, McNeal retired through injury. From 1926 to 1927, McNeal served as Albion's coach on a part-time basis. He was licensee of the Nags Head, Dudley Street, West Browmwich from 1927 to 1949.

McVITIE George

Right winger 5'10"
Born *7/9/1948 Carlisle*
Playing career: *Carlisle United, West Bromwich Albion (Cost £33,333 52 appearances 5 goals Aug 1970 – Aug 1972), Oldham Athletic, Carlisle United, Queen of the South (1965-1982) England schoolboy and Youth International. Went on FA XI tour of Ireland & Australia playing three games.*

McVitie's club of longest service was Carlisle United for whom he played in two spells, 1965-70 and 1976-81 playing 241 league games scoring 41 goals. Alan Ashman ex-Carlisle manager, took him to West Bromwich Albion in August 1970 for £33,333. In two season he played 42 games scoring 5 goals. George was a right winger of many skills but a player who did not always seem up to the standards of First Division football. McVitie went on FA XI tour of Ireland & Australia in May and June 1971 playing three games. He moved to Oldham Athletic.in 1972 for £15,000, playing 113 games scoring 19 goals in four years. He then returned to Carlisle for his second spell. In the close season he worked for ESK Brickworks in Brisco, where they made bricks for Laings the builders. He loaded bricks into piles for the forklift truck. He ended his senior career playing in Scotland for Dumfries club, Queen of the South playing 21 league games. He became a milkman when he hung up his boots in 1980, before running a sub post office outside Carlisle. In honour of his sterling service, he has a bar named after him at Brunton Park, home of Carlisle United.

"DID YOU KNOW?"

"At 552 feet, the Albion Ground at the Hawthorns is the highest ground above sea level in the English League."

MELLON Michael 'Micky'

Midfielder 5'10"

Born *18/3/1972 Paisley, Scotland*

Playing career: *Bristol City, Cork City (loan), West Bromwich Albion (Cost £75,000 47+10 sub appearances 7 goals 1993 – 1994), Blackpool, Tranmere Rovers, Burnley, Tranmere Rovers, Kidderminster Harriers, Witton Albion, Lancaster City (1989 – 2006).*

Mellon began his career in 1989 as a 17-year-old with Bristol City gaining promotion to the old Second Division, then managed by Joe Jordan. In 1991, he was loaned out for two months to League of Ireland club Cork City, making his League of Ireland debut on 20th October 1991. He made eleven league appearances scoring three goals. He spent four years at Ashton Gate, totalling 35 league appearances. He joined West Bromwich Albion in 1993 for a fee of £75,000. Micky was a tough tackling, energetic and reliable midfielder. He played 47 games plus another 10 substitute appearances scoring seven goals in their promotion season ending in a Play-Off Final victory over Port Vale at Wembley, which he missed after being sent off in the second leg Semi-Final against Swansea. A move to Blackpool for a fee of £50,000 in 1994 saw Mellon establish himself as a regular on the team and scoresheet. Under Sam Allardyce's guidance, Mellon made 125 league appearances and scored 14 goals. He was voted the club's Player of the year in the 1995–96 season. The season following Allardyce's sacking in 1997, Mellon moved up a division to join Tranmere Rovers, who were then playing in Division One, for a fee of £300,000. He spent two seasons at Prenton Park, followed by another two with Burnley, whom he joined for £350,000 gaining promotion finishing second to Preston North End. He returned to Tranmere Rovers in March 2001 initially on loan, and then on a free transfer. He was released in May 2004. Mellon joined Kidderminster Harriers in August 2004, signing a two-year contract. After leaving Harriers, Mellon spent a short spell at Witton Albion in 2005 before joining Lancaster City. Mellon was appointed assistant manager of Lancaster City in June 2006 but left in October due to financial reasons. He joined Burnley as Youth Team Coach. In September 2008 he was appointed manager of Fleetwood Town but was sacked in December 2012.

Joined Barnsley the same month, as coach and later assistant manager. He was sacked in March 2014 but was appointed manager of Shrewsbury Town in the May. He left in October 2016 after a poor start to the season. Became manager of Tranmere Rovers and oversaw their return to the Football League after winning the play off final against Boreham Wood in May 2018. Won promotion again in May 2019 after winning the play off final at Wembley. By March 2020, the team were within the relegation zone, but with a game in hand on their nearest rivals and on a run of three successive victories. The cancellation of fixtures due to the COVID-19 pandemic meant that the season could not be completed, and a vote was taken by League One clubs on 9 June to resolve promotion and relegation issues on a points per game (PPG) basis. This meant that Tranmere would be relegated to League Two for the 2020/21 season. Mellon was appointed as manager of Scottish Premiership club Dundee United on 6 July 2020.

MERRICK Alan

Defender 5'10"

Born *20/6/1950 Selly Oak, Birmingham*

Playing careers: *West Bromwich Albion (156 + 13 sub appearances 5 goals July 1968 – June 1975), Peterborough (loan), Minnesota Kicks, Pittsburgh Spirit, Los Angeles Aztecs, San Jose Earthquakes, Minnesota Kicks, Toronto Blizzard, Team America. England Youth International.*

A loyal club servant who showed toughness, stamina and determination in an array of defensive positions, ranging from full back to wing half to centre half. He never really established himself in Albion's first team but whenever he did play, he always gave 100% effort. Alan joined the Albion in July 1966 signing professional forms in August 1967. Alan Merrick made 169 appearances including 13 as a substitute, scoring 5 goals. He made his debut versus Peterborough in the 3rd round of the League Cup in September 1968 and was capped 3 times in the same year for England Youth. In September 1975 he went on loan to Peterborough followed by a move to Kidderminster and finally to the US where he made over 250 appearances for Minnesota Kicks, Los Angeles Aztecs, San Jose Earthquakes and Toronto Blizzard.

In 1983 he was capped by the USA when he played against Haiti. He lived in Minnesota for many years and is currently the head coach of the University of Minnesota men's club team, and ran his own academy.

In his own words: *"One year after retiring from playing I became Head Coach of the Minnesota Strikers playing indoor soccer on an artificial grass field placed on top of an ice rink. During the same period, I was owner of a Pool Hall with 35 tables. After 5 seasons the franchise folded and I started work as the National Sales Manager for a Toxicology Reference Laboratory in Minnesota – I also ran a Soccer Company and conducted coach and player education. We coached as many as 15,000 players a year. I have been the Head Coach of the University of Minnesota Men's Soccer team since 1999. I was a Realtor in Minnesota for several years and I am presently the Sales and Content Director for MOTI Sports in Minnesota. We have a mobile e-Platform of 3D Animation and Motion Capture to educate coaches and players of Soccer Education."*

MILLARD Leonard 'Len'

Left back /wing half 5'9"

Born 7/3/1919 Coseley, Staffordshire

Died 2/3/1997 Coseley, Dudley.

Playing career: *Coseley Town, Bilston Town, Sunbeam FC, West Bromwich Albion (626 appearances 18 goals Sep 1942 – June 1958)*

Len the dependable was Albion's left back for a number of years. Len started off as a centre forward, scoring two hat-tricks in wartime football, one against the Wolves. He then switched to the number 3 shirt in 1949 replacing the long-serving Harry Kinsell. He helped Albion gain promotion from the Second Division in 1949, continuing to hold a regular place in the top flight until his 39th year. He skippered the side in the 1954 FA Cup Final win over Preston North End. Indeed, but for a late run of defeats, due at least partially to an injury crisis, West Bromwich might have won the League Championship, too. Nicknamed the 'Agitator' Len appeared in 626 matches in all competition including Wartime League football, scoring 18 goals. He won a Midland Wartime Cup Winners' medal in 1944 beating Nottingham Forest in the Final. He played in 436 league games, 40 FA Cup ties and the Charity Shield match. Len also made 17 appearances for the reserves.

He was without a shadow of a doubt, a great servant to West Bromwich Albion, staying with the club through thick and thin for a duration of 21years. Len was a defender who stuck to his task. Always fair in the challenge, strong and clean with his kicks and honest in his keen and thoughtful approach to the professional game. In 1958 Millard moved to the non-League Stafford Rangers, whom he served as manager until 1961. After that he continued to shun the limelight, working in the West Midlands until his retirement in the early 1980s. He had a leg amputated in 1988-89. Filled many positions during his time at the Hawthorns..

MILLER Alan

Goalkeeper 6'4"

Born 27/3/1970 Epping, Essex

Playing career: *Arsenal, Plymouth Argyle (loan), West Bromwich Albion (loan 3 appearances Aug 1991), Birmingham City (loan), Middlesbrough, Huddersfield Town (loan), Grimsby Town (loan), West Bromwich Albion (loan then signed Cost £400,000 110 appearances Mar 1997 – Dec 2000), Blackburn Rovers (2000-2003), Bristol City (loan), Coventry City (loan), St. Johnstone (loan) (1988-2002).Retired with a slipped disc back injury. Went to the England Soccer School of Excellence, aged 14. England U-21 International.*

Miller attended the England Soccer School of Excellence at Lilleshall in Shropshire. He was an apprentice at Arsenal winning the FA Youth Cup in 1988 and four caps for the England under-21 team. However, with John Lukic and then David Seaman, first-team opportunities were rare. He had loan spells with Plymouth Argyle, West Bromwich Albion, playing 3 games at the start of the 1991/92 season, and Birmingham City. At Arsenal he won FA Cup and League Cup winners' medals in 1992/93 and a European Cup Winners' Cup medal in 1993/94, as an unused substitute each time. In summer 1994, wanting first team football, Miller moved to Middlesbrough for £500,000, winning a First Division winners' medal in his first season. In 1997, he signed for West Bromwich Albion in a £400,000 deal after a second loan spell. Tall and athletic, with a commanding presence in the penalty area, athleticism and good distribution, Miller was a popular figure at the Hawthorns. After three years at the Hawthorns, he moved to Blackburn Rovers in January 2000 for £50,000.

He only played two games during his time at Ewood Park. He went on loan to Bristol City and Coventry City during 2000/01. In October 2001, he was loaned out again, this time to St Johnstone. He was recalled to take his place on the bench as Blackburn won the 2002 Football League Cup Final at Wembley, providing back-up to Brad Friedel. Miller retired in 2003 after failing to overcome a back injury. In 2003 he moved to Mallorca running a company providing bespoke holiday services to tourists, for seven years. He owned a couple of racehorses when he was a footballer. He had a horse racing friend who had taken over the Nelson pub in Burnham Market, which he had renamed The Jockey. Alan & his partner Nerida Britton, took on the pub for 5-6 years, before they both started to work within the Holkham Estate in Norfolk. As development manager, Miller helped oversee the transformation of Wells Beach Café, seeing it become a thriving venue, with an emphasis on being dog-friendly. The venue won the national Kennel Club's Be Dog Friendly Award in 2015 He has two black Labradors of his own.

MILLINGTON Anthony 'Tony

Goalkeeper 5'10"
Born *5/6/1943 Hawarden, Wales*
Died *5/8/2015 Wrexham Maelor aged 72*
Playing career: *West Bromwich Albion (40 appearances July 1960 – Oct 1964), Crystal Palace, Peterborough United, Swansea City, Glenavon in Ireland (1961-1973) Welsh U-21, U-23 and Full International.*

Nicknamed 'Milly'. Tony Millington, Albion's Welsh international goalkeeper of the early 1960s, was pretty remarkable even by goalkeeping standards. Best described as a showman, he clearly believed that his job description extended beyond shot stopping. Millington, it appears, saw himself as an entertainer, and more power to him for that. Tony was born in Hawarden, and joined the Albion, initially as an amateur, in the summer of 1959. With bags of natural ability, it seemed as if the game came all too easily to him and concentration was an issue he sometimes struggled with. That could not disguise his talent and by 1961/62, he had forced his way into the Albion side at the age of 18, good enough to play ahead of Ray Potter and Jock Wallace, to make a first team

debut in a 2-2 draw at home to Manchester City on the last day of September 1961.He went on to rack up 24 games that season as Archie Macaulay replaced Gordon Clark as manager, before he and Ray Potter shared the number one jersey the following season. That was the year when Millington forced his way into the Welsh side, his debut coming in Cardiff against a strong Scotland side. Playing behind a defence that included club colleague Stuart Williams and the great John Charles, now back from his time with Juventus, Millington had to fish the ball out of the net three times as the Scots won 3-2, Denis Law one of Scotland's scorers. Millington was selected to play in goal at Wembley in the home internationals. England were rampant, winning 4-0. November 1962 was a tough month for Millington given that Albion had shipped five goals at home to Blackburn. We then proceeded to lose 4-1 at home to Nottingham Forest which led to the return of Ray Potter to the team. Potter stayed between the sticks that season, except for one game where injury kept him out. Millington steeped into the breach and was promptly mown down by Wolves who won 7-0 at Molineux. That was the end of his Albion career, not least because shortly after, Jimmy Hagan arrived to take charge as manager. Of all managers, Hagan was the least likely on earth to take to a showman goalkeeper, the kind who would celebrate a goal with a handstand, or swap sweets with supporters behind the goal while Albion were attacking. Millington's showmanship which, occasionally saw him making a save or two for the cameras.

Tony spent the next 18 months in the reserves before he was transferred to Crystal Palace in October 1964 for £7,5000, which reenergised his career, ensuring that for the rest of the 1960s, he would do battle with Dave Hollins and Gary Sprake for the goalkeeping job with Wales. After two seasons at Selhurst Park, Tony was sold to Peterborough United in March 1966 along with Derek Kevan for a combined fee of £15,000. He soon became established as the first-choice goalkeeper and made 118 league appearances over three years before moving to Wales to join Swansea Town for a £5,000 fee in July 1969 where he became a huge crowd favourite. Millington was always popular with crowds, for his humour and for his compassion. One story from his Swansea days sums him up. Warming up before the game, he suddenly chased off the field only to return carrying a chair. He'd spotted an elderly supporter on crutches in the crowd and ushered him into the disabled supporters' enclosure and sat him down to watch the game. Another old Swans fan once reported that one of Tony's party-pieces to entertain kids behind the goal was to swing on the crossbar monkey-style. He stopped doing this when this distraction caused him to miss a back pass and conceded an own goal. They do say you should never meet your heroes though, and for Tony, that was true. A big fan of the former Manchester United man Harry Gregg, now Swansea manager, the appreciation was not mutual, the stern Northern Irishman cut from the same cloth as Hagan and he moved on again to Glenavon in Northern Ireland to work in his Father-in-law's business. Millington met his wife Hazel in Khartoum in Sudan, after he travelled to the country for a club international match. She was an airline stewardess, and the couple married on October 15, 1973, three months after they first met. He suffered a horrific crash when he was driving a car, which clipped the kerb and rolled over. He suffered a dislocated neck and was left paralysed and wheelchair-bound following a year in hospital. car crash in 1975 left him wheelchair-bound for the rest of his life, and in need of constant care. Tony retired in 1975 after the car accident age 32. He settled in Wrexham and helped run the Wrexham FC disabled supporters club with his brother, Grenville, who had played in goal for Rhyl & Chester. He became the club's disability officer. Tony died of pneumonia after years of battling infections linked to a car accident which took place almost four decades earlier.

MILLS David

Attacker 5'8"
Born *6/12/1951 Whitby, North Yorkshire*
Playing career: *Middlesbrough, West Bromwich Albion (Cost £516,000 55+21sub appearances 6 goals Jan 1979 – Jan 1983), Newcastle United (loan), Sheffield Wednesday, Newcastle United, Middlesbrough, Darlington, Whitby Town. (1968-19886) England schoolboy and U-23 International.*

At school Mills represented England Schoolboys. He attracted interest from several clubs but moved to local team Middlesbrough, after missing close to a year due to injury, and signed for the club in July 1968. He was part of Middlesbrough's 1973/74 Second Division championship side, he scored the goal that earned the side promotion in the 1–0 victory over Luton Town. Mills came to the attention of the England Under 23 selectors, earning eight caps and scoring three goals. His best season in terms of goals was 1976/77 when he scored 18 times in 41 games, making him top scorer that season. He retained that title the next season. In December 1976, Mills asked for a move and so was transfer listed at a value of £200,000, but nobody came in for him. Two years later, his form had again caught the attention of other managers, and so in 1979, Ron Atkinson paid £516,000. to take him to West Bromwich Albion, breaking the English transfer record and making Mills Britain's first 'half million-pound footballer'. Atkinson gambled at the time, hoping that David would replace the veteran striker Tony Brown at the Hawthorns. Mills scored on his first full appearance for Albion. The gamble never paid off, with Mills never able to live up to the price-tag which Albion had placed upon his head. A hard-working inside right or centre forward with a distinctive knack of scoring goals, Mills had netted 94 goals in over 340 games for Middlesbrough before journeying south. It was anticipated that he would continue to find the net but that was not so. He tried but never quite fitted the bill and after four years and 76 outings for the Baggies he was loaned out to Newcastle United 1981/82.

At the end of the loan, he moved to Sheffield Wednesday for just £30,000, but he only remained there for a short time, moving back to Newcastle on a permanent transfer. In June 1984, Willie Maddren, Middlesbrough manager, re-signed him for one season, in which he finished top scorer with 14 goals. He suffered an Achilles tendon injury and a broken arm the following season and did not play. He had a short spell after this playing for Darlington, where he ended his career as a player in 1987. He was seriously injured in a car crash on Tyneside, which claimed the life of his father. He worked as a freelance journalist for local press, T.V. and radio, and was a print consultant. Then he got back into football as chief scout for Newcastle United, where he worked under seven different managers. In April 2008 he returned to Middlesbrough to boost the recruitment team along with Gordon McQueen. He has since worked closely with Steve Walsh at Hull City and Leicester City as chief scout.

MONAGHAN Derek

Forward 5'10"
Born *20/1/1959 Bromsgrove*
Playing career: *West Bromwich Albion (17 + 7 sub appearances 3 goals Jan 1977 – July 1984), Port Vale, Redditch United.*

Derek joined Albion from Astwood Bank in January 1976, signing professional terms in January 1977. He was part of the FA Youth Cup for Albion, playing just one game although his contribution to winning the cup was important, as he stepped in for Steve Lynex in the final and scored a goal. After the final, the team were presented with medals however they only had 12 medals to present, so Derek didn't get one. The former Baggie and England youth international would eventually get his medal, belatedly presented him at a supporters' club dinner in 2006. He made just 17 first team appearance plus 7 as a substitute scoring 3 goals. He went with the senior squad on the tour of China in 1978. Derek made his debut in UEFA Cup tie at home to Carl Zeiss Jena. Unfortunately, injuries meant his Albion career was finished in 1984 when he was given a free transfer and joined Port Vale where he played just 7 league and 2 cup games for Vale, having again suffered badly with injuries. He was given a free transfer in 1985 and moved to Redditch United. They won promotion out of the Southern Football League Midland Division in 1985/86. After retiring from football, Monaghan set up his own financial consultancy business in Warwickshire.

Derek Monaghan

His great claim to fame, whilst with Albion, was being arrested as a ticket tout outside White Hart Lane, the police thought he was selling tickets when he was only handing out complimentary tickets to players family & friends. Today he lives in Alcester with his wife Anita and daughter Poppy. He is a great supporter of the Old Baggies Former Players' Association.

MORLEY Anthony 'Tony'

Left winger 5'8½"

Born *26/8/1954 Ormskirk, Lancashire*
Playing career: *Preston North End, Burnley, Aston Villa, West Bromwich Albion(Cost £75,000 Dec 1983 - Aug1985), Birmingham City (loan), FC Seiko in Hong Kong (loan), Den Haag in Holland, West Bromwich Albion (Total 69 + 1 sub appearances 14 goals July 1987 - 1989), Burnley (loan), Tampa Bay Rowdies in USA.(1972-1988), Hamrun Spartans in Hong Kong. England Youth, U-23, 'B' International and six Full caps.*

Morley turned professional at Preston North End in August 1972. He played in 84 league games scoring 15 goals before he moved across Lancashire. In February 1976 to join Burnley for a £100,000 fee. In 91 league games he scored 5 goals. He joined Aston Villa for £200,000 in June 1979. A skilful, nippy winger, Morley enjoyed the best days of his career at Villa Park. He was seen as a wayward genius but was moulded by manager Ron Saunders into one of the most dangerous players around. He was a vital part of the Villa side that won the League Championship in 1980/81 and the European Cup in 1982. His brilliant dribble and cross set up Peter Withe for the winning goal against Bayern Munich in the final. His full Villa record was 170+10 substitute appearances, 34 goals. After adding a European Super Cup Winners' medal to his collection, he was transferred from Villa to local rivals West Bromwich Albion for £75,000 in December 1983. He was a classy right footed winger who played on the left. He was able to turn up the flow of a game in one sweeping run. Hu hugged the touchline and drew defenders to him before taking them on, crossing and creating chances galore for his colleagues. He spent two seasons at the Hawthorns appearing in 33 league games and scoring 4 goals. He briefly went on loan to another Midlands club, Birmingham City in November-December

1984 scoring 3 goals in 4 league games. He had a slightly nomadic career from then on, joining Seiko in Hong Kong and then Den Haag for £25,000, with whom he won a runners-up medal in the Dutch Cup, scoring in the final. Then there was a return to West Bromwich Albion in July 1987 where he played 28 more league games scoring 7 goals. He was loaned out to Burnley October-November 1988. In 1989 he moved to USA to play for Tampa Bay Rowdies, before finishing his career at Hamrun Spartans in Malta. Morley was a regular on the 'Villa Old Stars' circuit. He also provides colour commentary for radio broadcasts on Aston Villa's website. He has worked as a salesman and coached kids in the West Midlands. He had been among a group of former Villa players, including several of his European Cup-winning team-mates, making phone calls to check-in with elderly supporters during the Corona Virus pandemic. **Personal note**: *Although still a Villain, Tony phoned a relative of mine, Alan Coates who was suffering with cancer, in June 2020. They chatted about Rotterdam and other Villa days and it meant a lot to Alan, who sadly passed away a few weeks later and his funeral was two days after Villa's 'great escape' on the last day of the 2019/20 Premier League season.*

MOSES Remi

Midfielder 5'6"

Born *14/11/1960 Miles Platting, Manchester*
Playing career: *West Bromwich Albion (73 appearances 6 goals Nov 1978 – Sep 1981), Manchester United. (1979-1989) England U-21 International*

Remi was a midfield played who worked tirelessly, always on the go, prompting, teasing and harassing defenders into mistakes. West Bromwich Albion under the management of Ron Atkinson in the late 1970s, were enjoying a strong run of form which saw them finish in the top five for all but one season between 1977 and 1981. He made his first team debut 26th January 1980 at Crystal Palace in a 2-2 draw, playing the final 18 league games of that 1979/80 season. Then Moses only missed one game all season in 1980/81, appearing in 50 games in all competitions, his only full season with the Baggies. Whilst a West Bromwich Albion player he played in a benefit match for Len Cantello, that saw a team of white players play against a team of black players.

He was allowed to leave just after establishing himself in the Albion's midfield, playing 73 games in all competitions, in September 1981, Moses was transferred from West Bromwich Albion to Manchester United for £500,000, arriving at Old Trafford a month before Bryan Robson who went for a club record £1.5 million. At United he played in 150 league games scoring 7 goals. Bad injuries, an ankle problem kept him out for 11 months, then a couple of years later a knee injury forced him to retire from football at the age of 28. Since retiring from the game, he has been a property dealer in Alkrington, in Greater Manchester. In his spare time, he has coached Manchester Warriors under-20's, an inline skating team. Has also coached at Old Trafford occasionally as part of the in the 'unity in the community'. Born in England to Nigerian parents, he could claim to be the first Nigerian footballer to play for Manchester United although Odion Ighalo is actually the first Nigerian International player to do so.

MULLIGAN Patrick 'Paddy'
Right back 5'9"
Born *17/3/1945 Beaumont, Dublin*
Playing career: *Bohemians, Shamrock Rovers, Boston Rovers in USA (guest), Boston Beacons in USA (guest), Chelsea, Crystal Palace, West Bromwich Albion (130 appearances 2 goals Sept 1975 – Aug 1979), Shamrock Rovers, Galway United. Represented League of Ireland XI, U-23 and 50 caps at Full International level for the Republic of Ireland.*

Mulligan started his senior career playing for Bohemians in 1963. However, after only two games he signed for Shamrock Rovers in December 1963. He won the FAI Cup in 1965, 1966, 1967 and 1969. During the 1963/64 season he was part of the side which won seven trophies. He represented Rovers in European competition 10 times. In the summer 1967 he was part of the Rovers team that represented Boston in the United Soccer Association league. In 1968, they sent him on loan to the Boston Beacons of the North American Soccer League. On 22 October 1969, Mulligan signed for English club Chelsea for £17,500 where he played 58 league games scoring twice in three years. He featured in Chelsea's UEFA Cup Winners' Cup success in 1971, making a late substitute appearance in the first final against Real Madrid in Athens.

He also played in Chelsea's League Cup final against Stoke City a year later, though they lost 2–1 at Wembley. He played in 58 league games scoring 2 goals between 1969 – 1972 with Chelsea. Mulligan left in 1972 for Crystal Palace for a fee of £65,000. He stayed with the South London club for three years appearing in 57 league games scoring two goals between 1972 - 1975. He joined West Bromwich Albion's Irish contingent In September 1975, helping the club win Promotion in the 1975/76 season. Paddy was an attacking right back, an expert at over-lapping, steady and thoughtful, a player with ability who was never completely dominated by a winger. He made 109 league appearances scoring one goal for Albion between 1975 – 1979. He moved to Shamrock Rovers and then Galway United before retiring from playing. He then went to Greece to become assistant manager of Panathinaikos 1980-81 alongside Ronnie Allen. He was an Insurance Agent in Leighton Buzzard He returned to Ireland and managed Galway United 1983/84 and Shelbourne 1985/86. He applied to manage The Republic of Ireland National team but lost out to Eoin Hand by one vote. Opened his own Accountancy/Insurance Business. Occasionally appears as a soccer analyst with Channel TV3 on Irish television and a pundit for Dublin based Newstalk Sport.

MURPHY James 'Jimmy'
Right half 5'8"
Born *8/8/1910 Hawarden, Wales*
Died *14/11/1989 Manchester aged 79*
Playing career: *West Bromwich Albion (228 appearances Feb 1928 – Mar 1939), Swindon Town, 15 Welsh International caps.*

Nicknamed 'Spud' or 'Twinkletoes' was a vigorous attacking wing half, skilled in tackling and a glutton for hard work. In 1924 he represented Wales in a schoolboy international against England in Cardiff. He turned pro in February 1928 when he joined West Bromwich Albion as a 17-year-old. Murphy made his debut in a 1–0 defeat away to Blackpool on 5 March 1930 and played one further league game during his first season. In the following season, 1930/31, West Bromwich Albion won the FA Cup and promotion from the Second Division, but Murphy had yet to establish himself in the team and again made just two appearances.

Stuart Naylor

He became a regular in the Albion side upon the club's return to the First Division; He developed his game so well that he became a regular Welsh International and from 1931/32 to 1934/35 he appeared 149 times in league and cup for Albion, helping his team to achieve four consecutive top ten finishes, including fourth place in 1932/33. The 1934/35 season saw Murphy miss just one match all season, and he helped Albion to reach the 1935 FA Cup Final, which they lost 4–2 to Sheffield Wednesday. Murphy played 228 times for Albion without scoring a goal, before moving to Swindon Town in 1939, but the Second World War ended his spell at Swindon almost as soon as it had begun having played just 4 league games. During WW2 'Spud' served overseas with the Eighth Army, and there in Bari, Italy in 1945 he first met Matt Busby. Murphy was giving a speech about football to a band of troops, and in attendance was Matt Busby. Busby was so impressed by Murphy's speech that, upon his appointment as manager of Manchester United, he made Murphy the first signing of his tenure at the club. Murphy had the role of "chief coach" from 1946 until 1955, and became assistant manager in 1955 after Manchester United won their third FA Youth Cup in a row. It was Murphy's responsibility at the club to train the young footballers who were to become the "Busby Babes", which included Duncan Edwards and Bobby Charlton. After the Munich air disaster of 6 February 1958, he temporarily took over as manager while Matt Busby recovered from his injuries and, having assembled a substitute team, steered United to the 1958 FA Cup Final. Murphy had been in charge of the Welsh National team and was unable to travel with United. Hence, he was not involved in that tragic crash. Murphy had not been on the fatal flight because he had been away managing the Welsh team in a World Cup qualifying game. Murphy managed Wales at the 1958 FIFA World Cup in Sweden when they reached the quarter-finals. They lost 1–0 to Brazil, the eventual winners, to a goal by a 17-year-old called Pelé. Despite being approached to manage Brazil, Juventus and Arsenal, he remained as assistant manager at Old Trafford until 1971. Murphy chose never to become manager of the club because of his hate of the limelight.

He loved working in the background but never aspired to fulfil the job of manager. From 1973, Murphy scouted for Manchester United, most famously during the managerial reign of Tommy Docherty, when Murphy urged Docherty to sign wingers Steve Coppell and Gordon Hill.

Personal note: *I wrote to Jimmy Murphy at Manchester United in March 1983 as I was researching information about my Grandfather, Fred Everiss, former Albion Secretary/Manager. Mr Murphy replied a few days later. This is part of that letter. "Your Grandfather was the Club Secretary, he, I thought, ran the club generally. He was held in high esteem at top & players level. Mr Everiss accompanied me in my first International at Wrexham, Wales v England. A point of interest Mr Everiss approached me on several occasions to take over as manager at the Hawthorns." What might have been?*

NAYLOR Stuart

Goalkeeper 6'4"
Born *6/12/1962 Wetherby. West Yorkshire*
Playing career: *Lincoln City, Peterborough United (loan), Crewe Alexandra (loan x 2), West Bromwich Albion (Cost £110,000 409 + 1 sub appearances Feb 1986 – Aug 1996), Crewe Alexandra, Bristol City, Mansfield Town, Walsall, Exeter City, Rushden & Diamonds. England Youth and 'B' International. He retired 2001*

Stuart started his career at Lincoln City in 1980 and made 49 league appearances for the Imps in 5 years. In between he had loan spells at Peterborough United in 193 playing 8 games, Crewe Alexandra 1983/84 playing 38 league games and another loan spell with the Alex the following season 1984/85 playing another 17 league games. When Ron Saunders took over as manager at the Hawthorns in 1986, his first signing was Stuart Naylor, paying out £110,000 which at the time was the highest fee Albion had ever paid for a goalkeeper. He made his debut away at Old Trafford on 22nd February in a game Albion lost 3-0, thanks to a Jesper Olsen hat-trick. He played another 11 league games in that season 1985/86 that saw Albion finish bottom of Division One, relegated with Birmingham City. Nicknamed 'Bruiser' Stuart was tall, well built and with good reflexes. He gave Albion sterling service through some very difficult years in the Club's history.

He was an important squad member of the Promotion winning side of 1992/93 playing in 38 league and cup games but missed out on the Play Off Final at Wembley when his place was taken by Tony Lange. He made a total of 468 games for Albion and was capped at England Youth and 'B' team levels. He was granted a testimonial match against Coventry City and then released on a free transfer. He moved to Bristol, City, making 37 league appearances in three years. Stuart then had a spell at Exeter City sandwiched in between loan spells at Mansfield and Rushden & Diamonds, where Brian Talbot was manager. In a 22-year career he played 543 league games. At the end of his playing career, Naylor moved into coaching, joining Rushden & Diamonds permanently as a goalkeeping coach and back-up goalkeeper. In March 2004 Rushden's manager Brian Talbot departed for Oldham Athletic and Naylor followed him. In July 2005 he moved as goalkeeping coach to Bristol City. Then in March 2013, Naylor moved to Bristol Rovers until the end of the 2012/13 season. His contract was extended in May 2013. He still resides in Bristol with wife Debbie but was now Coach at the other Bristol side Rovers in 2016.

NICHOLL James 'Jimmy'

Full back 5'9½"
Born *28/12/1956 Hamilton, Canada*
Playing career: *Manchester United, Sunderland (loan), Toronto Blizzard, Sunderland, Toronto Blizzard, Rangers (loan), West Bromwich Albion (Cost £65,000 Nov 1984 – Aug 1986), Rangers, Dunfermline Athletic, Raith Rovers, Bath City, Rangers player/coach 2nd XI 1987. (1971-1996). 73 Northern Ireland caps.*
Jimmy Nicholl was born in Ontario, Canada, to Northern Irish parents. His family moved back 'home' when he was 3. Nicholl started his career as a junior player at Manchester United. His senior career started in 1974. He helped the club win the 1977 FA Cup Final and collected a runners-up medal in 1979.In 1981, he left the club to join Sunderland on a permanent contract after a loan spell. Played 32 games in one season before moving to Toronto Blizzard in Canada for £250,000, where he scored 11 goals in 77 games before signing for Rangers. In November 1984, he returned to England to sign for West Bromwich Albion a player exchange for Bobby Williamson, a deal valued at £65,000.

Jimmy played the easy game from right back; never flashy, usually steady and always seeking to find a man with his clearances. He stayed at the Hawthorns until Albion's relegation from the First Division in 1986, then returning to Rangers for three years, helping them win two Scottish league titles in the process. After leaving Rangers, he signed for Dunfermline Athletic in 1989 before moving to a player-manager role at Raith Rovers, having originally joined them on 27 November 1990. Following his time at Rovers, Nicholl played one game for Bath City in February 1996. Jimmy has twice managed Raith Rovers 1st as player/manager, then Millwall 1996/97, Cowdenbeath 2010/11, Hibernian as caretaker manager 2013, Cowdenbeath manager 2013-2015, Rangers caretaker 2018. He was assistant manager at Dundee but was sacked as part of their cost-cutting in 2020. Appointed assistant-manager of Northern Ireland national team in June 2020.

NICHOLLS John 'Johnny'

Inside forward/striker 5'8"
Born *3/4/1931 Wolverhampton, Staffordshire*
Died *1/4/1995 West Bromwich*
Playing career: *West Bromwich Albion (145 appearances 64 goals Aug 1951 – May 1957), Cardiff City, Exeter City, Worcester City, Wellington Town, Oswestry Town, Sankey (1951 – 1962) England U-23 and 2 Full International caps.*
Nicknamed 'Johnny on the spot'. Nicholls was born in Wolverhampton, Staffordshire. He joined West Bromwich Albion as an amateur in August 1950 and turned professional a year later. He was one of Albion's greatest post-was strikers. Johnny 'Poacher' Nicholls was a player who could run into the right place at precisely the right moment and score a vital goal. He had an instinctive knack of 'poaching' crucial goals and he did this so regularly during his stay with Albion. He could also unleash a cracking shot, or delicately flick the ball home with either foot, or head, back to goal or not. He formed a magnificent 'twin-striking' partnership with Ronnie Allen. The deadly duo scored 105 goals in two seasons 1953- 1955. John was part of the Albion 1954 FA Cup winning team beating Preston North End 3-2 at Wembley. He later admitted that he had one of his worst games in the striped shirt that afternoon.

He was the league's top scorer with 28 goals in 38 games also winning two England caps in the same year. His overall record for Albion was a grand one, and for the reserves too he netted frequently, grabbing 46 goals plus another 50 for the intermediate third team and 40 for the juniors. In 1956/57 he lost form and suffered with knee problems and in May 1957 he joined Cardiff City for £4,000, but moved on to Exeter City just six months later. In a total of 225 first class games he scored 95 goals. Lived in Exeter for a while before moving back to Wolverhampton. He used to collect insurance. He suffered a stroke, followed by a heart attack in the mid 1970's but was still a regular visitor to watch Albion at the Hawthorns. Had to use walking sticks for a number of years. He died in West Bromwich in 1995.

NICOL Steve

Right back/midfielder 5'10"

Born *11/12/1961 Troon, Scotland*

Playing career: *Ayr United, Liverpool, Notts County (player/coach), Sheffield Wednesday, West Bromwich Albion (loan 9 appearances Jan 1998 – June 1998), Doncaster Rovers, Boston Bulldogs player/manager*

(Mar 1999 – Sep 1999), New England Revolution manager (Sept 1999 – Nov 1999), Boston Bulldogs manager (Jan 2000 – Dec 2001), England Revolution manager (May 2002 – Oct 2011).27 Scottish International caps plus 14 U-21 appearances.

Nicol began his career with Ayr United in 1979 and spent just over two seasons with the Scottish side, racking up 70 league appearances, before Liverpool manager Bob Paisley decided to pay what turned out to be a bargain price, £300,000, to bring Nicol to Anfield in October 1981. Nicol stayed at Liverpool until January 1995 when he took on a player-assistant coach role at Notts County after being recruited by County's former Everton manager Howard Kendall. He stayed at Meadow Lane for just 10 months, playing 32 times. Nicol next moved to Sheffield Wednesday in November 1995. Nicol went on to make 49 league appearances before spending a spell on loan at West Bromwich Albion during the 1997/98 season where he played nine games, winning just two, as a defensive midfielder, adding some bite and experience to Albion's midfield. He then had a short spell with Doncaster Rovers before heading to the U.S. to take a player-coach position with the Boston Bulldogs of the A-League in 1999.

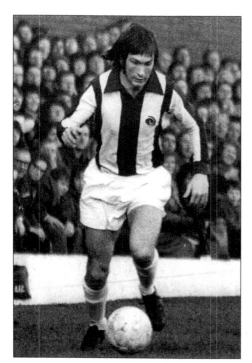

Gordon Nisbet

Peter Odemwingie

In September of that year, he took over as interim player-coach with the New England Revolution of Major League Soccer for the final two games of the season, winning both. He returned to the Boston Bulldogs as player-coach for the 2000 and 2001 seasons before re-joining the Revs in 2002 as an assistant coach. In 2002, Nicol took over as head coach of the New England Revolution, leading the team to the MLS Cup final that season and was named MLS Coach of the Year. The team advanced to the MLS Eastern Conference Finals every year during his tenure and returned to the MLS Cup final in 2005, 2006 and 2007, losing all four. On 24 October 2011, Nicol and the Revolution mutually decided to part ways, ending his 10-season stay. Commentator for ESPN's football coverage in the USA as well as a regular contributor with talkSPORT in the UK. Released his autobiography in 2016, '5 League Titles and a Packet of Crisps'.

NISBET Gordon

Full back/goalkeeper 5'10"
Born *18/9/1951 Wallsend*
Playing career: *West Bromwich Albion (167 appearances 1 goal Sept 1968 – Sept 1976), Hull City, Plymouth Argyle, Exeter City. (1969-1988) Nisbet was caretaker manager of Plymouth Argyle alongside Alan Gillett for two games in 1992. 1 England U-23 cap.*
'Nizza' signed for West Bromwich Albion, when he left school at the age of eighteen in 1969. He made his Albion debut as a goalkeeper in 1969. Prior to breaking into the first team on a regular basis, Gordon had right half and centre forward as well as goalkeeper for the reserve team. but under Don Howe's shrewd management, he was successfully converted into a right back. He played a total of 136 league appearances and a further 31 in various cup competitions scoring one goal. Gordon also played for Hull City making 193 league appearances between 1976-1980. He moved to Plymouth Argyle playing 281 league games between 1980 – 1987 scoring 14 goals. His final club was Exeter City where he played just 12 games in 1987/88. He played non- league football and became a company director of the Bealon Group in charge of property but then became a police officer with the Devon & Cornwall Police. He is retired and now lives in the coastal resort of Sao Martino do Porto on the silver coast in Portugal.

ODEMWINGIE Peter

Striker, Right winger 5'10"
Born *15/7/1981 Tashkent, Uzbekistan*
Playing career: *Bendel Insurance in Nigeria, La Louvière in Belgium, Lille in France, Lokomotiv Moscow in Russia, West Bromwich Albion (Cost undisclosed fee Aug 2010 - Aug 2013), Cardiff City, Stoke City, Bristol City (loan), Rotherham United, Madura United in East Java (2000-2018) 62 Nigeria Full International caps, Nigerian Olympic team*
Odemwingie was born in Tashkent, Uzbek SSR, Soviet Union to a Nigerian father and a Russian mother, both of whom were medical students. He moved with his family to Nigeria when he was two, before completing his secondary education in Russia. At the age of 17 he moved back to Nigeria and after spending a short time with amateurs AS Racines Lagos he became a professional with Nigeria Premier League side Bendel Insurance, where he scored 19 goals in 53 league appearances from 2000 - 2002. He signed for La Louvière in 2003 and made his mark by helping the club to win the Belgian Cup in his first season. He made 44 league appearances scoring 9 goals. Ligue 1 side Lille signed him and he played 75 league games scoring 23 goals. Odemwingie helped Lille fight for the league the following season and scored five league goals for them in the 2006/07 season inlcuding two against A.C. Milan at the San Siro to take Lille to the UEFA Champions League knockout stages. In July 2007, he signed for Lokomotiv Moscow for a reported fee of US$14 million. In three seasons for Lokomotiv, Odemwingie became one of their most important players. During his time at Lokomotiv Stadium, Odemwingie managed 21 goals in the Russian Premier League from 75 games. On 20th August 2010 Odemwingie signed for Premier League club West Bromwich Albion for an undisclosed fee. A day later, he scored the 81st-minute winning goal on his Premier League debut, a 1–0 win against Sunderland. Shortly after signing for West Bromwich Albion, photographs showed Lokomotiv Moscow fans celebrating the sale of Odemwingie through the use of racist banners targeted at the player. One banner read "Thanks West Brom". Before Albion's game against Tottenham Hotspur in September 2010, it was announced that West Brom fans would unfurl a banner to counter the racist one.

It read 'Thanks Lokomotiv' and is accompanied by a picture of Odemwingie celebrating his winner on his debut against Sunderland. On 30th April, Odemwingie became the first player in the Baggies' Premier League history to score in four consecutive games. Odemwingie ended the 2010–11 Season as West Bromwich Albion's top goalscorer with 15 league goals. On 12th February, Odemwingie scored his first Premier League hat-trick for the club in a 5–1 victory over Black Country rival Wolverhampton Wanderers, firmly entrenching him in Albion folklore. 25th February he scored 2 goals in a 4–0 win against Sunderland. His performances in the month of February led him to be named the Premier League Player of the Month for the third time in his career. Odemwingie headed in the winner against Chelsea on 17th November, pushing West Bromwich Albion to a 2–1 home victory, their sixth win from seven home games to start the season. Later in the season Odemwingie scored against Aston Villa to make it 2–2 in the 83rd minute after West Brom had been 2 goals down at half-time in an enthralling match. 25th January 2013, West Brom announced they had rejected a formal transfer request from Odemwingie. Peter's future at West Bromwich Albion came under doubt when he launched a tirade against his club on Twitter, in addition to accusing them of "reaching into his pocket", reiterating his wish for a move elsewhere. On 31st January 2013, transfer deadline day, Sky Sports cameras pictured him outside Loftus Road, in an attempt to sign for Queens Park Rangers, but he was refused entry, as no offer had been accepted by Albion Chairman Jeremy Peace. He was widely criticised for his attempt to join QPR with the Albion chairman saying he acted "unprofessionally". After initially being sent home from training on his return to Albion, Odemwingie was later disciplined by the club for his actions on transfer deadline day and resumed training, while also publicly apologising for his behaviour. He returned to the side against Sunderland on 23rd February 2013 coming on as a substitute in the final few minutes and was jeered by some Albion supporters. Steve Clarke continued to use Odemwingie as a substitute which caused him to attack the club on Twitter.

At the end of the season Steve Clarke stated that he expected Odemwingie to leave the Hawthorns in August 2013. On 2nd September 2013, Odemwingie signed a two-year contract with Cardiff City for £2.25 million. He scored 1 goal in 15 league games for the Bluebirds before Odemwingie joined Stoke City on 28th January 2014 in a player-exchange with Kenwyne Jones. He scored 5 goals in 27 league games for the Potters. He had a loan at Bristol City playing 7 league games scoring twice in March 2016. In October 2016, Odemwingie signed a short-term contract until 25th January 2017 with Rotherham United. He played 7 games without scoring. Odemwingie left Rotherham United at the end of his short-term contract, informing his manager via text message that he would not be staying at the club. On 3rd April 2017, Odemwingie joined Indonesian Liga 1 side Madura United as a marquee player. He scored on his league debut, successfully netting a penalty in a 2–0 triumph against Bali United on 16 April. He scored a hat-trick against Semen Padang on 12 April 2017. Odemwingie announced his retirement on 3 April 2019. He stated his ambition was to become a professional golfer. In 2020 he was part of a group of present and former players who sent messages or made phone calls to senior season ticket holders during the Corona Virus pandemic.

O'REGAN Kieran
Midfielder/full back 5'9"
Born *9/11/1963 Cork, Ireland*
Playing career: *Brighton & Hove Albion, Swindon Town, Huddersfield Town, West Bromwich Albion (Cost £25,000 44 + 10 sub appearances 2 goals July 1993 – June 1995), Halifax Town, Altrincham. 4 full Republic of Ireland team caps and played for U-21's.*
O'Regan was signed by Brighton and Hove Albion in 1982 from Tramore Athletic. Whilst at Brighton he gained 4 caps for the Republic of Ireland team in 1984. He played a season for Swindon Town before getting a transfer to Huddersfield Town in 1988.

"DID YOU KNOW?"

"In 1953/54 Albion won the FA Cup but were runners-up in the League to local rivals Wolves."

He spent six seasons with Town making 199 league appearances. He had a two-year spell at West Bromwich Albion, signed for £25,000 by Keith Burkinshaw in July 1993. A versatile footballer, who worked hard in midfield. He started 1993/94 in the first XI, playing the first 22 games, wearing various shirt numbers, starting with 10, then 2, 11, 4, 8, 7, and once a substitute wearing number 12. The following season 1994/95 12 league games, mainly at right back, and a further 8 substitute appearances. In July 1995 he returned to West Yorkshire to join Halifax Town. He made 135 league appearances scoring 7 goals between 1995-1998. Kieran was joint manager of Halifax Town with George Mulhall from Feb 1997-Aug 1998 during which time he also captained the team. O'Regan became sole manager when Mulhall retired in August 1998.however he was sacked in April 1999. He was a summariser on Huddersfield Town games on BBC Radio Leeds. He also worked selling carpets at Carpet Clearance Centre in Huddersfield.

OSBORNE John

Goalkeeper 6'2"
Born *1/12/1940 Barlborough, Derbyshire*
Died *7/11/1998 7/11/1998 Worcester aged 57*
Playing career: *Chesterfield, West Bromwich Albion (Cost £10,000 312 appearances in two spells 1967 – June 1972 and April 1973 – July 1978), Walsall (loan), Shamrock Rovers. English schoolboy International*
Nicknamed 'Ossie'. John had been an England Schoolboy International, playing at left half playing alongside John Talbut. He started his professional career at Chesterfield where he played 110 games in between 1960 – 1966 where he had followed Gordon Banks as number one. He joined West Bromwich Albion in January 1967, signed by Jimmy Hagan for £10,000 but was unable to play in

the League Cup Final at Wembley as he was cup-tied, having already played for Chesterfield in earlier round. He was in competition with Ray Potter and Dick Sheppard. He had a plastic joint inserted into one finger after an injury in the Charity Shield at Manie Road, Manchester in 1968. This earned him the nickname 'Bionic' 'Ossie' occasionally performed miracles between the posts for Albion and was undoubtedly one of the finest post-war keepers the club has had.

He was tall, had a safe pair of hands, was alert in positioning, excellent at taking the ball high in the penalty area. He was an incredibly courageous and dedicated clubman. John was a key member of the Albion FA Cup winning team of 1968, beating Everton 1-0 at Wembley. He was a runner up in the 1970 League Cup Final against Manchester City. Ossie was competing for a short period with Peter Latchford and he retired in June 1972, being reinstated by Albion in April 1973. He had the Grand National Winner Red Rum paraded around the pitch prior to his testimonial in 1978, netting £32,000 – a record at the time for a Midlands footballer. He loved a cigarette, even being pictured once smoking during a game. He loved training but didn't enjoy the actual game. He was commercial manager at Worcestershire CCC 1986 - 1995, later worked in the promotions side at the Sandwell Evening Mail. He also went into business in the Sports Outfitters trade with Jim Cumbes. He loved ornithology, bird watching. He was a star member of Albion's TV Quizball team Sadly John was the first of the '68 Cup winners to die, of cancer, in 1998, aged 57. John Osborne was arguably the finest goalkeeper to have ever played for West Bromwich Albion. In 2004, he was named as one of West Bromwich Albion's 16 greatest players, in a poll organised as part of the club's 125th anniversary celebrations.

OWEN Gary

Midfielder 5'9"
Born *7/7/1958 St. Helens, Lancashire*
Playing career: *Manchester City, West Bromwich Albion Cost £465,000 (225 + 4 sub appearances 26 goals May 1979 – July 1986), Panionios (Greece), Sheffield Wednesday, Hammarby (Sweden), APOEL (Greece) England U-21 and 'B' International*

Gary Owen

Owen started his career with Manchester City, turning professional in 1975 making his debut aged 17. He went on to make 103 league appearances scoring 19 goals for City between 1975 – 1979. In May 1979 Owen was sold, by City manager Malcolm Allison, to West Bromwich Albion for £450,000, despite being a strong fans' favourite. At Albion, he was a regular, and although a midfielder, was awarded the number 10 shirt usually reserved for a striker, and he was also the club's first choice penalty taker. A skilful left sided midfielder and auality ball player, often seen covering the left back position as the raiding Derek Statham made lung bursting runs forward. He certainly had the craft, the knowledge and the know-how and confidence to dictate the midfield arena. He had five excellent seasons with Albion 1979 – 1984 but after breaking his shin at West Ham in 1984 and later a gashed calf which required a skin graft plus a torn thigh muscle, marred the final two years of his time at the Hawthorns. In 1985/86 he lost his place in the side due to his injuries and the team were relegated. For West Bromwich Albion, Gary made 187 league appearances scoring 11 goals between 1979 – 1986. Owen joined Panionios in Greece for 1986/87, playing 23 league games. For the 1987/88 season he returned to England for a year with Sheffield Wednesday, playing just 14 league games. He then played two games for Swedish club Hammarby IF in 1988. Owen ended his career in season 1988/89 with APOEL in Cyprus, playing 16 league games. Gary was a journalist providing opinion on Manchester City in the Manchester Evening News and on local radio station Century FM. He had an art dealership 'Gary Owen Fine Art'. He now works for a company that helps with cost reduction for electricity & gas and other fuels.

In his own words: *"I was an art dealer from the age of 25, whilst still playing, and I did that for 15 years. I was a radio show host. Had a newspaper column. I worked for an Isle of Man company on behalf of certain players including Ravanelli, Emerson & Juninho. Since 2002 I have been managing director at GTC a Cheshire based cost reduction consultants. My Business partner is the secretary of the official Manchester City Supporters Club. On match days I work at City in the executive boxes. I live in Worsley and walk a lot with my German Shepherd."*

PAILOR Bob
Centre forward 6'0"
Born *7/7/1887 Stockton-on-Tees*
Died *24/1/1976 Hartlepool, County Durham age 88*
Playing career: *West Bromwich Albion (92 appearances 47 goals October 1908 – May 1914), Newcastle United 1914-15.*

He turned professional with West Bromwich Albion in October 1908, making his debut in January 1909 in a Division Two match against Bradford Park Avenue. Pailor was a player made for scoring goals. His hefty build, allied with ace and agility, made him such an effective and useful centre forward, one of the best around at that time. He averaged a goal every two games for Albion, including 40 in 79 league outings, and 16 in season 1912-13. In 1912 he helped Albion reach the FA Cup Final by scoring a last-gasp winner against Blackburn Rovers in the Semi Final replay. He topped Albion's scoring charts in two successive seasons 1911/12, scoring 10 league goals in 20 league games as well as in 1912/13 when he netted 16 league goals in 24 games. During his six years associated with Albion, Bob won many friends both on and off the field. He left Albion in 1914 after Alf Bentley arrived from Bolton Wanderers. In May 1914 he joined Newcastle United for a £1,550 fee. He had a kidney complaint, causing him to retire in May 1915, aged 28. He was a successful bookmaker in the Hartlepool area but in later years he was forced to hand over his licence when he became blind.

Bob Pailor

Carlton Palmer

PALMER Carlton

Midfielder/defender 6'2"

Born *5/12/1965 Rowley Regis.*

Playing career: *Chelsea youth, West Bromwich Albion (131+8 Sub appearances 5 goals Oct 1984 – Feb 1989), Sheffield Wednesday, Leeds United, Southampton, Nottingham Forest, Coventry City, Watford (loan), Sheffield Wednesday (loan), Stockport County, Dublin City, Mansfield Town, Staveley Miners Welfare (1984-2013). England U-21, 'B' and 18 Full Caps.*

Palmer started his career at West Bromwich Albion, joining as an apprentice in July 1983 before turning professional in December 1984. Carlton was a lanky, long striding youngster who made the breakthrough into big time soccer in splendid style. He occupied several different positions in Albion's senior side but preferred the number 2 shirt at right back or a place in midfield, a job he always wanted. He played in 121 league games scoring 4 goals for Albion. A serious shoulder injury prevented Carlton from gaining England U-21 honours in 1988. He skippered the side in 1989 in the Toulon International Tournament. After joining Sheffield Wednesday in February 1989 when ex-Albion boss Ron Atkinson signed him in a swap deal involving Colin West moving to West Bromwich Albion, Carlton played 205 league games scoring 14

goals for the Owls. In September 1997 he was signed Southampton for a fee of £1.0 million. In the dressing room he was described as abrasive, awkward and argumentative, but on the football pitch he was determined, hard-working and persistent and his long legs made him a most difficult player to compete against. Southampton manager Dave Jones said of Palmer "He covers every blade of grass out there, but that's only because his first touch is so crap". In January 1999 he was transferred to Nottingham Forest for a fee of £1.1 million. He later played for Coventry City, who in turn loaned him out to Watford for three months in 2000–01. He also had a loan spell at Sheffield Wednesday, before joining Stockport County in November 2001 where he was player-manager but was later sacked in September 2003. Palmer briefly played for Dublin City in Ireland, whom he joined in August 2004. He was appointed manager of Mansfield Town in November 2004. He resigned in September 2005. Later he worked as a television football pundit. He owned an online estate agency in Sheffield which ceased trading in 2008. He worked in Dubai for Repton School. He set up his own Football Academy in 2012 teaching football and PE. Was director of Sport at Wellington College Shanghai from 2014. In December 2016 he required a life-saving heart operation. He has since made a full recovery. His biography 'It Is What It Is' was released in October 2017 and contains some industrial language.

PEARSON Harold

Goalkeeper 6'1"

Born *7/5/1908 Bolehall, Tamworth, Staffs*

Died *31/10/1994 Sandwell*

Playing career: *Nuneaton Town, Tamworth Castle, West Bromwich Albion (303 appearances May 1927 – Aug 1937) Guest West Ham United in WW2. 1 England schoolboy appearance, 1 Full England International cap.*

Nicknamed 'Algy', Harold joined West Bromwich Albion as an amateur in April 1925 and turned professional a month later. His father Hubert Pearson was also a goalkeeper and the two were together on Albion's books until Hubert's retirement in May 1926. Harold Pearson made his debut in December 1927, in a Division Two match against South Shields.

In 1930/31 he helped the club to achieve promotion to the First Division and played in the 1931 FA Cup Final, in which Albion beat Birmingham 2–1. In 1932 he earned his only cap for England alongside his Albion team mate George Shaw, marking the occasion with a clean sheet in a 3–0 win over Scotland at Wembley Stadium. Pearson kept goal in the 1935 FA Cup Final, but this time earned only a runners-up medal as his team lost 4–2 to Sheffield Wednesday. After making 303 appearances for West Bromwich Albion, he joined Millwall for a £300 transfer fee in August 1937. He helped them win the Third Division South in 1937/38. He remained with Millwall until his retirement in 1940, although he did appear as a guest player for West Ham United later in Second World War. He married Doris Phillips in September 1939. He was the Son of Hubert Pearson of West Bromwich Albion, and Cousin of Harry Hibbs of Birmingham and Blackpool's Horace Pearson. Harold worked for a small arms firm during WW2, transferring to Webley and Scott of Great Barr. He died in October 1994 at the age of 86

Personal note: I met Harold a few times, once at the Hawthorns in the Halfords Lane stand prior to a game and twice I visited him at his home in Oldbury Road, West Bromwich in 1983. First impression when I shook hands with him was, wow his hands are massive. He could easily pick up a football with one hand. He was always willing to chat about football and enjoyed being recognised out and about around West Bromwich town centre. He always carried his FA Cup winners medal in his pocket. He told me that in the 1930-31 season the players were on £1 per week with a £1 bonus for a draw or a £2 bonus for a win. For the FA Cup Semi-Final against Everton, the players were paid their basic £1 plus a bonus of £4 for the win and in the FA Cup Final against Birmingham they received basic pay of £1 plus an £8 bonus per player. Harold showed me some of his medals, jerseys and replica FA Cup plus an engraved gold pocket watch.

PEARSON Hubert

Goalkeeper 5'11"
Born *15/5/1886 Kettlebrook, Tamworth, Staffs*
Died *October 1955 Tamworth, Staffs*
Playing career: *West Bromwich Albion (371 appearances 2 goals Feb 1905 – May 1926)*

A broad-shouldered goalkeeper, efficient, sound and dependable, Hubert's usefulness was not confined to the goal line. He would advance some distance to avert danger, fly-kicking the ball to safety if need be, but he was never regarded as being reckless. Hubert participated in Albion's 1912 FA Cup Final team, when they lost 1-0 after a replay against Barnsley. A junior international for England in 1907, Pearson senior was once selected for the English squad in 1923, to play against France, at the age of 37, but was forced to miss the fixture due to injury. However, he did play twice for the Football League in 1914 and 1922 plus he represented the Football League side and the FA. He spent his entire professional career with West Bromwich Albion spanning 18 years,1907-1925, making a total of 371 appearances and in 1911/12 season he scored two goals, both penalties. Pearson was the father of Albion keeper Harold Pearson, and the uncle of Harry Hibbs goalkeeper for Birmingham. It's interesting to know that between Hubert and his Son Harold, Pearson, they won every honour in the game available at that time : First, 1919/20 Second 1910/11 & Third Division (S) 1937/38 (Millwall) championship medals; First 1924/25 and Second Division runners up medals 1930/31; FA Cup winners 1931 and runners-up medals 1912 & 1935; FA Charity Shield Winners 1920 and runners up 1931.

PEMBERTON James 'Jimmy'

Right back 5'9"
Born *30/4/1916 Wolverhampton, Staffs*
Died *10/2/1996 Wolverhampton*
Playing career: *West Bromwich Albion (172 appearances Aug 1938 – Mar 1951)*

Jim was a strong, confident right back, hard and wiry, with a fine physique, solid kick and excellent positional sense. He was pretty fast too, one of the fastest full backs Albion have ever signed. During the war, Jimmy served as a Lance Corporal, R Fusiliers, based in North Africa and Italy. He played for the Army v Italy, Yugoslavia, England XI, Switzerland and Greece. A prominent member of Albion's Second Division promotion side of 1948-49, he was virtually an ever present in the side during the first four post-war League seasons, missing just 7 games out of 168.

He was then sorely injured playing against Aston Villa at Villa Park in the opening match of the 1950-51 season, and sadly he never played again. He lived in Wolverhampton in his retirement and was almost completely blind.

PENDREY Garry

Left back/defender 5'9"
Born *9/2/1949 Birmingham, England*
Playing career: *Birmingham City, West Bromwich Albion (Cost £30,000 18 appearances Aug 1979 – Aug 1981), Torquay United, Bristol Rovers & Walsall. (1966 – 1983)*

He signed for Birmingham City in 1965 as an apprentice defender, before agreeing professional terms in October 1966. Pendry played for the club until 1979, making 360 appearances in all competitions and scoring five goals. He then had a spell playing for West Bromwich Albion as a cover for Derek Statham, playing 18 games for Ron Atkinson's team in 1979/80. With his permed hair, a feature of the day, Pendrey was known for his tough tackling and no-nonsense clearances. It was something of a surprise when Atkinson signed him for Albion. Garry did not feature at all the following season and moved on to Torquay United in August 1981. Bristol Rovers was his next stop in December 1981 but onlymade just one appearance. He finished with 8 games at Walsall in the 1982/83 season. Pendrey went in to coaching whilst still playing at Walsall & then became assistant manager from 1983 to 1986. He joined Wolverhampton Wanderers as coach in November 1986. Garry managed his first club Birmingham City between June 1987 – April 1989. Upon getting the sack he re-joined Wolves as a coach in July 1989-1994. From 1996 until 2010 Pendrey had been an assistant to Gordon Strachan at Coventry City, Southampton, Celtic & Middlesbrough. Retired from active involvement with football.

"DID YOU KNOW?"

"West Bromwich Albion are the only team to have ever won the FA Cup and Promotion in the same season 1930/31."

PENNINGTON Jesse

Left back 5'8"
Born *23/8/1883 West Bromwich, Staffs*
Died *5/9/1970 Kidderminster aged 87*
Playing career: *Dudley Town, West Bromwich Albion (March 1903 – May 1922), Oldbury Town (guest), Notts County (guest) 25 England International caps, played for the Football League and for an England XI.*

One of the greatest names in the annals of West Bromwich Albion Football Club, Jesse 'Peerless' Pennington. Born in Maria Street in West Bromwich in August 1883. In the 1891 census, his family were living in Dartmouth Road, Smethwick. In the 1901 census Jesse was the 2nd of six children now living in St George's Street in Smethwick. He was a superbly equipped left back and scrupulously fair in his play. Notably quick in recovery and a defender with a beautiful balance, a keen eye and a splendid kick down the line. According to the 1911 census, Jesse was listed as a professional footballer, married to Nelly with one child and one servant. They were living at 33 High Street, Smethwick which was a cycle and outfitters shop until at least 1934. He was a magnificent club captain wonderful sportsman and indeed a grand clubman of the highest calibre. Jesse played 455 league games and appeared in 39 FA Cup ties including the 1912 Final, when Albion lost to Barnsley in a replay. He guided Albion to the Second Division championship in 1911. In 1913, Pennington was approached by Pascoe Bioletti who offered £5 per player for Albion corruptly to endeavour not to win their forthcoming game against Everton on 29th November. Pascoe's son, William Bioletti, was operator of a football betting business in Geneva. Pennington alerted the police and after the game, which ended in a draw, he met Bioletti, to collect the payoff, at which point the police moved in to arrest Bioletti who was sentenced to 5 months' imprisonment in 1914. As it happened, Albion and Everton drew the match. During WW1 he was employed in Coventry to work in a munition's factory, Guested for Coventry City in the 1918/19 Football League Midland Section. Jesse led Albion to the First Division League Championship in 1919/20. In his entire playing-career he never scored a goal – he did miss a penalty though. He was only ever dropped once and his displays were always edged with genius.

In 1910 he had a pay dispute with Albion and actually signed for Kidderminster Harriers. That dispute was sorted out thankfully and the appropriate forms cancelled before they were posted. Jesse had a sports and fishing tackle shop, also described as a cycle and outfitters shop, at 33, High Street, Smethwick where his family lived between 1912 until 1934 when the Co-operative bought the premises. Jesse retired from professional football in August 1922. He was a coach at Albion, Kidderminster Harriers & Malvern College. In 1936 Jesse was living in Shrawley, Worcestershire. In the 1939 register he was living at the Tanhouse, Worcester Road, Titton, Stourport. He was a scout for Wolves, managed Kidderminster Harriers, and scouted for Albion 1950 – 1960. He was living at 3, Hazeldine, Hartlebury, Stourport between 1968 – 1970 until his death in Kidderminster Hospital in September 1970. He was made a life member at WBA in 1969.
Personal note: *I went with my parents to meet Jesse at his cottage in Hartlebury in 1964. He was such a charming man. He knew my Mom, who was Fred Everiss' daughter, from his time with the Albion. He reminded me that he pronounced his name as Jess, even though it had an 'e' on the end, it was not Jessie. I told Jesse that Fred Everiss, former Albion secretary/ manager, was my Grandfather but he died a year before I was born and I never met my other Grandfather either, Jesse said, "You can call me Grandad!"*

PERRY Charles 'Charlie'

Centre half 5'11"
Born *3/1/1866 West Bromwich*
Died *2/7/1927 West Bromwich*
Playing career: *West Bromwich Albion (210 appearances 15 goals Aug 1885 – May 1896) Won three England Caps & represented the League XI*
Charlie was a superb player and grand captain. He had a polished style, was determined in everything he did, cool under pressure, and a man who marshalled his defence magnificently from the centre half position, which was undoubtedly his best. He made his first team debut, replacing the injured Fred Bunn, in the 1886 FA Cup Final against Blackburn Rovers at The Oval, a match that finished 0–0. Perry collected a runners-up medal after Albion lost 2–0 in the replay.

He was on the losing side once more in the 1887 final, in a 2–0 defeat to Aston Villa. He picked up his first winner's medal in 1888 as Albion beat Preston North End 2–1. Charlie Perry had another winner's medal in the 3–0 win over Aston Villa in 1892. However, he missed the 1895 FA Cup Final due to an injury that later forced his retirement in May 1896. He was also director of the club between 1898 and 1902. He kept the 'Golden Cup' public house on Cross Street West Bromwich until George 'Spry' Woodhall took it over in 1905. Brother of Walter & Tom. Charlie was Albion's first 'great' centre half and all told he served the club in 210 competitive games, being a regular in the side from 1888 to 1895.

Mick Perry

PERRY Michael 'Mick'

Midfielder 5'10"

Born *4/4/1964 Wimbledon, London*

Playing career: *West Bromwich Albion (17 + 6 sub appearances 5 goals Feb 1982 - Oct 1984), Torquay United (loan), Northampton Town (loan, Mansfield Town (loan), Torquay United, Port Vale (.*

Mick joined the Albion in June 1980 as an apprentice having represented Kingston-upon-Thames Schools. He signed professional forms in February 1982 and made his debut v Watford at home in April 1983. Perry had 5 years at the Hawthorns but spent some of the time on loan at Torquay making 5 league appearances in 1984, Northampton Town making 4 league appearances 1984, and Mansfield before signing in March 1985 for £5,000 by Torquay United. He played in 18 league games scoring one goal 1984/85. He had a brief spell at Port Vale on trial, then drifted into non-league football with Wealdstone, Worcester, Slough and Redditch before he retired and became part of a sales team for GM Coachwork who specialise in converting vehicles so wheelchair users can drive or be a passenger. Mick still lives locally in Great Barr with his partner Bea and his two stepsons. Mick has attended numerous AGM's of the Old Baggies' Former Players Association in recent years.

PERRY Thomas 'Tom'

Half back 5'9"

Born *5/08/1871 West Bromwich*

Died *18/7/1927 West Bromwich*

Playing career: *Stourbridge, West Bromwich Albion (280 appearances 15 goals July 1890 – Oct 1901), Aston Villa. Played for England once the League XI*

Stalwart, right half for Albion during the ten years leading up to the club's move from Stoney Lane to the Hawthorns. Tom Perry was a capable, efficient and extremely enthusiastic performer, whose hard graft and dedicated approach to the game made him such a key figure in the 1890's. Made his debut as outside left, but soon moved to half back. He was right half in the 1895 FA Cup Final which was his best role. In all he played 280 competitive games for the club. Moved to Aston Villa in October 1901 and retired in 1903. Brother of Walter & Charlie. Tom died two weeks after Charlie, and his Walter passed on a year later in 1928.

PERRY Walter

Wing half / Inside Forward 5'9"

Born *11/10/1868 West Bromwich*

Died *21/9/1928 West Bromwich*

Playing career: *West Bromwich Excelsior, West Bromwich Albion (Aug 1886 – Dec 1889), Wolverhampton Wanderers, Warwick County, Burton Swifts, West Bromwich Albion (Total 15 appearances 7 goals Oct 1894 – Nov 1895), Burton Swifts.*

A naturally gifted, versatile footballer, Walter Perry, who could occupy both wing–half and inside–forward positions, had two spells with West Bromwich Albion but never really established himself as a regular in the first team. His first club was West Bromwich Excelsior for which he signed in 1885. He then signed for West Bromwich Albion in August 1886 and made his League debut on 29 September 1888 at Stoney Lane, the club's home ground at that time. The visitors were Burnley and the home team defeated the visitors 4–3. Walter Perry also scored his debut League goal in this match. Perry left for Wolverhampton Wanderers in December 1889 having got no first–team action at Albion. He appeared in eight League matches for the 'Wolves' and scored three League goals. In May 1890 he left for non–League Warwick County. By August 1891 he was back in the Football League, but a Second Division club Burton Swifts, where he appeared 47 times for 40 League and seven FA Cup, scoring 12 goals, seven in the league and five in the FA Cup. He returned to Albion in October 1894, where he made one more top–flight appearance, retiring in 1900. Brother of Charlie & Tom. He returned to 'Albion' in 1906 as reserve team manager, leaving in 1907 and was a Football League linesman from 1909–12. He was taken ill shortly after World War 1 ended and never fully recovered his health, passing away on 21 September 1928.

"DID YOU KNOW?"

"Tony Brown is Albion's record goal scorer with 279, although W.G.Richardson scored 328 for WBA, 100 of them were in War-Time competitions which don't usually count. "

PESCHISOLIDO 'Paul' Paolo Pasquale

Striker 5'7"

Born *25/5/1971 Scarborough, Ontario, Canada*
Playing career: *Toronto Blizzard, Kansas City Comets (indoor), Birmingham City, Stoke City, Birmingham City, West Bromwich Albion (Cost £600,000 41 + 10 sub appearances 21 goals July 1996 – Oct 1997), Fulham, Queens Park Rangers (loan), Sheffield United (loan), Norwich City (loan), Sheffield United, Derby County, Luton, St Patricks Athletic in Dublin. (1990 – 2009) Canada U-17, U-20, U-23 and Full International 53 caps.*

Peschisolido, nicknamed 'Pesch', began his professional playing career when still a high-schooler with Archbishop Denis O'Connor Catholic High School in Ajax, Canada. He led the team to OFSAA finals in his last year then moved on as a trainee with the Toronto Blizzard of the Canadian Soccer League, where he was named the "Rookie of the Year" in 1989. He also played the 1990/91 Major Indoor Soccer League season with the Kansas City Comets, being named the league's 'Newcomer of the Year'. After spending a year with the Juventus academy, returning homesick saw him offered the opportunity to join Birmingham City for £25,000. He was joint top scorer in each of his two seasons with the club. In August 1994, he moved on to Stoke City in a £400,000 plus player exchange deal involving Dave Regis. In 1995, Peschisolido married Karren Brady, now Baroness Brady, who was at the time managing director of Birmingham City. He was top scorer with 15 goals for the 1994/95 season, and remained at Stoke until March 1996, when he returned to Birmingham until the end of the 1995/96 seasons. Peschisolido signed for West Bromwich Albion in a £600,000 deal in July 1996. Rarely have Albion fans been so pleased to sign a player because in the seasons leading up to him joining the Baggies, if 'Pesch' was on the opposition's team sheet, you could guarantee that he would stick the ball into the Albion net on at least one occasion, home or away, come rain or shine. Quick off the mark, devastating over 10 or 12 yards, Peschisolido was always a livewire player in and around the 18-yard box, a player who would run the channels all day, who would chase down lost causes and would be a living nightmare to defenders.

Feisty and fiery, 'Pesch' was a complete handful. He made his first appearance for the club in the 3–1 home League Cup defeat to Colchester United on 3rd September 1996. Four days later, Paul scored just nine minutes into his Albion league debut, as the Midlands side ran out 2–0 winners at Queens Park Rangers. 'Pesch' and Andy Hunt were useful strike partners up front, later joined by a young Lee Hughes. He was joint top League scorer that season for the club. After 51 appearances and 21 goals for West Brom, he dropped down a division to join Fulham in October 1997, for a £1.1 million transfer fee. Peschisolido was loaned to Queens Park Rangers in November 2000. In January 2001, he went on loan again, this time to Sheffield United, before spending a further loan period at Norwich City. He later re-joined Sheffield United in a permanent deal for £250,000, after agreeing to a wage cut. He was a key player in the 2002/03 season, helping the club reach the semi-finals of the 2003 FA Cup and League Cup and the Division One play-off final. In March 2004, Peschisolido joined Derby County in a swap deal, with Izale McLeod moving to United on loan for the rest of the season. In July 2007 Peschisolido signed for Luton Town on a one-year deal. He played just four league matches and one cup match for Luton, scoring once in the Football League Trophy against Northampton Town, before an ankle problem kept him out of action from September onwards. After the injury failed to respond to injections it was confirmed in December that he would require an operation, ruling him out for the rest of the season. Luton released Peschisolido at the end of the 2007/08 season, following their relegation to League Two. By the time he announced his retirement from playing football, he had accumulated 447 League appearances and 118 goals over 16 years, predominantly in the second tier of English professional football. He also made 76 cup appearances, scoring 22 goals. On 15th January 2009, he was appointed as Jeff Kenna's assistant manager at League of Ireland club St Patrick's Athletic. Both Kenna and Peschisolido registered as players for the 2009 season in case of emergency. On 15th May 2009, he resigned from this post for "personal reasons" with immediate effect.

Three days later, 18th May 2009, he was appointed manager of Burton Albion taking over from caretaker manager Roy McFarland, who had taken the club to promotion to League Two after the departure of Nigel Clough. He was dismissed in March 2012 following a poor of games which left Burton in 17th position.

PHELAN Mike

Midfielder 5'11"

Born 24/9/1962 Nelson, Lancashire
Playing career: *Burnley, Norwich City, Manchester United, West Bromwich Albion (Free transfer 20 + 3 sub appearances July 1994 – Jan 1995) (1979-1995).*

Haing been born in Nelson, Lancashire, he started his playing career at Burnley where he played 168 league games scoring 9 goals between 1979-85. Burnley were relegated to the Fourth Division, and Phelan moved to Norwich City for £60,000 in July 1985, where he played another 156 league games scoring 9 goals. His success for the Canaries drew the attention of larger clubs and he followed Steve Bruce to Manchester United for £750,000 on 1st July 1989. At Manchester United, he finally won his first international cap, against Italy in 1989, and an FA Cup winner's medal in his first season. This was followed by the FA Charity Shield in 1990, European Cup Winners' Cup in 1991 and the League Cup in 1992. Phelan was often deployed at right-back during his first season at Manchester United, but following the arrival of Denis Irwin in 1990 he mostly played on the right or in the centre of midfield. He had played on the right side of midfield before Irwin's arrival, most notably in the FA Cup final win over Crystal Palace in May 1990, when Paul Ince was switched from central midfield to right-back. With the younger players stepping up at Old Trafford, Phelan was given a free transfer at the end of the 1993/94 season, signing for West Bromwich Albion, where he spent 18 months. In the first season he made 19 appearances plus 3 as a substitute. He had lost his pace and it was obvious that his best footballing years were behind him. The next year, with his first-team chances limited by younger players such as Kevin Donovan and Lee Ashcroft, who were more favoured by new manager Alan Buckley, appointed in the autumn following the dismissal of Keith Burkinshaw.

Phelan, having made just one further appearanc as a substitute, retired from playing at the end of the 1995/96 season. He returned to Carrow Road in December 1995, as assistant manager to Gary Megson and managed the club's reserve team. When Megson was fired and subsequently joined Blackpool, Phelan followed him to take up a similar role, returning to his native North-West. A year later, he followed Megson to Stockport County. Phelan moved on shortly afterwards, accepting a post at Manchester United's Centre of Excellence. With Steve McClaren's departure to Middlesbrough in the summer of 2001, Phelan was promoted to first-team coach. He was appointed assistant manager of Manchester United on 3rd September 2008, replacing Carlos Queiroz who had left to manage the Portugal national football team. Phelan was Sir Alex Ferguson's right-hand man during three Premier League title wins, a Club World Cup, two League Cups and two runs to the final of the UEFA Champions League. He departed the club shortly after Sir Alex Ferguson's retirement. In November 2014, Phelan was announced as a first-team coach at Norwich City. Following the resignation of Neil Adams on 5th January 2015, Phelan was named caretaker manager of the Norfolk side. On 9th January 2015, Norwich appointed Hamilton Academical manager Alex Neil, and Phelan returned to his first-team coaching duties. On 20th January 2015, Phelan left the club by mutual consent. On 5th February 2015, Phelan was named assistant manager at Hull City. In July 2016, following the resignation of fellow ex-Manchester United player Steve Bruce, the club confirmed that Phelan would act as caretaker manager. In October 2016, Phelan was appointed first-team manager on a permanent basis. This only lasted until 3rd January 2017, when Hull City released a statement stating that the club and Phelan had parted company due to a desire for a fresh approach. 16th July 2018, Phelan was appointed Sporting Director at Central Coast Mariners in Australia. On 19th December 2018, Phelan was appointed as a first-team coach for Manchester United's caretaker manager, Ole Gunnar Solskjær. On 10th May 2019 he was appointed as United's assistant manager.

PHILLIPS Kevin

Striker 5'7"

Born *25/7/1973 Hitchin, Hertfordshire*
Playing career: *Baldock Town, Watford, Sunderland,
Southampton, Aston Villa, West Bromwich Albion
(Cost £700,000 68 + 13 sub appearances 46 goals Aug
2006 – June 2008)),Birmingham City, Blackpool,
Crystal Palace (loan then signed), Leicester City (1991
– 2014) 1 England 'B' cap and 8 Full England
International caps*

He started his footballing career at
Southampton being taken on as an
apprentice in 1989. As a youth, Phillips was
considered to be too small to play up front
and was played at right back, in which
position he made two reserve team
appearances in 1990. He failed to make the
grade at Southampton and was released by
manager Chris Nicholl, and returned to
Hertfordshire where he signed for non-
League semi-professional side Baldock
Town in the summer of 1991. Here, he was
initially played as a defender until an injury
crisis resulted in manager Ian Allinson
playing Phillips as a striker, scoring twice in
his first match in his new role. He was
signed by Watford in December 1994 for an
initial £10,000, plus four additional
payments of £5,000. He suffered a foot injury
in March 1996, initially diagnosed as a
hairline fracture of the ankle and later
discovered to be a hole in a ligament in his
foot, that kept him out for a year. In July
1997, Phillips signed for Sunderland for a fee
of £325,000, potentially rising to more than
£600,000, just after their relegation from the
Premiership. In the 1997/98 season, Phillips
set or equalled club records by scoring in
seven consecutive matches and in nine
consecutive home matches, became the first
Sunderland player since Brian Clough in
1961/62 to score 30 goals in a season, and
finished the campaign with 35 goals in all
competitions, the most by any Sunderland
player in one season since the Second World
War. After scoring Sunderland's second goal
in the Play-Off Final, Phillips was
substituted after 73 minutes with an injury,
so missed the remainder of the 4–4 draw
with Charlton Athletic which Sunderland
lost 7–6 on penalties. Promotion was
confirmed in April 1999 as Phillips scored
four of Sunderland's five goals in an away
game against Bury, and he ended the season
with 23 goals from only 26 league games,

and 25 goals in all competitions. His form
earned him an international call-up for
England, and he made his debut in the
starting eleven in a friendly against
Hungary. In January 2001, Phillips scored
his 104th goal for Sunderland, breaking the
club's post-war goalscoring record. As the
season wore on, Kevin suffered both a lack
of form and disciplinary problems. Phillips'
goals contribution to Sunderland's 2001/02
season fell to 13. He had played in 235
matches for Sunderland, and scored 130
goals at an average of better than a goal
every two games. In August 2003, following
Sunderland's relegation from the Premier
League, Phillips moved to the south coast to
join Southampton for a fee of £3.25 million.
He continued to score regularly in his
partnership with new signing Peter Crouch.
29th June 2005, he departed from
Southampton after two years and 22 league
goals to join Aston Villa in a £1 million deal.
Phillips shared front-man duties with Juan
Pablo Ángel and fellow new signing Milan
Baroš, but illness and further injuries
disrupted his season, in which he
contributed only five goals. He began the
2006/07 season with Villa, but on 22nd
August, he signed for West Bromwich
Albion for a £700,000 fee. He scored 22 goals
in his first season with West Brom, including
two hat-tricks, one in a 5–1 win at Ipswich
Town and the second in a 7–0 defeat of
Barnsley on the final day of the regular
season that confirmed Albion's place in the
play-offs. Phillips scored twice in the first leg
of the Play-Off Semi-Final against
Wolverhampton Wanderers, and headed the
only goal of the second leg at the Hawthorns
to ensure their progression to the Final at
Wembley, which they lost 1–0 to Derby
County. He missed six weeks of the 2007–08
season because of a knee injury sustained in
early November, but rediscovered his
goalscoring form on his return to win the
Championship player-of-the-month award
for December. Described by Albion manager
Tony Mowbray as "a natural goal-scorer
with great awareness and vision", Phillips
scored his 200th League goal in a 1–1 draw
with Crystal Palace on 13th March 2008. For
the last match of the season, away to Queens
Park Rangers, fans of West Bromwich Albion
chose to dress up as superheroes in honour
of Phillips, who is nicknamed "Super Kev".

Stuart Phillips

Albion won the match 2–0 to win promotion to the Premier League as champions. Phillips won numerous awards over the season. He received Player-of-the-Year awards from both the West Bromwich Albion Supporters Club and from the club itself, after scoring 24 goals from 30 starts and finishing as the Championship's second top goalscorer. At national level, he was chosen Championship Player of the Year at the annual Football League Awards. He made 71 league appearances scoring 38 goals for the Baggies. When his contract with West Bromwich Albion expired at the end of the 2007/08 season, the club offered Phillips a one-year deal, with an additional second year if he made 19 or more league appearances. He rejected the offer, preferring to sign a two-year contract with Birmingham City, newly relegated from the Premier League. He signed a one-year contract extension ahead of the 2010–11 season, but missed the start through injury.

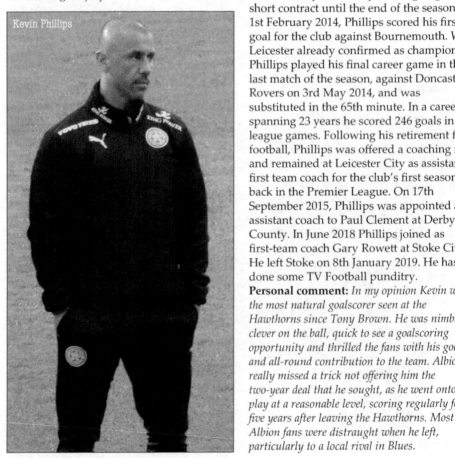

Kevin Phillips

He went on to make five league starts, but his major contribution came in the League Cup. Facing League One club Brentford, Phillips scored a stoppage-time equaliser and converted his penalty in the shootout by which Birmingham progressed to the quarter-final. They went on to reach the final, where Phillips received his first winners' medal in a cup competition, albeit as an unused substitute, as Birmingham defeated favourites Arsenal 2–1. In July 2011, Phillips signed a one-year deal with Championship club Blackpool. Phillips finished the season as the club's top scorer, with 17 goals in all competitions. Phillips took up the option to extend his Blackpool contract for a further year, but scored only twice from 18 appearances before following manager Ian Holloway to Championship rivals Crystal Palace, initially on loan then signed a one-year deal. However, after 18 league games and 6 goals he left for Leicester City in January 2014 signing a short contract until the end of the season. On 1st February 2014, Phillips scored his first goal for the club against Bournemouth. With Leicester already confirmed as champions, Phillips played his final career game in the last match of the season, against Doncaster Rovers on 3rd May 2014, and was substituted in the 65th minute. In a career spanning 23 years he scored 246 goals in 580 league games. Following his retirement from football, Phillips was offered a coaching role and remained at Leicester City as assistant first team coach for the club's first season back in the Premier League. On 17th September 2015, Phillips was appointed as assistant coach to Paul Clement at Derby County. In June 2018 Phillips joined as first-team coach Gary Rowett at Stoke City. He left Stoke on 8th January 2019. He has done some TV Football punditry.

Personal comment: *In my opinion Kevin was the most natural goalscorer seen at the Hawthorns since Tony Brown. He was nimble, clever on the ball, quick to see a goalscoring opportunity and thrilled the fans with his goals and all-round contribution to the team. Albion really missed a trick not offering him the two-year deal that he sought, as he went onto play at a reasonable level, scoring regularly for five years after leaving the Hawthorns. Most Albion fans were distraught when he left, particularly to a local rival in Blues.*

PHILLIPS Stewart

Centre Forward 6'0½"

Born *30/12/1961 Halifax, England*

Playing career: *Hereford United, West Bromwich Albion (Cost £25,000 15 + 1 sub appearances 4 goals Mar 1988 – Jan 1989), Swansea City, Wrexham, Sudbury Town, AFC Sudbury, Worcester City, Newport County (1977 – 1994)*

He signed as an amateur for Hereford United in July 1976 becoming a full professional in November of that year. In two separate spells with Hereford, Stewart Phillips proved to be a talented goalscorer, and will remain in the record books forever. Stewart was the first player to score a hat-trick in an away match for the club in the Football League, and was also the first to score 100 goals for United in the league era. Stewart went on to be the Bulls' top scorer in four successive seasons, 1981/82 16 goals, 1982/83 14 goals, 1983/84 19 goals and 1984/85 22 goals. Phillips is remembered for his contribution to the Whites v Blacks game in 1978. The showing of the BBC documentary of the Len Cantello testimonial reminded us that Stewart played in this game at the tender age of 17 years and scored one of the 3 goals in the 3-2 win for the Blacks. Stewart Phillips spent nearly 10 years at Hereford before signing for the Albion in March 1988 for £25,000. He made his debut v Middlesbrough in the same month. He helped Albion stave off the threat of relegation from the Second Division. Although he did not make many appearances for the Albion, he has fond memories of his time with Albion, 15 + 1 as a substitute scoring 4 goals, Phillips said "I really enjoyed my spell at the Hawthorns. It was just unfortunate Ron Atkinson and Colin Addison went to Atletico Madrid. I was just caught up in it really. It was all about timing…right place, wrong time. I didn't doubt my ability at that level at all. I'd had a good scoring record at Hereford, and I was getting used to playing in the Second Division." After 15 appearances plus 1 as a substitute and 4 goals he moved onto Swansea in February 1989 for £25,000. Stewart returned to Hereford in August 1990 followed by a short stint at Wrexham. Upon finishing his career Stewart remained in Hereford where he lives with his wife Joanne, he has 2 grown up sons Ashley & Alex and has his own Property Development Business. A keen follower of the Old Baggies Former Players' Association, a regular at the Golf Day and often seen in the Regis Suite on match days.

Personal note: *Stewart scored a terrific goal at St Andrews in what turned out to be his final match for Albion as they beat Birmingham City 4-1 on October 15th 1988 with the other goals coming from Hopkins 2 and Gary Robson. However, as Stewart himself put it, it was a case of "right place, wrong time"*

PIGGOTT Gary

Striker/forward 6'0"

Born *1/4/1969 Warley, West Midlands*

Playing career: *Dudley Town, West Bromwich Albion (3 + 2 sub appearances 1991 – 1992), Shrewsbury Town (1992 – 1993), Willenhall Town, Tamworth*

Gary Piggott started his footballing career at Dudley Town. Signed by Bobby Gould in the Summer of 1991 made his debut away at Darlington in a Division Three match that Albion won 1-0 with a Don Goodman goal. He made 3 league starts and 2 substitute appearances without scoring. Really, he did nothing in Bobby Gould's poor team other than possess a great fans' chant: "I'd rather have a Pig than a Bull', referring to Steve Bull of course. He moved to Shrewsbury Town for the 1992/93 season and in another uneventful spell, he made 4 league appearances without scoring. He went back into non-league football with Willenhall Town and the Tamworth. After football he became an electrician.

POTTER Graham

Left back 6'1"

Born *20/5/1975 Solihull*

Playing career: *Birmingham City, Wycombe Wanderers (loan), Stoke City, Southampton, West Bromwich Albion (Cost £300,000 32+15 sub appearances Feb 1997 – June 2000), Northampton Town (loan), Reading (loan), York City, Boston United, Shrewsbury Town (loan), Macclesfield Town. (1992-2005). Played once for England at U-21 level*

Potter began his career as a trainee at Birmingham City, making 25 appearances scoring twice. After a loan spell at Wycombe Wanderers and three appearances, he moved on to Stoke City. In three years he played 45 games for the Potters, scoring once. He had one season with Southampton during the 1996/97 season but only played in 8 games for the south coast club.

He joined West Bromwich Albion in 1997, making 32 appearances plus 15 as a substitute. A tall left sided full back but not the quickest or most skilful. After three-and-a-half years at the Hawthorns, which included two loan spells at Northampton Town, playing 4 games, and Reading another 4 appearances, he signed for York City. At the Yorkshire club, he seemed to find his footballing level and a place to play regularly , notching up a total of 114 league games, during which, he scored 5 goals in his three seasons at Bootham Crescent. Potter moved from York City to Boston United in the summer of 2003 but joined Shrewsbury Town on loan just a few months later in November of the same year. In 2004, he moved on a free transfer to Macclesfield Town, where he finished his senior playing career. He became a beneficiary of the PFA's Education scheme and graduated with a 2:1 in Social Sciences from the Open University, He then became Football Development Manager at Hull University, coaching the University teams and developing football within the community. He also worked at York City coaching the Under 14s at their Centre of Excellence. At this time, he also acted as ssistant coach for the England Universities Squad. He then joined Leeds Metropolitan University in July 2008 as Football Coaching Manager. In December 2010 he was appointed coach for Ostersunds FK. In Sweden. In 2013, after two successive promotions, Potter extended his contract with the club for another three years. On 13 April 2017, Potter's team won the Svenska Cupen, beating Norrköping 4–1 in the final. Potter was appointed manager of newly relegated Championship club Swansea City on 11 June 2018 on a three-year contract. The Swans finished 10th in the league, after a strong end of season run. Swansea initially offered Potter a new contract to remain at the club, which would have made him one of the Championship's highest earning managers. However, the club eventually granted permission for Potter to begin talks with Brighton, who would reportedly pay Swansea about £3m in compensation for Potter and his backroom staff. Potter was appointed head coach of Premier League club Brighton & Hove Albion on 20 May 2019, signing a four-year contract.

POTTER Raymond 'Ray'

Goalkeeper 6'0"

Born *7/5/1936 Beckenham, Kent*
Died *7/8/2005 aged 69*
Playing career: *Crystal, Palace, West Bromwich Albion (Free transfer 238 appearances July 1958 – June 1967), Portsmouth (1951 – 1970).*

Ray Potter started his professional career at Crystal Palace where he played 44 league games in 5 seasons. After the halcyon days when Jim Sanders and Norman Heath had been fighting it out for the goalkeeping jersey in the early 1950s, Albion had struggled to find a long-term successor, Sanders in his final season sharing that berth with Colin Jackman for much of the 1957/58 season. Ray was tempted north on a free transfer to West Bromwich Albion and given a chance to play in the top flight rather than Division Four where Palace were labouring, as he fought his way into the first team. He had competition from Jackman and, later on, Jock Wallace and the youthful Tony Millington, but Potter was as tenacious as they come, always fighting his way back into a starting eleven that, in his early days, included the likes of Bobby Robson, Don Howe and Derek Kevan. Potter tended to stay on his line, leaving it to Stan Jones, Terry Simpson and Chuck Drury to command the box, a surprise given Potter was powerfully built enough to give as good as he got in the rough and tumble of the penalty area. Looked on as a "steady Eddie" of a goalkeeper, Potter came into his own from 1962/63 onwards A model of consistency, ever present in the following two seasons.

Potter was an important stabilising force at the back for the Baggies as they gradually evolved into the formidable cup fighting force that would lay waste to the rest of the country in the late 1960s. With a team that tried to pour forward at every opportunity, the goalkeeper had a big part to play, not least when we got our hands on our first piece of silverware in a dozen years by beating West Ham United over two legs in the League Cup final of 1966.The first game was at Upton Park and Potter was outstanding, making a couple of fine saves, as Albion were trailing just 2-1 after the 1st leg, setting the team up for the blitzkrieg that destroyed the Hammers 4-1, winning the cup 5-3 on aggregate. That was Ray Potter's finest hour at the Hawthorns. He wasn't a barmy, larger than life character like John Osborne, the man who eventually put paid to Ray's Albion career on his arrival from Chesterfield. Instead, Potter was a quiet, thoughtful man, modest, a footballer who was happy to do his job with the minimum of fuss, quietly keeping the ball out of the net, pleased that somebody else was being forced into the spotlight. He left the Hawthorns in May 1967, signing for Portsmouth, where he spent three seasons, making just 3 league appearances, before retiring in 1970. He became Assistant Commercial Manager at Colchester United in August 1970. Moved to Bournemouth as Assistant Commercial Manager & P.R.O. Secretary 1970 – 1975. Later Ray joined the administration team at Portsmouth.

POTTER Ronald 'Ron'

Centre half 5'10"
Born 5/12/1948 Wolverhampton
Playing career: *West Bromwich Albion (8 appearances Dec 1966 – Nov 1970), Swindon Town. (1964 – 1975)*
Ron was an enthusiastic centre half whose 8 appearances for Albion spanned six seasons when he covered for Stan Jones and John Talbut. He moved on to Swindon Town in November 1970. At the County Ground he played 91 games plus two substitute appearances. Between November 1970 and May 1975. He had an unsuccessful trail at Hartlepool in 1975 He was in the antiques business in Quatt, Near Bridgnorth. Moved to live in the Portsmouth area.

QUASHIE Nigel

Midfielder 5'9"
Born 20/7/1978 Southwark, London
Playing career: *Queens Park Rangers, Nottingham Forest, Portsmouth, Southampton, West Bromwich Albion, West Ham United, Birmingham City (loan), Wolverhampton Wanderers (loan), Milton Keynes Dons (loan), Queens Park Rangers, IR in Iceland, Bl / Bolungarvikm in Iceland. England U21 & 'B' International plus 14 caps for Scotland*
Quashie was born in the London Borough of Southwark to a Ghanaian father and an English mother. He was married for ten years to Joanna, with whom he had a daughter and a son, who died shortly after birth in 1999. After a divorce and his move to West Bromwich Albion, he started a relationship with Kerry Clarke, who in September 2005 gave birth to his son. He began his career in London as a trainee with Queens Park Rangers in August 1995 making 58 league appearances. Quashie joined Premier League side Nottingham Forest for £2.5 million at the start of the 1998/99 season. He played in 43 league games for Forest. Quashie joined Portsmouth in August 2000 for a fee worth up to £600,000, signing a three-year contract. He seemed to have settled well with Pompey playing 148 league games scoring 13 goals. Quashie joined rivals Southampton for a fee of £2.1 million in January 2005 where he made 37 league appearances before moving again to West Bromwich Albion in January 2006 for £1.2 million. He was charged with misconduct by the Football Association after being sent off against Middlesbrough three weeks later for alleged use of foul and abusive language towards the referee's assistants as he left the pitch and was given a one-game ban in addition to a four-game ban for the sending off, his second of the season, and a £5,000 fine after admitting misconduct. Albion were relegated at the end of the season. Quashie achieved the rare distinction of being relegated from the Premiership in two successive seasons. Following relegation, Quashie was allowed to leave in the January 2007 transfer window as he expressed a wish to return to the Premier League and manager, Tony Mowbray, wanted to raise some revenue to bring in new players. After 30 appearances plus one goal for Albion, he joined West Ham United on a three-and-a-half-year contract for an initial fee of £1.5

Nigel Quashie

RAVEN Paul
Centre back 6'0"

Born *28/7/1970 Salisbury*

Playing career: *Doncaster Rovers, West Bromwich Albion (Cost £150,000 294 +10 sub appearances 21 goals May 1989 - July 2000), Doncaster Rovers (loan), Rotherham United, Grimsby Town, Carlisle United, Barrow (1988-2006). England schoolboy and Youth.*

Raven started at Doncaster Rovers signing professional in July 1988. After his first full season with Rovers, where he made 52 league appearances, he moved to West Bromwich Albion for £150,000. Raven played for Albion for the next eleven years, while also spending time on loan with former club Doncaster playing 7 games in 1991/92, and Rotherham United playing 11 games 1998/99. Nickname 'Raves', he was a strong determined defender, who could occupy right back or centre back berths. Paul was a member of the Albion team that won the play off Final at Wembley in 1993. He played in 259 league games, totalling 294 appearances plus 10 as a substitute in all competitions scoring 21 goals. In July 2000, Raven joined Grimsby Town on a free transfer. Grimsby were managed by Alan Buckley for whom he had previously played at the Hawthorns. Although Buckley was sacked eight weeks later, Raven played for three years at Blundell Park. In the summer of 2003, he joined Carlisle United along with fellow Grimsby player Steve Livingstone. During his time at Carlisle he scored once against York.

million, rising to £1.75 million after West Ham successfully avoided relegation in the 2006/07 season. A persistent foot injury meant that Quashie did not play a single competitive match during 2007/08. Quashie trained with Birmingham City of the Championship for several weeks to regain fitness, before signing on loan, initially for a month, in October 2008, but returned to West Ham in January, having played 11 times for Birmingham. He had short spells with Wolverhampton Wanderers, MK Dons & made a return to Queens Park Rangers. On 13th April 2012, Quashie joined Icleandic side Íþróttafélag Reykjavíkur on a two-year contract as both a player and as assistant manager to Andri Marteinsson. He was also a coach in the ÍR academy. Following the dismissal of the manager on 21t August 2012 with ÍR at the bottom of the division, Quashie was appointed to take charge of the team until the end of the 2012 season. In January 2013, Quashie signed a 3-year contract with Icelandic club BÍ/Bolungarvík. He also served as assistant coach in all three seasons. He retired from playing football following the 2015 season. Although born in London and having played for England at U-21 and 'B', International levels, he opted to play for Scotland after declaring that his Grandfather was born in Glasgow. He made 14 appearances in the Blue of Scotland.

Paul Raven

After Carlisle, he played out the last two years of his career at Barrow. Following his retirement Paul worked in the sportswear industry representing brands such as Mitre, Prostar and Uhlsport as a Key Account Manager before joining the PFA as an advisor and project worker for the education department. Educated to degree standard Paul is ideally placed to impart his own knowledge and experience to future, current and former members. Paul is a very supportive member of the Old Baggies Former Players' Association. He lives in Doncaster.

RAW Henry 'Harry'
Wing half / inside forward 5'8½"
Born 6/7/1903 Tow Law, County Durham
Died Nov 1965 Tow Law, County Durham
Playing career: *Huddersfield Town, West Bromwich Albion (Cost £1,500 27 appearances 7 goals Feb 1931 – July 1936), Lincoln City (1925-1939)*
Nicknamed 'Harry' he was a schemer with go-ahead ideas, a player of commendable steadiness, who played for Huddersfield Town in their Championship year side of 1925/26 and in their FA Cup team of 1930, playing in 63 league games for the Terriers scoring 11 goals. Harry's first professional contract, signed on 14th May, 1925. With this came the signing-on fee, a massive £10 and then a weekly wage of £5. He moved to the Hawthorns February 1931 as cover for Joe Carter and Tommy Magee, but he spent most of his time in Albion's Central League side, gaining three championship medals with the second XI in the 1930's, to go with the two he won with Huddersfield Town. He moved to Lincoln City for £250 in August 1936 until retiring in 1939. He always regarded Huddersfield Town as his big love and stayed close to Billy Smith, Tommy Wilson, Roy Goodall, and Marshall 'Bon' Spence. He even wore the badge from his FA Cup Final shirt on a blazer when he managed Crook Town in the 1940's. Harry ended up at the steel works latterly. Stayed involved with Tow Law Town all his life.

"DID YOU KNOW?"

"Neil Clement and Chris Brunt have both appeared in three promotions whilst playing for Albion."

RAWLINGS James 'Sid'
Outside right 5'8½"
Born 5/5/1913 Wombwell, South Yorkshire
Died July 1956 Penarth, South Wales aged 43
Playing career: *Preston North End, Huddersfield Town, West Bromwich Albion (Cost £600 10 appearances scoring 1 goal Mar 1935 – June 1936), Northampton Town, Millwall, During WW2 guested for Clapton Orient, Rochdale, Preston North End, Bury, Liverpool, Southport, Stockport County and was loaned to Everton then signed by them, Plymouth Argyle (1932 – 1948)*
Rawlings nicknames 'Sid', played for Preston North End, between 1932-34 appearing in 12 league games. He moved to Huddersfield Town for 1934-35 season playing 11 league games before signing for West Bromwich Albion for £600 in March 1935. Son of Archie Rawlings, former Preston North End FA Cup winger from 1922, Sid was a brisk, penetrative outside right who was signed as cover for Tommy Glidden. He only played 10 league games for Albion, scoring once, as his first team chances were limited. He travelled a lot during his career moving to Northampton Town in July 1936 for £500 playing 48 league games, scoring 18 goals. Northampton were playing in Division 3 (South) at the start of the 1936/37 season. The moved proved successful and he never missed a game all season playing in all the league and cup games. Although they finished 7th in the league, they were humiliated in a first round FA Cup match when they were beaten 6-1 at non-league Walthamstow. Sid never seemed to settle in one place and at the end of the season was off again, this time to fellow Division 3 (South) team Millwall in December 1937. Once again, the move proved to be a success with his new team finishing the 1937/38 season as champions. At Millwall he played 53 league games, scoring 27 goals. Despite playing in a higher division Syd continued to play first team football and scored regularly as well. This brought him to the attention of Division 1 team Everton, where he went on loan at the end of the 1938/39 season and signed for them permanently in 1940. Unfortunately, the Second World War stopped all football for four years with 26-year old Sid in his prime. He made guest appearances in WW2 for Clapton Orient, Rochdale, Preston North End, Bury, Liverpool, Southport, Stockport

County as well as a loan at Goodison Park before being Signed by Everton. He moved to Plymouth Argyle in 1946 making 56 league appearances scoring 20 goals before retiring in 1948, aged 34. After ending his professional career at Plymouth Argyle, he continued to play locally for Tavistock and subsequently managed them for a short period. He died prematurely in 1956 from leukaemia aged 43.

READER Josiah 'Joe'

Goalkeeper 6'0"
Born *27/2/1866 West Bromwich, Staffs*
Died *8/3/1954 West Bromwich, Staffs*
Playing career: *West Bromwich Albion (370 appearances Aug 1885 – Apr 1901) 1 England International cap*

Reader was born in West Bromwich, the fourth of five children, where he attended Beeches Road School and St Phillips School. In the 1871 census he was living with his parents and his 4 siblings at Old Meeting Street, Wednesbury. In the 1881 census Josiah is the younger of two sons now living at home with a boarder at Hargate Lane, Wednesbury. He joined West Bromwich Albion as an amateur in January 1885 and turned professional in August of the same year. Joe was a goalkeeper to rank with the finest the game has produced. Superb in handling with marvellous reflexes, he used his feet as much as anything else to divert shots or headers. Reader made his league debut in October 1889 in a Division One match away to Aston Villa. In the 1891 census he was married to Dorcas and they lived in Trinity Road, West Bromwich. He won an FA Cup winners medal with Albion when they beat Villa 3–0 in the 1892 final. In 1894 he won his only England cap, in a 2–2 draw with Ireland in Belfast and also represented the Football League side three times as well as the League XI once. He helped Albion reach the FA Cup Final once more in 1895, but this time was on the losing side as Aston Villa won 1–0. It is believed that Joe was the last of the goalkeepers to discard the customary long white trousers, doing so in the mid 1890's. He had taken over from the great Bob Roberts and was superseded by Ike Webb. He really was a dedicated club man, whose love for the club was enhanced when he turned out in one match with his arm in a sling.

Nicknamed 'kicker', Reader became the only player to have represented the club in a competitive match at three different grounds, namely Four Acres, Stoney Lane and The Hawthorns. After 370 senior appearances for Albion, Reader retired from playing football due to illness in April 1901, after a 16-year career. In the 1901 census he was living in Thynne Street, West Bromwich, with a daughter Ivy. In the 1911 census Josiah and his wife Dorcas still lived lived in Thynne Street. They had two other children who had died. Josiah was listed as a County Court Bailiff. He then took up the role of trainer-coach at the club until shortly before WW1, when he became a ground steward at the Hawthorns until 1950. In the register of 1939, Joe and Dorcas were living at Stanway Road, West Bromwich. Josiah is listed as a retired County Bailiff. His association with West Bromwich Albion spanned 65 years. A grand clubman. He died in West Bromwich in March 1954, aged 88.

REED Frederick 'Fred'

Centre half 5'11"
Born *March 1894 Benwall & Scotswood-on-Tyne*
Died *December 1967 West Bromwich*
Playing career: *Newburn, Wesley Hall, Benwell, Lintz Institute, West Bromwich Albion (157 appearances 5 goals Feb 1913 – July 1927), Guested for Newcastle United in WW1. (1909 – 1927)*

Fred's displays at centre half for Albion were typical of a rugged North Easterner, especially in the tackle where he was solid, determined and so efficient. When he arrived at the Hawthorns in 1913, he was understudy to Sid Bowser, and had to wait almost ten years, including the war years, as WW1 interrupted many-a-playing career, before establishing himself as a regular in the first team. Reed served as a sergeant in the Royal Fusiliers during World War One. He guested for Newcastle United during the war. Reed made one appearance in the first XI during the Championship Winning season of 1919/1920. He amassed well over 150 appearances for Albion's 2nd XI before becoming a permanent fixture in the senior side as skipper. He had three and a half seasons as first team pivot, totting up 138 appearances at League level before standing down in favour of a younger man, Ted Rooke. He retired from playing in 1927 to become Albion trainer until 1950.

Personal note: *In the early 1960's Fred was living in Walter Road, Smethwick and his garden backed on to my garden in Devonshire Road. He would chat over the hedge as he frequently returned my over-hit football.*

REED Hugh 'Hughie'

Right winger 5'4"

Born *23/8/1950 Dumbarton, Scotland*
Died *1/11/1992 Crewe,Cheshire aged 42*
Playing career: *West Bromwich Albion (6+4 sub appearances 2 goals Aug 1967 – Nov 1971), Plymouth Argyle, Brentford (loan), Crewe Alexandra, Hartlepool United.*

Hughie joined Albion at the same time as Asa Hartford in 1967 and signed a professional contract the following year . He made his professional debut against Stoke City in November 1968. Opportunities on the wing were few and far between for Reed and he made just 10 appearances before being released. In November 1971 Hughie signed for Third Division club Plymouth Argyle for a £12,000 fee. where he made 58 appearances and scored 11 goals. Reed then joined Fourth Division club Crewe Alexandra in July 1974 after a loan spell at Brentford. Reed had a short stint with Fourth Division club Hartlepool between October and November 1976 and ended his career in non-league football, before retiring in 1982. After his retirement from football, Reed settled in Crewe. He was found dead at his home on 1st November 1992, aged 42.

REES Ronald 'Ronnie'

Right winger 5'8½"

Born *4/4/1944 Ystradynlais, Wales*
Playing career: *Coventry City, West Bromwich Albion (£65,000 40+2 sub appearances 12 goals Mar 1968 – Jan 1969), Nottingham Forest, Swansea City, Haverfordwest (1962-1975). 39 Welsh International caps & U-23 International*

When Jimmy Hill was Coventry City manager, he found he had an outstanding 18year-old winger in the reserves called Ronnie Rees. Hill's gamble in promoting the Welsh youngster to the first team in September 1962 paid off and for the next six years he was a virtual ever-present in the team making 262 appearances and scoring 52 goals. In the 1963/64 promotion season he scored 15 goals, including a hat-trick in the 8-1 thrashing of Shrewsbury.

His goalscoring prowess was soon rewarded with an international call-up - Ronnie first won Under 23 honours and in 1964, after being an ever present in the Division Three championship side, then won the first of his 39 full caps. Three years later in 1967 he was a major influence as the Sky Blues won promotion to Division One. In 1968, with Noel Cantwell keen to strengthen the side in the club's first of many relegation battles, Ronnie was the only saleable asset and was allowed to join West Bromwich Albion for £65,000 in March. Albion were on a FA Cup run but Rees was cup-tied, having already featured in the competition for Coventry. He played in 10 of the final 12 league games of the 1967/68 season, scoring three goals, usually on the right wing or occasionally on the left deputising when Clive Clark was out injured. The forward line was exciting with two such fast, thrilling wingers as Rees and Clark, and striker Jeff Astle thrived on the service, including scoring two hat-tricks in three days against Manchester United and West Ham United. Rees started the 1968/69 season as first choice winger, without Clive Clark who had suffered a bad injury on the tour to East Africa in the summer, where Rees himself was sent off in one game. Ron was a two footed winger who could play on either flank. Fast and direct in style, always eager to have a shot at goal. Maybe if he had joined Albion before the FA Cup run, he would have made a real name for himself at the Hawthorns. After another 24 league games and 1 substitute appearance, during which time the back of the net was found six times, he was allowed to move on to Nottingham Forest in March 1969 for £60,000. He made another 76 league appearances scoring 9 goals for Forest before being transferred to Swansea City in January 1972 for £26,000. He played 89 league games scoring 5 goals before moving along the Gower Peninsula in South Wales to non-league Haverfordwest. Ronnie finally hung up his boots in 1975 and worked behind the scenes at Cardiff City before taking a job at the Ford motorworks in Bridgend. He was forced to retire in 1995 at the age of 51, after suffering a stroke in 1995, sadly leaving him unable to walk or talk. As a result, he became a resident at Hengoed Court Care Home in Swansea.

Cyrille Regis

REGIS Cyrille MBE
Centre forward 5'11½"

Born *9/2/1958 Maripasoula, French Guiana*
Died *14/1/2018 Birmingham aged 59*
Playing career: *Molesey, Hayes, West Bromwich Albion (Cost £5,000 + £5,000 after 20 appearances 297+5 appearances 111 goals) Coventry City, Aston Villa, Wolverhampton Wanderers, Wycombe Wanderers & Chester-City. England U-21, 'B', & 5 Full International caps*

After leaving school, Regis trained as an electrician, earning a City and Guilds diploma. Cyrille continued to practise the trade until his move into professional football. The 1975/76 season saw Regis move to Athenian League club Molesey, for whom he scored around 25 goals during his one campaign for the club. He went on to join semi-professional Hayes of the Isthmian League, signing on 7 July 1976. Regis was spotted by West Bromwich Albion's chief scout Ronnie Allen, who recommended that the First Division club should sign him. With the Albion directors unsure of paying a four-figure fee for such a young, unproven player, Allen offered to fund any initial payment from his own pocket, so sure was he that Regis would make it in the top tier of English football. The transfer took place in May 1977, for an up-front fee of £5,000, plus another £5,000 after 20 appearances. Regis made his first team debut in a League Cup match against Rotherham United on 31 August 1977, becoming an instant hit with the fans, scoring twice in a 4–0 win. He became only the second Albion player to score a penalty on their debut, the first being Bobby Blood in 1921.Three days later Regis made his league debut in a 2–1 victory over Middlesbrough. Again, he found the net, taking the ball from the halfway line to the penalty area before scoring with a right-foot drive. Middlesbrough's David Mills, who later became a teammate of Regis at Albion, described it as "a goal of sheer brilliance." He continued to find the net on a regular basis scoring some spectacular and breath-taking goals on the way. Indeed, Cyrille created a club record by scoring on his Albion debut in five different competitions League, League Cup, FA Cup, Tennent Caledonian Cup and Central League. Big Cyrille, nicknamed 'Smokin Joe' was strong, muscular and aggressive, he had a terrific shot. His heading ability was top-class, and he could leave opponents standing with his devastating speed over 25-30 yards. He would often collect the ball around the half way line and head towards goal, brushing aside opponents with his powerful shoulders, before unleashing a cannonball shot. He was certainly a snip of a buy. Cyrille was voted PFA Young Player of the Year in 1979, and he was runner up to Footballer of the Year, Steve Perryman, in 1982, He had seven wonderful years at the Hawthorns during which time he scored 140 goals in 370 matches, including friendlies and tour games. As a West Bromwich Albion player, he played in a benefit match for Len Cantello, that saw a team of white players play against a team of black players. John Giles allowed Cyrille to leave for a rather paltry £300,000 when he joined Coventry City in October 1984. This came as somewhat of a shock to Albion fans and Cyrille himself said it was a wrench to leave the Hawthorns. He soon settled down at Highfield Road and scored 5 goals in a Milk Cup game against Chester. Regis won the only major trophy in his career, the 1987 FA Cup. In 7 years with the Sky Blues, Cyrille scored 56 goals in 238 league appearances, including a goal for Coventry at the Hawthorns on 24th November 1984, on his return to the Hawthorns just two months after leaving, in a league match that Albion won 5-2. Peter Barnes added City's other goal. Big Cyrille had spells at Aston Villa between 1991-93 making 52 league appearances scoring 12 goals; Wolverhampton Wanderers 1993/94 when in September 1993 he came on as a substitute at the Hawthorns to rapturous applause from Albion fans, for the injured Steve Bull. Played 19 league games scoring 2 goals; Wycombe Wanderers 1994-95 35 appearance in the league and scored 9 goals; Chester City 1995/96 scoring 7 goals in 29 league appearances. He amassed 614 league games scoring 158 goals in 21 years as a professional footballer. In 1989 he became a born-again Christian after the death of his friend and former team mate Laurie Cunningham in a car crash in Spain. He attended the Renewal Christian Centre in Solihull and was a trustee of Christians in Sport. He was awarded an honorary fellowship by the University of Wolverhampton in 2001.

He and his wife Julia supported charities such as Water Aid having visited Ethiopia in 2007. He was awarded the MBE in 2008. A football agent until his death from a heart attack in January 2018. His brother Dave was a professional footballer, his cousin John was an International sprinter. His nephew Jason Roberts, for who Cyrille was his agent, later played for WBA. Regis's death was announced on 15 January 2018; he was 59 and is survived by his second wife, Julia. Two of his former clubs West Bromwich Albion and Coventry City, played in a friendly match dubbed the 'Regis Shield'; West Bromwich won 5–2.

Personal Note: *In April 2008 my daughter Deborah, an Albion fan since birth, married Mike, a Coventry fan. I wanted to find some way of 'uniting' the two football-mad families. The Old Baggies Former Players' Association contacted Cyrille, on my behalf, and asked if he would attend the reception in Solihull. He agreed and as my daughter and her new husband were about to take their first dance, I introduced a very special guest, Cyrille Regis, who played so heroically for both Albion and Coventry.*

I took some photos of him in his Albion kit and his Coventry kit, which Cyrille duly signed for some of the wedding guests also posing for photos. What a Gentleman.

REID Nicholas 'Nicky'

Right back/defender 5'10"
Born *30/10/1960 Davyhulme, Lancashire*
Playing career: *Manchester City, Seattle SoundersBlackburn Rovers, Bristol City, West Bromwich Albion (Free transfer 17+9 sub appearances 1 goal Jan 1993 – Dec 1993), Wycombe Wanderers, Bury, Sligo Rovers (1977 – 1997)*

Nicky played for Manchester City from 1977 – 1987 making 216 league appearances scoring 21 goals. He moved to Blackburn from 1987 – 1992 making a further 174 league appearances scoring 9 goals. After a short spell with Bristol City, he joined Albion in January 1993 and was a member of the Albion team that won the Play Off Final at Wembley in 1993, scoring one of the goals in a 3-0 victory over Port Vale. He left Albion in January 1994 after appearing in 26 games with just that one goal, at Wembley. Reid had a spell with Wycombe Wanderers.

Nicky Reid

Then he became player/manager at Sligo Rovers in Ireland when Jimmy Mullen left in July 1997. He left in 1999, and moved back to England where he studied part-time for a degree in Sports Rehabilitation with the University of Salford. Reid was appointed assistant physiotherapist at Burnley in 2000. He left in 2004 to take up a position with Manchester City, where he stayed until 2005. He was part of Chief Physiotherapist Jim Webb's staff and was involved mainly with the club's reserve side. Reid joined Barrow AFC as their fitness coach in October 2005, before joining Bury FC as Chief Physiotherapist in February 2006. He left them in July 2007 by mutual consent and became physio at Hyde United, and in January 2008 became Paul Lake's replacement as Macclesfield Town Physio. He completed a second degree at the University of Salford in 2008, this time in Physiotherapy. After suffering with arthritis, he now lives in Withnell Fold, and has a pub in Chorley, The Masons Arms in Harpers Lane, brewing his own Masons Pale Ale.

Steven Reid

REID Steven

Defender/midfielder 5'11"

Born *10/3/1981 Kingston upon Thames, London*
Playing career: *Millwall, Blackburn Rovers, Queens Park Rangers (loan), West Bromwich Albion (loan then signed on Free Transfer 76 + 12 sub appearances 4 goals Mar 2010 – July 2014), Burnley. (1998 - 2015) England schoolboy international, Republic of Ireland U-21 and Full International 23 caps.*

Steven started his career at Millwall, and made his professional debut in the 1997/98 season at the age of 17. He was part of the successful 2000/01 team that gained promotion to the English First Division. Reid gained a reputation for his strong, driving runs and phenomenal long-range shooting ability. After 5 years and 139 league games scoring 18 goals, he moved for £1.85 million move to Blackburn Rovers in July 2003. Reid missed the majority of the 2006/07 season through injury. A back injury limited him to three appearances before he sustained cruciate ligament injury in January, which kept him out for the rest of the season. In 7 years with Rovers he played 113 league games scoring 6 goals. On 19th November 2009, Reid signed on loan for Queens Park Rangers in an attempt to recapture his career from injury.

The loan lasted until midway through December 2009. On 5th March 2010, West Bromwich Albion signed Reid on a one-month loan. He made his debut against his previous loan club, Queens Park Rangers, on 6th March 2010, playing at right back in the 3–1 defeat at Loftus Road. On 26th May 2010, Reid joined Albion following their promotion to the Premier League on a permanent basis after signing a two-year contract. He officially joined on 1st July 2010 after a medical and had the option of a further 12-month extension on his contract. A confident, strong tackling, former midfield player who added a degree of skill to Albion's back line. He was well liked by the fans and the club managed his injury problems with personal training programme. After a match against Chelsea which Albion won 1–0 on 3rd March 2012, Reid missed the rest of the season after injuring ankle ligaments. In 4 years at the Hawthorns he played in 92 league games scoring 3 goals, having played most of the time at right back. After being released by West Bromwich Albion at the end of the 2013/14 season Reid was initially considering taking up a coaching role at the Hawthorns.

However, after being approached by newly promoted Burnley, he opted to stay on playing and signed a one-year contract at Turf Moor. 18th May 2015, with Burnley relegated, having played just 7 league games, Reid announced that he would retire at the end of the season, and enter coaching. In June 2015, Reid was appointed in the role of first-team coach at Championship club Reading. Reid left on 27th July 2017, in a bid to pursue new challenges. In September 2017, he joined Crystal Palace, as first team coach working alongside his former manager Roy Hodgson. Reid left Palace in August 2018, with manager Hodgson indicating that Reid had cited personal issues and wished to take time away from football. He then briefly coached at AFC Wimbledon, leaving in December 2018. In April 2019, he was appointed to assist caretaker manager Jimmy Shan at West Bromwich Albion. He worked for the Baggies until the end of the 2018/19 season, before joining Steve Clarke's backroom staff with the Scottish National team.

Steven Reid Coaching: A new venture to offer help, support and guidance to those in football and beyond for issues on and off the field. These could include things such as stress and anxiety, new working environment, homesickness, pressure to perform, dealing with enjoyment of the game and contract concerns. All ages and levels of the game will be welcome. Visit: https://www.stevenreidcoaching.com/

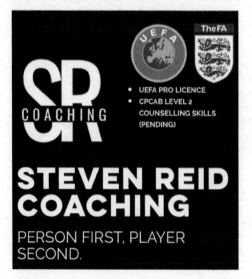

REILLY George

Centre forward/centre half 6'4"
Born *14/9/1957 Belshill, Lanarkshire, Scotland*
Playing career: *Northampton Town, Cambridge United, Watford, Newcastle United, West Bromwich Albion (Cost £100,000 Dec 1985 – June 1988), Cambridge United, Barnet (1976-1989).*

A Scot, he moved to Corby as a lad with his parents. It was with Corby Town that he began to score goals, which continued throughout his career. Nicknamed 'Mother' by some fans, George started his professional career with Northampton Town in June 1976, scoring 23 goals in the 1977/78 season. Cambridge United paid £140,000 for him in November 1979. Graham Taylor took him to Watford for £100,000 in August 1983. Reilly scored the winning goal for Watford against Plymouth Argyle in the 1984 FA Cup Semi-Final at Villa Park and played in the 1984 FA Cup Final. He moved to Newcastle United in February 1985 for £200,000. Reilly moved to West Bromwich Albion in December 1985. In that first season he made 20 appearances scoring just 4 goals, in a team that included Garth Crooks and Imre Varadi, but failed to prevent Albion being relegated from the top division, finishing 22nd in the League with only 4 wins all season. One of the tallest strikers to ever play League football. He was awkward-looking, lanky-legged and appeared disinterested at times. He has certainly put the wind up a few players over the years. He usually played at centre forward although he made a few appearances for Albion at centre half. Once sent off after only 75 seconds in Albion's Bass Charity Cup tie with Burton in July 1987. George left Albion on a free transfer in July 1988 to re-join Cambridge United. He moved to Barnet the following year. He scored 134 goals in 447 senior appearances, scoring in all four divisions. He was a bricklayer when in 2003 on a building site in Corby, he was attacked by another worker who bit part of his right ear off, before whispering "Plymouth" in his other ear by way of explanation. George is now living with the fear his cherished memories of that afternoon below the famous Twin Towers will soon be lost as he battles dementia. He was officially diagnosed in 2014 with the condition aged just 57 but was showing tell-tale signs of brain damage years before it was confirmed.

George bristles with anger when describing how he was dumped by the game after telling football union bosses he faced the toughest fight of his life. George Reilly claims the Professional Footballers' Association (PFA) made "vague promises" about getting him counselling after the devastating diagnosis. Since then, George, who during his career acted as a rep for the union, says he's been met with a wall of silence. It has only been the support of a charity and his new wife that has helped get him through his ordeal. George's dementia has been blamed on damage suffered at the back of his brain, meaning his deterioration is slower than had it been at the front. Living in his modest home in Kettering, Northamptonshire, he wants Britain's football associations and the PFA to do much more to help players hit with the illness and other brain conditions.

RICHARDSON William

Centre half 5'10"

Born 14/2/1908 Great Bridge, Tipton
Died 19/8/1985 West Bromwich aged 77
Playing career: *West Bromwich Albion (352 appearances 1 goal Nov 1926 – May 1937), Swindon Town, Dudley Town, Vono Sports. Retired June 1941*
Bill was a shade casual at times, yet all in all he was a splendid pivot, unflagging and especially good in the air. He turned professional in August 1926, when he joined West Bromwich Albion. He first set foot inside the Hawthorns when the centre half and wing half positions were causing the management some concerns. Bill buckled down to the task ahead of him and soon settled into the team's style of play without much ado and made his league debut in December 1928 in a Division Two match away at Middlesbrough. He had little Tommy Magee on the right and Len Darnell on his left, forming a steady and reliable middle line. He also played right half and left half. In his first two seasons at the Hawthorns. Bill played consistently well apart from the odd hiccup here and there. He was a popular player and very reliable. In 1930/31, still playing alongside Tommy Magee but with Jimmy Edwards on his left, he helped the club to achieve promotion to the First Division and played in the 1931 FA Cup Final, when Albion beat Birmingham 2–1. Richardson also appeared in the 1935

FA Cup Final, but this time earned only a runners-up medal as his team lost 4–2 to Sheffield Wednesday. He gave Albion 11 years grand service, making 352 appearances for West Bromwich Albion. He joined Swindon Town for £200 in May 1937 playing just 9 league games, before moving on a free transfer to Dudley Town in September 1939. He joined Vono Sports F.C. in August 1940 but spent just one season with the club prior to his retirement in June 1941. His older brother, Sammy also played for West Bromwich Albion 1913 – 1927, and was part of Albion's 1919/20 Championship winning team.

Personal note: *During the early 1960's Albion created a Development Association and formed the Albion Pools Bill was an Agent for the Pools and would often stop and chat in the Office, where I worked during school holidays, in the Smethwick Corner when bringing in his paying-in book every week.*

RICHARDSON William 'Ginger

Centre forward 5'8"

Born 29/5/1909 Framwellgate Moor, County Durham
Died 29/3/1959 Perry Barr, Birmingham aged 49
Playing career: *Hartlepool United, West Bromwich Albion (Cost £1,250 444 appearances 328 goals June 1929 – Nov 1945), Shrewsbury. Guested for Derby County & Walsall in WW2. 1 England International cap.*
In the 1911 census 'WG' was listed as being the youngest of six children living with his Mom Rebecca, and Dad George, at Newcastle Row, in Framwellgate Moor. Before signing for Albion, he had worked as a bus conductor for the United Bus Company in Hartlepool. He also played for the Bus Company's football team. He played 29 league games for the Hartlepool scoring an impressive 19 goals, prompting Albion to pay £1,250 for his services on 11th June 1929. On his day 'WG' had few equals and no superiors at snapping up half chances, especially those which flew across the face of goal, from either wing, deflected or not. A truly dynamic centre forward who depended on alertness rather than his height and weight. He was quick, assertive and pretty sharp inside the box, a place where he scored most of his goals. He made his Albion debut against Millwall on Boxing Day in 1929 scoring in a 6-1 win. During the 1930's 'WG.' was always hitting the headlines.

The 'G' standing for Ginger, his hair colour, was added to avoid confusion with another William Richardson who was centre half in the same 1930's side. He was part of the great cup and promotion winning team of 1930/31, scoring both Albion goals to win the 1931 FA Cup Final at Wembley against Birmingham. He also scored the match winning goal in the final game of the season at the Hawthorns, beating Charlton Athletic 3-2 to clinch promotion. He once scored 4 goals in 5 minutes at West Ham in 1931; hit three in six minutes v Derby County in 1933; set an Albion record with 40 League and Cup goals in 1935/36, a record that still stands as of 2020. 'WG' scored 14 hat-tricks in major league and cup football including four 4's. In wartime he scored 125 goals in 106 games including friendlies. In the 1939 register, Bill is listed as a professional footballer and a war reservist with the Police Force. He and his wife Olive, were living in Springfield Crescent, West Bromwich, the same Crescent where years later, Jeff and Larraine Astle lived at the time of Albion's 1968 FA Cup win. During WW2 'W.G.' twice scored six in a match versus Luton Town and against the RAF 1941/42. He notched five against Swansea Town in 1941 and another five v Aston Villa in 1943. He won just one England cap against Holland in 1935. Transferred to Shrewsbury Town for £250 in November 1945 he scored 55 goals in 40 outings for the Shrews before returning to the Hawthorns as coach/assistant trainer in June 1946. He died of a heart attack whilst playing in a charity match, aged 49. His son Brian spent a year as a professional with the Albion 1957/58 before moving to Walsall.

RICKABY Stan

Right back 6'0"

Born *12/3/1924 Stockton-on-Tees, County Durham*
Died *8/2/2014 Perth, Western Australia aged 89*
Playing career: *Middlesbrough, West Bromwich Albion (Cost £7,5000 205 appearances 2 goals Feb 1950 – June 1955), Poole Town player/manager, Weymouth, Newton Abbot Spurs (1946-1964). He played once for England*

In WW2 Stan was an Army Infantryman with the Dorsetshire Regiment, reaching the position of sergeant. He was a tall, strong, accomplished right back, good in the tackle with a powerful kick.

He turned professional with Middlesbrough in July 1946. In February 1950 After playing just 10 league games for Middlesbrough, he joined Albion for £7,5000 in February 1950, initially as cover for Jim Pemberton. Within six months he had replaced the injury-stricken right-back and held his place in the side until just before the 1954 FA Cup Final. He had a bad thigh injury, sustained in the Cup semi-final against Port Vale, which meant that Rickaby missed the Final, but he nevertheless received a winner's medal along with Norman Heath who was also injured, having played in all the previous rounds of the competition. He made his only appearance for England on 11 November 1953, in a 3–1 win against Northern Ireland at Goodison Park. He took up the role of player-manager at Poole Town in June 1955 before moving on to Weymouth. Rickaby transferred to Newton Abbot Spurs in August 1963 before retiring as a player a year later. Even whilst playing he had an eye to the future, studying in the field of accountancy.

Liam Ridgewell

He also sold furniture with Ray Barlow. They marketed a gramophone cabinet with a unique system of tabulation. He sold life insurance in Birmingham. Later worked in accountancy before retiring. Rickaby emigrated to Australia in 1969 to work with Aboriginal communities and published his autobiography 'Up Over and Down Under' in 2002.

RIDGEWELL Liam

Left back/Centre back 6'2"

Born *21/7/1984 Bexleyheath, London*

Playing career: *Aston Villa, Bournemouth (loan), Birmingham City, West Bromwich Albion (Cost undisclosed but thought to be about £1.5 million 76 + 2 sub appearances 2 goals Jan 2012 – May 2014), Portland Timbers in USA, Wigan Athletic (loan), Brighton & Hove Albion (loan), Hull City, Southend United (2002 – 2020). England U-19 and U-21 International.*

Ridgewell began his career with West Ham United, without making a league appearance moving to Aston Villa in February 2001. He had a brief loan spell with Bournemouth in 2002 appearing in 5 league games. He was part of the team that won the 2002 FA Youth Cup Final against Everton. On 10th April, in a 1–1 draw with rivals West Bromwich Albion, he and opponent Jonathan Greening were sent off for headbutting each other. Ridgewell completed a move to Birmingham City for a fee of £2 million on 3rd August 2007, becoming the first player to transfer between the bitter rivals since Des Bremner in 1984. In April 2009, Ridgewell suffered a broken leg after a challenge by Plymouth Argyle midfielder Jamie Mackie. He made an unexpectedly quick return to the side five months later, usually a centre back, but playing in the less familiar position of left back. He continued in that role and played there as Birmingham went on a club-record 12-match unbeaten run in the top division and set a Premier League record by fielding the same starting eleven for nine consecutive games. He played the full 90 minutes as Birmingham beat favourites Arsenal 2–1 in the 2011 Football League Cup Final, thus earning qualification for the Europa League. Liam played in the Play-Off round first leg against Portuguese club Nacional, Birmingham's first participation in major European competition for nearly 50 years, in an unfamiliar holding midfield position.

Ridgewell signed a two-and-a-half-year contract with Premier League club West Bromwich Albion on 31st January 2012. The transfer fee was undisclosed but thought to be close to £1.5 million. On 12th February, he made his debut in a 5–1 away win over Wolverhampton Wanderers. He made his home debut a week later as West Brom beat Sunderland 4–0 at The Hawthorns. Liam was a centre back who was converted to a left back, powerful and strong in the tackle but in his last season at the Hawthorns part of the crowd seemed to get on his back. On 16th May 2014, West Bromwich Albion announced that they would not take up the option of extending Liam's contract and he was released from the club. Ridgewell was signed as a Designated Player for the Portland Timbers of Major League Soccer in June 2014. In 8th January 2015, Liam signed for Wigan Athletic on a six-week loan. Returning to the USA, Timbers qualified for the 2015 MLS Cup Play Offs, in which Ridgewell opened the scoring in a 3–1 first leg win over Western Conference regular season champions FC Dallas, as the team eventually reached MLS Cup 2015. In the decisive match on 6th December away to the Columbus Crew at Mapfre Stadium, he captained the Timbers to a 2–1 win. In December 2015, Ridgewell agreed a short-term loan with Championship team Brighton & Hove Albion. Back in the USA, he was sent off on 30 September 2018 at the end of a goalless draw at home to FC Dallas. The Timbers made the 2018 MLS Cup Play Offs. In the Western Conference Semi-Final, they defeated rivals Seattle Sounders on penalties, though Stefan Frei saved Ridgewell's attempt. The Timbers lost the MLS Cup 2018 2–0 at Atlanta United in Ridgewell's final game. On 31st January 2019, he joined Hull City for the remainder of the 2018/19 season. Released by the Tigers at the end of the season. In August 2019, Ridgewell signed a one-year deal with EFL League One club Southend United. He made his debut the next day in the season opener, a 3–1 home loss to Blackpool, starting on the left of a three-man defence and being replaced after 52 minutes. Manager Kevin Bond said his decision may have been "unfair" to start Ridgewell after he had not played any friendlies in the summer. Liam left Southend on 31st January 2020.

ROBBINS Walter

Outside left/Forward 5'10"

Born *24/11/1910 Cardiff, Wales*

Died *February 1979, Swansea*

Playing career: *Cardiff City, West Bromwich Albion (Cost £3,000 91 appearances 31 goals Apr 1932 – May 1939) 11 Welsh International caps. Went on Welsh International tour of Canada in 1929.*

Prior to professional football, Robbins worked for a local brewery as a lorry driver. He was serving a motor mechanic apprenticeship when he rose to attention scoring 68 goals in the 1927/28 season for Ely United in the Cardiff & District League. He signed for Cardiff shortly afterwards in 1928/29 season. He toured Canada with the Welsh FA in 1929.With Cardiff he won a Welsh Cup winners' medal in 1930. On 6 February 1932, Robbins scored five goals during a 9–2 win over Thames, which remains the club's record league win. Playing 86 league games he scored 38 goals for the Bluebirds. Robbins was sold to West Bromwich Albion for £3,000 in April 1932. Walter, with his 'Errol Flynn film-star-like looks', was a competent outside left with tree trunk legs which enabled him to release a thunderbolt shot. He was a member of Albion's reserve side that carried off the Central League Championship kin three successive season 1932-35. He joined Albion as a deputy to Stanley Wood but found he had to contest the left-wing position with Wally Boyes as well. Robbins had a few games at inside left before finally settling for a more controlled role, later in his career, as a central midfielder. He actually played two games at centre half for Albion in 1938. He spent 8 years at the Hawthorns before the outbreak of World War II. Post WW2, he was briefly trainer at Newport County moving to Cardiff City as trainer in 1945, training them to promotion in 1946/47 and again in1951/52. Then moved to Swansea Town as Chief Scout 1958, then as Trainer in 1960 sitting on the bench for the 1964 FA Cup Final against Preston North End, also Assistant Manager 1968-71, finally as Chief Scout 1971 – 1978, when he retired through ill health. In the 1950's he was trainer to the Welsh National team. In May 1971 Walter was granted a well-earned Testimonial Match by Swansea and Albion were the visitors at the Vetch Field.

ROBERTS Graham

Defender/midfielder 5'8"

Born *3/7/1959 Southampton, Hampshire*

Playing career: *Portsmouth, Dorchester Town, Weymouth, Tottenham, Rangers, Chelsea, West Bromwich Albion (Cost £220,000 41 appearances 6 goals) Stevenage Borough, Chesham United, Slough Town (1978 – 1999) England 'B' and 6 Full International caps.*

Roberts was born in Southampton, and joined his local club as a schoolboy in October 1973, but failed to make the grade. He joined Portsmouth in March 1977. He moved to Dorchester Town where he impressed before joining local rivals Weymouth. From there he was sold to Tottenham Hotspur in May 1980 for £35,000. Roberts was a member of the successful Tottenham Hotspur side of the early 1980s, winning two FA Cups and a UEFA Cup in 1984. In 6 years at Spurs he played 209 league games scoring 23 goals. He moved to Rangers in 1986 for £450,000 and won the Scottish Premier Division in his first full season and the Scottish League Cup a year later. He made 55 league appearances scoring three goals for the 'Gers. He joined Chelsea in August 1988 for £475,000 and helped the side emphatically win the Second Division championship in 1988/89. He played 70 league games for Chelsea scoring 18 goals before he moved to West Bromwich Albion in July 1990, signed by Brian Talbot to bring some toughness and experience to the team. Roberts made his debut at the Hawthorns on 17th November 1990 in a 2-0 win against Blackburn. He was part of the Albion team that was humiliated at the Hawthorns in the 3rd Round of the FA Cup January 5th 1991 losing 4-2. To non-league Woking. Roberts was voted as Albion Supporters' Player of the Season 1990/91, playing 27 league games scoring 4 times when the team was relegated to Division Three for the first time in the club's history. Noted for dying his grey hair black, every few months, he played a further 12 Division Three league games in 1991-92 scoring twice. He left Albion to become player/ manager at Enfield from March 1992 until 1994. Returned to playing at Stevenage Borough 1994/95 then went to Yeovil Town as player/ manager 1995-98. He was later manager of Chesham United during the 1998/99 season. Roberts was appointed manager to Hertford

Town in 2000, but left in February 2001 when he became manager of Isthmian League club Boreham Wood. Despite leading the club to Division One title, he resigned and was appointed manager of Carshalton Athletic, who he guided to the Isthmian League Division One South title in 2002/03. Roberts briefly managed Braintree Town at the end of the 2003/04 season. In 2005 he was appointed manager of Clyde. In August 2006 he was sacked for allegedly making racist remarks. An employment tribunal found these allegations 'either exaggerated or possibly not true' and Roberts was awarded £32,000 in compensation for unfair dismissal. He wrote his autobiography 'Hard as Nails' in 2008. In September 2010 he was assistant coach then later head coach of the Pakistan national football team. From January 2011 to March 2012 he was Nepal national team coach He does after dinner speaking. He has worked as a media pundit for the likes of Sky and Talksport. He is on YouTube discussing all things football with Micky Hazard and Abbi Summers and on Twitter @GrahamRoberts4 .

ROBERTSON Alistair 'Ally'

Centre back 5'9"

Born *9/9/1952 Philipstoun, Scotland*

Playing career: *West Bromwich Albion (622+4 sub appearances 12 goals Sept 1969 – Sept 1986), Wolverhampton Wanderers. (1969 – 1990) Scotland schoolboy and Youth International.*

Robertson joined as an apprentice in July 1968 and turned professional in September 1969. He made his league debut at home in a 2-1 win against Manchester United in 1969 as a 17-year old. He was a steady, unobtrusive central defender, sending in challenges with his powerful shoulders and getting in some crunching tackles. When only 18 Ally broke a leg playing against Charlton Athletic in a League Cup tie at the Hawthorns. He bounced back in style and went on to become one of Albion's finest defenders. He had a fine understanding with fellow-defender John Wile and together they appeared in 573 games in Albion colours, helping the club win promotion in 1975/76, reach three cup semi-finals as well as containing some of the best strikers in European football in the UEFA Cup.

Ally Robertson

181

He remained with the club until 1986, making 626 appearances in all competitions in the heart of the team's defence and playing under managers such as Alan Ashman, Don Howe, Johnny Giles, Ronnie Allen, Ron Atkinson, Ron Wylie, Nobby Stiles and Ron Saunders. The club spent all but three seasons in the top flight during his playing days. A tough defender, he held in high regard by the club's fans. However, he never won a Scotland cap. After 18years service Ally Robertson said farewell to Albion and joined rivals Wolverhampton Wanderers on a free transfer at the start of the 1986/87 season after being told by manager Ron Saunders that he would not fit into his future plans. In five seasons 1975-80 he only missed 7 league games out of a possible 210. He won Fourth Division Championship and Sherpa Van Trophy Final medals in 1987/88 and Third Division Championship medal in 1988/89 as skipper of the club After retiring from league football in 1990 he became player/manager of non-league Worcester City, and later took up the reigns at Cheltenham Town. He lived in Stourbridge and was a business manager for Sytner Oldbury, a BMW car dealership. He later arranged finance as business manager. Retired but helped out few days a week driving for Rybrook car sales company. He had a column in the Express & Star newspaper. He is a staunch supporter of the Old Baggies Former Players' Association. In 2020 he was part of a group of present and former players who sent messages or made phone calls to senior season ticket holders during the Corona Virus pandemic.

ROBINSON Paul

Left back/centre back 5'9"

Born *14/12/1978 Watford, Herts*
Playing career: *Watford, West Bromwich Albion (Cost £3750,000 Oct 2003 – July 2009), Bolton Wanderers (loan then signed), Leeds United (loan), Birmingham City (1996-2018)*

Nicknamed 'Robbo', Robinson began his football career in the youth system of his hometown town club, Watford. He made his first-team debut as a second-minute substitute in a 1–1 draw against Luton Town on 29 October 1996, aged 17. In a match against Port Vale on 29th April 1999, Robinson made a poor tackle on Vale player

Stewart Talbot, breaking both bones in Talbot's lower leg. The injury kept Talbot out of the game for 10 months and resulted in a "six-figure" out-of-court settlement. Out of 252 Watford appearances he was booked 63 times and sent off three times. One of these dismissals came in the 1998/99 Play-Off Semi-Final against Birmingham City, which saw him miss the second leg. He did feature, however, in the club's 2–0 Play-Off victory against future employers Bolton Wanderers. Robinson made 32 appearances for Watford in their 1999/2000 FA Premier League season, and stayed with the club when they were relegated to Division One. In 7 years at Vicarage Road he scored nine goals from 252 appearances in all competitions. In October 2003 Robinson was sold to West Bromwich Albion for an initial £250,000 fee, potentially rising to £375,000 depending on appearances and Albion being promoted to the Premiership. He made his West Brom debut in a 1–0 win against Norwich City on 18th October. Initially played as a wing-back with Albion adopting a back three, but he struggled in that role, not being the most skilful player. When Bryan Robson took over from Gary Megson as manager, he reverted to a back four, playing 'Robbo' at left back a position he was accustomed to. A strong and powerful tackler and a great motivator, he was a success in that role. Robinson was touted as a potential England left back by Bryan Robson. His first goal for West Bromwich Albion was a memorable one, an injury-time headed equaliser at Villa Park in April 2005 which earned him the club's Goal of the Season award. He was an integral part of Albion's "Great Escape" from relegation. On 28th October 2006, Birmingham City captain Damien Johnson's jaw was broken in two places in a collision with Robinson during a local derby, for which he received a straight red card. The incident drew criticism from Birmingham manager Steve Bruce, who believed Robinson's use of the elbow to be a deliberate act. Robbo was the subject of a £1.5 million bid from Premiership team Wigan Athletic in August 2007 as a replacement for Leighton Baines, who had been sold to Everton. The move fell through when he failed a medical. Robinson was named in the Professional Footballers' Association Championship Team of the Year, alongside teammates Jonathan Greening and Kevin Phillips, after helping Albion win promotion to the Premiership as league champions. On 12th July 2009, Robinson completed a season-long loan move to Bolton Wanderers, where he was reunited with his former manager Gary Megson. The player explained that he had joined Bolton on a three-year contract, the first year being on loan and the deal to become permanent in the summer of 2010 when Bolton would pay West Brom a fee of £1 million. The deal was made permanent in January 2010. In two years with Bolton Wanderers he played in 67 league games. In March 2012, Robinson joined Leeds United on a month's loan, playing in 10 league games. Championship club Birmingham City, Robinson signed a one-month contract with the latter in September 2012 which was extended until the end of the season. Robinson signed a one-year contract, with an option for a further year, ahead of the 2013/14 season, and was appointed both club and team captain for the season. In May 2014, it was announced he had agreed a player/coaching role with Birmingham.

Robinson was given a three-match ban after he was "seen to aim a kick" at Aston Villa captain James Chester in April 2017. The incident was missed by the match officials and dealt with using video evidence. In February 2018, Robinson announced that he would retire at the end of the 2017/18 season. He made a brief appearance in Birmingham's last game of the season, as a 91st-minute substitute in their 3–1 victory over Fulham.

ROBSON Bryan

Midfielder 5'11"

Born *11/1/1957 Chester-le-Street, County Durham*
Playing career: *West Bromwich Albion (252 + 7 sub appearances 46 goals Aug 1974 – Oct 1981), Manchester United, Middlesbrough. England U-21, 'B' and 90 Full England International caps*

Nicknamed 'Pop', Bryan had great stamina, aggression and an abundant supply of skill with his feet. Able to read a game and see opportunities to pass to his forward colleagues. Bryan made his debut in April 1975 away at York City in a 3-1 victory for the Baggies and played the final 3 games of the 1974/75 season scoring in each game.

Paul Robinson

183

Robson played 16 times in the Promotion-winning season 1975/76 even appearing at centre half and left back. He suffered three broken legs during the 1976-77 season when he was trying to establish himself in Albion's first team. Thankfully he recovered full fitness and helped the Baggies gain a place in Europe via the UEFA Cup. Bryan won England Youth international honours, then added U-21, 'B' and full caps to his wardrobe, whilst with the Albion, as he fast became one of the most gifted footballers in European circles. He was Sports Argus/Sportsco, Footballer of the Year in 1979 Midland Footballer of the Year, and Midland Sports Writers' Player of the Year in 1980. His Brother, Gary joined Albion as an apprentice just before Bryan left the Hawthorns. After 259 games and 46 goals for Albion, Robson became Britain's costliest footballer when he joined Manchester United in October 1981 for a fee of £1.5 million, but the whole deal was worth £2 million including Remi Moses moving with him. Regarded by many as the best midfield player in England since the war, Bryan had been plagued with injuries over the previous few years and after starting England's World Cup challenge in Mexico, he had to sit out the rest of the competition with a damaged shoulder. At Old Trafford, he won the Premier League twice, the FA Cup 3 times, the Charity Shield twice and the European Cup Winners' Cup. After playing in 345 league games, almost 500 in all competitions, scoring 99 goals in all competitions, he moved to Middlesbrough. in May 1994 when he accepted the role of player-manager at Middlesbrough. From 1994 to 1996 he combined the role with that of England assistant manager under Terry Venables, and was linked with the manager's job when Venables announced his intention to quit after Euro 96, only to rule himself out of the running. Robson played his final game as a player on 1st January 1997, in a Premier League game against Arsenal at Highbury 10 days before his 40th birthday. He claimed in his autobiography that he knew it was the right time to retire as his whole body ached for two weeks afterwards trying to keep up with the livewires Dennis Bergkamp and Ian Wright. Robson made a dream start to his managerial career as Middlesbrough won the Division One title and promotion

to the Premier League in their final season at Ayresome Park before relocation to the new 30,000-seat Riverside Stadium on the banks of the River Tees. He was assisted by Viv Anderson, another former Manchester United player. In 1996/97, Robson led Boro to both domestic cup finals but they lost both, losing 1–0 in a replay to Leicester City in the League Cup Final and 2–0 in the FA Cup Final to Chelsea, while they suffered relegation in the Premier League. The board kept faith in Robson and he repaid their loyalty with automatic promotion back to the Premiership in 1997/98. Again, the club missed out on cup success at the final hurdle with a 2–0 defeat against Chelsea in the League Cup final. A month later The Boro' brought in Terry Venables as head coach to assist Robson, who remained as manager. Robson left the club "by mutual consent" in June 2001. Robson accepted the manager's job with Division One strugglers Bradford City. Bradford took only 22 points from 27 games under Robson and were relegated in 23rd position.

Bryan Robson

Robson's third management job began on 9th November 2004, when he agreed to return to his old club West Bromwich Albion as manager, 23-years after his departure as a player. Albion were bottom of the Premiership on Christmas Day, a position from which no team had previously escaped relegation from the Premiership. The team were also bottom going into the last game of the season. However, Robson and his players defied all the odds to stay up thanks to a 2–0 home win over Portsmouth on the final day of the season, coupled with favourable results from elsewhere. Despite some significant new signings in the 2005 close season, his team failed to build on this achievement in 2005/06 though, and Albion were relegated with two matches left to play. They had failed to win any of their final 13 Premier League games. Robson left the club "by mutual consent" on 18th September 2006, following a disappointing start to the season. On 22nd May 2007 it was announced at a press conference that Robson and Brian Kidd would be the new choice of management at Sheffield United. 14 February he was "relieved of his first-team duties" before later in the day leaving Sheffield United.

In March 2008 he he returned to Manchester United as an ambassador for 12 months, to promote the club's commercial and charitable arm, alongside Bobby Charlton. On 23rd September 2009, Robson agreed to become coach of Thailand national team. He resigned as manager on 8th June 2011, and has since returned to his role as an Official Club Ambassador for Manchester United.

ROBSON Gary
Midfielder 5'5"
Born *6/7/1965 Pelaw, County Durham*
Playing career: *West Bromwich Albion (213 +43 sub appearances 34 goals April 1983 – June 1993), Bradford City, Gateshead (1982 – 1998)*

Gary Robson joined the Albion in May 1981 as an apprentice signing professional forms in May 1983. After Albion's relegation in 1985/86 Albion and Robson junior, spent the next seven years in a side failing to make an impact in the second tier and then falling into the third. He witnessed a managerial change almost every year from Atkinson to Allen, through to Wylie, Giles, Stiles and Saunders. Gary spent 12 years at the Hawthorns making 256 appearances including 43 substitute appearances, scoring 34 goals.

Gary Robson

He was a versatile player who appeared anywhere from full back to outside left. Robbo made his debut as a substitute versus Southampton in May 1983 and made his final appearance in February 1993 against Port Vale. He was a substitute for the 1993 Play Off Final squad but unfortunately was not called upon. In July 1993 he joined Bradford City playing in 75 leagues games scoring 3 goals. He signed for Gateshead in 1996 to play alongside brother Justin. Then in July 1997 he became Player-coach at Gateshead, leaving the club when they were relegated at the end of the 1997/98 season. Gary Robson was Assistant Manager at Durham Alliance's Whitehill F.C. in 2011. He is the younger brother of former Albion and England player Bryan. Gary is a regular supporter of the Old Baggies Former Players' Association functions in particular annual golf days & annual general meetings. Gary had his own business Chauffeuring Fleet Business and was living in Chester-le-Street with wife Claire.

In his own words: *"I've had four operations and have been seeing a specialist for five years. 3 cartilage operations and microfracture surgery, as there's no cartilage left. It's all down to putting your body on the line playing football." He bears no ill-will to Ardiles for not letting him off the bench for the final few minutes of the 1993 Play Off Final win against Port Vale at Wembley. Gary had recovered from a broken arm sustained against Port Vale in February 1993 and was about to join former coach Stuart Pearson at Valley Parade, Bradford after 256 appearances and 34 goals for the Baggies. "It was disappointing not to get on. I was cleared by the FA to wear a light cast on my arm and with us being 3-0 up it would have been nice to play at Wembley for the last few minutes. I bear no malice to Ossie. There's no grievance. I've seen him a few times and he's a lovely guy."*

ROBSON Sir Robert 'Bobby' CBE

Right half/inside forward 5'10"
Born *18/2/1933 Sacriston, County Durham*
Died *31/7/2009 County Durham*
Playing career: *Fulham, West Bromwich Albion (Cost £25,000 257 appearances 61goals Mar 1956 – Aug 1962), Fulham, Vancouver Royals (1950 – 1968 20 England International caps.Played in both 1958 & 1962 World Cup squads*
Before playing professional football, he started as an electrician's apprentice for the

National Coal Board in the Langley Park Colliery. His first professional club was Fulham where he played 152 league games scoring 68 goals between 1950-56. He signed for West Bromwich Albion in March 1956 for £20,000. A model competitor whose overall play was full of self-confidence. Bobby's temperament was a shining example to the rest of his team-mates. He was a hard grafter, always full of fight, showing the right spirit at the right moment, he inspired his fellow men and proved to be a tireless performer. He played alongside some fine Albion players including Ronnie Allen & Derek Kevan, before he was converted from a goal-scoring inside right into a creative right half by manager Vic Buckingham. Even whilst still playing for WBA & England, he worked for an Engineering Company in West Bromwich, in the afternoons. He played in 239 league games for Albion, scoring 56 goals before returning to Fulham in August 1962 for £20,000. In the next 5 seasons he played 192 league games scoring 9 goals, Released by Fulham in June 1967, Bobby became trainer/coach at Oxford University. He had a brief spell as player/manger in Canada with Vancouver Royals 1967. He managed Fulham Jan 1968 – November 1968. Then he scouted for Chelsea Nov 1968 – Jan 1969. He became manager of Ipswich Town 1969 - 1982, Managed abroad PSV Eindhoven 1990 -1992, Sporting CP 1992-1994, Porto 1994-1996, Barcelona 1995-1997 and Newcastle United 1999 - 2004. Managed England B and Senior team 1982 -1990.

His last management role was as a mentor to the manager of the Republic of Ireland national team. He was created a Knight Bachelor in 2002.He suffered recurrent problems with cancer and in March 2008 put his name to the Bobby Robson Foundation, a cancer research charity. In August 2008 his lung cancer was confirmed as termina and he died in 2009.Bobby was a fine cricketer, playing for Sacriston, Worcester Park, London and for West Bromwich Dartmouth. He also enjoyed golf and tennis.

ROSLER Uwe
Centre forward 6'1"
Born *15/11/1968 Altenburg. East Germany*
Playing career: *FC Lokomotive, BSG Chemie Leipzig, FC Magdeburg, Dynamo Dresden, FC Nuremberg, Dynamo Dresden, (loan), Manchester City, FC Kaiserslautern, Tennis Borussia Berlin, Southampton, West Bromwich Albion (loan 5 appearances 1 goal October 2001), SpVgg Unterhacing, Lillestrom (1987-2003) 5 full East Germany caps & U-23 player.*

A centre forward in his playing career, Rösler played for several clubs, most notably Manchester City, where he was the leading goalscorer for three consecutive seasons 1994/95 1995/96 and 1996/97. He also played for 1. FC Kaiserslautern, where he played in the UEFA Champions League. He was a footballing nomad, appearing for 10 clubs plus another two on loan, including a spell with West Bromwich Albion, whom he joined towards the end of October 2001 and played 5 games scoring just once but it was a winning goal against Nottingham Forest in a 1-0 win at the Hawthorns. He set off on a celebratory run behind the goal at the Smethwick End of the ground, endearing him to the Albion faithful. Rosler was forced to retire when he was diagnosed with lung cancer in 2003, with an X-ray discovering that he had a tumour in his chest. Rosler made a full recovery after chemotherapy and obtained his coaching badges whilst in remission. In 2005 he was appointed manager of Lillestrom, but left a year later to manage Viking in 2006. He left the club in November 2009. Molde hired him on a short-term contract in August 2010, replaced by Ole Gunnar Solskjaer in November 2010. Brentford took him on as manager in June 2011 on a two-year contract. In December 2013 he moved to Wigan Athletic as manager. He was sacked in November 2014.

In May 2015 Uwe was appointed as head coach of Championship side Leeds United. He was sacked in October with Leeds in 18th position. In July 2016 he was appointed manager of League One side Fleetwood Town. He was sacked again in February 2018 after 7 straight defeats. In June 2018 Rosler was announced as the new head coach of Swedish title holders Malmo FF. He left after two seasons. On 29th January 2020 Rosler was appointed the new head coach of German Bundesliga side Fortuna Dusseldorf, his first German club in his coaching career.

ROWLEY George Arthur (known as Arthur)
Inside left/outside left 6'0"
Born *21/4/1926 Wolverhampton*
Died *19/12/2002 Shrewsbury*
Playing career: *West Bromwich Albion (41 appearances 15 goals May 1944 – Dec 1948), Fulham, Leicester City, Shrewsbury Town player/manager (1946-1964). Guested for Manchester United, Middlesbrough, Brighton & Hove Albion, Lincoln City, and Wolverhampton Wanderers in WW2. Played for England 'B' and the Football League side.*

Rowley was nicknamed "The Gunner" because of his explosive left-foot shot, Rowley scored a record 434 league goals between 1946 and 1965. He signed professional for West Bromwich Albion in May 1944. He began playing as an outside left for Albion, where he made 41 appearances scoring 15 goals between 1944-1948. It is hard to understand why England 'B' and Football League honours were not followed by a full international cap, so great was Arthur's marksmanship. Why did Albion let him go when they did? He matured with Fulham in between 1948-1950, scoring 27 goals in 56 league games. He developed into a great striker with Leicester City who signed him for £14,000 in July 1950. He holds the club record for the most goals in a single season at Leicester City scoring 44 goals in 42 league matches 1956/57. He scored a total of 251 goals for the Filberts between 1950 – 1958. He moved to Shrewsbury Town for £7,000 in June 1958 as player/manager scoring 38 goals in 43 games for Shrewsbury in 1958/59. He is also Shrewsbury's record league goal scorer with 152 league goals in 236 games. In between 1946 – 1965 he amassed 434 league goals.

During this time, he scored 20 or more in ten successive seasons between 1950 and 1960. After Shrewsbury, he managed Sheffield United July 1968 to August 1969, Southend United March 1970 until May 1976. Then went to Telford United as assistant manager 1978/79, Oswestry Town manager July 1979-October 1980. He became a district manager for Vernons Pools and lived in Shrewsbury until his death in December 2002. He was the younger brother of Manchester United footballer Jack Rowley.

RUSHBURY David 'Dave'
Defender/left back 5'10 "
Born *20/2/1956 Wolverhampton*
Playing career: *West Bromwich Albion (31 appearances July 1974 – July 1979), Sheffield Wednesday (loan then signed), Swansea City, Carlisle United, Gillingham, Doncaster Rovers, Carlisle United (loan), Bristol Rovers, Cambridge United (1974-1987).*
Dave was a stylish, hard-working defender who occupied positions 2- 6 inclusive during his professional career. He had one good season with Albion when he replaced Ally Robertson in the middle of defence in 1974/75. After 28 league games, he moved to Sheffield Wednesday for £60,000 after a loan. In three years at Hillsborough he played 112 league games scoring 7 goals. He moved to Swansea in July 1979 for £60,000 making 52 league appearances 1979-81. Carlisle United was his next stop, moving in August 1981 for £40,000. He played 129 league games in four years. He had a brief spell at Gillingham who paid £15,000 for him in March 1985, playing just 12 league games. In July of the same year he moved to Doncaster Rovers for £10,000. In 2years he played another 66 league games, scoring twice. He had a brief loan spell with Carlisle before signing on a free transfer for Bristol Rovers in February 1987, playing 16 league games. He had short spells at Cambridge United and Goole Town. Rushbury took both the UEFA A licence and the FA treatment diploma in sports injuries. He was Physiotherapist at Chesterfield, caretaker manager after Nicky Law left, then manager until April 2003. Appointed director of football at non-league Alfreton Town. Obtained a BSc (Hons) in sport science and since 2001 worked at Chesterfield College lecturing in Sport Therapy and other BTEC qualifications. He lives in Chesterfield.

RYAN Reginald Alfonso 'Paddy'
Inside forward/wing half 5'9"
Born *30/10/1925 Dublin County Dublin, Ireland*
Died *13/2/1977 Sheldon, West Midlands*
Playing career: *Nuneaton Borough, Coventry City, West Bromwich Albion (272 appearances 31 goals Apr 1945 – June 1955), Derby County, Coventry City (1944 – 1960) Ryan was also a dual international, playing for both Ireland teams, the FAI XI and the IFA XI*
Nicknamed 'Paddy' due to his Irish heritage. Ryan initially played gaelic football at School in Dublin while growing up, but then switched to soccer after moving to Blackpool during the early years of the Second World War. He played with Claremount School, Blackpool Boys, various factory teams and had trials with both Sheffield United and Nottingham Forest before joining Nuneaton Borough. In April 1943 he signed for Coventry City as an amateur and during the 1942/43 season he played 2 games in wartime regional leagues. He then turned professional in August 1944 and made a further 4 appearances for the club during the 1944/45 wartime season. In April 1945 Ryan signed for West Bromwich Albion and during the 1945/46 season, he made 17 appearances in the Football League South. He made his debut for the club against Millwall in November 1945. Together with Davy Walsh and Jackie Vernon, he helped Albion gain promotion to the First Division in 1949. In 1954, together with Ronnie Allen and Frank Griffin, he was a member of the West Bromwich Albion team that finished as First Division runners-up and FA Cup winners. He also helped the Baggies share the FA Charity Shield when he scored in a 4-4 draw with Wolverhampton Wanderers. Ryan signed for Derby County in June 1955 for a fee of £3,000. He was appointed team captain and in three seasons with the club missed only three matches – two because of injury one because of international duty. He was a member of the side promoted as champions of the Third Division North to the Football League Second Division in 1956/57. In 1955 he also played for an English Division Three North XI against an English Division Three South XI. Ryan played 133 league games for County, scoring 30 goals. He also played a further 6 games for the club in the FA Cup, scoring a further goal.

He returned to City in September 1958. He then helped the club win promotion from the newly formed Division Four, after they finished as runners-up in 1959. During his second spell with City he played 70 times in all competitions. After retiring as a player in November 1960, Ryan worked as a pools' supervisor for both Coventry City between 1960–1961 and West Bromwich Albion between 1961–1962. From September 1962 to October 1976 he was chief scout for Albion. He later worked as a scout for various clubs including Aston Villa, Derby County, Hereford United and Leeds United before retiring in 1994.

Personal note: *My Dad, Chas Atkins, worked with Paddy Ryan setting up the Albion Pools in the early 1960's. I used to help out in the school holidays. Paddy said to me when I was in Junior School, "If you pass your 11 plus exam, I will give you an International cap." Well a few months later, I was successful in passing the exam for entry my local school Holly Lodge Grammar. True to his word, Paddy gave me a wonderful green velvet Irish International cap, of which I am still the very proud owner.*

SAKIRI Artim

Midfielder 5'10"

Born 23/9/1973 Livada, Struga, SR Macedonia

Playing career: *Karorman & Vardar (both in Macedonia), Halmstad in Sweden (loan), TeBe Berlin in Germany (loan), FC HIT & Korotan in Slovenia (both in Slovenia), Malatyaspor & CSKA Sofia (both in Turkey, West Bromwich Albion (Cost £250,000 11 + 22 sub appearances 1 goal July 2003 – July 2004), AaB Aalborg in Denmark, Inter Turku in Finland,FC Vaduz in Switzerland, Shkendija in Macedonia, Besa Kavaje in Albania, Qarabag,Azerbaijan. 73 Macedonia caps.*

Artim Sakiri. In 1997, he moved from Vardar to Swedish side Halmstads BK, a team that won the Swedish premier league Allsvenskan the same year. In 2003, he moved for £250,000 from Bulgarian club CSKA Sofia to West Bromwich Albion in England. A ball playing balding midfielder, he made his debut in a 4–1 defeat away at local rivals Walsall. In his first home league match for Albion, Sakiri scored a spectacular long-range goal, helping his team to a 4–1 win over Burnley which was, however, his only goal for the club. He made 30 appearances during 2003/04, but the next season he only played three games and left the club.

He was set to move to Burnley, but the move fell through as his work permit wasn't renewed. Instead, Sakiri went to AaB in Denmark. He was released by AaB in 2006. In Autumn 2006, he signed for Finnish club FC Inter. He made five Veikkausliiga appearances and scored three times, but his contract was not renewed. In 2007, he signed for FC Vaduz. At the beginning of the season 2008 he has signed for Azerbaijani side Qarabağ FK. Artim retired from playing in 2009 after a 22-year career in which he played over 300 league games scoring 64 goals in 10 different countries for 14 teams. He became Manager of Shkendija in Macedonia but left with the club in financial difficulties. 2014/2015 he was manager of Albanian club Kukesi. In 2019 Sakiri was manager of Flamurtari in Azerbaijan.

SANDERS James 'Jimmy'

Goalkeeper 5'11"

Born 5/7/1920 Hackney, London

Died 11/8/2003 Tamworth, Staffordshire

Playing career: *Charlton Athletic, West Bromwich Albion (Cost £2,250 391 appearances Nov 1945 – June 1958), Kettering Town, Coventry City, Hinckley Athletic (1941-1960) for West Bromwich Albion, Southampton, Chelsea, West Ham United, Fulham & Liverpool during WW2.*

Jim signed professional for Charlton in September 1941. Like so many players of his era, Jim did his national service in the RAF during WW2. He flew 120 operational flights as Rear Air Gunner, but was shot down and his resulting injuries although healing, caused him terrible pain. He was told he would never play football again. He proved everyone wrong by regaining full fitness. He joined Albion for £2,250 in November 1945. He was a very consistent goalkeeper, never acrobatic but always steady and helped them win promotion in 1948/49. He went on to play 391 first team matches and he was the Albion keeper in the FA Cup winning side of 1954, replacing Norman Heath had suffered a bad neck and back injury in March at Sunderland. Sanders was a bit of an expert saving penalties, stopping 25 in his 19-year career. He became a publican first in Derby, then in Birmingham. He always wore his '54 Cup Winners medal around his neck on a gold chain, as well as his trademark dicky bow. Lived in retirement in Tamworth until his death in August 2003 aged 83.

SANDFORD Edward 'Teddy'

Inside left/centre half 5'9"

Born *22/10/1910 Handsworth, Birmingham*
Died *13/5/1995 Great Barr aged 84*

Playing career: *West Bromwich Albion (317 appearances 75 goals May 1930 – March 1939), Sheffield United, Morris Commercial FC (1930 – 1943)*

Edward Sandford was born in October 1910 at 367 Holyhead Road, Handsworth, just a 'stones-throw' from the Hawthorns. In the 1911 census Ted was the youngest of three children still at the same address. His Father was a railway wagon maker. In October 1929, while still an amateur, Sandford joined West Bromwich Albion, the club that his uncle Abe Jones had represented between 1896 and 1901. He turned professional in May 1930. He arrived at the club when there was an abundance of inside forward talent at the Hawthorns and he spent his first term in the reserves before scoring on his senior debut in November when Albion beat Preston North End 3–2. He played in every match from then on during 1930/31 his first season. He was a key member of the Albion side that won promotion to the First Division and that also beat Birmingham 2–1 in the 1931 FA Cup Final. In November 1932 he won his only England cap, in a 0–0 draw with Wales at Wrexham, although he was selected as a reserve for 2 other games. He also had to withdraw from an England tour of Scandinavia in 1937 due to injury. He also was an FA Cup Final runner up in 1935, scoring one of Albion's goals in a 4-2 defeat by Sheffield Wednesday. A player of the quiet brigade, never flashy, Teddy was nevertheless an excellent goalscoring inside left who was exceedingly quick to pounce and dispossess an opponent, who in turn found it hard to dispossess Ted. He had an enviable physique which held him in good stead later in his career when he lined up as centre-back to good effect. He was the club captain in the 1937 FA Cup Semi Final defeat to Preston just a couple of days after the death of Albion legend Billy Bassett. Teddy had ten fine seasons with Albion. He joined Sheffield United for £1500 in 1939. In the 1939 register, Teddy and his wife Lily were living at Hall Green Road, West Bromwich and his profession was noted as, a body builder in wood. He finished his footballing career with Morris Commercial F.C., retiring in May 1943.

Ted was a coach for Albion 1950-57 and then scout 1961-67. Teddy later owned a cafe on the Birmingham Road, next to the Woodman Inn. He latterly lived in Queslett Road, Great Barr, where he died in May 1995 aged 84.

In his own words: *Ex-Albion player and Chairman Billy Bassett died on 8th April 1937, two days before the 1937 FA Cup Semi Final when Albion played Preston at Highbury. Teddy, the club's captain said, "We were all too full up to play. Mr Bassett's death stunned the whole team – even the supporters. He was such a well-respected person. He taught me a lot and I must admit that I was tearful for most of the first half following the minute's silence before the kick-off." Albion lost the game 4-1.*

Personal note: *I was fortunate enough to visit Teddy Sandford in September 1983 at his home in Great Barr. He was rather a shy guy but loved talking about his football days with West Bromwich Albion. We talked about the FA Cup and Promotion winning team. He was the youngest member of the squad. In his later years he was suffering with arthritis in his legs.*

SANKEY Jack

Wing half 5'10"

Born *19/3/1912 Winsford, Cheshire*
Died *14/3/1985 Sandwell*

Playing career: *Windsford United, West Bromwich Albion (287 appearances 27 goals Nov 1930 – Oct 1945), Northampton Town, Guested for Walsall 1945-46, Hereford United. (1928 – 1953)*

Jack Sankey played for Winsford United in Cheshire before joining Second Division West Bromwich Albion in November 1930. He eventually made his first team debut in an FA Cup tie at Chelsea in January 1934. His League debut coming a week later against Blackburn Rovers in a First Division match. He immediately established himself as a regular in the first XI playing 20 league games and 2 FA cup games although he was not selected for the 1935 FA Cup Final team who lost 4-2 to Sheffield Wednesday, having lost his place in March to Jimmy Edwards. He was part of Albion's 1937 FA Cup semi-final team that lost to Preston North End at Highbury and he continued to play until peacetime football was abandoned due to the outbreak of WW2 in September 1939. By then Jack had scored 5 goals in 160 appearances. Jack was an industrious and highly efficient wing half or inside forward who let the ball do most of the work.

His overall play was characterised by some powerful long-range shooting and he could defend as well as attack. He spent three seasons and more in the second XI 1930 – 1933. Including matches played during the war years, Sankey played a total of 287 games for West Bromwich Albion scoring 27 goals. He joined Northampton Town in October 1945 for a fee of £500. He moved to Hereford United in 1947 and stayed there until he retired in 1953. He was assistant trainer/coach at Hereford 1953/54. He was granted a Testimonial Match in 1954 when Hereford beat West Bromwich Albion XI 10-5, with 4,500 fans in attendance. West Bromwich Albion coach between 1955 and 1964. Later he was an Albion scout 1965-66. He retired from football related activities to work at a cycle factory in Handsworth.

SCHARNER Paul

Midfielder/defender 6'3"

Born *11/3/1980 Scheibbs, Austria*

Playing career: *Austria Wein, SG Untersiebenbrunn (loan), SV Salzburg, SK Brann in Norway, Wigan Athletic, West Bromwich Albion (Free transfer 52 + 12 sub appearances 7 goals Aug 2010 – July 2012), Hamburger SV, Hamburger SV II, Wigan Athletic (loan). 12 Austria U-21 appearances and 40 Full Austrian International caps also an U-21 International.*

He operated mainly as a defender, although he could play almost every midfield position as well. He was known for his great positional versatility and haircuts.

Scharner started his professional career with Austrian Bundesliga sides Austria Wien and SV Salzburg, before moving to Norwegian Tippeligaen club SK Brann in late 2004. In January 2006, joined Premier League Wigan Athletic for £2.5 million. Paul was noted for his positional flexibility, having played every outfield position for Wigan except left back. In two spells with the Latics, Paul made 159 league appearances. On 30th August 2010, Scharner joined newly promoted Premier League side West Bromwich Albion on a two-year deal. Having played as a central defender, he made the switch to the Hawthorns when manager Roberto Di Matteo told him he will be used as a midfielder. He received seven yellow and one red cards that season. The next, his final year in the Premier League, he played 29 games for the Baggies, mostly as a starter, scoring three goals, while receiving six yellow cards. A feature of his play is his great professionalism and focus, planning his training, goals and achievements meticulously on flip-charts. He was a tall, powerful hard tackling midfield player who wanted eventually to move to centre back. He became a legend with Albion fans by scoring against Aston Villa and lifting his football shirt revealing a T-shirt with a large Albion badge. After not meeting a clause in his contract that would trigger a twelve-month extension, Scharner announced that he would be leaving the Hawthorns.

Paul Scharner

He had started 52 games and made 12 substitute appearances scoring 7 goals. After a short time as a free agent, he transferred to Bundesliga veteran club Hamburger SV in August 2012, before returning to Wigan Athletic on loan in January 2013 - winning the FA Cup in May beating Manchester City. He announced his retirement, at age 33, in September 2013. Paul Scharner is married to Marlene and has three sons: Constantin, Benedict and Paul Jr. He has received vocational education in the field of electrical engineering and lists skiing, reading, motorcycling and billiards as his personal interests.

SCIMECA Ricardo
Midfielder/Full back 6'0"
Born *13/6/1975 Leamington Spa*
Playing career: *Aston Villa, Nottingham Forest, Leicester City, West Bromwich Albion (£100,000 33 + 7 sub appearances July 2004 –Jan 2006), Cardiff City (loan then signed) (1995 – 2009)*

Scimeca started his career at Aston Villa, coming through the club's youth system, as a central defender and was largely a squad player until his move to Nottingham Forest in 1999 for £2.5 million.

Stephane Sessegnon

He spent four seasons at the City Ground, He moved on to Leicester City in 2003, on a free transfer after failing to agree a new deal. At Leicester he scored once in a 4–3 defeat to Wolverhampton Wanderers on 25th October 2003. Scimeca then moved on a free transfer to West Bromwich Albion a year later by activating a get-out clause in his contract which allowed him to leave Leicester. He was part of the 'Great Escape' squad who escaped relegation from the Premier League on the final day of the season. He did not play in that game against Portsmouth but he did play 27 games and made another 6 substitute appearances. His versatility was his main quality, appearing in five different positions at the Hawthorns. He moved to Cardiff City in early 2006 where he played 70 league games between 2006-09. Ricardo retired in 2009 following a groin injury. Scimeca joined the veteran's team of his home town club, Leamington, in the Central Warwickshire Over 35's Premier League in 2013. In April 2015 he joined Solihull Moors in a role as youth coach.

SESSEGNON Stephane
Midfielder/Winger 5'6"
Born *1/6/1984, Allahe, Benin*
Playing career: *Requins de l'Atlantique in Benin,Creteil, Le Mans, Paris Saint-Germain (all in France), Sunderland, West Bromwich Albion (Cost £5.5 – rising to 6 million with extras 74 + 18 Sub appearances 8 goals Sep 2013 – June 2016), Montpellier, Genclerbirligi. 82 full caps for Benin.*

Sessegnon began his career in Cotonou with Benin Premier League side Requins de l'Atlantique. He moved to France to join Créteil, where he played 68 league games scoring 10 goals. Sessegnon signed a three-year deal with Le Mans on 19 May 2006. Initially used as a holding midfielder, playing 61 league games scoring 6 goals at Le Mans. Sessegnon was given a more advanced role for the 2007/08 season, often starting on the right side of the midfield or as an attacker. He remained in France by signing a four-year deal with Paris Saint Germain. The fee was said to be in the range of €8–10 million. He played 77 games for PSG scoring 9 goals. On 29th January 2011, Sessegnon departed Paris Saint-Germain to join English club Sunderland. He signed a three-and-a-half-year contract and the transfer fee was priced at £6 million.

He became a fan favourite at the Stadium of Light, playing 87 games scoring 17 goals. On 2nd September 2013, Sessegnon joined West Bromwich Albion for a club record fee of £5.5 million, rising to £6 million with extras. He was a fan favourite at the club and his substitution in matches has often led to a negative reaction from the fans. After almost leaving the club at the end of the season after falling out with manager Tony Pulis over selection issues, Sessegnon would return to the first team in the 2015/16 season with consistent performances. He played 79 league games for Albion scoring 8 goals, mainly playing in a wide right position. 18th May 2016, it was announced that Sessegnon and Victor Anichebe would both leave the club for free having cost a combined total of around £12 million. In September 2016, Sessegnon signed for Ligue 1 side Montpellier, playing 43 league games scoring 3 goals. In January 2018, Sessegnon signed a one and a half-year contract with Süper Lig side Gençlerbirliği in Turkey, playing 75 league games scoring 10 goals.

SETTERS Maurice

Wing half/inside forward 5'6"

Born *16/12/1936 Honiton, Devon*

Playing career: *Exeter City, West Bromwich Albion (Cost £3,000 132 appearances 10 goals Jan 1955 – Jan 1960), Manchester United, Stoke City, Cleveland Stokers, Coventry City, Charlton Athletic. (1954-1970).*

Maurice, nicknamed 'Mo-Mo', made more than 400 appearances in the Football League for Exeter City, West Bromwich Albion, Manchester United, Stoke City, Coventry City and Charlton Athletic, and in the United Soccer Association with the Cleveland Stokers. His favoured position was wing half. Setters started his career with Exeter City making his debut towards the end of the 1953/54 season. He made 10 appearances for the "Grecians" in 1954/55 and impressed enough to tempt First Division West Bromwich Albion to acquire his signature in January of 1955 for £3,000. With his bandy legs and crew-cut hairstyle, Maurice Setters looked what he was on the field of play – a real terrier, as hard as nails, determined, fearless, reckless at times. A real tough nut. Under the guidance of Vic Buckingham Setters became a regular as the "Baggies" finished in 4th in 1957/58 5th in 1958/59 and 4th again in 1959/60.

Maurice, gained England schoolboy honours, one Youth cap for England, 16 appearances at U-23 level, also playing for the FA XI and Young England but never played a full international, although Setters was included in England's 1958 FIFA World Cup squad as a reserve player, but did not travel to the tournament or play in any matches. He went on Albion's tour of Canada and USA in 1959 but had some problems and a disagreement with travelling director Jim Gaunt and he was dropped from the final games of the tour. After playing 120 league games for Albion scoring 10 goals, in January 1960, he was transferred to Manchester United for a fee of £30,000. Matt Busby signed Setters as a replacement for the injured Wilf McGuinness. Setters developed his reputation for being one of footballs 'hard men' and his combative style earned him the captaincy. A poor 1962/63 league campaign saw Manchester United nearly relegated in the Second Division but they did beat Leicester City 3–1 in the 1963 FA Cup Final. A much improved 1963/64 season brought a 2nd-place finish behind Liverpool. A 7–0 win over Aston Villa early in the 1964/65 season was Setters final game for United. In total, he made 159 league appearances scoring 12 goals before he was sold to Stoke City for £30,000. On a tour in America, Setters played nine times for the Cleveland Stokers scoring three goals. He missed just three matches For Stoke in 1965/66 playing in 45 fixtures. His run in the first team continued in 1966/67 until he sustained injury against Liverpool on 4 March 1967 which allowed Alan Bloor to take his place. After failing to dislodge Bloor, after 86 league games for Stoke, Setters joined Coventry City in November 1967. He made 51 league appearances for Coventry in just under three years at Highfield Road and ended his career with a four-month spell with Second Division Charlton Athletic playing 8 league games. He went into management with Doncaster Rovers from 1971 – 74, before in 1978 becoming Jack Charlton's assistant at Sheffield Wednesday. He was Rotherham United assistant manager 1983/84, Newcastle United chief Scout 1984-85, then re-joined Jack Charlton as his assistant manager of the Republic of Ireland national team for ten years. Lived in retirement in Tichill, Doncaster.

Craig Shakespeare

SHAKESPEARE Craig

Midfielder 5'10"

Born *26/10/1963 Birmingham*

Playing career: *Walsall, Sheffield Wednesday, West Bromwich Albion (Cost £275,000 120 + 8 sub appearances 16 goals July 1990 – June 1993), Grimsby Town, Scunthorpe United, Telford United, Hednesford Town (1981 – 2000)*

Craig was an attacking midfielder, who favoured his left foot and his preferred position was on the left side of midfield. He signed as a professional for Walsall in November 1981. In 1987/88 he helped Walsall to win promotion to Division Two via the Play Offs. He played well over 350 games for the Saddlers, scoring 59 goals, and in 1989 he moved to Sheffield Wednesday, then in the First Division, for a fee of £300,000. He spent less than a year at Hillsborough, before moving to West Bromwich Albion for £275,000. He stayed at Albion for over three years, making 128 appearances in total and became the team's first choice penalty taker. He scored twice from the penalty spot in Albion's first ever game in the Third Division, a 6–3 victory over Exeter City in August 1991 Albion were promoted in 1993, but Shakespeare moved to Grimsby Town, re-joining Alan Buckley, under whom he had played at Walsall. In 4-years he made 106 appearances in the league for the Mariners scoring 10 goals. He later moved on to Scunthorpe United 1997/98 playing 4 league games, and also played non-league football with Telford United and Hednesford Town, before retiring. In 1999, he re-joined West Bromwich Albion as Football in the Community Officer. In this role, he was responsible for promoting football at grass roots level in the local community. He later took up the post of academy coach, then in 2006 became Reserve Team Coach. In October 2006, following the departure of Bryan Robson and then his assistant Nigel Pearson, who had been caretaker manager for a period of four weeks, Shakespeare was given charge of the first team for one game pending the arrival of Tony Mowbray. The game was away to Crystal Palace; Albion won 2–0. Shakespeare left Albion in June 2008 to become Pearson's assistant manager at Leicester City, a move that was confirmed on 1st July. As well as having worked together on the West Bromwich Albion coaching staff, the two had also played together at Sheffield Wednesday. Shakespeare once said that Pearson was the best captain he had ever played under. Shakespeare then followed Pearson to Hull City, which lasted until 2011. He then again followed Pearson back to Leicester City when the latter was reappointed manager there in November 2011. Following Pearson's sacking in July 2015, Shakespeare remained as assistant manager to incoming manager Claudio Ranieri. When Ranieri was sacked on 23 February 2017, Shakespeare took over as caretaker manager. On 12th March, he was named as the new manager of Leicester City. On 8 June, Shakespeare signed a 3-year deal to be the permanent manager for Leicester City. On 17th October 2017, he was fired after poor performances left the club in the bottom three of the standings and in danger of relegation. On 1st December 2017, Shakespeare was appointed first team coach at Everton following the appointment of Sam Allardyce as manager the previous day. He re-joined Nigel Pearson at Watford in 2020 until, along with Pearson, was sacked with 2 matches left to play after the break for Covid-19 pandemic. Watford were relegated at the end of the 2019/20 season. He was appointed as assistant head coach at Aston Villa in August 2020

SHAW Cecil

Full back 5'9 ½"

Born *22/6/1911 Mansfield*

Died *January 1977 Handsworth, Birmingham*

Playing career: *Wolverhampton Wanderers, West Bromwich Albion (Cost £7,500 251 appearances 14 goals Dec 1936 – June 1947), Nottingham Forest & Blackpool during WW2, Hereford United (1930 – 1949)*

He turned professional in February 1930 when he joined Wolverhampton Wanderers. He helped them win promotion to Division One in 1932/33. After 183 competitive appearances for Wolves, Shaw, who was Wolves' captain moved to their local rivals West Bromwich Albion in December 1936. Albion broke their transfer record to secure his services, paying the £7,500 fee in two instalments. He went straight into the Albion team, making his Albion debut the same month, in a 2-1 win against Liverpool at Anfield.

Cecil was a tough full back, a resolute and robust tackler. He was a solid man, able to withstand any challenge. He kept his place comfortably until the war and partly through it. He is one of only a handful of players to have represented Albion before, during and after the hostilities of 1939-45. Towards the end of the 1930's he lined up alongside his namesake George Shaw in the two full back positions for Albion. In 1935 Cecil represented the Football League and was reserve for England on two occasions. During the Second World War he continued to represent Albion, as well as making guest appearances for Nottingham Forest and Blackpool. Shaw scored 14 goals in 251 competitive games for West Bromwich Albion. In 1947 he left the club to join Hereford United, where he played until his retirement in 1949. He later refereed in the Oldbury & District leagues 1959/60 and worked as a scout for West Bromwich Albion between 1961 and 1964.

SHAW (George) David

Striker 5'10"

Born *11/10/1948 Huddersfield, Yorkshire*

Playing career: *Huddersfield Town, Oldham Athletic, West Bromwich Albion (Cost £77,000 78 +18 sub appearances 21 goals Mar 1973 – Dec 1975), Oldham Athletic (loan then signed) (1967-1978) Retired through injury.*

David was a striker who played for Huddersfield Town, Oldham Athletic and West Bromwich Albion. He was the grandson of David Steele, triple championship winner and later manager of Huddersfield Town, so it was hardly surprising that David Shaw should begin his career with his home town club in 1966. However, after playing just 24 games and scoring 3 goals, in September 1969 he was part of an exchange deal in which Les Chapman moved to Leeds Road from Oldham Athletic and Shaw moved across the Pennines to join the Lancashire club. His speed off the mark and eye for a goal soon made him a favourite with the Boundary Park faithful, and his partnership with Jim Fryatt in the 1970/71 season, when he scored 23 goals and Fryatt scored 24, made a major contribution to the Oldham club's promotion from Division 4. His continued success over the next two seasons led to a big-money transfer in March 1973.

He moved to West Bromwich Albion for a fee of £77,000. Playing at a higher level, he did not achieve quite the same success as he had in the lower divisions, scoring 21 goals in 74 starts and 18 substitute appearances for the Midlands club. He was nicknamed 'super-sub' as he seemed to have the knack of scoring when he came off the bench. Shaw was a dangerous striker, full of energy but perhaps lacked ball control in tight situations. He was already starting to suffer from niggling injuries towards the end of his time there, and in October 1975 he moved back to Oldham on a free transfer. He maintained a more than reasonable strike rate on his return to the club, netting 21 goals in his 59 appearances over the next three years, but he was troubled by a knee injury for much of this time and was forced to retire in 1978. After running a pub for eight years he worked for an engineering firm, Hopkinson's Values, as a storeman for fifteen years then took on driving jobs for around eight years before retiring due to trouble with both his hips which needed replacing.

SHAW George

Right back 5'10

Born *13/10/1899 Swinton, West Riding*

Died *10/3/1973 Doncaster*

Playing career: *Gillingham, Doncaster Rovers, Huddersfield Town, West Bromwich Albion (£4,100 425 appearances 11 goals Nov1926 – May 1938), Stalybridge Celtic player/manager, Worcester City player/manager, Floriana in Malta player/manager*

In the 1901 census George was living in Mexborough and his Father was a miner. In the 1911 census George Shaw was the oldest of five children, having one brother and three sisters. One other sibling had tragically died. His Father was still a miner and the family lived in the Goldthorpes area of Rotherham. George served the Navy from 4th June 1918 primarily on HMS Victory. Shaw played for Gillingham for two seasons appearing in just 3 league games before moving back home to play for his local club Doncaster Rovers. Between 1922 – 1924 he played 64 league games and scored 6 league goals, 5 of them penalties. In 1922/23 a season which saw Doncaster end as runners-up in the Midland League and win the Wharncliffe Charity Cup. The following season, 1923/24, Rovers were selected for promotion back to the Football League for the first time since 1905. In their first match of the season Shaw managed to send his penalty kick into the stand, thus missing out on scoring their first return goal and failing to win the match. His last match for Doncaster was at Walsall on 26th January 1924, after which he transferred to Huddersfield Town. George was an occasional player in Huddersfield's three successive First Division Championship seasons 1923/24, 1924/25, 1925/26 making 24 appearances in those three seasons. Nicknamed 'Teapot', and the 'Singer' George 'Cocky' Shaw gave long and loyal service to the club. Admirably built for a full back, he was dominant in the air, strong on the ground and decidedly safe and sure with his kicking. He was a grand volleyer of the ball and a useful penalty taker, as well as a free kick specialist. Leaving Huddersfield, he signed for West Bromwich Albion at a cost of £4,100 which was then a club record fee. He proved to be worth every single penny, and more. With Albion he won Promotion to Division One and an FA Cup winners' medal in 1931 and a runners-up medal in the 1935 FA Cup Final. He played once for England along with fellow clubman Harold Pearson at Wembley v Scotland in 1932. He had an outing for the Football League XI and went on two FA Tours to Belgium, France & Spain in 1921 and to Canada in 1931. He was one of 18 players who left Liverpool on 11th May 1931 heading for Montreal in Canada on board the Duchess of Richmond. He returned on 27th July 1931 via Southampton on the Empress of Britain. He said goodbye to the Hawthorns' fans shortly after the end of the 1937/38 season having amassed 425 appearances scoring 11 goals. He joined Stalybridge Celtic as player/manager in June 1938, moving on to Worcester City also as player/manager in March 1939. In the 1939 register, George is married to Dorothy and was an assurance agent living in Barnsley Road, Scawsby, near Doncaster. After the War, George settled in Malta as Manager of Floriana from 1948 until 1951. They were Maltese League Champions 1949/50, Malta Cup Winners 1948/49 & 1949/50, Caesar Cup Winners 1949/50 and Main Congress Cuyp Winners in 1949. Shaw brought his Floriana team to the Hawthorns in 1951 when Albion won 2-0 in a Festival of Britain match.

He retired in June 1951 and returned to Hamworth Colliery near Doncaster. George was an ex-Navy man and beside singing he was a dab hand at mat making. He was the elder brother of Wilf Shaw, who also played full back for Doncaster Rovers, until he was killed in action in World War II.

SHEARMAN Ben

Outside left 5'8"
Born *2/12/1884 Lincoln*
Died *1/10/1958*
Playing career: *Rotherham Town (Midland league), Bristol City, West Bromwich Albion (Cost £100 143 appearances 11 goals June 1911 – July 1919), Nottingham Forest, Gainsborough Trinity, Norton Woodseats. (1905 – 1938)*

Shearman was signed by Rotherham Town 1906 -1909. Renowned as a speedy winger with an accurate crossing ability. He was transferred to Bristol City 1909-1911 with whom he made his Football League debut in 1909. After two seasons at Bristol, they were relegated in 1911, he moved to West Bromwich Albion where he enjoyed the most successful spell of his career, featuring in the 1912 FA Cup Final where the Baggies eventually lost to Barnsley in a replay at Bramall Lane. With the outset of World War 1 he moved back to Sheffield to work in steel production at Tinsley whilst making regular guest appearances for Sheffield United before eventually joining the British Army. Ben was an elusive outside left, quick off the mark and strikingly accurate with his deep crosses both high or low hit from the touchline. He played in 143 games for Albion. He played for the Football League XI on two occasions in 1911. Following the end of the war he was bought by Nottingham Forest for £250 but stayed only one season before moving into non-league football with Gainsborough Trinity and then Norton Woodseats as trainer/coach until 1937. Despite missing four years of his career due to World War I he made 217 appearances in the Football League, totalling more than 250 games in all competitions.

"DID YOU KNOW?"

"Albion's first £10 million player was Brown Ideye from Dynamo Kiev in July 2014."

SHEPPARD Richard 'Dick'

Goalkeeper 5'11"

Born *14/2/1945 Bristol*

Died *18/10/1998 Bristol aged 53*

Playing career: *West Bromwich Albion (54 appearances Feb 1963 – June 1969), Bristol Rovers, Torquay United (loan), Fulham (loan), Weymouth, Portway FC Bristol. Retired October 1975.*

He joined the professional ranks at West Bromwich Albion in 1963 and went on to play 39 League games in six years with Albion. Dick was a capable goalkeeper of sound build and splendid reflexes, who was somewhat unfortunate to be with Albion at the same time as Tony Millington, Ray Potter and John Osborne. He was perhaps a few inches shorter than most keepers. He collected a runners-up tankard in the 1967 League Cup Final at Wembley, where QPR's Mike Keen left a boot imprint on Sheppard's chest in the lead up to Rangers' winning goal. He made 54 appearances in all competitions for Albion. He moved back to his home city of Bristol in 1969 to join Bristol Rovers. It was Dick Sheppard's penalty save in the Watney Cup Final of 1972 against Sheffield United, in which Rovers won 7-6 in a do-or-die penalty shoot-out, that gave Rovers their first ever major trophy. Sheppard also famously saved a George Best penalty at Old Trafford in 1972 as Bristol Rovers beat Manchester United 2-1 in a League Cup replay after a 1-1 draw at Eastville. Dick made 151 League appearances before suffering a skull fracture in January 1973 in a match against Tranmere Rovers at Eastville Stadium.

It was eleven months before he was to play again, when he joined Torquay United on loan in December 1973. He played just two games for Torquay, and it was a further year before he finally made it back into the Bristol Rovers line-up. His only appearance for The Pirates after breaking his skull came against Bristol City in December 1974, and after conceding four goals in the second half his professional career came to an abrupt end, aged 29. Although he was sent out on loan to Fulham later in the season, he never played in the League again. In the summer of 1975, Sheppard joined Weymouth, where he spent a year, followed by a year with Portway Bristol. He moved to Paulton Rovers in 1977, and in January 1980 became the goalkeeping coach for his former club Bristol Rovers. He died in 1998 at the age of 53.

SHINTON Frederick 'Fred'

Centre forward 5'11"

Born *7/2/1883 Wednesbury, Staffs*

Died *11/4/1923 Wednesbury aged 40*

Playing career: *West Bromwich Albion (68 appearances 46 goals April 1905 – December 1907), Leicester Fosse, Bolton Wanderers, Leicester Fosse, Wednesbury Old Athletic.*

Fred turned professional with West Bromwich Albion in April 1905. He was a deadly marksman who scored a goal every 125 minutes of League football for Albion, during his eighteen months association with the club. A very sporting character, he played with dash and tenacity; he had a never-say-die attitude and simply loved scoring goals. Nicknamed 'Appleyard' and 'Tickler' by his team mates, he had the superb knack of finding the net. He was recruited by Albion following the many problems the club had with the centre forward position, when no fewer than six different players had been tried there. Fred came along and fitted in a treat, making a big impact with the fans almost immediately. He remained with Albion until November 1907, when he joined Leicester Fosse for £150.When he left the Hawthorns several hundred supporters were so upset that they rebelled outside the ground. He was the Second Division top scorer in 1909/1910 scoring 31 goals in 38 matches. In August 1910 he moved to Bolton Wanderers for a £1000 fee, but re-joined Leicester Fosse just five months later, for £750.

Shinton was not offered a contract by Fosse at the end of the 1910–11 season and instead joined Wednesbury Old Athletic, playing for the club in the Birmingham & District League. He featured in the club's Wednesbury Charity Cup winning side v Darlaston in March 1912, but although captaining the side at the start of the following season, he appears to have made no further appearances after October 1912. He died at home in Wednesbury in April 1923 after a long illness.

SHOREY Nicholas 'Nicky'

Left back 5'9"

Born *19/2/1981 Romford, Essex*

Playing career: *Leyton Orient, Reading, Aston Villa, Nottingham Forest (loan), Fulham (loan), West Bromwich Albion (Cost £1.3 million 2010 – 2012), Reading, Bristol City, Portsmouth, Pune City in Indian Super League, Colchester United, Hungerford Town. 2 England caps. 1 England 'B' appearance.*

Shorey started his career at Leyton Orient playing 15 league games before he moved to Reading in 2001 for £25,000 where he made just under 300 appearances over seven years

Larus Sigurdsson

while helping the team reach the Premier League. He joined Aston Villa in 2008 for reported fee of £3 million, but was limited to 24 league appearances over two seasons. While with Villa, Shorey was loaned out to Nottingham Forest 9 games and Fulham 9 games. He joined West Bromwich Albion for £1.3 million in July 2010, as a solid, strong-tackling left back, making 53 Premier League appearances over two seasons with the club. After four years away, Shorey re-joined Reading on a free transfer in July 2012, but could only manage 17 league appearances 2012/13. He then joined Bristol City the following season 2013/14 playing14 games in just five months with before joining Portsmouth in January 2014. He played 41 league games for Pompey and then Indian Super League club Pune City in the summer of 2015. After playing in every match for Pune City, Shorey returned to England in January 2016 with League One club Colchester United playing 15 league games. He finished his playing career with National League South club Hungerford Town in 2016. In October 2018, Nicky and Glen Little, were appointed joint managers of Isthmian League Premier Division side, Wingate & Finchley. This was short lived as on the 29 October he left his managerial role due to personal reasons. On 2 July 2019, Shorey returned to Reading, taking up the role of Academy Lead Scout but he was made redundant by the club shortly after Christmas 2019 in cost cutting measure by the club.

SIGURDSSON Larus

Central defender 6'0"

Born *4/6/1973 Akureyri, Iceland*

Playing career: *Þór Akureyri in Iceland, Stoke City, West Bromwich Albion (Cost £350,000 114 + 14 sub appearances Sep 1999 – Nov 2004), Þór r Akureyri, I Akraness (1990 – 2010) 42 Iceland International caps.*

Larus played with Þór Akureyri along with his father Sigurdur Larusson who later became the manager. His cousin Þorvaldur Örlygsson who was playing in England for Stoke City recommend him to manager Lou Macari and he joined Stoke on trial then signed, playing 23 times in 1994/95 and his performances were so good he won the 'Player of the Year' award. He was an ever-present in 1995/96 as Stoke lost the play-offs to Leicester City.

He missed just one match in 1996/97 in final season at the Victoria Ground. He played in all but three matches in 1997/98 as Stoke suffered relegation to the third tier. Larus played 43 times in 1998/99 as Stoke failed to gain promotion. After making 228 appearances for Stoke he was sold to West Bromwich Albion in August 1999 for a fee of £350,000. He was a key member of Albion's squad that won promotion to the Premier League for the first time in 2001/2002 where he formed a sold centre back partnership alongside Phil Gilchrist. Sigurdsson played 42 league games plus 1 as substitute during that season. He suffered three different knee injuries during his time at The Hawthorns. The first problem came in 2000 when Sigurdsson ruptured his left anterior ligament. In 2003 in his last competitive game he damaged a cartilage. Then when making his comeback, he ruptured an anterior ligament. He had to step down from top-flight football. Sigurdsson went home to his old club, Þór, and played 15 games for them in 2005. In summer 2006, he was appointed player-manager at Þór, a position he held until 31st May 2010 when he resigned after conflict with the board. On 20th July 2010, he joined ÍA, the club he played in as a youngster. At the start of the 2011 season Larus was appointed as the manager of KF, retiring as a player.

In his own words: *In 2018 he returned to the Hawthorns to collect the 'Cap' the club were presenting to every former player. "It's been a while since I've been asked for an autograph," he said, on his return to The Hawthorns. "It's the first time my youngest son has seen me give an autograph and I don't think he could really understand why people were asking me! It was really special, it's a fantastic place, and a great club, with fantastic supporters. I'm really grateful for how the club treated me, my wife and our youngest son. We're over the moon."*

SIMMONS Charles 'Chippy'
Centre forward 5'11"

Born *9/9/1878 West Bromwich, Staffs*
Died *12/12/1937 Wednesbury, Staffs aged 59*
Playing career: *Oldbury Town, Worcester Rovers. West Bromwich Albion (Total 193 appearances 81 goals April 1898 – July 1904), West Ham United, West Bromwich Albion Cost £600 (May 1905 – March 1907), Chesterfield Town, Wellington Town, Royal Rover in Canada.*

Charles Simmons, nicknamed 'Chippy' was born in West Bromwich and turned professional with West Bromwich Albion in April 1898. He was a regular scorer for Albion from either inside right or centre forward. He teamed up splendidly with Billy Bassett and later Jimmy McLean and Fred Buck. A player with a lethal shot, 'Chippy' had plenty of pace and craft, and he always seemed to find plenty of space as well. He was a big favourite with the fans, especially the ladies, and it is reported that he had a personal fan club. On 3 September 1900 Simmons became the first Albion player to score at The Hawthorns, when he equalised Derby County player Steve Bloomer's goal in a 1–1 draw. He scored 75 league goals for Albion in 8 seasons, winning a Second division Championship medal in 1902. This same year he figured in an international trial, and later represented the Professional of the South v The Hawthorns of the South in 1905. He was an England reserve on three occasions during 1901/02 season. He became the top scorer in First Division 1901/02 by scoring 23 goals. He moved to West Ham United for £700 in July 1904, but returned to Albion for £600 just ten months later. When he returned to the Hawthorns for a second spell, he did marvellously well with Fred Shinton.

Chippy Simmons

Indeed, in season 1905/06 'Chippy' and Fred between them netted no fewer than 34 league goals. In his two spells with Albion, 'Chippy' scored 81 goals in 193 games. He joined Chesterfield Town and went on to play for Canadian side Royal Rovers in 1910. He retired in 1922, returning to West Bromwich, where he became a publican. He died in Wednesbury in 1937.

SIMPSON Terence 'Terry'
Left half/centre back 5'11"
Born *8/10/1938 Southampton, Hampshire*
Playing career: *Southampton, Peterborough United, West Bromwich Albion (Cost £6,000 77 appearances 4 goals May 1963 – Mar 1967), Walsall, Gillingham (1957-1973).*
Terry started his professional career with Southampton in July 1957, playing 22 league games, scoring once in 5 years. He moved to Peterborough United in June 1962 playing 45 league games scoring 4 goals in the 1962/63 season. Jimmy Hagan signed him for Albion in May 1963 for £6,000. Terry was a durable left half who later tried his luck at right back. A strong tackler who loved to go forward. During four years at the Hawthorns he played 72 league games scoring 4 goals. He moved to Walsall in March 1967 for £2,000, playing in 51 league games scoring 3 goals for the Saddlers between March 1967 and July 1968. After breaking a leg playing, Simpson was forced into early retirement. Gillingham made him a trainer for 12 months. He then returned to his area of birth, Southampton and worked at Union Castle on the docks for 3 years, then spent 29 years working for Ford Motor Company at Swaythling before retiring in 2003.

SINGLETON Martin
Midfielder 5'9"
Born *2/8/1963 Banbury, Oxfordshire*
Playing career: *Coventry City, Bradford City, West Bromwich Albion (16 + 5 sub appearances 1 goal Dec 1986 – Nov 1987), Northampton Town, Walsall, Worcester City, Aylesbury United. (1981 – 1991) England Youth International 6 caps*
Singleton played for Coventry City making 23 league appearances scoring 1 goal between 1981- 84, Bradford City paid £20,000 in December 1984. Whilst at Bradford, he won the League Division Three title in 1984/85 but on the last day of that successful season, while playing against Lincoln City, the day was turned into a nightmare when 56 spectators were killed in a horrendous stand fire. Stuart Naylor was in goal for Lincoln. He played 71 league games for City scoring 3 goals, before moving to West Bromwich Albion for £30,000 in December 1986. Signed as a utility player he played in shirts numbered 4, 6, 10, & 11 plus used as a substitute. Making 16 appearances plus 5 as a substitute, he scored 1 goal before moving on to Northampton Town in November 1987. He played 50 league games for the Cobblers scoring 4 times. His final League team was Walsall where he made 28 league appearances in 1990/91. He had spells in non-league football with Worcester City and Aylesbury United. Lived in Buckinghamshire.

SMITH David
Winger/Left back 5'8"
Born *29/3/1968 Stonehouse, Gloucestershire*
Playing career: *Coventry City, AFC Bournemouth (loan), Birmingham City, West Bromwich Albion (Cost £90,000 91+26 sub appearances 2 goals Jan 1994 – Jan 1998), Grimsby Town, Swansea City. (1986 – 2003) 10 England U-21 International caps*
Smith started his career at Coventry City after signing professional terms with the club in 1986 and he soon became a Sky Blue's fan favourite due to his fast and exciting wing play. After a very brief loan spell at Bournemouth where he made one league appearance in 1993, he moved to Birmingham City where he spent a season 1993/94 playing 38 league games scoring 3 goals. He moved to local rivals West Bromwich Albion under Alan Buckley for £90,000. He was a small, sprightly winger but he could easily fade out of games.

Sometimes asked to perform in midfield but not big enough in physique nor strong enough in the tackle. He spent four years at the club making 102 league appearances scoring 2 goals. Smith re-joined Grimsby Town and Alan Buckley who paid £200,000 halfway through the 1997/1998 season. In four years at Blundell Park he played 112 league games scoring 9 goals. He moved to Swansea City for the 2002/03 season on a 12-month deal playing in the Third Division. Several injuries prevented him from making an impact and he only managed four appearances all season, scoring once. He left Swansea at the end of the season and soon after retired. Upon retiring from professional football in 2003, Smith returned to Grimsby where he briefly worked in a local car dealership, before going into marketing. He was appointed as the assistant commercial manager at Grimsby Town in 2003. He eventually became the commercial manager.

SMITH Keith

Striker 5'9"

Born *15/9/1940 Woodville, Derbyshire*
Playing career: *West Bromwich Albion (70 appearances 34 goals Jan 1958 – May 1963), Peterborough United, Crystal Palace, Darlington, Orient, Notts County, Kidderminster Harriers, Tamworth, Bromsgrove Rovers 1972-75.*

Born in Derbyshire, Smith played professionally for West Bromwich Albion between January 1958-May 1963. Not ideally built for a striker, being rather small-looking and fragile, but Keith was pretty smart and elusive around goal, carrying a fair shot and excellent positional sense. His striking rate was excellent with Albion, scoring 34 goals in 70 appearances. Keith formed a potent partnership with Derek Kevan. While at WBA, he and his wife owned and ran the chip shop in Chapman Street. Peterborough United was his next stop in an exchange deal for Terry Simpson plus £6,000 cash. In 1963/64 he played 55 league games scoring 28 goals before signing, in November 1964, for his former Albion manager Dick Graham, now managing Crystal Palace. He notched up another 50 league games and 14 goals. On 28th August 1965, Smith became the club's first ever substitute when he replaced Ian Lawson. He also scored Palace's fastest ever goal, a six-second strike against Derby County, away from home on

12th December 1964. Smith was transferred to Darlington in 1966 playing another 17 league games scoring 2 goals before seeing out his professional career with Leyton Orient 3 games in 1967 and Notts County playing 89 league games scoring 7 goals between 1967-1970. Keith has worked in the Lottery Department at Aston Villa and Birmingham City. Later joined West Midlands Police Force in Wednesbury until retiring.

SNEEKES Richard

Midfielder 5'11"

Born *30/10/1968 Amsterdam, Netherlands*
Playing career: *Ajax, Volendam, Fortuna Sittard, FC Locarno in Switzerland, Bolton Wanderers, West Bromwich Albion (Cost £400,000 231 + 22 sub appearances 34 goals Mar 1996 – Sep 2001), Stockport County, Hull City, Herfolge BK in Denmark, , Hinckley United (1984-2007).22 appearances for Netherlands schoolboys and Netherlands U-21's.*

Sneekes made his debut for Ajax at the age of 16, and broke through into the Netherlands U-21 team, but never quite fulfilled his potential for the club and was transferred out at the age of 21. After a short spell at Volendam Sneekes signed for Fortuna Sittard and spent four years at the club after which he moved to FC Locarno in Switzerland before being transferred to England. Sneekes signed for Bolton Wanderers in August 1994 for £200,000. He was part of their team that won promotion to the Premier League that season, but was a casualty the following season when Bolton struggled in the Premier League and was transferred shortly before the end of the season. Alan Buckley signed the Dutchman for West Bromwich Albion in March 1996 for £400,000. Sneekes almost immediately became a cult hero at The Hawthorns. He was an overnight sensation, and many of the Baggies crowd took to wearing long blonde wigs. Sneekes finished his first season with ten goals from thirteen games, arguably for some Albion fans saving them from relegation. He spent seven seasons at West Bromwich Albion playing 231 games plus 24 substitute appearances, scoring 32 goals. He was transferred at the start of the 2001/02 season moving to Stockport County on a free transfer in September 2001, but played only 10 league games, staying just two months before a move to Hull City.

He made 25 appearances in the league without scoring before he left the club in May 2002. A further year was spent with Danish club Herfølge BK, before retiring from the professional game at the age of 34. He played a few games in non-league football for Hinckley United and Dudley Town. In May 2010, Sneekes was announced as an assistant Academy Coach at Tamworth developing youth talent. In July 2011, Richard was announced as a First Team Coach at League Two Hereford United. He left the club once his contract ran out at the end of June. 2012. In May 2014, he was unveiled as the new manager of Rushall Olympic. This was Sneekes first solo role as manager of a senior club. He was be assisted by Steve Hinks, with CB radio support from Daryl Burges. In November 2016 he was named as the new manager of Sutton Coldfield Town until 2018.

He and his wife owned an Italian restaurant in Angelo's Italian Restaurant in Wylde Green Sutton Coldfield.

Now he is teaching in the Sutton area. He is a good supporter of the Old Baggies Former Players' Association. Often heard on local radio giving his constructive comments on the Albion games.

SPEEDIE David

Striker/forward 5'7"

Born *20/2/1960 Glenrothes, Scotland*

Playing career: *Barnsley, Darlington, Chelsea, Coventry City, Liverpool, Blackburn Rovers, Southampton, Birmingham City (loan), West Bromwich Albion (loan9 appearances 2 goals Jan-Feb 1993), West Ham United (loan), Leicester City, Crawley Town, Atherstone United, Hendon, Stamford, Harrow Borough, Crook Town, Darlington Railway Athletic, Rainworth Miners Welfare (1978-2007). Scottish International*

At Barnsley 1978-80 he played 23 league games without a goal. With Darlington 1980-82 he played 88 league games scoring 21 goals. Chelsea signed him for £80,000 and between 1982-1987 he played 162 league games scoring 31 in 5 seasons.

Keith Smith (c)

Richard Sneekes

He moved on to Coventry City for £750,000 in July 1987. Playing alongside Cyrille Regis, he scored 31 goals in 122 league games. He made 12 appearances in the league for Liverpool scoring twice in 1991 then moved to Blackburn Rovers from 1991/92 playing 36 games scoring 23 goals. Next, he went to Southampton for £400,000 but only made seven appearances having a loan spell at Birmingham, 11 games without a goal. Then he joined Albion on loan between January 1993 – February 1993. The fans were excited by his aggressive, energetic and dynamic style of play. He scored the winner at Bournemouth on 26th January 1993. He played 7 games wearing the number 7 shirt, scoring two goals. Albion fans wanted him to stay but his wages and any likely transfer fee was out of the question to a third level team. He had another loan spell with West Ham united playing 11 games, scoring 4 goals. He moved to Leicester City prior to the start of the 1993/94 season, playing 37 league games scoring 12 goals. In a 16-year career in league football he played for 11 clubs, three on loan, he played over 500 league games scoring 148 goals. He then 8 years in non-league football. He played Church league football in Dublin for Francis AFC, having tried his hand at football agent and recruitment agencies. He worked for Setanta and RTE in Ireland. Speedie was living in South Yorkshire where he was a taxi driver and relaxes playing golf.

SPINK Nigel

Goalkeeper 6'1"
Born *8/8/1958 Chelmsford, Essex*
Playing career: *Chelmsford City, Aston Villa, West Bromwich Albion (Free transfer 24 appearances Jan 1996 -- Sept 1997), Millwall, Forest Green Rovers (1976-2001) One England Cap.*
Spink had a big break when early in the European Cup Final of 1982 Villa Keeper Jimmy Rimmer got injured and Nigel replaced him as Villa won the trophy, having only made one previous senior appearance. He went on to make 460 appearances for Villa in almost two decades before moving to neighbouring club West Bromwich Albion in January 1996. Spink made 24 appearances in all competitions for Albion, and became the oldest goalkeeper to appear for the club when, at the age of 39 years and 19 days, he kept goal in a League

Cup tie against Cambridge United on 27th August 1997, a record since broken by Dean Kiely at 39 years, 189 days. A £50,000 move in September 1997 took him down a division to Millwall in Division Two, and he continued playing at The Den for another three seasons making 44 league appearances until he finally retired in June 2000, just before his 42nd birthday. He worked as a goalkeeping coach at West Bromwich Albion before being appointed manager of non-league Forest Green Rovers in 2000. He left in 2002 and has since struck up a strong friendship with Steve Bruce, acting as goalkeeper coach under Bruce at Birmingham City, Wigan Athletic and Sunderland, leaving here in 2011. In February 2012 he was appointed goalkeeping coach at Bristol City until the end of 2012/13 season. He has since started his own courier business S&M Couriers. He does after dinner motivational speaking.

STATHAM Derek

Left back 5'5 ½"
Born *24/3/1959 Wolverhampton, Staffordshire*
Playing career: *West Bromwich Albion (372+1 sub appearances 11 goals Apr 1976 – Aug 1987), Southampton, Stoke City, Walsall, Telford United (1976-1991) Won three Full England International Caps& played for the U-21 and 'B' sides*
Derek began his career with West Bromwich Albion where he earned a reputation as a solid, classy defender with excellent passing ability. He was possibly the finest left back in England in the early 1980's but he had Arsenal's Kenny Samson to contest the England number 3 shirt, winning a paltry 3 caps for all his effort, skill and enthusiasm. He was in the Albion team that won the Youth Cup in 1976. He was Midlands Sport Writers Young Player of the Year in 1978. Derek was a cheerful, buoyant character who could tackle tigerishly and loved to attack. Derek made 373 appearances including 1 as a substitute and scored 11 goals for Albion. He struggled with injuries over a couple of seasons and a £250,000 move to Liverpool was cancelled after an unfavourable medical report. He was transfer-listed at the end of the 1986/87 season by Ron Saunders. He moved to Southampton for £100,000 in August 1987. Between 1987-89 he played 64 league games for Saints scoring twice.

He then spent two seasons at Stoke City 1989-91 playing 41 league games scoring 1 goal. He moved to Walsall and between 1991-93 he played 50 league games. He finished his career with Telford United making 34 appearances in 1993/94. Derek now lives in Puerto de la Duquesa on the Spanish Costa del Sol where he runs his own business selling spas and hot tubs. Derek, born in Wolverhampton, made a hurried return to the city on March 12th before 'lockdown' began, to spend time with his 91-year-old mother, Mary. He was by her side when she died and stayed for her funeral on 21st April 2020. Mary was not a victim of the pandemic but had been ill for some time. On April 23rd he flew from Heathrow to Gibraltar but was not allowed in to travel to Spain due to the 'lockdown' and was forced to return to London, even though his wife had the paperwork necessary but was across the border. Thankfully, Derek managed to fly home the following day thanks to feverish calls from Judith, his wife, to the Spanish authorities. That flight cost him an extra £400.

STEGGLES Kevin

Right back/ Defender 6'0"
Born *19/3/1961 Ditchingham,*
Playing career: *Ipswich Town, Southend United (loan), Fulham (loan), West Bromwich Albion (on loan Feb 1987 then signed 16 appearances Mar 1987 – Dec 1987), port Vale.* Steggles began his career at Ipswich Town in 1980 but was a bit-part player making 50 league appearances in 6 seasons. He had loan spells at Southend United and Fulham before leaving Portman Road in February 1987 to spend the rest of the season in the Second Division with West Bromwich Albion. Having been relegated the previous season, Albion were struggling in the lower half of Division Two when Steggles arrived possibly as cover for the injured Martin Bennett. He was a natural 'sweeper' who could read a game well. He played 7 consecutive games but Albion lost 4 and drew three. His chances were very limited from then on. After just 16 appearances, he joined Third Division Port Vale for £10,000. He made twenty league and five FA Cup appearances in 1987/88, before losing his place in April. Manager John Rudge handed him a free transfer May 1988, and Steggles moved on to play for Southern

League side Bury Town, and then Eastern Counties League clubs Brantham Athletic, Great Yarmouth, Woodbridge Town, and Felixstowe & Walton United.

STEPHENS Kenneth 'Kenny'

Right winger 5'7 ¼"
Born *14/11/1946 Bristol*
Playing career: *West Bromwich Albion (24+3 sub appearances 3 goals Nov 1964 – Dec 1968), Walsall, Bristol Rovers, Hereford United, Gloucester City, Almondsbury Greenway, Bath City, Keynsham RSC, Kingswood FC (1964 – 1985)*
He joined West Bromwich Albion as an apprentice in 1962, before turning professional in 1964. Ken was a useful, skilful, tricky player who could occupy the right wing and inside right positions. He probably lacked that extra yard of pace to get away from defenders. He went on to play 22 League games for Albion, scoring twice. In the 1967/68 season, he played 18 league games and 1 sub appearance as well as twice coming on in FA Cup replays against Liverpool. Ken also played in the Semi Final, Albion beating Birmingham City 2-0 to get to the FA Cup Final. He seemed all set to play for Albion in the FA Cup Final, at Wembley, his name appearing in some editions of the Final matchday programme. On receiving the news that Graham Lovett would play, Stephens surprisingly and unaccountably, disappeared. I don't think Ken ever came to terms with that disappointment and never made his peace with West Bromwich Albion. He was subsequently transferred to Walsall for £5,000. After playing seven games for Walsall, who he joined in 1968, he retired from football to become a newsagent in the West Midlands, but was tempted out of retirement to join his home town club Bristol Rovers in 1970. He went on to play in 225 League games for Rovers and scored eleven goals in a seven-year spell with the club. He ended his League career with Hereford United, for whom he made 60 appearances between 1977 and 1980, then made 35 appearances for Gloucester City in the Southern Football League before dropping down to non-League football to join Hanham Athletic in 1982. He managed Hanham Athletic 1986/87 and went on to be their chairman. He lived in Bristol, and was set up as a newsagent.

Derek Statham

STRODDER Gareth 'Garry'

Defender/centre half 6'1"
Born *1/4/1965 Cleckheaton, West Yorkshire*
Playing career: *Lincoln City, West Ham United, West Bromwich Albion (Cost £190,000 148 + 18 sub appearances 9 goals July 1990– June 1995), Notts County, Rotherham United (loan), Hartlepool United, Guiseley. (1982 – 2001)*

Garry joined Lincoln City in 1982, spending five years at the club and was voted the club's player of the year before signing for West Ham United. After three years in East london, Gary Strodder joined the Albion in March 1987 for £190,000. He made his debut in a 1-1 draw at Portsmouth at the start of the 1990/91 season. He was a strong, powerful centre half, good in the air and strong in the tackle. He was in the Albion side that was humiliated by non-league Woking in the FA Cup in January 1991 and he played in 30 league games plus 4 as a substitute in a disastrous season when Albion were relegated to the Third Division for the first time in the club's history. Just 2 seasons later he was part of the successful 1993 Play-Off Final team against Port Vale at Wembley. He played 140 league games for Albion between 1990 – 1995 before he joined Notts County for a fee of £145,000. Strodder made 121 league appearances for County scoring 10 goals in between 1995-1999. He had a spell on loan at Rotherham and in March 1998 playing 3 games. A further transfer ensued to Hartlepool in February 1999 where he played 61 league games then dropped into non-league football with Guisley in July 2001. He amassed a total of 522 league appearances scoring 26 goals in a career spanning 19 years. After retiring from playing he worked for the community development section at Leeds United, before going into business in Menorca. He now lives in Wetherby.

SUGGETT Colin

Inside forward/Striker/midfielder 5'7 ½"
Born *30/12/1948 Chester-le-Street , County Durham*
Playing career: *Sunderland, West Bromwich Albion (Cost £100,000 165 + 5 sub appearances 30 goals July 1969 Feb 1973), Norwich City, Newcastle United. (1966-1978) England schoolboy and Youth.*

Suggett began his career as an apprentice at Sunderland, with whom he twice won the FA Youth Cup. He represented England Schools, and later the England Youth team.

Between 1966–1969 he played 86 league games for the Black Cats, scoring 24 goals. He moved to West Bromwich Albion in July 1969 when Alan Ashman signed him for a club record fee of £100,000. Nicknamed 'Suggo' he got off to a flying start with the baggies scoring twice on his debut at Southampton in August 1969. Colin started as a striker alongside Jeff Astle but later dropped into a deeper lying midfield role. He was a member of Albion's League Cup Final side that lost in the final at Wembley to Manchester City 2-1 after extra time He arrived at West Bromwich with a big reputation as a goal-scorer and he left, converted to a highly-efficient midfielder. He made 165 appearances plus 5 as a substitute scoring 30 goals. He then joined Norwich for a £70,000 fee in February 1973. He was voted Norwich City player of the year in 1975. Keen pigeon fancier. Enjoyed a wager on horses & dogs. Owned a greyhound whilst at West Bromwich Albion. He became a youth coach at Newcastle United 1981, reserve team manager and even caretaker manager for a short while following the departure of Willie McFaul, 2nd November 1988–4th December 1988. Then he became Director of Coaching at Ipswich and later chief scout, a position he also later held at Carlisle United in 2006.

Kevin Summerfield

SUMMERFIELD Kevin

Striker/Forward 6'0"

Born *7/1/1959 Walsall, West Midlands*

Playing career: *West Bromwich Albion (7 + 4 sub appearances 4 goals April 1976 – May 1982), Birmingham City, Walsall, Cardiff City, Plymouth Argyle, Exeter City, Shrewsbury Town. (1977 – 1996)*

He began his career with West Bromwich Albion as a forward, making his first team debut in 1977. He was a 'string bean' of a footballer, but a skilful one. Kevin never really got the opportunity to show his true value with Albion despite playing a low-key role in the club's FA Youth Cup winning season of 1975/76. before joining Birmingham City five years later. In 1982/83 he played just 5 league games for Blues scoring one goal. A few months later, he signed for his hometown club Walsall and enjoyed a successful 18 months there, scoring 17 league goals, which led to a transfer to Cardiff City in 1984 where he played 10 league games scoring once. He signed for Plymouth Argyle six months later, where was converted into a Midfielder, and was an important member of the squad for the next five years. He played 139 league games scoring 26 goals between 1984-1990. A broken leg sustained in January 1989 led to a year on the sidelines. After regaining full fitness, he spent time on loan with Exeter City playing 4 games. He ended his playing career with Shrewsbury Town making 163 league appearances scoring 21 goals between 1990-1996. He returned to Plymouth Argyle in 1997 as the club's youth team coach, and was appointed caretaker manager three years later. He became the club's assistant manager after the arrival of Paul Sturrock and led the club to the brink of promotion to the Football League Championship before joining Sturrock at Southampton. He gained promotion two more times with Sturrock, at Sheffield Wednesday in 2005, and at Swindon Town in 2007, before returning to Plymouth Argyle once again. He then spent two years as assistant manager at Tranmere Rovers, before moving to Burton Albion to take up the same role. In October 2014, he followed Burton manager Gary Rowett to Birmingham City, again as assistant manager, where they remained for two years, and in March 2017 joined Derby County, again as assistant to Rowett.

SUMMERS Gerald 'Gerry'

Wing half 5'8"

Born *4/10/1933 Small Heath, Birmingham*

Playing career: *West Bromwich Albion (25 appearances Aug 1951 – May 1957), Sheffield United, Hull City, Walsall.*

Gerry started his professional career with West Bromwich Albion signing professional terms in August 1951. He had so many good players in front of him in the Albion first team especially the great Ray Barlow, and had to wait for his debut on 24th December 1955 at home against Manchester United in a 4-1 defeat. He played in 20 of the final 21 league games and in three FA Cup matches in 1955/56 season. He played just twice the following year. Summers was sold to Sheffield United signed by Joe Mercer in May 1957 for £3,5000. He played in an FA Cup Semi-Final and helped United win promotion finishing runners up in Division Two behind Ipswich Town in 1960/61. He played 260 League games as attacking wing-half. He moved again in April 1964 to Hull City for £14,000. Whilst with the Tigers he spent 2 or 3 weeks doing preliminary and full badge coaching courses as a staff coach for the FA. He spent time at Lilleshall in Shropshire which was the school of coaching. Having joined Walsall in a £10,000 move, Summers then joined Ronnie Allen at Wolverhampton Wanderers. He was appointed as manager at Oxford United from 1969 to 1975. Then moved to manage Gillingham from 1975 to 1981. He later returned to the Hawthorns to assist Ronnie Allen during his second spell as Albion manager. He coached at Leicester City, then became Youth Development Officer at Derby County, but his knees had 'gone', so Jim Smith switched him to scouting from his home in a Leicestershire village.

In his own words: *Talking about Ronnie Allen, "Ronnie was my golf partner. He was playing off scratch. He was always opening doors. We met Peter Allis at a golf club in West Bromwich. He introduced me to Seve at the Belfry at one of the Ryder Cups in the 1980's. We went to see Frankie Vaughan in West Bromwich, or Wolverhampton, when he was relatively unknown. We me him backstage." Then talking about Bobby Robson when he was England Manager, "I went to several games at Wembley as his guest and there would be a parking space and a four-course meal laid on."*

Brian Talbot

SWAIN Kenny
Full back/midfielder 5'11"

Born *28/1/1952 Birkenhead, Liverpool*

Playing career: *Wycombe Wanderers, Chelsea, Aston Villa, Nottingham Forest, Portsmouth, West Bromwich Albion (loan 7 appearances 1 goal Feb - Mar 1988), Crewe Alexandra. (1973-1992).*

Swain began his professional career with Chelsea, signing from Wycombe Wanderers in the summer of 1973. As he had been a non-contract player with Wycombe, having joined them from college football, his signing-on fee was just £500. He made his League debut for Chelsea in 1974. His most successful season with the club came in 1976/77, when the young side won promotion back to the First Division. He remained with Chelsea until 1979, when they were relegated, and then signed for Aston Villa for £100,000. With Villa, Swain was switched to full-back and was a part of the team which won the league championship and European Cup in consecutive seasons. After playing 143 league games scoring 4 goals, he left Villa in 1983 and had spells with Nottingham Forest 1983-85 playing 112 games scoring twice. Then he joined Portsmouth 1985-88 playing 113 league games. He helped Pompey win promotion from Division Two in 1987. Kenny Swain was a steady, positional player originally an inside right, converted to full back at Villa Park. He joined Albion on loan in February and March 1988, at a crucial period in the season, when he appeared in 7 games at right back, along with other experienced pro's Andy Gray and Brian Talbot, scoring on his final appearance away at Huddersfield as Albion won 3-1 in front of just 4,503 spectators, as he helped Ron Atkinson's team avoid relegation to Division Three. He signed for Crewe Alexandra in August 1988 as player/coach helping Crewe achieve promotion from Division Four. He was a member of Villa's Championship winning side 1981 and the European Cup win of 1982. He went into management with Wigan Athletic 1993/94, then Grimsby Town 1996/97. Between 2002 and 2004, Swain was Director of Football at Thomas Telford School and scouted for a number of clubs. From 2004 to 20114 he was FA coach worked with the national under-16's and 2012/2013 with the under 17's.

TALBOT Brian
Right half/midfielder 5'10"

Born *21/7/1953 Ipswich, Suffolk*

Playing career: *Ipswich Town, Toronto Metros (loan in 1971 & 1972), Arsenal, Watford, Stoke City, West Bromwich Albion (Cost £15,000 73+10 sub appearances 6 goals Feb 1988 – June 1990), Fulham & Aldershot (player/manager).6 England International caps, 6 'B' caps and one U-21 appearance.*

Brian was an exceptional midfielder, who, when signed for Albion, had already chalked up over 650 appearances in League and Cup football for Ipswich, Arsenal, Watford and Stoke City. He won FA Cup winners' medals with Ipswich Town 1978 and Arsenal 1979 and played in Arsenal's losing FA Cup Final and European Cup Winners Cup Finals of 1980. He was a vital cog in the centre of midfield with each club that he served giving the forwards excellent service. A worker with skills and determination, Brian's presence in the side certainly went a long way in staving off the threat of relegation in 1988. Talbot signed for West Bromwich Albion by Big Ron for £15,000 to add great experience to the midfield. Then he was given the player/manager job between February 1989 – January 1991 at the Hawthorns after Ron Atkinson left. At times the football was exciting in his first term but he seemed to find the transition more difficult than he imagined. Some of his transfer dealings were not too successful including Ian Banks, Ronnie Robinson and Steve Parkin. Albion managed to avoid relegation in his second season but he was sacked in January 1991 after Albion lost 4-2 to non-league Woking in the FA Cup 3rd Round at the Hawthorns. After leaving Albion, he joined Fulham and played five times in the Third Division, scoring once, before being appointed player-manager of Fourth Division strugglers Aldershot, who were deep in debt. After a dismal start to the 1991/92 season, Talbot left the Shots in November 1991, four months later the club went bust and were forced out of the Football League. Talbot then led Maltese Premier League club Hibernians to the league title in 1993 and 1994. He returned to English club football in 1997 as part of the coaching staff of Rushden and Diamonds, then in the Football Conference. After a spell as head coach he was appointed manager before the start of the 1999/2000 season.

At the end of the 2000/01 season Rushden secured promotion to the Football League under his management and reached the Division Three Play Offs in 2002 but lost in the Final. In their second season in the League they secured the 2002/03 Division Three title, but were relegated the following season. Talbot having left the club in March 2004 after seven years to take over at Oldham Athletic. He signed a two-year contract as manager of Oxford United before the final game of the 2004/05 season. After an unsuccessful stint in charge, Talbot was sacked in mid-March 2006 with the team 22nd in League Two, destined to lose their League status at the end of the season. Talbot made a quick return to management in Malta with Marsaxlokk, and guided them to the domestic league title and a place in the UEFA Champions League. Talbot remained with the club until early 2011 in the role of technical director. In February 2011, he joined English Premier League club Fulham as European scout. He was promoted to chief scout and assistant director of football operations in February 2017.

TALBUT John

Centre half 6' 1½"
Born *20/10/1940 Headington, Oxfordshire*
Died *14/08/2020 Mechelen, Belgium*
Playing career: *Burnley & West Bromwich Albion (£30,000 192+1 sub appearance 1 goal Dec 1966 – May 1971), player/manager at Belgium club K V Mechelen Played for England at schoolboy and U-23 levels.*

Nicknamed 'Big T'. Talbut initially made his name with Burnley, through the club's youth system and established himself as a first team regular. In December 1966 Jimmy Hagan paid £30,000 to take Talbut to West Bromwich Albion and he soon replaced veteran Stan Jones at the heart of Albion's defence, proving to be worth every penny. Talbut was an experienced centre half having already played 138 league games for Burnley. He signed at the same time as John Osborne and both players were cup-tied, being unable to play in the 1967 League Cup Final at Wembley. Talbut, and Osborne, were winners with the Baggies in the 1968 FA Cup Final but also featured on the losing side in the 1970 Football League Cup Final. John never scored a league goal for the club but did find the net once against A.S. Roma in the Anglo-Italian Cup in 1970.

Although a strong presence in the air Talbut was at times found wanting on the ground and the arrival of John Wile in late 1970 left him surplus to requirements at the Albion. No longer able to gain a first team spot he left Albion in the 1971 close season to take up the position of player-manager with Belgian second division club KV Mechelen. In a 13-year career in England he made 282 league appearances without a single goal between 1958-1971. He continued to play for KV Mechelen and between 1971-76 made 148 league appearances scoring 6 goals. He remained in Belgium for many years running pubs, one called 'Kup Winna' in Mechelen. He was also a leisure centre proprietor near Brussels. Sadly, John was suffering from Alzheimers in recent times and passed away on 14th August 2020. Sincere condolences go to his wife Ena, Daughters Nicola and Debbie and Son Mark and to his 8 grandchildren and two great grandchildren. A giant of a centre half and a wonderful man.

TAYLOR Robert 'Bob'

Centre forward 5'10"
Born *3/2/1967 Easington, County Durham*
Playing career: *Leeds United, Bristol City, West Bromwich Albion (Cost £300,000 Jan 1992 – July 1998), Bolton Wanderers (loan then signed), West Bromwich Albion (Cost £90,000 Total appearances 299 + 78 sub appearances 131 goals Second spell Mar 2000 – May 2003), Cheltenham Town, Tamworth, Kidderminster Harriers (1986 – 2007)*

At the age of 17 Taylor joined his local non-league club, Horden Colliery Welfare. In March 1986, after only a few months there, Taylor turned professional by signing for Leeds United. He gradually worked his way into the Leeds first team, making his professional debut against Millwall on 12th April 1986, and was part of the Leeds squad that lost the 1986/87 Division One Play Off Final, losing to Charlton Athletic in a replay. By the 1987–88 season he had become a regular in the side. However, when Howard Wilkinson succeeded Bremner as Leeds manager in 1988, the young centre-forward found himself surplus to requirements. In March 1989 Taylor moved to Bristol City, with Carl Shutt moving to Leeds as part of the deal. Taylor made an instant impact at his new club, scoring eight goals in 12 games during the remainder of the season.

Bob Taylor

His immediate importance earned him the deferential nickname of 'God'. In 1989/90, his first full season at City, he helped the club achieve promotion to Division Two. Taylor finished as Division Three leading goalscorer with 27 league goals, plus another 7 in cup games, and was also named Bristol City Player of the Year. The following season proved to be less prolific for Taylor, but it was a major surprise when Bristol City agreed to sell Taylor to West Bromwich Albion. It was Albion manager Bobby Gould who brought him to The Hawthorns for a £300,000 fee in January 1992, as a replacement for Don Goodman, who was sold to Sunderland earlier in the season. Taylor scored on his debut against Brentford in a 2–0 Hawthorns win, and added another two on his away debut as Albion beat local rivals Birmingham City 3–0 at St Andrew's. Initially nicknamed "Trigger" due to a resemblance to the TV character in Only Fools and Horses, Taylor soon became known as "Super Bob", a nickname he was first given by Bristol City fans during his spell there. He scored eight times in 19 games during the second half of 1991/92. During the 1992/93 season, Taylor capitalised fully on the attacking football Albion played under manager Ossie Ardiles, finishing as Division Two's top goalscorer with 30 league goals, scoring 37 in all competitions. When Andy Hunt arrived at Albion in March 1993, he and Taylor quickly forged a successful striking partnership that would last several seasons. Hunt and Taylor were part of the Baggies team that beat Port Vale at Wembley in the Division Two playoff final, to secure promotion to Division One. Taylor scored 37 goals in 57 games during the 1992/93 season. He was the club's top league goalscorer once again in 1993/94, scoring 18 goals. His only hat-trick for Albion, in a 4–4 draw against Watford on 12th March 1996, helped him to finish as Albion's top league goalscorer for the third time, finding the net on 17 occasions in 1995/96. He captained the side for the second half of that season and scored his 100th goal for the club in the final league game of the campaign, against Derby County. Things changed however in 1998, when Denis Smith succeeded Ray Harford as manager. Recovering from an ankle injury and struggling with his fitness, Taylor was sent out on loan to Premiership club Bolton Wanderers. When Albion were only prepared to offer him a one-year contract, Taylor moved to Bolton permanently in July 1998 for a £90,000 fee. He was the Wanderers' top scorer in the 1998/99 season. With West Bromwich Albion struggling near the foot of Division One, manager Gary Megson re-signed Taylor in March 2000 in a £90,000 deal, making the striker one of four deadline-day signings by the club. Taylor's return to the Hawthorns paid off as he scored five goals in eight games, including one in a last day 2–0 victory over Charlton Athletic, to keep Albion in Division 1. His goal against former club Bolton, an overhead kick in a 4–4 draw, was voted as Albion's 'goal of the season' for 1999/2000. The following season 2000/01 then saw Albion exceed all expectations, reaching the Division 1 playoffs, where they lost in the semi-final to Bolton. Taylor became the 100th Albion player to be sent off in a first team match when he received a red card against Barnsley on 28th October 2001. After scoring vital goals in the final few games of the 2001/02 season against Nottingham Forest, Coventry and Rotherham, he sealed Albion's promotion to the Premiership with the second goal in a final-day 2–0 win over Crystal Palace. Taylor's emotive comment was "I've got my beloved Baggies to the promised land." In March 2003, he was unhappy with his lack of first team action, saying that he was forced to train with the Albion youth team, and that he hadn't spoken to manager Gary Megson for four months. Albion were already relegated by the time Bob Taylor made his 377th and final appearance for them, in a 2–2 draw against Newcastle United on 11 May 2003. In what was only his second start of the season, Taylor was substituted due to injury after half an hour, but left the field to a standing ovation. He then spent a season at Cheltenham Town, playing league 28 games scoring 7 goals. He then joined Tamworth in 2004. Scoring 19 goals in 60 league games During 2005/06, Taylor received a conviction for drink-driving; Tamworth gave him two weeks leave to deal with personal matters. In May 2006, following his release from Tamworth, Taylor linked up with Kidderminster Harriers for pre-season training and signed a non-contract deal with the club in September 2006.

He left Kidderminster in January 2007 having made three appearances as a substitute. He subsequently retired from professional football, playing for Turnpike FC in Lichfield Pub League, and has since set up his own promotions company, Super Bob Events. Bob started studying for his UEFA coaching licence. He installs linographic mezzanine flooring. Has worked for a pallet racking company. In 2020 he was part of a group of present and former players who sent messages or made phone calls to senior season ticket holders during the Corona Virus pandemic.

TCHOYI Somen
Attacking Midfielder/Winger 6'2"
Born *29/3/1983 Douala, Cameroon*
Playing career: *Union Douala in Cameroon, ODD Grenland in Finland, Stabaek in Norway, Red Bull Salzburg in Austria, West Bromwich Albion (Cost £2.7 million 17 +30 sub appearances 8 goals August 2010 – July 2012), FC Augsbrg in Germany, Austria Salzburg, Arema FC in Indonesia, SV Austria Salzburg, Markt Allhua in Austrria, SV Burmoos inAustria, ASV Taxham in Austria, SC Konstanz-Wollmatingen in Germany (2004 2019)*

Tchoyi signed for Odd Grenland in time for the 2005/2006 season from Union Douala. He played less due to not mixing too well on the field and due to restrictions on non-EU players in Norway. Subsequently, Tchoyi was sold to Stabæk during the 2006–2007 season for 3.000.000 NOK approx. £330,000. In July 2008 he signed for Red Bull Salzburg for a fee in the region of £1.8 million. On 20th August 2010 he signed for newly promoted West Bromwich Albion, on a two-year deal for an undisclosed fee, believed to be around £2.7 million. He made his debut for the club when he came on as a substitute in a 1–0 defeat to Liverpool on 29 August 2010. He scored his first goal for the club against Manchester United at Old Trafford on 16 October 2010. In a feat revered as 'Tchoyi Story 3' by Baggies fans after the film Toy Story 3, he scored a hat-trick against Newcastle United at St. James' Park on the last day of the 2010–11 season, rescuing a point for the Baggies after being down 3–0 early into the second half. Following 47 games 30 as a substitute, at West Bromwich Albion, netting 8 goals, Tchoyi was released on a free transfer and he subsequently signed a contract with FC

Ausburg in the Bundesliga in January 2013 until end of the season. In December 2014 he joined Arema FC in Indonesia until July 2015. Moved back to Austria to play for Austria Salzburg, July 2015-January 2016. He then signed for Markt Allhau July 2016 – January 2017. In January 2018 he signed for Barmoos until July 2018. Moved to Taxkam July 2018–Aug 2019. His last known team was SC Konstaz-Wollmatingen in Germany where he was still playing aged 37.

THOMAS Jerome
Left winger/forward 5'10"
Born *23/3/1983 Wembley, London*
Playing career: *Arsenal, QPR (loan x2), Charlton Athletic, Portsmouth (loan then signed), West Bromwich Albion (Free transfer 89 + 17 sub appearances 13 goals Aug 2009 – June 2013), Leeds United (loan), Crystal Palace, Rotherham United, Port Vale. England at U-17, U-19, U-20 & U-21 levels.*

He began his career with Arsenal, but never played in the first team despite winning two FA Youth Cup titles with the youth team and being capped up to England under-21 level. He had two loan spells with Queens Park Rangers, playing 10 league games scoring 3 goals. He was transferred to Charlton Athletic for £100,000 in February 2004. He played 70 Premier League games for the club, before Charlton were relegated at the end of the 2006/07 campaign. After a total of 103 league games in four years at the Valley, he was sold to Portsmouth in August 2008, initially on loan, then signed for an undisclosed fee. Jerome only played three first team games for the club. He struggled to return to full fitness after fracturing his spine and was released by Portsmouth in July 2009. He signed with West Bromwich Albion in August 2009. His injury problems were carefully managed at the Hawthorns. Jerome Thomas nicknamed 'J.T.', was one of the most entertaining and thrilling wingers to play for Albion in recent years. He could use both feet and was a dribbling ball player. His crossing was good, regularly creating chances for the strikers. He was a player who could get you off your seat, along with Jason Koumas when they were both at their his best. He went on to record a career high tally of eight goals in 29 appearances in the 2009/10 season to help Albion to secure promotion to the Premier League with a second-place finish.

On 25th September 2010, he provided an assist for Peter Odemwingie and then went on to score the winning goal in a 3–2 win over Arsenal at the Emirates Stadium. On New Year's Day, he helped West Brom to beat Manchester United 2–1 in what proved to be right-back Gary Neville's final game as a player. Jerome made 31 appearances in the 2011–12 season, scoring two goals. Between 2009-2013 he played 106 games for Albion in scoring 13 goals. However, he found first team games hard by come under new head coach Steve Clarke after recovering from injury early in the 2012/13 season, as the good form of Zoltan Gera kept him out of the side. He spent six weeks on loan at Leeds United, making 6 league appearances. Thomas returned to the Hawthorns and featured in 12 games for West Bromwich Albion in the second half of the season, but was released upon the expiry of his contract in May 2013. He joined Crystal Palace on a free transfer in July 2013. He played just ten Premier League games over the course of two seasons, before he joined Rotherham United in February 2016, following a six-month period spent as a free agent. He made 6 appearances for the Millers. Thomas signed with Port Vale in July 2016, and spent one season with the club playing 23 league games scoring one goal, being released in May 2017. Recently working for Chelsea.

THOMAS Michael 'Mickey'
Winger 5'6"
Born *7/7/1954 Mochdre, Wales*
Playing career: *Wrexham, Manchester United, Everton, Brighton, Stoke City, Chelsea, West Bromwich Albion (Cost £100,000 28 appearances 1 goal Sep 1985 – Aug 1986), Derby County (loan), Wichita Wings in USA, Shrewsbury Town, Leeds United, Stoke City, Wrexham, Porthmadog (1972-1994) 51 Welsh International caps*

Thomas began his career with local side Wrexham where he spent eight seasons appearing in 230 league games scoring 33 goals. He earned a move to Manchester United signing for £300,000 in November 1978. After three seasons at Old Trafford making 90 league appearances scoring 11 goals, Thomas had short spells at Everton signing in a deal worth £450,000 plus a swap for John Gidman in August 1981 playing just 10 league games. In Nov 1981 he moved to Brighton & Hove Albion for £400,000, playing 20 league games. He joined Stoke City for £200,000 in August 1982. After one and a half seasons at the Victoria Ground and 57 league appearances plus 14 goals, he moved on to Chelsea for £75,000 in January 1984, with whom he helped gain promotion at the end of the 1983/84 season. He then moved to West Bromwich Albion for £100,000 in September 1985 playing 20 games in a poor Albion side that was relegated at the end of the 1985/86 season.

Garry Thompson

John Giles had left, Nobby Stiles was interim manager, replaced by Ron Saunders. When he suggested Mickey Thomas should move house to live nearer to the ground, Mickey refused and he was loaned out to Derby County from March-May 1986. Thomas was a hard-working, industrious midfield dynamo, a super ball player, sometimes a bit of a showman, tricky and skilful, who had been in League football 14 years when he joined Albion. He spent two years in the United States playing indoor football for Wichita Wings who paid Albion £35,00 for his services. He moved back to England in 1988 to play for Shrewsbury Town 1989/89 and Leeds United 1989/90 before making a return to Stoke City 1990/91 and then to Wrexham 1991-93. Thomas finished his playing career at Porthmadog. In the Football League Mickey played 603 league games scoring 77 goals in a 21year career. He was a youth coach at Wrexham until doing a stretch at Her Majesty's pleasure for his part in a counterfeit money scam where he laundered the money through Wrexham's trainees. North Wales Police arrested him in 1993, and after a trial he was sentenced to 18 months in jail. In August 1992, Thomas was attacked by two men in a country lane at Dyserth, Clwyd. He was in his Volkswagen with a 29-year-old woman, when his window was smashed and he was assaulted with a hammer and a screwdriver. Thomas was admitted to hospital with 15 stab wounds to his left buttock. In February 2019 he made it public that he had stomach cancer. Thomas currently provides analysis on Manchester United matches on Key 103 and Piccadilly Magic 1152. He also works as an after-dinner speaker.

THOMPSON Garry

Striker 6'0"

Born *7/10/1959 Kings Heath, Birmingham*
Playing career: *Coventry City, West Bromwich Albion (Cost £225,000 105 appearances 45 goals Feb 1983 – Aug 1985), Sheffield Wednesday, Aston Villa, Watford, Crystal Palace, Queens Park Rangers, Cardiff City, Northampton Town. (1977 – 1997)*

Nicknamed 'Thommo', Garry Thompson started his career with Coventry City signing professional terms in June 1977. He scored 49 goals in 158 outings for the Sky Blues. He joined West Bromwich Albion in February 1983 for £225,000.

He formed a terrific partnership alongside Cyrille Regis, albeit for a short period of time. A tall striker, powerful in the air, sharp and decisive on the ground, scored goals as regular as clock-work, until leaving the Albion. He played 105 games in all competitions for the Baggies, scoring 45 goals and he played his best football at the Hawthorns. He was voted 'Player of the Year' 1984/85. The Albion fans were somewhat annoyed he was allowed to leave the Hawthorns so soon after his partner up-front Cyrille Regis. Thompson, who is a Villa fan, wanted to go to Aston Villa but Albion Directors refused to sell him to their local rivals. He went to Sheffield Wednesday in August 1985 for £450,000 staying just one season, scoring 7 goals in 36 league games. He did eventually join Aston Villa in July 1986 for £430,000 scoring 17 goals in 60 league games. He later had spells at Watford 1988-90. Crystal Palace 1990-91, QPR 1991-93, Cardiff City 1993-95 and Northampton Town 1995-97. In a 20-year career 'Thommo' played 487 league games scoring 124 goals. Thompson began his coaching career while still a player at Northampton Town and later moved to Bristol Rovers as a coach and reserve team manager. In January 2001, after the sacking of manager Ian Holloway, Thompson was named in caretaker charge and managed the first team until the end of the 200/01 Second Division season but was unable to prevent the Gas' relegation to the Third Division. Thompson became assistant to new manager Gerry Francis in June 2001 and after Francis' resignation in December 2001, he took over the role as permanent manager on a 2.5year contract. By 9th April 2002 and with relegation into non-league football looking likely, Thompson was sacked. In October 2002, Thompson was named as assistant to manager Wally Downes at Second Division club Brentford. He continued in the role until 15th March 2004, when, with the prospect of relegation looming, Downes was sacked. Thompson was named caretaker manager and his one match in charge resulted in a 1–1 draw with Blackpool the following night. He left the club on 18th March. Thompson served as a coach at struggling Conference Premier club Farnborough Town during the 2004/05 season and quit the club on 31st March 2005.

In February 2006, Thompson joined Conference North club Hucknall Town as assistant to manager Kevin Wilson. He was released from his contract in December 2006. He has worked in PR. He was also a driver. Garry was a summariser for BBC WM giving his comments on Aston Villa games.

TOWNSEND Andy

Midfielder 5'11"
Born 23/7/1963 Maidstone, Kent
Playing career: *Welling United, Weymouth, Southampton, Norwich City, Chelsea, Aston Villa, Middlesbrough, West Bromwich Albion (Cost £50,000 17+3 sub appearances Sept 1999 - June 2000) (1980-2000) Republic of Ireland International, captaining the side at the 1994 World Cup Finals.*
Started his career at Welling United and then joined Weymouth in 1984 for £13,500. In January 1985, he was signed by Southampton for £35,000 and made his professional debut at home to Aston Villa on 20 April 1985 as Southampton qualified for Europe, only to be banned in the aftermath of the Heysel Stadium disaster. Over the next season, he was in and out of the team but broke his leg in a pre-season friendly against his old club Weymouth in August 1986. He fought his way back to fitness and re-joined the side the following January In the 1987/88 he was a virtual ever-present in the Southampton midfield. He was a hard-tackling, hard-working midfielder with an eye for goal. It was a shock when Southampton sold him to First Division rivals Norwich City in August 1988, for a fee of £300,000. He was a member of the Canaries' 1988/89 side that finished fourth in the top flight and reached the semi-finals of the FA Cup. Norwich made a handsome profit when they let Townsend join Chelsea for £1,200,000 in July 1990. After making a total of 138 appearances for Chelsea, scoring 12 goals but winning no trophies he transferred to Aston Villa in July 1993 for £2.1million. He finally won some silverware when Villa won the 1994 League Cup, beating Manchester United 3–1. He captained Villa when they reclaimed the trophy in 1996 with a 3–0 victory over Leeds United. In August 1997, just after the start of the 1997/98 season, he transferred to Bryan Robson's Middlesbrough for £500,000 having made 134 league appearances for the Villains, scoring eight league goals. He made

37 appearances in his first season on Teesside, scoring twice as Boro' won promotion to the Premier League. In the 1998/99 season, he formed a useful partnership with Paul Gascoigne as Middlesbrough finished comfortably in mid-table in their first season back in the Premiership. In the following season, he found it harder to get into the first team and on 17 September 1999 he moved down a division to West Bromwich Albion for £50,000. In his one season at West Bromwich Albion he only made 17 league appearances before a recurrent knee injury forced his retirement in July 2000, after a season in which Albion narrowly avoided relegation to Division Two. He has since worked as a pundit for ITV Sport, moving to BT Sport in 2015. In April 2016, Townsend joined Bolton Wanderers as a consultant. He presented BBC Radio 5 Live and written columns for the Daily Mail. radio presenter for Talksport. He has featured in several EA video games as commentator alongside Clive Tyldesley. He was a football consultant for property company "Harlequin Property" where he helped set up soccer schools at their Caribbean resorts.

TREACY Ray

Centre forward 5'9"
Born *18/6/1946 Dublin, Republic of Ireland*
Died *10/4/2015 aged 68*
Playing career: *West Bromwich Albion (June 1964 – Feb 1968), Charlton Athletic, Swindon Town, Preston North End & Oldham Athletic, West Bromwich Albion (In two spells Total 24+43 sub appearances 7 goals Aug 1976 – May 1977), Shamrock Rovers, Toronto Metros in Canada, Shamrock Rovers assistant manager 1978-80, Drogheda United player/manager Jan 1981- Feb 1983) (1964 – 1983) 41 Republic of Ireland International caps and played for the League of Ireland. A schoolboy, Youth and U-23 International.*
As a youth Treacy played with Home Farm, before joining West Bromwich Albion as a youngster in August 1961, signing professional terms in June 1964. He made 5 first team appearances for West Bromwich Albion, scoring one goal in 4 years, before joining Charlton Athletic in February 1968 for £17,500. Later moving to join Swindon Town in June 1972. He joined Preston North End in December 1973 for £30,000 and had a loan spell at Oldham Athletic in March 1975. He returned to West Bromwich Albion

joining Johnny Giles' Irish contingent at the Hawthorns, where he finished his English career. A bouncy, short striding striker, aggressive at times, with good skills and reasonable speed. In his career in England Treacy made 290 league appearances and he scored 78 goals. He then joined Shamrock Rovers in 1977 under Johnny Giles. He was player/manager at Drogheda United for two seasons from 1980 until resigning on 19th December 1982. He then managed Home Farm. He was granted a testimonial against the full national side in May 1989. Controversially, he was one of the backers behind the baffling move to install "Dublin City" into the Scottish Second Division in 1990 despite managing in the League of Ireland at the same time. He resigned from the Farm in September 1990. He returned to Rovers as manager in January 1992 and won the title in the 1993/94 season. He ran a successful sports travel agency in Dublin for 30years, retiring in October 2009. He died in 2015 after a short illness, aged 68.

TRENTHAM Herbert 'Bert'

Left back 5'9"
Born *22/4/1908 Chirbury, Shropshire*
Died *June 1979 in Birmingham aged 71*
Playing career: *Hereford United, West Bromwich Albion (Cost £600 271 appearances April 1929 – May 1937) Hereford United, Darlaston (1926 – 1942) He won Junior International Honours and represented the Football League in 1933.*

Nicknamed 'Corker'. Bert joined Albion in April 1929 for £600 from Hereford United. He was a useful full back, able and willing to try anything from either the right or left back positions. A model of consistency, he was sound rather than outstanding, and always played with a handkerchief wrapped around his withered right hand He formed a great full back partnership with George Shaw and together they played in over 230 senior games for Albion during the 1930's, lining up in Albion's Promotion winning and FA Cup winning side of 1930/31 and the 1935 FA Cup Final. During his fine career he won Junior International honours in 1929 and represented the Football League in 1933. He never scored a goal for the Baggies in 271 appearances but he did have the misfortune of scoring three own-goals. Bert also appeared in 54 reserve team games for Albion.

After leaving the Hawthorns in May 1937 he returned to Hereford United on a free transfer, before finishing his career with Darlaston 1939 - 1942. He retired from football in 1942 to concentrate on his ironmongers' business in Ward End in Birmingham.

TREWICK John

Midfielder 5'9"
Born *3/6/1957 Stakeford Nr. Bedlington, Northumberland*
Playing career: *West Bromwich Albion (116 +18 sub appearances 11 goals July 1974 – Dec 1980), Newcastle United, Oxford United (loan then signed), Birmingham City, Bromsgrove Rovers, Gateshead, Tamworth. England schoolboy and youth international.*

John Trewick, nicknamed 'Tucker', was a determined midfielder grafter who put in some good performances during his 6year professional career at the Hawthorns. He played 134 times including 18 as a substitute scoring 12 goals. John Trewick joined the Albion as an apprentice in July 1972 signing professional forms in July 1974. "Tucker" made his debut versus Hull in November 1974. He also played six times in the UEFA Cup during the 1978/79 season, scoring one goal against Galatasaray.

John Trewick

He left The Hawthorns in December 1980 for Newcastle United for £234,000. 4 years in the North East then saw a move to Oxford United where he gained a League Cup Winners medal when Oxford beat QPR in the final. A move to Birmingham City in 1987 was followed by spells in non-league including Bromsgrove Rovers, Gateshead and Tamworth. He coached at West Bromwich Albion from 1993, moving to Derby County in 2001. After leaving Derby he worked as a coaching educator and youth coach at Wolverhampton Wanderers before joining Hereford United in June 2004. The 2007/08 season saw Hereford consistently place in the top five of League Two, and they secured automatic promotion with a match to spare. He was offered the role of manager at Hereford, which he accepted on 24 April 2009, after Graham Turner announced his resignation. Trewick offered his resignation after failing to win any of the first seven League games in the 2009/10 season, but was persuaded to stay on by Turner. The club remained in the lower reaches of the division, with their lowest ever Football League gate of 1,266 on 23 February at home to Northampton. On 8th March 2010 Trewick was sacked, with chairman and former manager Graham Turner taking the job on a temporary basis. Following the sale of Hereford United, Turner became manager of Shrewsbury Town and hired Trewick as a Senior Coach.

Imre Varadi

In his own words: *During West Brom's visit to China in 1978 he entered football history in his reply to a question about the Great Wall remarking, "Impressive, isn't it? But once you've seen one wall, you've seen them all!" Trewick maintains the TV documentary gave the wrong impression and he was merely joking.*

VARADI Imre
Striker/winger 5'8"

Born *8/7/1959 Paddington, London*
Playing career: *Sheffield United, Everton, Newcastle United, Sheffield Wednesday, West Bromwich Albion (Cost £285,000 39 + 2 sub appearances 13 goals June 1985 – October 1986) Manchester City, Sheffield Wednesday, Leeds United, Luton Town (loan), Oxford United (loan), Rotherham United, Mansfield Town, Scunthorpe United. (1977-1995).*

Nicknamed 'Ray', Imre was born in Paddington to a Hungarian Father and an Italian Mother. He served his apprenticeship at Sheffield United 1978/79 scoring 4 goals in 10 games, before moving to Everton for £80,000 in March 1979. In two years, he scored 6 goals playing 26 league games. Further moves saw him move for £125,000 to Newcastle United between 1981 and 1983 scoring 39 goals in 76 games in the league. In August 1983 he signed for The Owls. Costing £150,000. He scored 33 goals in 76 league matches for Sheffield Wednesday. Imre Varadi joined the Albion in June 1985 for £285,000 signing from Wednesday. He made his debut on first match of the 1985/86 season versus Oxford United., scoring in a 1-1 draw. Ray made 41 appearances including 2 as a substitute scoring 13 goals in a struggling team, that was relegated from the First Division at the end of the 1985-86 season. Imre stayed at the Hawthorns for just over 12 months and moved on to Manchester City by Albion manager Ron Saunders, in a deal that saw Robert Hopkins join the Baggies. At City between 1986 and 1988 he scored 26 goals in 65 league games The City fans nicknamed him Imre 'Banana' and threw lots of inflatable bananas onto the pitch. Another stint at Sheffield Wednesday from 1988 to 1990 scoring 3 goals in 22 games was followed by moves to Leeds, Luton (loan), Oxford United (loan), Rotherham United, Mansfield Town, Boston United, Scunthorpe United and Matlock Town, whom he also managed between 1995 and 1997.

He finally finished his career in football at Stalybridge Celtic where he was Assistant Manager/Coach. In a playing career spanning almost 20 years 'Ray' played over 400 league games scoring 150 goals. Imre joined the PFA but for many years. He was fully licenced FIFA agent from 2004 working Northern England representative for The Stellar Group. Provided commentary on games for PA Sport and BBC Radio Sheffield, where he lives and he is an active supporter of the Old Baggies Albion's Former Players Association.

Personal note: *I recall watching Albion v Sheffield Wednesday at the Hawthorns on 15th September 1984. It was a tremendously entertaining end to end game of football. Wednesday played with three forwards, Brian Marwood on the right, Lee Chapman at centre forward and Imre Varadi on the left kept storming forward and Varadi looked a world beater, scoring one of the Wednesday goals in a thrilling 2-2 draw. Garry Thompson had scored the two Albion goals. Gary Shelton scored a late equaliser I wrote to Howard Wilkinson, then Wednesday manager, stating that Wednesday's performance was one of the best and most entertaining that I had ever seen at the Hawthorns by an opposing team. I even suggested that Varadi was good enough to play for England. Wilkinson wrote back to me thanking me for my kind words and said he had put my letter up in the dressing room for the players to read. Within a few months Albion signed Varadi and Thompson went to Sheffield Wednesday.*

VERNON John 'Jackie'

Centre half 5'11"
Born *26/9/1918 Belfast, Northern Ireland*
Died *24/8/1981 Belfast., Northern Ireland*
Playing career: *Belfast Celtic, West Bromwich Albion (Cost £9,500 200 appearances 1 goal Feb 1947 – June 1952) Shamrock Rovers (guest), Crusaders player/ manager. Dual international Northern Ireland 20 caps & Republic of Ireland 2 caps. (1939 – 1954)*

Known as Jack or Jackie, John Vernon was nicknamed 'Twinkletoes' due to his small size 5 feet. He won Irish Cup winners' medals in 1941, 1943 & 1946 with Belfast Celtic. Albion signed Jack on a five-year agreement in 1947, handing over a then record cheque to Celtic for £9,500. "Money well spent" said Albion Secretary/Manager Fred Everiss.

Owing to the bitterly cold weather which gripped Britain that winter, Jack had to wait 5 weeks before making his debut at West Ham United, losing 3-2 with Hammers centre forward Frank Neary scoring a hat-trick. However, unperturbed, Jack soon settled down into the routine of commanding the back division, a job he did successfully, not only for Albion, but also for Northern Ireland. Jack Vernon was unquestionably one of the finest centre halves, fine in defence, supreme in the air and masterful on the ground. He was a true sportsman of the highest calibre. He led Albion to Promotion in 1948/49 and totalled 200 appearances for Albion scoring once, 1948 on Christmas Day, a present in a 1-0 win against Sheffield Wednesday at the Hawthorns. On leaving the Hawthorns he returned to Northern Ireland to play for Crusaders, appearing in 44 league games between 1952-56. He represented the Irish FA Select side on several occasions, and the Irish Regional League 12 times between 1941-1946. Jack played 22 times for Ireland (2 for the Republic) skippering the Northern Ireland team on 17 occasions. Jack made 2 appearances for the FAI XI in 1946. He also played twice for the Great Britain XI in 1947 v Europe XI at Hampden Park and in 1951 he captained the team against Wales as the FA of Wales celebrated 75th anniversary. He returned to his Father's family Butchers business in Belfast until his death in 1981. His wife died 24 hours later.

VOLMER Joost

Defender 6'3"
Born *7/3/1974 Enschede, Netherlands*
Playing career: *Twente, Helmond Sport, VVV-Venlo, MVV Maastricht, Fortuna Sittard, AZ Alkmaar, West Bromwich Albion (Free transfer 12+6 sub appearances July 2003 – June 2004), Den Bosch, De Graafschap (1993 – 2009)*

Joost was a tall, strong Dutch centre back who signed by Gary Megson for Albion on a free transfer from Fortuna Sittard for the 2003/04 season. After playing in the first six games, five of which were won, he rarely appeared again, making a total of 12 starts and 6 substitute appearances. Tommy Gaardsoe and Darren Moore took the centre back positions. Albion were promoted to the Premier League at the end of the season and this prompted a review of the squad.

Joost Volmer

Volmer was released and moved back to the Netherlands to play for Den Bosch. In a career spanning 16 years he played almost 350 league games mainly in Holland, with just the one season in England.

In his own words: *"After I retired from football I first worked as logistic manager for a clinic in Holland. I also was Europe scout for West Bromwich Albion (Holland, Belgium and Germany). At the moment I'm a Health Manager for a podiatry clinic in Holland called Podiatry Hermanns. I live in a little place called Meijel in the south of Holland."*

WALFORD Stephen 'Steve'

Defender 6'1"
Born *5/1/1958 Highgate, London*
Playing career: *Tottenham Hotspur, Arsenal, Norwich City, West Ham United, Huddersfield Town (loan), Gillingham (loan), West Bromwich Albion (loan March – May 1989),Lai Sun in Hong Kong, Wycombe Wanderers (1975-1990)*

Tall, athletic defender, a good reader of situations with an excellent left foot. Walford started his footballing career at Tottenham Hotspur in 1974. At Spurs he made only two appearances before being signed in 1977 by Arsenal to play under former Spurs manager Terry Neill in a deal worth £25,000. Walford went on to play as a substitute in Arsenal's victorious 1979 FA Cup Final side. He made 98 appearances and scored four goals for the Gunners altogether. In 1981, he moved to Norwich City for £175,000. Whilst with Norwich he helped the club avoid relegation and thereafter saw them being promoted to the First Division.

After 108 appearances for Norwich, Walford moved on to West Ham United in 1983 for a fee of £160,000. He played 115 times for the Hammers in four years. Towards the end of his West Ham career, he had loan spells at Huddersfield Town, Gillingham and then West Bromwich Albion between March and May 1989 making three league starts and one substitute appearance under Brian Talbot. He moved abroad to play for Lai Sun of Hong Kong in 1989 before returning to England to play for Wycombe Wanderers under Martin O'Neill the following year .He was appointed Youth development manager and then assistant manager to Martin O'Neill at Wycombe Wanderers 1990-95 but has since followed Martin O'Neill to Norwich 1995, Leicester City 1995-2000, Celtic 2006 – 2010, Aston Villa 2006 - 2010 and Sunderland 2011 – 2013. Then on to the Republic of Ireland with O'Neil again as his assistant for the national team 2013 – 2018. Finally, he moved to Nottingham Forest for a short spell in 2019.

WALLACE John 'Jock'

Goalkeeper 6'1"
Born *6/9/1935 Wallyford, Scotland*
Died *24/7/1996 Basingstoke*
Playing career: *Workington, Ashton, Berwick Rangers, Airdrieonians, West Bromwich Albion (Cost £10,000 Oct 1960 – June 1962), Bedford Town, Hereford United, Berwick Rangers (1952 – 1969) Played for the Scottish League.*

During his early career he also spent some time working in a local Workington pit. National Service with the King's Own Scottish Borderers spending some time in the Jungles of Malaysia.

He played for Workington in 1951-53 before moving to Ashton-under-Lyme. Berwick Rangers then took him in 1955/56 before he signed for Airdrieonians in September 1956. West Bromwich Albion paid £10,0000 for him in October 1959. He was not the greatest of keepers but a daring one who could be superb at times, yet he 'blotted his copybook' by dropping a clanger. During his time with the Albion, he coached Christ Church School at the King George V playing fields in West Bromwich. Jock joined Bedford Town in July 1962, then moved to Hereford United in August 1964. He began his management career in 1966 as player-manager of Berwick Rangers. He then coached at Hearts before Rangers appointed him coach under manager Willie Waddell in 1970. Jock took on the manager's role in 1972 winning multiple trophies. He unexpectedly resigned in 1978 and moved to Leicester City during which time, he made an audacious attempt to sign three- time European Footballer of the Year Johan Cruyff. After three weeks negotiating and with the player expressing a desire to play for city, the deal was never agreed. Motherwell were his next managerial stop off point in Nov 1982, but Rangers came calling again and he returned to Ibrox Nov 1983. He subsequently had short spells at Sevilla 1986-87 and Colchester United 1988-90. Wallace suffered with Parkinson's disease and died aged 60.

WALLWORK Ronald 'Ronnie'

Midfielder 5'10"
Born *10/9/1977 Manchester*
Playing career: *Manchester United, Carlisle United (loan), Stockport County (loan), Royal Antwerp (loan), West Bromwich Albion Free transfer (99+8 sub appearances 3 goals July 2002 – Jan 2008), Bradford City (loan), Barnsley (loan), Huddersfield Town (loan), Sheffield Wednesday, Ashton United (1993-2014) England U-20 International.*
Wallwork began his career at Manchester United, where he made his debut in 1997. He never fully established himself in the United first-team however, and was loaned out to Carlisle United and Stockport County. During a further loan spell at Royal Antwerp, he was banned from football for life for attacking a Belgian referee, although the ban was later substantially reduced. In 2002, Wallwork moved to West Bromwich Albion on a free transfer.

He was not always a regular in the side however, and spent time on loan at Bradford City, Barnsley and Huddersfield Town. His spell at Barnsley was cut short when he was stabbed in a nightclub, causing him to miss more than two months of the 2006/07 season. In almost 6 years at the Hawthorns he made 99 appearances plus 8 as a substitute, scoring 3 goals. Wallwork was transferred to Sheffield Wednesday in January 2008, but was released just four months later. He started a clothes business D&R Designers in Failsworth. This was burgled in 2007 and hundreds of pounds worth of goods were stolen. In December 2011 Wallwork was sentenced to 15 months in prison after pleading guilty to three counts of receiving stolen cars. Returned to football for a short spell at Ashton United in 2014.

WALSH David 'Davy'

Centre forward 5'11"
Born *28/4/1923 Waterford, Ireland*
Died *11/3/2016 Thurlestone, Devon age 93*
Playing career: *Limerick, Linfield, West Bromwich Albion (Cost £3,500 174 appearances 100 goals May 1946 – Dec 1950), Shamrock Rovers (loan), Aston Villa, Walsall, Worcester City (1942-1957). He played for both Ireland 11 caps and the Republic of Ireland 20 caps. He was a member of the Albion promotion team of 1948/49.* Walsh began playing youth football in Waterford before joining Limerick United in 1942. Despite Limerick finishing second from bottom in the competition Walsh scored 6 goals. At the end of a very successful goalscoring 1942/43 League of Ireland season he was loaned to Shelbourne for their Dublin and Belfast Inter-City Cup ties. In 1943 he moved north of the border and joined Irish League side Linfield. Walsh scored 122 goals in Ireland, including 73 during the 1945/46 season for Linfield. While at Linfield he helped them win the Irish Cup in 1945 and a Northern Regional League / Irish Cup double in 1946. In May 1946, Walsh joined West Bromwich Albion for a fee of £3,500, signed by Fred Everiss, and subsequently made a terrific start to his English League career by scoring in each of his first six games. Dave had an ideal build for a striker. He had speed and thrust and he continued to score regularly for Albion throughout his career at the Hawthorns. He was a key figure when they gained promotion in 1949.

Walsh went on to score 100 goals for WBA before moving to Aston Villa for a fee of £25,000 in December 1950. He made 114 appearances and scored 40 goals for Villa, averaging a goal every three games, before moving onto Walsall in July 1955. After one season there he joined Worcester City where he retired as a player in May 1957. He owned a sports shop and newsagents in Droitwich. Later ran holiday homes in Thurlestone and Kingsbridge near Plymouth. Retired in 1984 and lived in Thurlestone near Torquay. Sadly, suffered with dementia in the last few years of his life. Dave died in Devon in 2016 aged 93.

WARD Robert 'Bob'
Goalkeeper 6'1"
Born 4/8/1953 West Bromwich
Playing career: *West Bromwich Albion (10 appearances Mar 1973 – Sep 1977), Northampton Town (loan), Blackpool, Wigan Athletic. (1973 – 1981)*
Bob became an apprentice at his home town club before completing proforms in March 1973. Bob made just 10 appearances for the Albion, he was competing with John Osborne, Peter Latchford and Tony Godden for the No 1 shirt.

Bob Ward

In September 1977 he joined Blackpool for £15,000 and then in 1979 Wigan Athletic. A back injury which curtailed Bob's career and he was forced to retire in October 1981. At this point, Bob moved to Wales and became a physiotherapist at Rhyl General Hospital. Later combined his football and medical experience by returning to his former club Blackpool FC to become their physio. This was followed by seven years at Chelsea as physiotherapist, and a stint in the north-east with Middlesbrough. Bob then went into his own private practice

WATSON Steve
Right back/midfield 6'1"
Born 1/4/1974 North Shields
Playing career: *Newcastle United, Aston Villa, Everton, West Bromwich Albion (40+4 sub appearances 1 goal July 2005 - Feb 2007), Sheffield Wednesday (loan then signed) (1990-2009). He retired from playing in 2009 due to long-term injury problems.*
He began his career with Newcastle United. During his seven years at the club, he wore a jersey with every shirt number 2–11 at least once, earning a reputation as a key all round capable footballer He came on as a 77th-minute substitute at Wembley Stadium in the 1998 FA Cup Final, in which Newcastle were beaten 2–0 by Arsenal. Watson was transferred to Aston Villa for £4 million in October 1998. Watson signed for West Bromwich Albion on 5th July 2005 on a three-year contract on a free transfer. He joined Sheffield Wednesday on 9th February 2007 on loan until the end of the 2006/07 season, with opportunities at the Hawthorns limited. He was re-called by Albion on 26th April with two matches remaining, as cover for the injured Curtis Davies and the suspended Neil Clement. Watson signed for Wednesday permanently on 10th July 2007 on a free transfer. He was appointed Development Coach at Huddersfield in November 2010. Joined Birmingham City as coach in August 2012 but was dismissed along with manager Lee Clark in October 2014. Steve was appointed as the assistant manager at National League club Macclesfield Town on 4 July 2016. Watson was then appointed manager of National League club Gateshead in October 2017. He became manager of Northern League North club York City in January 2019.

WEST Colin
Centre forward 6'0"
Born *13/11/1962 Wallsend-on-Tyne*
Playing career: *Sunderland, Watford, Rangers, Sheffield Wednesday, West Bromwich Albion (Swap deal for Carlton Palmer 72+9 sub appearances 23 goals Feb 1989 – Jan 1992), Port Vale (loan), Swansea City, Leyton Orient, Northampton Town (loan), Rushden & Diamonds (loan then signed), Northwich Victoria, Hartlepool United. (1980 – 2001)*

Colin West hailed from Wallsend-on-Tyne and began his career at Sunderland in 1981, playing more than 100 games for the Black Cats before moving on to Watford in March 1985. He was sold on to Rangers the following year for £180,000, before he returned to England with Sheffield Wednesday in September 1987 for £150,000. Two years later he signed with West Bromwich Albion in a swap deal involving Carlton Palmer moving to Sheffield. Tall, blonde, powerful and aggressive striker with a proven goal scoring record. Collin was a member of the Albion team that was humiliated by non-league Woking in the FA Cup 3rd Round in January 1991. He played 73 league games for Albion, scoring 22 goals. He joined Swansea City in August 1992, following a loan spell at Port Vale. He was part of the Swansea team that lost over two legs in the Third Division play offs of 1992/93 and West was sent off at the Hawthorns in the second leg. He moved on to Leyton Orient in July 1993 and spent five years at the club. In 1997 he was loaned out to Northampton Town, before he switched clubs to Conference club Rushden & Diamonds. The next year he signed with Northwich Victoria, before signing with Hartlepool United in 2000. He made a total of 464 league appearances scoring 129 goals in 21 years. Colin went into coaching at Hartlepool United as assistant manager, Sheffield Wednesday as assistant manager, Stockport County as assistant manager and Millwall as reserve team coach. In December 2008 he joined Southend United as reserve team coach. Hartlepool United were next from June 2010 to February 2012 assistant coach. He had a spell with Notts County as coach. West joined Carlisle United in September 2014 as assistant manage. Northampton Town appointed Colin as assistant manager in October 2018.

WHITE (Eric) Winston
Right wing/midfielder 5'10"
Born *26/10/1958 Leicester*
Playing career: *Leicester City, Hereford United, Chesterfield, Port Vale, Stockport County, Bury, Rochdale (loan), Colchester United Burnley, West Bromwich Albion (Cost £35,000 17+3 sub appearances 1 goal 1991 – 1992), Bury, Doncaster Rovers, Carlisle, Wigan (1976-1993).*

He began his career with Leicester City, before signing with Hereford United three years later. In 1983, he ended up at Bury following brief stays at Hong Kong Rangers, Chesterfield, Port Vale and Stockport County. He helped the "Shakers" to win promotion out of the Fourth Division in 1984/85. Loaned out to Rochdale, he was allowed to sign with Colchester United on a free transfer in March 1987. He was sold on to Burnley for £17,500 in October 1988 and joined West Bromwich Albion for a £35,000 fee in 1991. Signed by Bobby Gould, along with Kwame Ampadu and Paul Williams (the tall one), in a bid to keep Albion in Division Two. It failed and the Baggies slipped out of the Division in 1990/91. White was a right winger, enthusiastic and willing to run at defenders but his final ball was not always well placed. In Albion's first ever season in Division Three, 1991/92, the club missed out on the play-offs by one place and three points under Bobby Gould, who was then sacked. White was released from his contract at The Hawthorns by new boss Osvaldo Ardiles in October 1992, and then had brief spells with Bury, Doncaster Rovers, Carlisle United, and Wigan Athletic. White made 529 league appearances with 13 different clubs in a 17-year career in the Football League. Winston co-owned a restaurant in Padiham before becoming Regional Sales Manager at Life Fitness UK. He gained a bachelor's degree in Business and studied for an MBA. White worked with a worldwide soccer agency and ran a health and fitness consultancy business.

WHITEHEAD Clive
Right back/right wing/midfielder 5'11"
Born *24/11/1955 Northfield, Birmingham*
Playing career: *Bristol City, West Bromwich Albion (Cost £100,000 183+13 sub appearances 9 goals Nov 1981 – July 1987), Wolverhampton Wanderers (loan), Portsmouth, Exeter City, Yeovil Town (player/ manager) (1973 – 1991). England Youth International.*

Clive Whitehead

In March 1973 Clive joined Bristol City and turned professional with the club five months later. He scored the winning goal to help the club to achieve promotion from the Second Division in 1975/76. After playing 256 games for the Ashton Gate team, Whitehead was transferred to West Bromwich Albion in November 1981, for a fee of £100,000. Clive, nicknamed 'scrumpy', was a good, gritty, unselfish professional, who could perform equally well at full back, central defender or in midfield. Early in his career he was a skilful left winger. In 1982/83 he filled six different positions for Albion but he always regarded the right back spot as his best position. After going through a bad spell immediately prior to Ron Saunders joining Albion in 1986, the new manager told him that he was the best number two in the League, if he put his mind to it. Clive was a good mimic and often fooled the lads with his phone imitation of Ron Saunders! During the 1985–86 season he was loaned to Albion's local rivals Wolverhampton Wanderers. He joined Portsmouth on a free transfer in July 1987, playing 65 league games, scoring twice. He moved on another free transfer to Exeter City in July 1989 playing 48 league games scoring 5 goals.

A move to Yeovil Town followed in October 1990, with Whitehead taking up the role of player-manager, but he was dismissed from the position in April 1991. He then worked as an academy coach and scout at his former club Bristol City. Later he worked for as a football agent. Clive lives in Somerset with his wife Heather, Clive was a fully qualified Financial Advisor with Openwork and he works in the Pensions Industry. Clive can occasionally be seen back at The Hawthorns on some match days in his role of Referees Assessor.

WHYTE Christopher 'Chris'
Centre back 6'1"
Born *2/9/1961 Islington, London*
Playing career: *Arsenal, Crystal Palace (loan), New York Express indoor USA, Los Angeles Lazers indoor USA, West Bromwich Albion (Free transfer 95 + 1 sub appearances 9 goals Aug 1988 – June 1990), Leeds United, Birmingham City, Coventry City (loan),West Ham United (loan), Charlton Athletic, Detroit Neon indoor USA, Leyton Orient, Oxford United, Rushden and Diamonds, Raleigh Express in USA, Harlow Town, Hyvinkään Palloseura in Finland (1979 – 2000) 4 England U-21 International caps*

Strong in the air and good at intercepting passes, the tall elegant Chris Whyte made his league bow for Arsenal in 1979 and gained 4 England U-21 caps. He then had a spell in the USA playing indoor soccer. He joined 2nd Division West Bromwich Albion in August 1988 on a free transfer from LA Lazers. He played 96 games for Albion scoring 9 goals. Chris was certainly one of the best 'footballing' centre halves seen at the Hawthorns. He was voted Baggies' Player of the Year in 1989. He moved to Leeds United for £450,000 signed by Howard Wilkinson. He was virtually an ever-present in the following three seasons, playing in a total of 146 games, helping Leeds win the First Division Championship in 1991/92. In 1993 he moved to Birmingham City winning the Second Division Title in 1994/95. He had a brief loan with Coventry City before moving to Charlton Athletic in 1996. He had another two seasons in the USA indoor league before joining Leyton Orient in 1997 for one league game. He moved to Oxford United in 1997 playing just 10 league games, Rushden & Diamonds for 2 seasons from 1997 to 1999 before trying his hand again in the USA with Raleigh Express.

Chris Whyte

He had one final try in English football with Harlow Town of Rymans League Division One. His final port of call was in Finland playing for HyPS in 2000, making 10 appearances, bringing to an end a career that spanned 22 years, 614 league games and 62 goals. Chris had a role Identifying, developing and promoting quality football talent – South American football talent. From 2011 he was Senior Partner at Old Pro Management LLP, where he helps to manage Professional Footballer interests, at Highbury Grove.

WILE John

Centre half 6'1½"
Born *9/3/1947 Sherburn, County Durham.*
Playing career: *Sunderland, Peterborough United, West Bromwich Albion (Cost £32,000 618+1 sub appearances 30 goals Dec 1970 – June 1983), Vancouver White caps (loan), Peterborough United. (1966-1985). John was player/manager of Peterborough United.*

Nicknamed 'Wiley', John Wile started as a central defender with Sunderland, although he did not play a Football League match for them. In 1967/68 he signed for Peterborough United. He made 130 senior appearances for The Posh between 1967 and 1970.

John then joined West Bromwich Albion in December 1970 for £32,000, making his debut v Blackpool at the Hawthorns that same month. He spent more than 12 years at Albion, and was club captain during and after Ron Atkinsons spell as manager. His most famous moment came when he played with blood pouring from a headwound during the 1978 FA Cup semi-final against Ipswich at Highbury. Big Wiley was a leader and admired by colleagues, a natural captain who lead the side through the very entertaining late 70's and the of course through the mid 70's when we won promotion from Division 2 and on many an entertaining European evening against the likes of Valencia, Bruges, Dunfermline to name but a few, Wile played in 500 league matches, a total of 619 appearances in all competitions for Albion. He played in the NASL for Vancouver Whitecaps in the summer of 1982. After leaving Albion in June 1983, John returned to Peterborough as player/manager. He was manager of Solihull Indoor Cricket school, and executive of Walsall and Cradley Heath Indoor Cricket schools. In August 1987 he came out of retirement to play for Sutton United.

John Wile

Graham Williams

Lived in Litchfield and owned a business which sold conveyors to the building industry. John returned to the Hawthorns as Chief Executive in March 1997 and stayed in this role until 2002. In 2004, he was named as one of West Bromwich Albion's 16 greatest players, in a poll organised as part of the club's 125th anniversary celebrations. John resides in Worcestershire with his wife Carole and is still working in a business partnership based in the West Midlands.

WILLIAMS Graham

Left back/left wing 5'7½"

Born *2/4/1938 Henilan, Denbighshire, Wales*
Playing career: *West Bromwich Albion (354 +6 sub appearances 11 goals April 1955 – April 1972), Weymouth, (manager 1972 – 1975). 26 Welsh caps*

Graham, nicknamed 'Willie', joined the Albion as an amateur in September 1954, becoming a professional in April 1955. He initially came under the eye of manager Vic Buckingham who made a great impression on the youngster: "Vic always said that football should flow, like chocolate, it shouldn't be all bump, bump, bump." Willie made 354 appearances for Albion as a left sided player scoring 11 goals. Graham made his debut as an outside left against Blackpool on 19th November 1955, but only became a regular in the team midway through the 1959/60 season, some four years later, when he switched to left back and replaced Stuart Williams in the side. There was a sense of transition about Albion at that point, Ronnie Allen and the great Ray Barlow coming towards the end of their time here, the likes of Don Howe, Derek Kevan and Bobby Robson the stars of the show and new faces such as Graham, Alec Jackson and David Burnside beginning to make their presence felt. Graham made the left full-back slot his own, with Stuart Williams heading for Southampton where he ended his playing career. Stuart would later return to The Hawthorns as a coach in the late 1960's. By this time Graham was not just the first name on the team sheet, but the captain to boot, a role he was made for. He was an inspirational leader who could get the team acting as one, on and off the field. Graham was the scourge of outside rights everywhere, a tough tackler who gave no quarter and was quite happy to deposit his opponent into the crowd if necessary.

That said, his early experience as a striker added an additional dimension to his game and with Don Howe also marauding forward from right-back. The Albion were among the first teams to deploy full-backs as a supplement to their conventional attack. He led the side to the 1966 League Cup win over West Ham United, scoring a stunning goal in the second leg of the Final at the Hawthorns. He also captained the side at Wembley in the 1967 League Cup Final loss to third Division QPR. Graham had to play in goal for part of the FA Cup fourth round replay at Southampton, after Ossie was injured, on the way to the Final at Wembley in May 1968. Albion claimed their fifth FA Cup win and it was left to Graham to climb the 39 steps to the Royal Box and collect the cup itself, the pinnacle of any professional footballer's life. He became the last captain to lead an Albion side to an FA Cup Final victory when they beat Everton by a single goal. Graham became a feature of the Welsh side through the 1960's. It was a team that featured some wonderful players, leaving him rubbing shoulders with the likes of Ivor Allchurch, Cliff Jones and, on brief occasion, perhaps the greatest Welsh footballer of all time, John Charles. 'Willie' was capped 26 times by Wales plus two he had games at under-23 level. He left the Hawthorns to become player/manager of Weymouth May 1972-June 1975. When he retired from playing, he was coach at Sports Klub Kuwait 1975/76, coached at OFI in Greece 1976/77, Managed Poole Town September 1979-June 1981. He became chief coach for Cardiff City November 1981 and later manager until February 1982 when he was sacked. Williams coached the Finnish team, RoPS. Graham was also assistant manager of the Welsh National side under Bobby Gould. He later scouted for Cheltenham Town and Newport County 1983/84. Graham has also coached in Nigeria with the Leopards FC, Finland with FC Rovantemen 1987-89 & Dubai. He had been scouting for Tottenham Hotspur. Graham Williams was the first Chairman of the Old Baggies Former Players' Association of which he is a great supporter. He was living in Oswestry, after the death of his wife Helen.
In his own words: *"I had a job with the Forestry whilst still playing for West Bromwich Albion. Lived in a club house in Hill Top.*

Also had 2 years of National Service, as did many other players of the time. Got paid a retainer in the Summer of £11 per week, £15 in the season, plus bonuses." Talking about the 1967 League Cup Final loss, "I think the League Cup Final at Wembley was pretty unlucky. Mike Keen would have been sent off today for what he did to Dick Sheppard. I played the second half with only one eye. I was at Moorfield's Hospital for a fortnight afterwards. Ken Foggo would have been the first substitute at Wembley, but the referee wouldn't let me go off. He said to me, 'The only way you go off is if I send you off.' We were in control, it was finished by half-time, but the second half turned into a nightmare. Going back out of the tunnel for the start of the second half, Jim Langley from their team turned to me and said, 'Christ, we've just been put on four grand per man to win this!' We were on 25 quid to win! Losing that one really hurt."

WILLIAMS Paul
Left back/Defender 5'8"
Born *11/9/1969 Leicester*
Playing career: *Stockport County, Coventry City, West Bromwich Albion (loan 1993 5 appearances Nov-Dec 1993), Huddersfield Town (2 loan spells), Plymouth Argyle, Gillingham Bury (loan then signed), Leigh FRML. (1989 – 2003)*

Paul left-back learned his trade at Stokport, playing 70 league games between 1989 - 1993, showing enough early promise to earn a move to the Premier League with Coventry City for £150,000. Unfortunately, he was unable to break through to the first-team, making just 14 league appearances in two years. He had a loan spell with West Bromwich Albion, when Keith Burkinshaw signed him playing five games between November and December 1993. He played left back which had proved a problem position during this season. He was an instant hit with Albion fans, often overlapping down the left side of the field with speed. It was surreal watching him run around the edge of the Hawthorns pitch high 5'ing fans at the end of his final game on December 19th a 1-1 draw against Barnsley. He totally convinced Albion fans that former manager Bobby Gould had indeed signed the 'wrong Paul Williams' back in 1991. (See the **Personal note** with the next Paul Williams). At that time, finances were so tight that the club could not affords to buy him.

He had a couple more loan spells both at Huddersfield Town, before Plymouth Argyle manager Neil Warnock convinced Williams to rebuild his career in the fourth tier, signing him for £50,000. His energy and enterprise were a sight to behold down the left flank. Williams left after relegation back to the fourth tier having played 131 league games scoring 4 goals and a Play Off winning Final at Wembley, signing for Gillingham and then Bury. Finished his football career Leigh RM in 2002/03. He appeared on the pitch at the Ricoh Arena in 2019 as part of their Legends Day.

WILLIAMS Paul

Striker 6'4"

Born *8/9/1965 Belfast, Northern Ireland*
Playing career: *Lisburn Distillery, Preston North End, Carlisle United, Newport County, Sheffield United, Hartlepool United, Stockport County, West Bromwich Albion (Cost £250,000 29 + 23 sub appearances 7 goals Mar 1991 – Jan 1993), Coventry City (loan), Stockport County, Rochdale, Doncaster Rovers (loan), Altrincham. 1 cap for Northern Ireland.*

Nicknamed 'Willow', he started at Leeds United as a Youth but failed to make the grade. He then played 110 games for Lisburn Distillery scoring 22 goals. Had a short spell at Preston North End playing 1 game at centre half, then was let go. At Carlisle he failed to appear in a league game. He moved to Newport County in 1987 for their last disastrous season in the league. Williams was a centre half but he ended up as centre forward as there was no one else. He played 26 league games scoring three goals. He then had a season at Sheffield United who signed him for £17,000 in March 1988 without scoring a goal. He moved to Hartlepool United in 1989 for £3,000 in a spell again without scoring a goal. He moved to Stockport County in 1990 on a free transfer, scoring 14 goals in 24 games before being signed by Bobby Gould in March 1991 for £250,000 from Stockport County, along with Winston White and Kwame Ampadu on transfer deadline day. There were two Paul Williams' at Stockport at the time and some people reckon Gould signed the wrong one! Paul was tall and gangly, looking very awkward at times, with poor close ball control. For someone so tall, he was not the greatest header of a ball. Gould took 'Willow' to Coventry City in 1992.

There he had a short spell on loan appearing in two premier League games. He was released by Albion for just £25,000 in January 1993 returning to Stockport County, playing a further 16 league games scoring 3 goals. County soon came to regret the signing. Williams was involved in controversy in a game when he launched a throw-in towards the penalty area, resulting in the winning goal against Chesterfield, after the ball had been put into touch for an injury. He also antagonised everyone at the club by flaunting his wealth after marrying the Chairman's daughter. On loan at Rochdale in November 1993, he made his debut in midfield away at Crewe and did absolutely nothing, apart from score a spectacular volley from the edge of the box. The following Monday he 'pulled a fast one' on both Rochdale and Stockport by telling each he was training with the other! He returned to Stockport but re-signed for Rochdale in February 1994. Rochdale ended up giving 'Willow' a 2.5 year contract and a big signing-on fee. As Stockport were so keen to offload him, they said he could have the transfer fee himself. In total, Williams played 37 league games in three years with Rochdale, scoring 7 goals. During this time, he did also have a short loan spell at Doncaster Rovers. A supporter from Rochdale wrote, "Paul was a massive bloke, 6'4" and over 14 stone, but actually not that good in the air because he couldn't get off the ground. His nickname was 'Willow', apt as he had the mobility of a tree, constantly berating his team-mates for not putting the ball within an inch of his boot. At Stockport, a former team-mate who shall remain anonymous, alleged that Williams used to arrange his sendings-off to suit his social calendar." In the summer of 1995, with his long expensive contract restricting options, the manager wanted to 'pay-him-off' but the Board refused to let the deal go through. Paul himself put a spin on it, that he wanted to stay and prove the fans wrong. When he eventually retired from football, he ran a sandwich shop with his wife. He made the news a couple of years later when he injured himself falling off a horse. He was the Son of Betty Williams, the Nobel Peace Prize Winner from Northern Ireland, who was widely perceived to have retired on the proceeds.

Personal note: *The wrong Paul Williams? Williams' transfer to West Bromwich Albion is still surrounded by rumour. Stockport County had another Paul Williams, a young 5'8" black defender and the story went out that Albion's assistant-manager Stuart Pearson had signed the wrong one, with manager Bobby Gould coming into the dressing room the next day and asking Paul, the 6'4" white striker, "Who the hell are you?" At the time Pearson and Gould were having a highly unprofessional and public feud, so that perhaps fed the flames.*

WILLIAMS Stuart

Full back 5'10"

Born *9/7/1930 Wrexham, Wales*
Died *5/11/2013 Southampton*
Playing career: *Wrexham, West Bromwich Albion (246 appearances 9 goals Feb 1951 – Sept 1962), Southampton. 43 Welsh International caps. (1949-1965)*

He joined Wrexham, where his father was a director, as an amateur in August 1949, making five league appearances before being signed by West Bromwich Albion in November 1950 as an amateur, signing professional forms in February 1951. Originally an inside right, Stuart converted to a grand full back who gave Albion 12 years of sterling service. At West Bromwich, he made his debut as a centre-forward before switching, firstly to wing-half, before settling into the full-back position. In 1954, Williams helped West Bromwich to reach the runners-up position in the Football League and seemed certain to replace the injured Stan Rickaby in the FA Cup Final, but manager Vic Buckingham opted instead for the more experienced Joe Kennedy. Stuart had a first-rate temperament, splendid positional sense and a sure kick. Williams later developed a great full-back partnership with Don Howe. After playing 226 league games in 12-years, in September 1962, he joined Southampton for a fee of £15,000. Williams made his debut on 19th September 1962, in a 2–1 victory over Chelsea, when he took over at right-back. He rarely missed a match over the next four years, although in 1965/66, he switched to left-back. Williams's final 150th league match for Southampton came on 22nd April 1966, shortly before the end of the season which saw the Saints celebrate promotion to the top flight for the first time.

He held various coaching and management positions at home and abroad including trainer at WBA 1967-69 sitting on the bench in the 1968 FA Cup Final. Stuart was Aston Villa trainer January 1970. He became manager of Payhaan in Iran August 1970. Stuart the went to Morton as trainer/coach 1970-71. He returned to Southampton as coach/assistant manager from August 1971 to April 1973. Williams then moved north to Carlisle United where he was a scout in 1973. Viking Stavanger of Norway appointed Williams as manager 1973/74. Stuart was selling machine tools for a local wholesale business in West Bromwich whilst still an Albion player, for a short while. He settled in Southampton and had 12 years as a commercial tyre salesman then worked as a financial controller with a transport company.

WILLIAMS William 'Bill'

Centre half 6'1"

Born *23/8/1942 Esher, Surrey*
Playing career: *Portsmouth, QPR, West Bromwich Albion (Cost £10,500 1 appearance May 1963 – Jan 1966), Mansfield Town, Gillingham, Maidstone United, Durban City in South Africa for 5 years. England schoolboy and Youth International.*

Started his football career playing just 3 league games for Portsmouth. He then moved to QPR in 1961 playing 45 league games. A tall steady centre half, signed by Albion manager Jimmy Hagan in May 1963 from QPR for £10,500 as cover for Stan Jones. He proved to be one of the few poor signings by Jimmy Hagan in his time as Albion manager. He only played one at home against Nottingham Forest in January 1965 a 2-2 draw. He moved on to Mansfield Town for £10,000 in January 1966. In two seasons he played 49 league games. Short spells at Gillingham and Maidstone followed before he moved to South Africa to Durban City as player/manager where he stayed for five years before retiring from playing. In 1979/80 he was coach to Sacramento Gold in NASL. In 1980/81 Bill was coach to Atlanta Chiefs NASL. He returned to Maidstone United as manager in November from 1981 to 1984. He returned to South Africa as manager of Durban United in 1984. He returned to the UK to Maidstone again, as manager in 1986/87, before becoming general manager from 1987 to 1991.

Williams took charge a third time as Maidstone manager for a short period in 1991 after the sacking of manager Graham Carr. In 1997 he took the manager's job at Dover Athletic in the Football Conference, leaving Dover in 2001. He spent a short time as manager of Kingstonian. He returned yet again to Maidstone United and has been a key member of the club for a number of years including roles as Chief Executive & Director of football, playing a major role in moving the club to the Gallagher Stadium. after 24 years of homelessness.

WILLIAMS William 'Billy'

Full back 5'10"

Born 20/1/1876 West Smethwick
Died 22/1/1929 1929 West Bromwich aged 53
Playing career: *Old Hill Wanderers, West Bromwich Albion (Cost £20. 204 appearances 12 goals May 1894 – June 1901) 6 England International caps*

Williams was born in Smethwick and played for various local clubs, ibefore being spotted by West Bromwich Albion, whom he joined in May 1894, signing for a £20 transfer fee. Billy was a brilliant defender, stylish, dedicated and above all, safe and sure under pressure. He possessed a long, raking kick and scored a few goals from distance. He was also an expert penalty taker. In 1894/95 Albion had a difficult league season, narrowly avoiding the end of season Test Match Play-Offs by a win on the final day of the season. They had more success in the FA Cup. In the Semi-Final against Sunderland, Williams scored from the penalty spot, thus helping Albion secure their fifth FA Cup Final appearance. In the Final, played at Crystal Palace against local rivals Aston Villa, Villa took a first-minute lead when Bob Chatt's shot was half saved by goalkeeper Joe Reader and John Devey bundled the ball over the line. This was the fastest goal in FA Cup history, scored after just 30 seconds. In the following season, Williams was ever-present in a defence that conceded 59 goals as Albion struggled throughout the year. They finished the season at the foot of the table and had to enter the end of season Test Matches involving the two teams finishing at the foot of the First Division and the two who finished at the top of the Second Division. Williams scored in a 6–1 victory over Manchester City and in a 2–0 victory over

Liverpool, and as a result Albion retained their First Division status with Liverpool replacing Small Heath. The 1896/97 season was yet again disappointing for Albion as they finished the season in12th place. The 1897/98 league season was more successful for the Baggies and at the end of March they still had faint hopes of a high finish, but four defeats in April, resulted in a seventh-place finish. He continued to play on for West Bromwich Albion until the 1900/01 season but the cartilage injury forced him to retire in June 1901. In his Albion career Billy played 180 league games, plus two in the Test Matches and 22 in the FA Cup, a total of 204 matches with 12 goals. After being forced to retire from playing through a cartilage injury, Williams became a trainer and later a scout for West Bromwich Albion. He subsequently became a licensee in West Bromwich for many years. He died in West Bromwich on 22nd January 1929, two days after his 53rd birthday.

WILLIAMSON Robert 'Bobby'

Striker 5'10"

Born *13/8/1961 Glasgow Scotland*
Playing career: *Clydebank, Rangers, West Bromwich Albion (Swap for Jimmy Nicholl 45 + 14 sub appearances 12 goals Aug 1986 – May 1988), Rotherham United, Kilmarnock (1980 -1995)*

Bobby Williamson started his professional footballing career with Scottish side Clydebank where he played 70 league games and scored 28 goals between 1980–1983. Glasgow Rangers paid £110,000 to take him to Ibrox. He broke his right leg on a night out whilst on an Australian tour just 5 months after signing for Rangers. He was out until December 1984. In three years, he played 41 league games scoring 12 goals at Ibrox. In August 1986 he moved to West Bromwich Albion, signed by Ron Saunders, in an exchange deal involving Jimmy Nicholl. He was part of a striking partnership with Stuart Evans. That did not go too well. Garth Crooks linked up with him later in the 1986/87 season. In two seasons at the Hawthorns he made 45 starts and 14 substitute appearances scoring 12 goals. A bustling, robust striker with good control but not the most powerful in the air. He moved to Rotherham United on a free transfer in 1988 and scored 49 goals in 93 league games for the Millers.

He went back to Scotland in 1990 and had 5 seasons with Kilmarnock scoring 38 goals in 145 league games. Bobby was appointed manager of Kilmarnock in 1996, winning the Scottish Cup a year later and guiding them into Europe during a six-year spell at Rugby Park. Two years at Hibernian 2002-04 were followed by a year at Plymouth Argyle 2004/05 before he arrived at Chester City in May 2007. A great first half of the season had Chester in the mix at the right end of League Two and Williamson was eyeing a promotion push. But the team suffered a post-Christmas slump and he left at the end of the season. Williamson was a hit in his five years 2008-2013 in charge of the Ugandan National team. They won the CECAFA Cup, an annual competition for nations from the Council for East and Central Africa Football Associations, four times in five years. In 2013 Uganda almost qualified for the 2013 African Cup of Nations, losing on a penalty shootout in the play-off tie with Zambia. But after a poor start to the 2014 World Cup qualifying campaign Williamson was sacked. Two months after leaving his Ugandan post Williamson was back in African football with Kenyan Premier League outfit Gor Mahia. In his season in charge 2013/14, he took them to their first national league championship for 18 years, paving the way for a job with the Kenyan national side in 2014. His stint lasted two years with Kenya. Williamson, despite living in Kenya, doesn't think he'll work in the country again. He was owed a substantial amount from the Kenya Football Federation and that was going to court in May 2019. When he was at Gor Mahia they won their first league title and he had still not received the bonus he was owed. Having spent most of his life in football, Bobby Williamson was enjoying the 'down time'. Able to bask in the Nairobi sunshine, the Scotsman who had made his home in Kenya for the past few years, had reasons to be positive about the future, regardless of whether that involves football. In late 2017 Bobby was left facing the biggest challenge of his life after receiving a cancer diagnosis. Cancerous cells had been found in his nasal passage which meant a gruelling 37 rounds of radiotherapy and seven chemotherapy sessions in India over a 3-month period.

Fast forward 14 months to February 2019, Williamson was in remission and things continued to look good. Williamson, who now lived in Kenya with his wife, Michelle, and daughter Saoirse. His wife was Kenyan and had a good job, his daughter was born in Uganda and was at school there in Kenya and it was her home and Bobby had friends there, and the sunshine helped.

In his own words: *"The people are great, too, some of them may not have much but they are happy with their lot."* Williamson said that *"Nairobi is quite a cultural and modern city and it's a nice place to live. I'm all about the shorts and flip flops so I can't imagine moving back to Scotland any time soon."*

WILSON Charles 'Tug'

Inside forward 5'10"

Born *20/7/1905 Heeley, Sheffield*

Died *8/4/1985 Kidderminster*

Playing career: *West Bromwich Albion (133 appearances 45 goals Nov 1922 – Feb 1928), Sheffield Wednesday, Grimsby Town, Aston Villa, Coventry City, Kidderminster Harriers, Worcester City, Kidderminster Harriers Guested for Charlton Athletic and Aldershot during WW2.*

Nicknamed 'Tug', Wilson joined West Bromwich Albion as an amateur in December 1920 and turned professional two years later. 'Tug' Wilson was an opportunist 'striker', with an unquenchable thirst for goals. He had film star looks and was a constant threat to opposing defenders. He could shoot from any angle and seemingly from any distance with either foot, and usually found the target. Curiously he had the habit of keeping himself clean on the muddiest of pitches, yet was still a worker, who moved back to left half later on in his career. He was only 16 years 63 days when he made his Albion debut against Oldham. In the 1920's he gained three Central League Championship medals with Albion and he assisted Wednesday in their First Division championship winning seasons of 1928/29 and 1929/30. 'Tug' linked up front splendidly with Stan Davies, George James and Joe Carter and he performed very well with his left-wing partners Arthur Fitton and Jack Byers. His best scoring season was in 1925/26 when he scored 17 goals in 30 league games. He made 133 appearances scoring 45 goals for Albion. In February 1928 he moved to Sheffield Wednesday for a £3,000 fee.

He moved on to Grimsby Town in March 1932, before joining Aston Villa in August 1933. In June 1934 he signed for Coventry City, and remained with the club until a move to Kidderminster Harriers in July 1935. Wilson joined Worcester City in August 1936, before re-joining Kidderminster in May 1937. He became a Publican in Kidderminster in 1947 retiring in 1971.

WILSON Ray

Left back/left winger5'8"

Born 8/4/1947 Grangemouth, Scotland
Playing career: *West Bromwich Albion (282+2 sub appearances 3 goals May 1964 - March 1977) Scottish U-23 International. Ray was forced to retire with a serious knee injury.*

Ray signed professional forms for Albion in May 1964. Ray made his debut on the left wing, versus Chelsea in October 1965. A stern tackler, quick to recover and confident on the overlap, he became Albion's regular left back in 1969 when displacing former skipper Graham Williams. He established himself as a fine left back, gaining Scottish under-23 recognition but like many Scots who played at the Hawthorns, did not get the full cap his talent deserved.

He was rewarded with a testimonial for his long service in May 1975 with Aston Villa as the opposition. Unfortunately, Ray had to retire due to injury, his last game being against Luton in December 1975. Ray made 282 appearances for Albion scoring 3 goals in a 13-year career. Wilson undertook a Glynwed International Training course whilst still playing, which stood him in good stead because upon retiring he joined Glynwed as a Regional Manager eventually becoming Regional Director for Glynwed Distribution. He then joined Edmund Walker, part of the Unipart Group, as Branch Operations Director 5 years. Later he joined GEC as Operations Director, then Wilson had 15 years with Finalist Group as Operations Director, Managing Director Autogem and Group Operations Director. He became MD of Vanda Careerwear. A keen golfer Ray has been both Captain and President of Walmley Golf Club. Lives in Sutton Coldfield with his wife Vanda and when not doing his bit selling work clothing, playing golf, supporting his football team he can think of nothing better than he and Vanda babysitting grandson Thomas. He was Chairman of the Old Baggies Former Players' Association.

Ray Wilson

Personal note: *Albion Scotland Scout, Dan Sharpe, was responsible for recommending Ray Wilson to the Chief Scout Paddy Ryan. When Dan visited the Hawthorns, I met him when I was a young boy, and he found out that I collected football programmes. Dan said that if I sent him a copy of the Sports Argus weekly, to follow Ray's career, he would send me the programmes from matches in Scotland that he scouted, which he did. I recall Ray Wilson lodging in Brisbane Road, Smethwick, living opposite to Devonshire Road Junior School opposite & Infants School in his early Albion career.*

WITCOMB Douglas 'Dougie'
Wing half 5'8"
Born *18/4/1918 Ebbw Vale, South Wales*
Died *6/8/1999 Newport, South Wales*
Playing career: *West Bromwich Albion (123 appearances 10 goals Nov 1937 – Feb 1947), Sheffield Wednesday, Leicester City (Guest), Newport County, Llandudno (19 37 – 1954) Guested for Grimsby Town, Leicester City, Swansea Town, Lovells Athletic and Newport County in WW2.Retired June 1956. Later played for Alloys & Alkmatic Works FC in South Wales 10 caps for Wales*

Stewart Woolgar

Dougie was a wing half of enormous talent, quick and cunning, a fine distributor under pressure, he tackled hard and possessed a powerful shot. He spent ten years at the Hawthorns. Like so many players of his era his footballing career was interrupted by WW2. He appeared in 123 games in all competitions including the Wartime League. He won 10 caps for Wales, including wartime internationals, and he represented the All British Team against the Football League in 1939 at Wolverhampton. In his career he amassed 303 league appearances. In February 1947 Witcomb moved to Sheffield Wednesday for £6,000. He played 224 league games scoring 12 goals at Hillsborough, helping the Owls win promotion from Division Two in 1951/52. He joined Newport County for the 1953/54 season in November 1953, making 25 appearances before joining Llandudno. He was living in Halesowen before moving back to South Wales.

WOOD Stanley 'Stan'
Outside left 5'8"
Born *23/7/1905 Winsford, Cheshire*
Died *17/2//1967 Halifax, Yorkshire aged 61*
Playing career: *West Bromwich Albion (281 appearances 66 goals April 1928 – May 1938), Halifax Town,1938--49. Guested for Huddersfield Town in WW2. Played for the Football League.*

Nicknamed 'Splinter' and the 'singing winger'. He was a wiry slippery outside left whose cleverness stood him in good stead for a decade with Albion. in April 1928. He made his Albion debut in September of the same year, in a Division Two match against Notts County. He established himself in 1928/29 taking over from Arthur Fitton. Stan was part of the Albion side that won promotion to the First Division in 1930/31 and beat Birmingham 2–1 in the 1931 FA Cup Final, playing 50 games and scoring 17 goals during that momentous season. He held his place until Wally Boyes came along in 1934. He still played a few more games, and went on to make 281 appearances for the club, scoring 66 goals, as well as 92 reserve team games when he scored 37 goals, helping the 'stiffs' win three successive Central League Titles in the mid 1930's. Stan always gave 100% effort. He really was a very fine footballer. In May 1938 Wood joined Halifax Town on a free transfer and represented them throughout WWII as well as appearing as a guest player for Huddersfield Town in 1941/42. He served as Halifax's trainer from 1946 to 1949. After playing, Stan worked in Holdsworth's Mill in Halifax, his Son Terry following him there before later becoming a teacher. Wood died in Halifax on 17th February 1967 aged 61.

WOODHALL George 'Spry'
Inside right//outside right 5'9"
Born *5/9/1863 West Bromwich*
Died *29/9/1924 West Bromwich*
Playing career: *West Bromwich Albion (74 appearances 20 goals May 1883 – July 1892), Wolverhampton Wanderers, Berwick Rangers (Worcester), Oldbury Town. 1883 – 1897). He played twice for England*

Nicknamed 'Spry' he was indeed a sprightly player, playing mainly at outside-right, moving to inside right to form a special partnership with Billy Bassett. He could centre with great accuracy and combined well in team work.

He played most of his career with West Bromwich Albion and was a member of the team that reached the 1886 and 1887 cup finals, going out 2–0 to Blackburn Rovers, in a replay, and Aston Villa respectively. In 1888, West Bromwich reached the final for the third consecutive year, when they met favourites, Preston North End at the Kennington Oval on 24 March 1888. Woodhall scored the winning goal with thirteen minutes remaining, when the Albion forwards outjumped Preston's defence and Woodhall pounced on the rebound, turning sharply to steer the ball between the posts, thus enabling his team to claim the first of their five FA Cup wins. He was a regular member of Albion's forward line for nine seasons. Woodhall represented England twice, making his debut against Wales in February 1888, when he scored the third goal in a 5–1 victory. Woodhall's goal was England's 100th international goal. He also played in the next match against Scotland which was won 5–0, the following month. He joined Wolverhampton Wanderers in August 1892 and played 18 league games before moving to Worcestershire club Berwick Rangers in 1894 He finished his career at Oldbury Town. With his delightful personality, 'Spry' was one of the most popular players of the 'old brigade', remembered as a generous and wholehearted sportsman, by the older generation who lived to tell the tales of his brilliant play down Albion's right flank. He took over the 'Golden Cup' Public House on Cross Street from Charlie Perry in 1905.

WOOLGAR Stewart
Midfielder 5'8"
Born *21/9/1952 Chesterfield*
Playing career: *West Bromwich Albion (3 + 3 sub appearances Sept 1969 – July 1974), Doncaster Rovers, Dunstable Town, Luton & Bedfordshire Police, Alvechurch, Dunstable Town.*

Nicknamed 'Woolie', Stewart played for Derbyshire Schools before being taken on as an apprentice at the Hawthorns in 1968, turning pro in September 1969. Stewart only made 6 appearances, 3 as a substitute. He made his debut against Manchester United in October 1972. He put in some fine performances for Albion's Youth and Central League sides but was never a force to be reckoned with in top company.

Upon retiring he joined the Luton & Bedfordshire Police Force but only did 12 months service before going into the Financial & Investment business. 'Woolie' is a great supporter of the Old Baggies Former Players' Association and loves nothing better than attending some Albion games with his granddaughter when he is not enjoying his retirement at his holiday home in Turkey.

YACOB Claudio

Midfielder 5'11"

Born *18/7/1987 Carcarana, Argentina*
Playing career: *Racing Club in Argentina, West Bromwich Albion (Free transfer 149 + 26 sub appearances 2 goals July 2012 – June 2018), Nottingham Forest, Nacional in Uruguay. 2 caps for Argentina at full level plus U-20 International.*

He began his career at Racing Club, and played two international games for Argentina in 2011. He moved to England's West Bromwich Albion on a free transfer in July 2012. Yacob signed a three-year deal. Yacob signed a new two-year contract with the Baggies on 10 July 2015. He signed a further deal on 29 September 2016. He made a total of 171 appearances over six Premier League seasons for Albion. Strong in the tackle and always giving 100% effort he became a fans favourite, as a ball winning midfielder, and he developed a strong partnership with Youssouf Mulumbu. Joined Nottingham Forest on a free transfer in September 2018 playing just 16 league games before returning to South America, signing for Uruguayan side Nacional in February 2020.

ZONDERVAN Romeo

Midfielder 5'9½"

Born *3/3/1959 Paramaribo, Suriname*
Playing career: *FC Den Haag, FC Twente Enschede, West Bromwich Albion (Cost £225,000 93+2 sub appearances 5 goals Mar 1982 – Mar 1984), Ipswich Town, NAZ Breda. (1977-1995). Netherlands 1 Full International cap as well as playing a U-21 and schoolboy.*

He played his early football with FC Den Haag and Twente Enschede. Played once for Netherlands at Full International level in a World Cup Qualifier against Cyprus in Feb 1981. He joined West Bromwich Albion for £225,000 in March 1982, a few months after his compatriot Martin Jol, playing together in the FA Cup Semi Final defeat by QPR at

Highbury in 1982. He was a talented right sided midfielder, good on the ball, but made his Albion debut at left back. He left Albion when John Giles returned for his second spell as manager. Zondervan played in 95 matches in all competitions for Albion. He moved to Ipswich Town for £70,000 in March 1984. Romeo played 274 league games for the Tractor Boys scoring 13 goals. He finished his playing career at NAC Breda back in Holland playing 26 league games. After football, he was part of Ipswich Town's scouting team in Europe, and working as a players' agent in Holland. He is a fully qualified pilot. He was arrested at British customs after they discovered a friend of his was carrying pornographic material from the Netherlands. Referred to by a certain tabloid newspaper as the 'Porno King'.

Pascal Zuberbuhler

ZUBERBUHLER Pascal

Goalkeeper 6'6"

Born *8/1/1971 Frauenfeld, Switzerlan*

Playing career: *Grasshoppers Club Zurich, FC Basel, FC Aarau (loan) in Switzerland, Bayer Leverkusen in Germany (loan), West Bromwich Albion (Free transfer 18 appearances July 2006 – Feb 2007), Neuchatel Xamax in Switzerland, Fulham (1992 – 2011) 51 Caps for Switzerland.*

Zuberbuhler played for Switzerland in the 2006 World Cup Finals and Euro 2008. He signed a two-year contract for Albion on a free transfer from Basel in July 2006. He was one of the tallest players ever to play for West Bromwich Albion. His first appearance was in a friendly against Motherwell, where he earned praise from his manager Bryan Robson. He then kept a clean sheet on his competitive debut as Albion beat Hull City 2–0. He then starred in a 3-0 victory over Wolves at the Hawthorns in October 2006. Zuberbuhler was dropped from the first team by new manager Tony Mowbray after starting the first 15 league games, apparently due to some the Albion fans booing and sarcastically applauding him when he played. He made 18 appearances for WBA. He left for Neuchatel Xamax on a free transfer. In 2008 when his former Switzerland national team boss, Roy Hodgson took him on loan, later signing a year-long deal at Fulham. As a goalkeeper coach, he has worked for various clubs, including Fulham, BSC Young Boys Berne, Servette FC and Derby County. He was goalkeeping coach to the Philippines national team on four occasions 2011, 2012, 2015 and 2015–2017. He has also been employed as a Swiss football pundit by Swiss pay-TV channel Teleclub since 2013. On 1 November 2017, former Swiss international goalkeeper Pascal Zuberbuhler took up a part-time role as a goalkeeper specialist at FIFA, where he was to oversee the education of goalkeepers around the globe. His main duties at world football's governing body would include the further development of goalkeeper training and the educational structures in place all around the world, particularly in areas where only basic work has been done so far. Hewould also assume the role of an observer and support the development of football and goalkeeping in particular.

ZUIVERLOON Gianni

Right back / centre back 5'11"

Born *30/12/1986 Rotterdam, Netherlands*

Playing career: *Feyenoord 2004-05, RKC Waalwijk(loan), Heerenveen in Holland, West Bromwich Albion (Cost £3.2million 69 + 7 appearances July 2008 – May 2011), Ipswich Town (loan), Mallorca in Spain, Heerenveen (loan), ADO Den Haag in Holland, Cultural Leonesa in Spain, Delhi Dynamos and Kerala Blasters in India 2019 Played 22 times for Netherlands U-21.*

Zuiverloon signed for Feyenoord, where Ruud Gullit was manager, in 2004 and stayed until 2006 appearing in 10 league games. He was loaned out to RKC Waalwijk for the 2005/06 season playing 28 league games scoring 1 goal. In June 2006 he moved to Heerenveen playing 60 league games scoring three goals in two years. In July 2008 Zuiverloon signed for West Bromwich Albion of the Premier League for £3.2 million. Rumours were that Manchester United were monitoring his progress. Gianni was strong and athletic but seemed to lack confidence at times. He made his debut for WBA in a 2–1 loss against Everton. Albion were relegated in 2008/09, back to the Championship after one season in the Premier League. In his second season, Gianni established himself in the first team under manager Roberto Di Matteo. Albion won promotion to the Premier League after finishing second place in the Championship in 2009/10. In his third season for West Brom, Zuiverloon's first-team opportunities were limited while he made three starts. He never fulfilled the early promise. He made 69 starts plus 7 substitute appearances for Albion, scoring 6 goals in three seasons. He had a loan spell at Ipswich in 2010 playing four league games. In July 2011, he signed a three-year deal for Spanish side Mallorca on a free transfer, playing just 9 league games. He had a loan spell with Heerenveen, playing 10 league games. He then signed a three-year deal with Eredivisie side ADO Den Haag as a free agent in August 2013, playing 70 league games, scoring 2 goals. In 2016 Gianni returned to Spain with Segunda División B club Cultural y Deportiva Leonesa, playing 50 league games scoring twice. In August 2018, Zuiverloon signed for Indian Super League club Delhi Dynamos, playing 17 games. In June 2019 he signed for Kerala Blasters FC.

Other WBA Resources

West Bromwich Albion Memorabilia
Run by Baggies' fan Barry Swash. Here you can buy and sell Albion memorabilia. Also looking for Albion programmes pre-1950. *See: Facebook group*

Look Back in Albion
A nostalgic look back at all things Albion (on Facebook). Run by Simon Wright Albion & Hereford fan, and Baggie Conrad Chircop.

Justice For Jeff
Dementia in football campaign Run by Dawn Astle, daughter of 'King' Jeff. *See Facebook group.*

1976 And All That

Albion photographer Laurie Rampling has his first solo book for sale. A limited edition of only 1000 copies, all profits are to be donated to the Albion Foundation, who do a fantastic job locally. *www.curtis-sport.com*

From Buzaglo to Balis
A new book by Chris Lepkowski Albion fan, former Evening Mail reporter and ex-Albion employee

Warwick Baggies
Albion Supporters Club.
E-mail WarwickBaggies@gmail.com
Facebook and Twitter @Warwick Baggies

Tony Matthews
Black Country Born and Bred
(an autobiography), available from Sports Trader (Rob Budd), 27 Berkeley Avenue, Clayhall, Ilford, Essex IG5 0UP. robertbudd4@aol.com.

Cyrille Regis, MBE
The Matches, Goals, Triumphs and Disappointments, is available from Apex Publishing Ltd (www. apexpublishing.co.uk) price: £8.99+P&P. E-mail: chris.cowling@ apexpublishing.co.uk

The Complete Footballer:
The Ronnie Allen Story
Reprinted: £1.50 + P&P per copy, contact: tony-matthews@live.co.uk or via Facebook

West Bromwich Albion
Former Players Association
Founded in 2003 with a view of bringing together former players of the football club to socialise, to meet as a group under an official banner but more importantly to assist and help those that may need financial, personal or moral support. With over 200 former players, it makes our Association one of the most progressive. With dinners, golf days, appearances and match day entertainment providing the funds should our members require assistance. We are always looking and welcoming new members, as long as an ex player made a first team appearance then they can join.

Photo Credits

A very big thank you to the Old Baggies for permission to use so many of their photos.

Damson, Chris. Daniel Bagshaw (Dan1980) **Victor Anichebe**. https://commons. wikimedia.org/wiki/File:Victor_Anichebe_ Bohemians_V_Everton_(5_of_51).jpg **Bednar, Roman**. Jameboy. https://commons. wikimedia.org/wiki/File:Roman_Bednar.jpg **Kevin Phillips**. Egghead06 https:// commons.wikimedia.org/wiki/File:Kevin_ Phillips_Leicester_City_coach.jpg **Astle Gates**, **The Three Degrees**, **Hawthorns Gates, Metro**. Elliott Brown https://www.flickr.com/photos/ell-r-brown

All: CC BY-SA (https://creativecommons.org/ licenses/by-sa/4.0)

Where Are They Now?
West Bromwich Albion
https://www.where-are-they-now.co.uk/club/ west-bromwich-albion
More players, comments, and memories. Please do visit the site and add yours!